Travels on the Green Highway

AN ENVIRONMENTALIST'S JOURNEY

NATHANIEL PRYOR REED

Reed Publishing Company LLC
11844 SE Dixie Hwy #C
Hobe Sound, FL 33455-5456

Designed by richworks graphics, Stuart, Florida
Cover designed by students of Walt Hines, Indian River State College, Ft. Pierce, Florida

Library of Congress Control Number: 2017900507

Dedication

For My Alita:

My wife, my companion, my advisor, mother of three, grandmother of five, whose love and support have been the essential, positive elements of my life.

And for Cindy Foley:

Who has kept me going as an assistant, a fact checker and a life friend.

Table of Contents

Table of Contents continues

Preface: Our Precious World

"We knew it was The Moment."

As I close the final chapter of my wonderful life, it is a great comfort to spend time with people who share my love and passion for this beautiful world. Together we have watched the rise of a trout in a mountain stream and witnessed indescribable sunrises in far away canyons, all the while striving to ensure that future generations will be able to feel the same delight in their hearts and souls.

I was reminded of this during a recent Oregon evening in the company of the International Federation of Fly Fishers. It was an event filled with awards for great contributors to the sport and for those who have fought for the protection and enhancement of rivers and lakes across the world.

I was touched to be among the honorees – accepting an award named for Jeanne and Frank Moore, two great individuals, two great naturalists, two great Americans.

Frank has devoted a significant portion of his life to his work as the volunteer Umpqua River Master, preserving a unique genetic stock of wild summer steelhead. Jeanne is one of the greatest experts on Oregon's wildflowers. Devoted friends, their lives and mine have intertwined since I first met them in the spring of 1971.

The number of great friends present at this event was overwhelming and included advocates for clean water, protectors of streams and river forests, fighters against unneeded dams, and combatants determined to stop poor fisheries management. I was given an opportunity to speak and recall the great battles we have engaged in to save America's wildlife and wild lands.

Many were overcome by my recitation of the era of great progress, and tear-filled strangers embraced me. They understood that my endeavors had encouraged their local efforts; we shared a life mission.

Each of us recognized our bond as a band of brothers and sisters who, although politically independent, appreciated the importance of a unique era in the late twentieth century in which we were able to rise above partisanship in order to do the right thing for America. We expanded national parks, created nature preserves, protected unique forests, and saved species from extinction.

It was a remarkable era, a period in which we joined forces – the concerned public, Congress, and extraordinarily gifted, determined and educated groups that crossed all political boundaries – to make things happen. We knew it was "The Moment," a unique age in which we were able to lay the groundwork of our nation's environmental foundation.

And I was so very, very fortunate to have played a part in it and be witness to events that shaped my life and country.

In many ways, it began with the first Earth Day on April 22, 1970, which is credited by many with launching the environmental movement that we have come to embrace as part of our lives.

It galvanized a national awakening and – for awhile – made presidents and members of Congress, governors and state legislatures, more aware of what was at stake in our natural world and much less circumspect about taking action to protect it.

Simply put: Earth Day was a trigger that ignited

the nationwide explosion of deep concern over pollutants in our nation's waters and our skies, and the deep concern over the mismanagement of land.

In the wake of that first Earth Day, I watched and advised a conservative, populist Republican governor of Florida, who evolved into a champion of the environment.

Together we stopped "business as usual" in the state – the sale of state-owned submerged lands and the destruction of important mangrove stands. We fought the creation of a jetport in the Everglades, opposed a federal barge canal across the state, supported the creation of what is now Big Cypress National Preserve, and objected to development that would have greatly damaged the wondrous Biscayne Bay, much of which is now a national park. I also worked with his successor to continue the mammoth job of cleaning-up Florida's vital waters.

Given the opportunity to serve on the federal level as Assistant Secretary of the Interior for Fish, Wildlife and National Parks, I worked with some of the nation's finest scientists, activists, politicians and staff to affect change. We toiled to implement environmental impact statements for federal projects in order to protect important natural systems.

Again in the afterglow of Earth Day, working under Republican Presidents Richard Nixon and Gerald Ford, we introduced new environmental laws, along with enforcement to compel compliance, including the Clean Water Act, the Endangered Species Act, the Marine Mammal Act and the Magnuson-Stevens Fisheries Act that extended our exclusive fisheries boundaries to 300 miles offshore.

As my fly fishing friends reminded me, we now live in an era in which very little environmental legislation is accomplished at federal and state levels. Instead, we are left with partisan bickering while our natural world faces threats that compound daily. People regularly ask how we can change this, if it is possible to return to the era of which I write – a time of bipartisan cooperation that seems like a distant memory.

I have seen how things can and should work and I hold faith that we may find such alliances again. We must because we can never, never give up the battle.

Too much is at stake.

The morning after the Oregon conference, I went fishing with my son and grandson. I relaxed on a green river bank and watched the perfection of their rhythmic casting at rising trout.

Looking at the nearby snow-capped mountains and the clarity of the stream's water that supported a surprising number of wild trout, a revelation came to me: Whatever the price, whatever the strains, disappointments and defeats, it has been a worthwhile life experience.

If my book invigorates young and old to passionately continue the task of facing seemingly insurmountable challenges to do the right thing for our environment, then I can face my final years knowing that my work will have made a significant difference in our world, our precious world.

Nathaniel Pryor Reed
Jupiter Island, Florida
October 2016

Foreword I

If you love wildlife and nature, drop everything and read this grand book by an ageless, tireless hero – one of the founding fathers of the environmental movement.

Nathaniel Reed has either led the charge or been in the front lines of most every major environmental battle during my adult life. He's older than I, but not by much. President Nixon appointed him Assistant Secretary for Fish, Wildlife and National Parks when Nathaniel was in his thirties. At that time, I was in my twenties and had just started writing about fish and wildlife for national publications. I regularly turned to Nathaniel for information, inspiration and support. I turn to him still, most recently in 2016 for facts about the global crisis facing Atlantic salmon. The best source he sent was his acceptance speech as honoree at a dinner hosted by the Atlantic Salmon Federation, which he has long served as an active and vocal board member. His energy and commitment remain undiminished.

I felt special gratitude for Nathaniel while recently wading the Snake River at Idaho's 11,000-acre Harriman State Park, casting tiny dry flies to well-educated rainbow trout as they sipped Tricos in the broad, slow flow. Nathaniel is called a "zealot," usually by developers and chamber-of-commerce types he's inconvenienced. While they don't mean it as a compliment, they're not wrong. What makes Nathaniel unique among zealots, however, is his world-class people skills. He knows how to build alliances even with those he dislikes. He knows when to take charge and when to delegate, when to shout and when to listen, when to demand prompt action and when to be patient. And he excels at deflecting credit and distributing it to others. That's why he was and is so effective. And that's why, more than anyone else, Nathaniel made Harriman State Park happen. (See details on pages that follow.) America is in desperate need of zealots like Nathaniel Reed.

In 1972 word came down that powerful polluters had prevailed on President Nixon to veto the Clean Water Act. Nathaniel, who had devoted many hours to preparation of that legislation, announced his resignation. But another environmental hero of the Nixon administration saved the day, convincing him to stay on because a Congressional override appeared likely. That hunch proved correct. And that hero was none other than Watergate co-conspirator, John Ehrlichman – Nixon's chief of staff, as devoted to America's fish and wildlife as he was to its president. Who knew? That's just one of the many important facts I learned and you'll learn from this book. Thanks Nathaniel (and thanks John Ehrlichman) for helping push arguably the most important environmental law ever passed to the point that a veto override became possible.

Nixon had scant knowledge of or interest in fish, wildlife or the environment. But he saw advocacy for such as a means of stealing thunder from the loathsome Democrats. Nathaniel instantly recognized the opportunity and made the most of it.

"What's this stuff called DDT I've been hearing about and what should we do about it?" Nixon asked Nathaniel before appointing him.

"Mr. President," Nathaniel replied, "it's a deadly, long-lasting biocide that's killing our wildlife and maybe us. You, Mr. President, have the authority and duty to ban a poison that is magnifying within the bodies of all wildlife and human beings."

Nixon replied: "Prove it so it can withstand legal attack, and I will ban DDT."

When Bill Ruckelshaus became the first administrator of the Environmental Protection Agency, the "Reed Team" of acknowledged experts presented him with data it had collected that proved DDT was menacing the world we live in. Based on this unassailable research, DDT was banned.

One of the great strengths of Reed's brilliant staff was its ability to work as a team and with other teams. That staff functioned well with Russell Train's people at the newly created Council on Environmental Quality and with those of Bill Ruckelshaus at the newly created Environmental Protection Agency. The resulting coordination and vision was unprecedented in the executive branch.

Reed attracted experts, never effectively utilized in the past, for input, criticism and recommendations. They came from universities, museums and environmental organizations. Never had the Interior Department fielded more devoted, well-trained environmentalists than those who served with Nathaniel from 1971-1977. They took advantage of the new National Environmental Policy Act which required all federal agencies to complete legally sound environmental impact statements for federal projects. No longer would Congressional add-ons be immune from legal review.

After the administration's stunning DDT victory Nixon made and kept a promise to approve the banning of Compound 1080, provided Nathaniel's team could make a case that would hold up in court. Reed supervised wildlife professionals who prepared an Environmental Impact Statement for the ban that survived aggressive legal challenge. One of the most destructive poisons ever developed, 1080 had been used to kill coyotes on federal lands for the subsidized sheep industry. But it subjected every mammal and bird that ate from thousands of poisoned baits strewn across the West to slow, agonizing death. The ban on production and use of Compound 1080 has saved millions of non-target animals including bald and golden eagles, foxes, badgers, bobcats, cougars and wolverines. Wolverines, in fact, had been extirpated from the contiguous states by 1080; now they're making a comeback. Thanks Nathaniel!

When the U.S. Army Corps of Engineers was converting wild rivers to straight, lifeless gutters Nathaniel Reed joined the successful fight to stop the practice. In this effort his most daunting challenge was stopping the partly completed Cross-Florida Barge Canal, one of the most brazen and destructive frauds ever perpetrated on U.S. taxpayers. As late as October 1970 Nixon was sufficiently clueless to ask Florida Governor Claude Kirk (for whom Nathaniel then worked as environmental advisor) to tell him all about "this controversial canal and its vocal opponents." Kirk, who had been a proponent until Reed explained the facts to him, didn't hold back; he informed the president that the canal was "an old-fashioned, reckless boondoggle that included a significant danger to a critical aquifer, a budget-busting, totally outdated public works project."

"Are you building it," Nixon inquired?

"No, you are," answered the governor.

Recently I canoed the Ocklawaha River, which the canal would have wiped out. Fed by clear springs, it is semi-tropical, canopied, ancient. It drains 2,800 square miles, much of it sanctuary for unique plants and animals rare or absent elsewhere. Around every bend Florida red-bellied cooters basked in the sun. Basking on higher ground were alligators. Ten feet down, largemouth bass, sunfish, Florida gar, bowfins, catfish, and golden shiners ghosted through and over waving eelgrass and coontail. Atlantic needlefish, iridescent green and silver, sliced the glassy surface. Snowy and great egrets stalked hummocks. Pileated woodpeckers and red-shouldered hawks laughed and shouted from dark woods. Flights of white ibises streamed overhead. All this and much, much more, including other equally wild and beautiful rivers and forests, would have been destroyed by the Cross-Florida Barge Canal had not Nixon, with a hard push from Nathaniel Reed and an impressive group of Floridians who combined sound science with politics, killed the project with an Executive Order. Thanks Nathaniel!

We should also thank Nathaniel for his leadership in converting Yellowstone grizzlies from garbage-eating circus animals to real bears that now function in a complex and complete ecosystem. Their recovery has been one of the greatest success stories of the Endangered Species Act.

The Reed Alaska Planning Team, headed by Curtis "Buff" Bohlen, was responsible for selection, mapping and accompanying ecological data that led to President Carter and Congress permanently protecting 154 million acres of Alaska's most magnificent and productive wildlife land and water.

Nathaniel joined a group of committed activists that defied public opinion and successfully fought efforts to create a megaport in Biscayne Bay which would have destroyed that magnificent natural asset accessible in minutes from downtown Miami. This was on my mind when my wife, Donna, and I left a family reunion at Florida's Pompano Beach. We couldn't wait to extricate ourselves from the wasteland of asphalt, cement and high-rise hotels. When we finally saw our chance we fled to Biscayne Bay where we spent a wonderful day casting flies to giant bonefish. Had it not been for Nathaniel and the dedicated allies he stood with and inspired, Biscayne Bay would look like Pompano Beach or worse. Instead it teems with aquatic and terrestrial life including one of the world's largest coral reefs and the East Coast's longest stretch of mangrove forest. How Nathaniel worked with both opponents and allies to win political support for the bay's protection as a national monument and then a national park is an inspiring story that you'll read in this book. Thanks Nathaniel!

Nathaniel was instrumental in saving and expanding Redwood National Park and Big Cypress National Preserve, in giving us the Marine Mammal Protection Act. Working with Council on Environmental Quality director Russell Train and his key staffers, Nathaniel helped develop the full range of legislation that is the foundation of our nation's environmental laws, including the Endangered Species Act.

Where I to detail all the gifts Nathaniel Reed has bequeathed on Americans and generations of Americans yet unborn, I'd need a book longer than this one. In his preface Nathaniel claims to be "closing out" his life. Don't believe it. He's as engaged today as he ever was, fighting for Everglades restoration, snail kites, neotropical birds, Atlantic salmon and other imperiled creatures that brighten this tired old planet.

Centuries hence Nathaniel and the rest of us won't be around; but his life will remain one that can never be closed out. Working with every advocacy group whose representatives had their own priorities required diplomatic skills and endless patience. The results speak for themselves.

Ted Williams
Grafton, Massachusetts
July 2016

Foreword II

In 1960, Florida was gripped in the clenches of well-financed developers who often were aided by Florida's politicians to clear vast mangrove jungles and fill life-sustaining swamps to make room for roads, waterfront property and gated golf course communities. Development at any cost was the goal of our politicians in Tallahassee, the state capital, and in Washington, D.C. The very attributes that lured so many people to Florida were being destroyed by uncaring state and local governments.

While touring Florida by plane and car to witness the devastation first-hand, Nathaniel Reed's life mission became to unite with fellow Floridians in a quest to stop unwanted development and mitigate ecological losses. He became a vocal environmentalist who spoke at public hearings, using scientific data to argue against construction projects capable of causing incredible damage to Florida's fragile ecosystem.

Nathaniel joined forces with several environmental societies, including Audubon, the Izaac Walton League, The Nature Conservancy, Sierra Club and Defenders of Wildlife because he was appalled by the discharge of untreated human sewage and toxic industrial waste into the ocean and Gulf of Mexico.

In 1965, he met Florida gubernatorial candidate Claude Kirk Jr., who Nathaniel admired for his stance on environmental issues, and campaigned with him for the last 75 days before the election. After Kirk's inauguration, Nathaniel became the first-ever governor's environmental counsel. With the vast majority of the state's newspapers and television stations as allies, and assisted by hundreds, if not thousands, of concerned, dedicated citizens who suddenly realized their "Eden" was being destroyed, Nathaniel took the opportunity to confront the real pollution disgraces that had been allowed to continue due to an indolent State Health Department.

In 1969, Gov. Kirk appointed Nathaniel as chairman of the newly formed Department of Air and Water Pollution Control, which later evolved into the Department of Environmental Regulation. Nathaniel continued in the position through the leadership of Gov. Reuben Askew and dramatically increased the size and power of the department.

In the spring of 1971, Nathaniel accepted an invitation from President Richard Nixon to become Assistant Secretary of Interior for Fish, Wildlife and National Parks. The next nearly five years in Washington, D.C., serving Presidents Nixon and Gerald Ford were a fascinating adventure.

By late 1971, an astonishing group of committed conservationists and environmentalists had been appointed to key positions in the Nixon administration and, along with a brilliant, committed staff, they accepted the challenges that made for an exciting, unique period in American environmental history. Guided by Russell Train, chairman of the President's Council on Environmental Quality, they worked together to establish the foundation of environmental law that remains today.

Some battles were lost to pure politics, but they never gave up, eagerly seeking new opportunities at a time when bipartisan members of Congress were willing to listen, work together and turn their efforts into the law of the land.

After his service with Interior ended, Nathaniel returned to Florida, where he remains a voice in conservation efforts by serving on countless environmental boards. Over the years, he received – and continues to receive – many state and national awards that run the gamut of his passions and interests.

Nathaniel's book of essays constitutes an account of many great environmental victories and a few defeats, mingled with amusing stories of oddities on the way through an incredible life's journey. His experiences always began with a singular desire to balance mankind's wants against the needs of our planet, and for that – and for his accomplishments – Nathaniel Pryor Reed has earned our praise and our gratitude.

Patrick Noonan
Potomac, Maryland
September 2016

Patrick F. Noonan is a noted American conservationist who founded The Conservation Fund in 1985 and still serves as its chairman emeritus. He also served as president of The Nature Conservancy and was a recipient of the Lady Bird Johnson Environmental Award. He received a MacArthur Foundation "genius" grant and the first Lufkin Award for outstanding environmental achievement. He organized and was the first president of The Conservation Fund. In addition, he has been an extraordinary advocate of Chesapeake Bay restoration efforts.

In the Beginning

"I hated what I found upon my return to Florida."

I grew up in a magical time and place. My childhood was spent roaming 125 acres of hillside property in Greenwich, Connecticut, punctuated by open fields and swamps, a six-acre lake, long, rocky ridges and deep woods underlain by acres of mountain laurel – all of it surrounded by a large National Audubon Sanctuary.

I was a natural. My mother once said I came out of the womb casting a fishing rod. I fished in our lake, prowled the woods, caught and mounted a vast butterfly and moth collection, and became a "birder."

We moved to Jupiter Island each year after Thanksgiving for the Christmas holiday. Every time I arrived, I knew I was stepping into Valhalla.

The south end of the Indian River, now referred to as the Indian River Lagoon, was at my front door. Every afternoon when I was a young boy, our family caretaker, Andy Ondich, took me trolling on the river, which teemed with sea trout, snook, ladyfish, and bluefish, all available to a young boy in pursuit. The abundance and variety of the lagoon's stock of fish is now a distant memory, but Andy and I forged a lifelong friendship.

The Atlantic Ocean, to the east of the island, was full of pompano, whiting, and croaker. I shared the cost of offshore charter fishing boats, caught my share of sailfish, kingfish and wahoo, and became an ardent fisherman.

By the time I was 7, I also was allowed to prowl the fields alone in search of birds and butterflies. When I was 15, I received a 20-gauge shotgun and began to explore the thousands of acres of palmetto-pine flat woods west of the island. I did very little damage to the quail population, but fell in love with hunting dogs and walks through the woods.

I was outdoors, and on the Indian River, every day, all day, throughout the vacations I took as a teenager and during college.

My parents encouraged me, giving me rare opportunities to explore nature. When I was only 14, a chauffeur drove me to the Everglades to join Frank Craighead, one of Florida's most famous early ecologists. We traveled together for three days across the southern end of the vast swamp just north of Tamiami Trail, which the Collier family had built in 1928 to lure potential real estate buyers to Naples.

I slept with Miccosukee Indian guides in their shelters under a mosquito net and saw thousands of wading birds that had made the Everglades world famous. The number of alligators, their sizes and indifference to us, was at first quite frightening, but I soon recognized them as an important link to the vast ecosystem – so vast that, despite repeated efforts to drain and "manage" it, it remained the Everglades.

My years at Deerfield Academy and Trinity College in the Northeast didn't teach me about the mysteries and realities of natural science, but I found ample time to walk deep in the woods of Massachusetts and Connecticut and spend endless hours fishing for trout and shad on spring weekends. In the fall and winter, I hunted pheasants with my future in-laws and wandered over Connecticut's deserted farms seeking ruffed grouse and woodcock.

After college, I served three years as an Air Force military intelligence officer stationed in and around Paris. My last seven months of duty were spent in the Middle East as an attaché to a ranking intelligence figure, an unforgettable experience. Military service gave me the opportunity not only to travel extensively in France, Germany, Norway, North Africa and the Middle East, but it also taught me the results of over-grazing by livestock and the ever-increasing desertification of North African countries. As populations grew, desert areas increased and tribal disagreements on grazing rights turned into armed conflict.

There never was any doubt where I would make my home when military service ended. Jupiter Island was my home ground. My parents owned most of the island, including the well-known Jupiter Island Club, which my mother managed with an iron hand. I worked as vice president of the company and managed and rebuilt the Hobe Sound Water Company. I built a beautiful golf course and played tennis or golf daily.

In the summer, I fished in Canada and the western United States and traveled with my family to splendid rental houses in England, France and Italy.

Still, it all was too comfortable. I knew something was missing, and I hated what I found upon my return to Florida in 1960.

The state was gripped in the clenches of well-financed developers who often were aided by Florida's politicians to clear vast mangrove jungles and fill life-sustaining swamps to make room for roads, homes and waterfront property. Thousands of freshwater wetlands were being drained. Standing water was considered a threat to development and a breeding ground for mosquitoes that was best drained. Productive farmlands for winter crops were rapidly being turned into gated golf course communities.

Low taxes, combined with the advent of air conditioning and relatively cheap air fare, encouraged a Florida real estate boom unrivaled since the 1920s. State and local governments encouraged growth at any environmental cost, determined to recover from the impacts of the Great Depression and previous building busts. Critics were declared "strange people in tennis shoes" who didn't understand the desire to transform Florida into a new playground inhabited by everyone from the ultra-wealthy to those who could barely subsist on Social Security.

Nowhere were the changes more obvious than in southeast Florida, home of the Everglades and some of the most valuable wetlands in the state. While I was away at college and overseas, a proposal to wall-in the Everglades with high dikes passed Congress. The Korean War was over, federal taxes had been dramatically reduced and the Army Corps of Engineers was staffed by hundreds of bright, well-educated engineers who were looking to design "public works" projects that were, in reality, massive drainage projects.

The creation of the Central and Southern Florida Flood Control District was a monster – a project that would keep the Corps involved for decades. From Orlando to Florida Bay, water was to be managed for potable water supplies and booming agriculture by digging hundreds of miles of drainage canals, designing and constructing the largest water pumps in the world.

The Corps and government officials declared that a sizeable portion of the Everglades would be drained for man's uses. The remaining Everglades would be controlled by compartmentalizing dikes,

'We have five years to set up laws before we lose all Florida to developers'

"I was horrified to learn how widespread water pollution is in Florida. I was horrified to find out that each year this disaster gets worse. And I was horrified, really horrified, when I calculated how much it is going to cost to solve our water pollution problem." — Nathaniel P. Reed

creating a series of manageable "lakes" where once was found slowly flowing water known as the "River of Grass." The miles of canals permanently disconnected water conservation areas from their headwaters at Lake Okeechobee. Lawmakers declared that the Everglades had to be dramatically reduced in size, tamed and managed by the levees, hundreds of miles of canals and massive pumps that could move millions of gallons of water in every direction, often at the whim of the managers.

Man was remaking my Florida with the heaviest of hands!

Development at any cost was the goal of our politicians in Tallahassee and Washington, D.C. There was not a single location in Florida outside the national parks, wildlife refuges and state parks that could be considered safe from yet another project to change what thousands of years had created.

Put succinctly: The quality of our air and water in several parts of our rapidly growing state was seriously threatened by industrial output, electrical utilities and vehicle exhaust.

In 1960, I began an exhaustive trip of Florida by plane and car to witness the devastation firsthand. My life's mission became to unite fellow Floridians in my quest to stop unwanted development and mitigate ecological losses. I became a vocal environmentalist who spoke at every public hearing I could attend, using scientific data to argue against construction projects with incredible impacts on our state's fragile ecosystem. I met hundreds of fellow citizens who shared my horror over what politicians and their Corps allies were both proposing and building.

I was being mentored by Dr. Arthur Marshall, Florida's most prominent ecologist, conservationist and educator. We spent hours together. His greatest admonition was, "Beware of unforeseen consequences of illiterate engineering and second-rate science." I also joined forces with several environmental societies, including Audubon, the Izaak Walton League, The Nature Conservancy,

THE MIAMI NEWS

A Cox Newspaper

- Pulitzer Prize For Editorial Cartoons In 1966
- Pulitzer Prize For International Reporting In 1963
- Pulitzer Prize For National Reporting In 1959
- Pulitzer Prize For Public Service In 1939

James M. Cox, Jr. *Publisher and President*	Daniel J. Mahoney, Jr. *Associate Publisher*	Sylvan Meyer *Editor*
Howard Kleinberg *Managing Editor*	Clarke Ash *Associate Editor*	Jack Kassewitz *Chief Editorial Writer*

10-A Tues., April 22, 1969 73rd Year, No. 290

Clarke Ash

Gov. Kirk's Smartest Move

A VIEW OF THE NEWS

A lot of people, Democrats as well as Republicans, will tell you that the smartest move Gov. Claude Kirk ever made was to appoint Nathaniel P. Reed as a special assistant.

Reed didn't want the job. He had a citrus ranch to manage, a comfortable home in Hobe Sound, a young family, and no particular concern about the source of his next paycheck. Most of all, he was not interested in becoming a politician.

Born to the silk, he had attended Trinity College, graduating in 1955, served a four-year hitch in military intelligence, and had come home to look after the family's sizable interests around Hobe Sound.

He had involved himself in Kirk's campaign only because the governor seemed to be making sense on a subject — conservation — that had become Reed's passion.

Reed's friends will tell you that he finally went to Tallahassee on the condition that he would have a free hand in implementing sound conservation policies without regard to the usual partisan pressures.

He has done so well that many of the state agencies, peopled with Democrats, regard Reed as a champion against the entrenched interests. And whatever else may be said about Kirk's administration, the governor's conservation policies cannot be faulted.

"I'm still not a politician," Reed told a recent visitor, "but nobody believes me." Seated in a cell-like office in a corner of the capitol, Reed waved an arm in the general direction of the governor's office. "Gov. Kirk has been very kind to me, and so has Lt. Gov. Osborne.

"I guess I became seriously interested in natural resources and their tremendous importance when I took over the management of the citrus ranch.

"In short order I learned about flood control, game and fish, water management, pollution . . . the whole picture."

Reed said he was enormously encouraged about Florida's progress in these areas when, shortly after Gov. Kirk's inauguration, the Legislature created the Pollution Control Commission. But before the commission can become fully effective, he said, two things must be accomplished. And with a characteristic disregard for the politics involved, he listed the requirements.

First, the state's sanitation engineers must be taken out of the Health Department. The sanitation engineers could become front line troops in the war against pollution. But as Reed said, "the Health Department is doctor oriented, and the doctors just don't understand the full pollution story."

The second necessary step, in Reed's view, is adequate funding for the Pollution Control Commission. Little more than token funding for the new agency came out of the economy minded Budget Commission, of which Gov. Kirk is the chairman.

"I love the governor," Reed said. "But it is inconceivable that a state like Florida would not invest at least $1 million in pollution control."

Reed's interest in pollution is universal throughout the state, but he is especially well versed in Dade County, possibly because Dade has so much to lose.

When the Homestead Air Base recently discharged raw sewage into a nearby canal, killing thousands of fish, Reed was one of the first to be notified. Dispensing with red tape, he quickly called the Secretary of the Interior, who called the Secretary of the Air Force, who began a sudden investigation.

"Dade has good anti-pollution laws," he said, "The problem is how to enforce them without stepping on everybody's toes.

"Leach (ex-Pollution Control Director Paul Leach) was a good man who hurt himself with an error. (Leach claimed a master's degree which he didn't have.) Now you need a good man to replace him. In fact, Dade County needs the best in America because it has the most to lose if its environment is destroyed."

Sierra Club and Defenders of Wildlife. I was appalled by the discharge of untreated human sewage and toxic industrial waste into the ocean and Gulf of Mexico. The very attributes that lured so many people to Florida were being destroyed by uncaring state and local governments.

I spoke in Tallahassee in front of numerous governors and cabinet members about continuing abuses by the Internal Improvement Fund, which declined to enforce primitive regulations on the clearing of mangroves and permits needed to dredge and fill wetlands.

Their reactions were always identical – inaudible disbelief. So many times I was dismissed as a "rich kid who wants Florida to look like Jupiter Island."

My life changed forever for the better in 1965 when I met Florida gubernatorial candidate Claude Kirk Jr. He was a maverick dismissed by newspapers as a "fool," but I admired his stance on environmental issues and campaigned with him for the last 75 days before the election.

He spent the majority of election night in my home and won the race easily.

After his inauguration, my wife, Alita, and I, were invited to a fried chicken luncheon on the floor of the governor's office. After taking the oath, Governor Kirk came to us and asked me to follow him down a corridor near his office.

We entered a small room with a desk, a desk chair and three modestly comfortable sitting chairs. He said, "Nathaniel, you've been screaming bloody murder about this state. Now do something about it. Here is your offer. I will make you a prominent member of my staff. You will have the assignment to correct the environmental ills that you have been preaching about. I cannot afford to pay you more than a dollar a year, as my budget is woefully inadequate. If you accept this offer, we will change Florida forever!"

I sat quietly behind the desk for a short while and then brought Alita, mother of our three young children, to the office and explained the governor's offer. Without hesitation, she asserted that this was "my moment to change from an ardent critic to a constructive agent of change."

"Take the position!" she implored me. "I will rent a furnished duplex near the Capitol tomorrow morning. I will fly home on the evening flight and have your clothes for winter and spring packed and a driver will bring them to you in Tallahassee in two days. You have enough clothes to get by for a couple of days. You will have to extend your stay in that miserable motel for three or four days, but you can catch a cab to the Capitol every morning after an early breakfast. Knowing you, you will find a place to dine near the governor's office. The green Ford sedan that you gave me will be yours in two days. I will fly up and settle you into the rented duplex.

"You will find ways to continue your efforts in South Florida, so we will see you on weekends. You can catch the Sunday afternoon commercial flight back to Tallahassee. When the children's school semesters are completed, I will have found a rental home for us within easy driving distance of the Capitol.

"Do it! It will change our lives, but for the better. You ache for the disgraceful pollution of our state's waters, the sale of submerged land, the filling of valuable mangroves.

"You have preached to me and across the state on those subjects. Now, this is an opportunity of a lifetime to work with the governor who listens to you, likes you and wants to turn the state upside down. Take the position!"

I stared at her recognizing that this was one of those moments when our joint lives would be changed forever.

Good to her word, we were comfortably housed in a duplex near the Capitol in just four days. Alita spent the next three days arranging for every other day maid service and even pouring hot water on the frozen windshield of my 'new' car.

I often enjoyed a cup or two of coffee with the governor at 7 a.m. My new life had begun."

Alita has never failed to be a loving wife, mother and the finest life companion for whom any man could wish. Her constant support and able criticism has marked our 50-plus years as life companions. None of the environmental successes I've enjoyed could have happened without her constant support.

B14—Palm Beach Post-Times, Sunday, March 22, 1970

"It is clear now in the 1970s our government has failed to protect our environment nationally and statewide."

—— Nat Reed

Stop the Polluters At Any Price –Reed

STUART— Gubernatorial aide Nat Reed has told conservationists here they must "move against polluters, at any price" if the area is to preserve its environment.

"It is clear now in the 1970s our government has failed to protect our environment nationally and statewide," Reed told the Martin County Audubon Society.

"Florida has the most delicate ecology of all the states, yet natural resources departments have ruled by 19th century ideals," said Reed.

He praised Gov. Claude Kirk for interceding to halt 90 years of such abuses.

Reed said he opposed re-election of most public officials, but made an exception in Kirk's case because, "he is a maverick — a maverick who doesn't like deals or the power structure."

"The crisis of the invasion is at hand. Everyone is coming to Florida. They are on the way and we can't bar the door. Florida had three million people in 1952, and there will be 24 million by 2003. The time has come to pause and consider, to make a blueprint," he said.

"Martin County now looks like a target in a battlefield," he said.

"I urge one or more conservationists to run for the County Commission. It would be a hell of a sacrifice, but we need at least one commissioner who knows, has the expertise, and the conscience to stop what we see coming," he said.

As the first-ever governor's environmental counsel, I had opportunities to confront the real pollution disgraces that had been allowed to continue due to an indolent State Health

Department.

In my new role, I worked tirelessly to bring Florida into compliance with national clean water and clean air regulations. It was a monumental task – I held hearings on these topics across the state and tried to convince rather uninterested municipalities that they needed to use advanced wastewater treatment systems before they dumped millions of gallons of untreated or under-treated sewage into Florida's waterways or off its sandy beaches.

We had hearing after hearing after hearing from the Keys all the way to northwest Florida. Every state had to write water quality rules around federal guidelines and there was not a single city or county in the state of Florida that met the federal rules in 1967 – and not a single industry had complied. We were creating new rules, a new permitting process, and there wasn't a single incinerator in the state that met the new federal standards for air pollution.

The Pensacola News

City, County Told to Formulate Program

PAUL TRAINER, JOHN WHITE, NAT REED, WATCH PROCEEDINGS
. . . pollution officials participate in area three-day conference

By MIKE HENDERSON
News Staff Writer

The federal government today ordered the City of Pensacola and Escambia County to quickly formulate a single program for the collection, treatment and disposal of waste waters in the Escambia River basin.

The action came at the conclusion of the Federal-State Enforcement Conference on Pollution of Escambia River and Bay.

Conferees said the city and county, in cooperation with the Escambia-Santa Rosa Regional Planning Council have already been at work on such a proposal.

"However, tangible results are not evident," said John A. White, director of Regulatory programs for the Environmental Protection Agency water quality office, in reading the findings of the group.

"The progress of the City of Pensacola waste abatement program has not been satisfactory," White said.

Nat Reed, chairman of the Florida Department of Air and Water Pollution Control, said "orders will be forthcoming. They will be stringent and with the full force of the state behind them."

He said the northeast treatment plant's operations is woefully inadequate.

He said the plant is "incapable of surviving as an entity."

Top engineers from the state will survey the northeast and Main Street plants operated by the city in an effort to divert flow of waste materials to the

Turn to ESCAMBIA—Page 2A

Escambia River Cleanup Ordered

FROM PAGE ONE

Main Street plant, Reed said.

"An extensive survey of the Main Street plant's capabilities will be made before such measures are implemented," he said, adding that discharges from the Main Street plant have not been altogether satisfactory.

Three area industries are planning to channel their waste through the Main Street plant by early July, but such action is likely to be delayed as a result of conference findings, Reed said.

"This has got to be faced. It is a critical issue. It's got to be face now or we're going to have continued problems," Reed said.

Vincent D. Patton, executive director of the state control agency, said that the industrial discharges from Armstrong Cork, Ashland Chemical and Tenneco have been channeled into Bayou Chico.

"We don't want to transfer the problem from Bayou Chico to Pensacola Bay," Patton said.

The Regional Planning Council was ordered to submit a progress report on the city-county pollution plan by April 15.

The governor supported campaigns against widespread sewage pollution and the improper sale of state wetlands and issuance of permits, which had allowed creation of instant waterfront property. Progress was slow, but with incredible assistance from a small team of federal experts in Atlanta, new water-quality regulations were developed and enforced.

The vast majority of the state's newspapers and television stations became allies. We tackled a number of abuses, and most were resolved during the terms of Governor Kirk and his successor, Governor Reubin Askew. We managed to pass a land-acquisition bond issue that, over time, became the most prominent such program in the nation. I persuaded Governor Kirk to challenge the proposed Cross State Barge Canal, to the dismay of its supporters. He joined President Nixon in canceling the expensive, ill-conceived Corps project.

I was assisted by hundreds, if not thousands, of concerned, dedicated citizens who suddenly realized their "Eden" was being destroyed.

In 1969, Governor Kirk appointed me chairman of the newly formed Department of Air and Water Pollution Control, which later evolved into the Department of Environmental Regulation. After Governor Kirk's reelection defeat, I was asked by Governor-elect Askew to remain in the job and dramatically increase the size and power of the department. To the surprise of many, Governor Kirk had proven to be the single most important person to change Florida from the days of the Old South to a modern state.

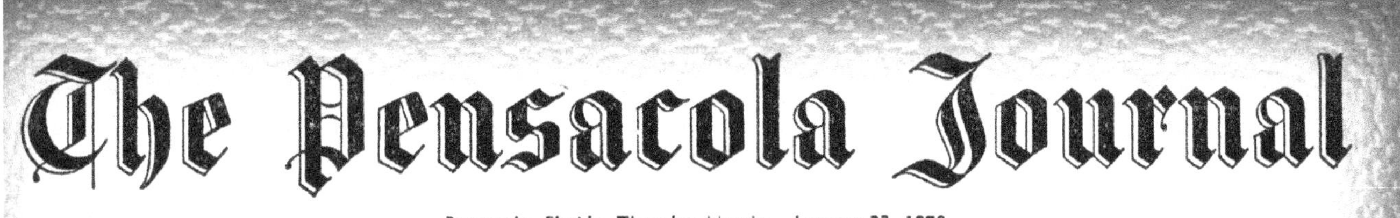

Pensacola, Florida, Thursday Morning, January 22, 1970

January 1973 Completion Date

Landmark Decision Sets Pollution Guidelines

MURRAY STEIN
. . . chairman

By MIKE ALBERTSON
Journal Staff Writer

State and federal officials Wednesday agreed on a landmark decision of pollution control regulations for Escambia River and Escambia Bay that would clean up the bay by controlling nutrient discharges more strictly than ever before.

The final product after two days of statements at the federal interstate pollution conference asked cutbacks of 94, 94 and 90 per cent respectively for carbon, nitrogen and phosphorus wastes.

In addition, the final agreement virtually halted all dredging operating in the bay until a comprehensive development plan for the estuary's shores can be drawn.

The final date for completion

By MIKE ALBERTSON
Journal Staff Writer

State and federal officials Wednesday agreed on a landmark decision of pollution control regulations for Escambia River and Escambia Bay that would clean up the bay by controlling nutrient discharges more strictly than ever before.

The final product after two days of statements at the federal interstate pollution conference asked cutbacks of 94, 94 and 90 per cent respectively for carbon, nitrogen and phosphorus wastes.

In addition, the final agreement virtually halted all dredging operating in the bay until a comprehensive development plan for the estuary's shores can be drawn.

The final date for completion
bled for the final agreement:

"You have some of the most delicious oysters in the world here, and we intend to restore that resource."

Southeastern Fisheries Association official Bob Jones, in Pensacola for the conference and Pensacola Seafood Wholesaler Clyde Richbourg were excited by the prospect:

Said Jones: "Do you realize that if all the oyster areas he is referring to (both in Escambia and Blackwater Bay) were opened, Pensacola would be the biggest oyster producing city on the Gulf Coast?"

In a final conference agreement with tougher wording in several places, the following requirements were set forth:

—The recommended waste abatement program was recommended to be accomplished "except as otherwise specified, by not later than Dec. 31, 1972."

—"There shall be (formerly recommendation was used) reductions of 94 per cent carbonaceous, 94 per cent nitrogeneous and 90 per cent phosphorus wastes discharged to Escambia River and Bay from major sources in Florida, including American Cyanamid, Escambia Chemical, Monsanto and the City of Pensacola Northeast sewage treatment plant."

—Due to the longer distance between Container Corporation of America and Escambia Bay, reduction requirements for carbonaceous and phosphorus wastes were relaxed slightly, to 90 per cent.

—No nitrogen cutback was required of Container Corporation, because nitrogens found in the outflow actually resulted from sewage discharge upstream from the plant on a creek.

—All waste sources shall (formerly recommended) remove settleable solids.

—Color in Escambia River at the Alabama-Florida State line as measured at the Highway 4 bridge near Century, shall be reduced to standards of federal and state governments.

—No further construction dredging shall be permitted in Escambia Bay or Mulat-Mulatto Bayou until a plan for development of the shoreline has been established.

—T e Louisville & Nashville Railroad Company bridge across Escambia Bay shall be rebuilt of modified (modified added to final agreement) by Jan. 1, 1973.

NAT REED

The Palm Beach Post

Published By Palm Beach Newspapers, Inc.

James M. Cox, Jr., Chairman — Robert W. Sherman, President
Cecil B. Kelley, Sr., Publisher — Gregory E. Favre, Editor
Robert J. Nangle, Associate Editor
David Lawrence Jr., Managing Editor

FRIDAY MORNING, MARCH 12, 1971

Gregory Favre

Nat Reed and the Alpha and Omega of Earth

Nat Reed, tall and thin and early Eastern collegiate in his blue blazer and white pants and rep tie, was reading from the Book of Genesis.

"In the beginning . . ." he read.

This was where it all started he was saying, where the earth was created, the air and waters and trees and mountains . . . all the gorgeous and life-giving and life-sustaining resources on this planet we inhabit.

This was where it started. Nat Reed, Florida's No. 1 pollution fighter who soon will be leaving to take a job in Washington, was talking about where it was going to end if something isn't done soon.

The alpha and omega of planet Earth.

Is it too late? Has man, as Reed asked, already laid the framework for self-destruction because of his ignorance and greed? Will he take the right path when he moves off this crossroad he currently occupies?

For four years Nat Reed has been trying to push that tiny portion of Earth called Florida in the right direction.

There have been some successes. Escambia Bay in Pensacola was allowed to become a cesspool and it will take years before it can be restored to its original state. But some regulations have been enforced and small gains can be seen.

Reed says white trout and sea trout are again being caught. A few shrimp are returning.

When Reed took on the state pollution problems he said he found that "the estuaries were being plundered. The weekly land sales were a national disgrace.

"The state government was cutting off water to the Everglades National Park after accepting $200 million of federal money to help construct the Flood Control District with one of the avowed purposes being to provide adequate water supplies to the park."

He talked of roads going through parks, of planned jetports and sewage flowing into the lakes and ocean.

Some of that has changed. Some hasn't. But there are more pluses now than minuses.

If this positive action is to continue, Reed said, citizens should make a simple checklist in order to keep an eye on progress or lack of it.

He said to watch the management of the estuaries and the trustees. Note how much acreage of public land is sold, the price for fill, the amount of land bought back by the state from old land sales, the incidence of law suits challenging the illegal operations which are underway and the increase in numbers and quality of the staff.

He said to determine if the Department of Air and Water Pollution Control remains a technical staff without political appointments and under the governor who must answer to the voters.

He said to see if the staff is increased as it needs to be and if the enforcement cases are pursued.

Some of his toughest checkpoints were reserved for the Department of Natural Resources. This department needs a highly trained director, he said. It needs a unified plan of action which includes a guaranteed supply of water to the Everglades National Park. It needs to revamp its marine lab and it needs new personnel with new ideas.

He also said the success of Conservation 70s could be used as a measuring stick.

But in the final analysis, he went on to say, it will be the enthusiasm and determination of the citizens, along with their tax dollars, that will ultimately be the go or no-go signal in this struggle.

"**If this state** doesn't continue its leadership as an example to the nation," Reed concluded, "then I think we may as well enjoy our lives as best we can and not worry about the future, as there will be none."

Nat Reed has done his part. He soon will be moving on to bigger challenges. He should go with the gratitude of all Floridians.

One late afternoon at the conclusion of a particularly stormy three days of air quality hearings in Jacksonville, Alita telephoned and said, "The White House is trying to reach you." When I called Washington, I talked with John Ehrlichman, the assistant for domestic affairs to President Richard Nixon. He asked me to go to the Everglades the next morning to meet with newly appointed U.S. Secretary of the Interior Rogers and fly over the national park.

I was exhausted and told Ehrlichman I was planning to go home and sleep for three days, but Alita disagreed. She said, "You will be there Saturday. You cannot turn down a Cabinet officer who's asked you to fly over the Everglades. You know all the problems of the Everglades. Here's your chance to explain it to the Secretary of the Interior."

I flew to Stuart in a state plane, slept, and flew to the helicopter pad in Miami's harbor in a float plane owned by the South Florida Water Management District.

After flying over the area in helicopters – a bald eagle trailed us part of the way and then seized a duck while we were watching – and I went back to the Miami airport where we had a big press conference, and a beer after it concluded. He said, man in the news

Millionaire A Bargain At $1 A Year

By TOM TWITTY
Sentinel Staff

Nathaniel Reed is a millionaire who thinks more about clean air and water than he does about money.

He proved it in Tallahassee. For more than four years, he led Florida's fight against pollution — serving as the unpaid head of the Air and Water Pollution Control Board and as a $1 a year adviser to governors.

He was first brought into the state fight against pollution by former Gov. Claude Kirk. Gov. Reubin Askew knows a bargain when he sees one, so he asked Reed to stay on at the same $1 a year.

THE 36-YEAR-OLD Reed, lanky, and nattily dressed, can claim credit for steering Florida away from the path of ecological destruction. And he's done it in a style which is the envy of the professional politician.

He seldom raises his voice, relying instead on facts and figures to carry the day. His open mind and urban manner make it difficult for opponents to get angry.

His methods are successful. He led the fight against Miami's proposed jetport on the edge of the Everglades, spearheaded the examination of the Cross-Florida Barge

NAT REED
. . . Clean thoughts

Canal which President Nixon finally halted, and put a crimp in the dredgers and fillers seeking to take over Florida's bays and other shallow waters.

LESS DRAMATIC, but perhaps the biggest accomplishment of all, is the anti-pollution program now on the way to reversing spillage o fthe state's precious water supply.

Air pollution, which never became a serious problem in Florida but loomed as one, has been stopped in its tracks.

Reed is scion of a wealthy New England family steeped in Republicanism which owns the exclusive Juniper Island Club off the coast at Hobe Sound—more as a hobby than anything else.

REED LIVES ON the island when he is not in Tallahassee or winging around the state on anti-pollution and conservation projects. He explains his interest in conservation thus:

"Our family has led out-of-doors lives and we naturally want to preserve those pleasures."

In June of 1968 Reed was the somewhat reluctant nominee in Gov. Kirk's effort to oust U. S. Rep. William C. Cramer as Florida's GOP national committeeman.

REED ENDEARED himself to organization Republicans when he withdrew gracefully before the divisive balloting could start.

He grew up in a political atmosphere. His uncle was campaign manager for Wendell Wilkie in 1940 and his mother managed President Eisenhower's Fairfield County, Conn., campaigns.

Reed came out of the Ivy League mold, attending Deerfield Academy and small but prestigious Trinity College. He served as an intelligence officer in the Air Force and won field promotions in Algeria and Lebanon.

"The president would like for you to be Assistant Secretary of the Interior. I want you to work with me. I want you to come to Washington now."

I returned home from Miami in the middle of the night and Alita was patiently doing some needlepoint. I sat down and said, "I was offered this job in Washington. I think it's absolutely insane."

She said, "Nathaniel, take the job. Let's go to Washington. Let's get you back to the birds and wildlife, fishes and get you out of this god-awful business of sewage and toxic chemicals and regulations, rules and lawsuits."

So, in the spring of 1971, I accepted the president's invitation to become Assistant Secretary of Interior for Fish, Wildlife and National Parks. My supportive wife sighed a great sense of relief, as the years of tackling sewage issues in Florida had taken a physical toll on me.

Every day during the next near five years in Washington, D.C., serving Presidents Nixon and Gerald Ford, as I left my car in the Interior Department's basement garage, I prayed I would accept the challenges that awaited me. Being able to select a brilliant, committed staff convinced me this was "the moment" in our collective lives when the stars were aligned and great opportunities awaited. It was up to us to accept the challenges that made for an exciting, unique period in American environmental history.

We were guided by Russell Train, chairman of the President's Council on Environmental Quality, and we worked together as a "Band of Brothers" to establish the foundation of environmental law that remains today.

We stopped the misuse of a coyote poison known as Compound 1080, which killed thousands of animals of all kinds, and prosecuted eagle-killers considered untouchable because of their political clout in the west. We formed an Interior team to ban the use of DDT and supported the creation of new national parks and wildlife refuges that added thousands of acres of public lands. We opposed dams and drainage schemes concocted by the Corps, Tennessee Valley Authority, Soil Conservation Agency and Bureau of Reclamation – outdated, environmentally destructive projects. Working with like-minded people in key federal agencies, we forged critical changes in environmental law ranging from pollution and endangered species protection to enhanced marine fisheries.

We lost some battles to pure politics, but we never gave up. We eagerly sought new opportunities at a time when bipartisan members of Congress were willing to listen, work together and turn our efforts into the law of the land.

After my Interior service ended, I returned to Florida to remain a voice in conservation efforts in my home state.

In all, I've served seven Florida governors of both parties on every conceivable committee and commission. I was elected town commissioner on Jupiter Island twice and appointed by three governors to sit on the South Florida Water Management District Governing Board. I've served on countless environmental boards and received many state and national awards that run the gamut of my passions and interests.

I hope that this collection of essays – stories that relate great environmental victories and some disappointing defeats, mingled with fond (and sometimes not particularly fond) anecdotes – can serve as inspiration for coming generations of Floridians and other Americans as we confront new, well-funded assaults on our land and our water and our air.

The work surely is hard – at times both thrilling and terrifying – but it is essential and it must be done, and I know that it will be done.

Of this I am certain: My stories illustrate Margaret Mead's famed observation, "Never doubt that a small group of thoughtful, committed citizens can change the world; indeed, it's the only thing that ever has."

For the People: Partisanship – and Bipartisanship
"You're My Mr. Clean"

The world of politics is always an interesting realm in which issues and personalities can change rapidly from one day to the next. In recent years, however, this has been complicated by the persistent friction generated by our two-party system.

These days, sadly and counterproductively, compromise and cooperation are held in low esteem.

However, when I first became deeply involved in politics there was a different atmosphere – one in which elected leaders often crossed the aisle to work together for accomplishments they felt were important for the citizenry.

This was absolutely true of environmental issues that arose in Florida during the 1960s and 1970s. Very often Republicans and Democrats collaborated to create legislation to protect the state's unique and valuable natural resources. My experiences in this field resulted in my work for two governors from different parties – something that might be unimaginable today.

I first became involved in government bureaucracy with the 1966 election of Claude Kirk as Florida's first Republican governor since Reconstruction.

When Kirk lost his 1970 reelection campaign, I was sure that I would be leaving Tallahassee. Reubin Askew, a Democrat, won the election and I believed he would bring his own staff to take over my role. I thought that was what I would hear when Askew called me into his office. Instead, he asked me to stay on.

I said, "Governor, I've got three little babies and my wife is despondent about my staying in Tallahassee."

Askew replied: "Bring her back. Stay on with me. I need you to keep cleaning up these messes. You're my Mr. Clean and I want you to stay."

So, I stayed on and I really enjoyed it. But the first big case I made in my role with the Askew administration caused a ruckus and it involved his home city, Pensacola.

After big rains, the city's sewage transfer stations would get overloaded and the city would just dump the sewage into Pensacola Bay, an important estuary. They'd dump the whole damn plant-full of sewage. They had done it four or five times when I came to them and said it had to stop.

I said, "OK, I got you a big federal grant. You're well along on cleaning up your sewage systems. You know perfectly well that you can bypass this transfer station and pump to your main holding tanks and holding ponds and run that sewage two or three days later so you do not have to dump it into the bay. Next time you run it into the bay, hellfire and brimstone is going to arrive and on top of it will be the biggest fine that I can possibly assess the city. Believe me."

Apparently city leaders didn't believe me because about 10 days after Askew took the oath as Florida's new governor, there was a big rain in Pensacola and the city once again dumped all undertreated sewage into the bay.

I was infuriated. When the news came that Pensacola had done it again, I issued a press statement. I flew to Pensacola, went to court and asked a judge to give me an injunction –

continued on next page

a restraining order against the city. My lawyers said the biggest fine we could assess was $25,000, so I asked the judge to fine Pensacola that amount.

The press went bananas. After the short flight back to the capital, the governor called and said, "I'd like to see you." I thought that perhaps my days in state government were finished. After all, I'd taken on his home city with vigorous enforcement.

When I arrived at his office, Askew stood up from behind his desk and very calmly said, "I understand. I've been briefed on what Pensacola did. I'm just going to say this one time to you. I have absolutely no sympathy for what Pensacola has done. All I want is, before you act, just call me and tell me what you're going to do first. I will not try to talk you out of doing it, but I want to know first."

"Governor, I apologize," I replied, relieved to still have the job. "Governor Kirk never cared one bit. I understand perfectly. It's a perfectly fair criticism and I guarantee it won't happen again."

Askew said, "I've got the mayor, I've got the chairman of the county commission, I've got all the industries of Pensacola screaming bloody murder. But I have informed them it is time to clean up!"

I had a wonderful relationship with Governor Askew for the next few months. Let's do the math: two administrations, two governors from opposing parties, one consistent effort to preserve our environment.

I want to make this point as clearly as I can: Politics is politics and, even back then, the battles often were fierce. But when something truly important came up, both parties often were able to reach an understanding, a compromise, a cooperative way forward so that we could serve the body politic.

We must find a way back to that form of governance. The future of our nation requires that we do.

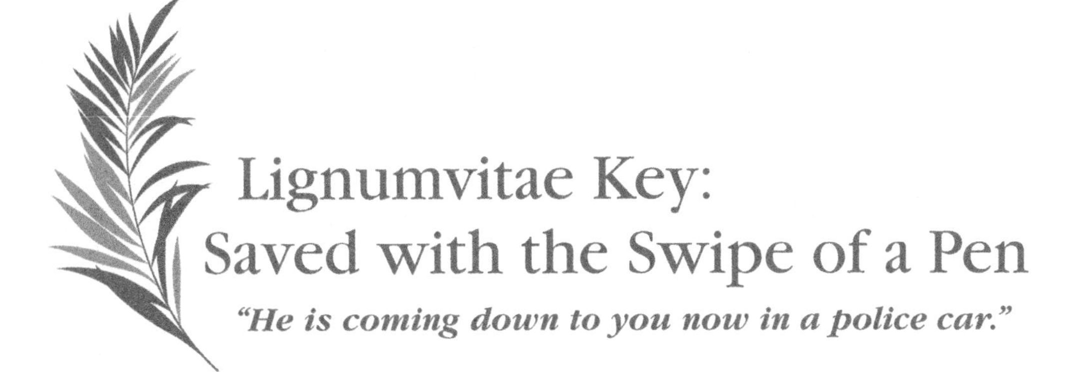

Lignumvitae Key: Saved with the Swipe of a Pen

"He is coming down to you now in a police car."

Lignumvitae Key is a small coral island located about midway along the Florida Keys archipelago. It is distinctive primarily because it contains one of the largest and least-disturbed tropical hardwood hammocks remaining in South Florida. The island has been an area of special interest for botanists and other scientists, fascinated by the incredible varieties of Caribbean hardwoods that had survived for centuries, despite hurricanes and infrequent but menacing cold weather.

It was otherwise little known until concerns arose over proposed plans for the development of an expensive residential community complete with clubhouse, pool and docks. It was to be accessed by a causeway connecting the island with highway U.S. 1, the primary route to and through the Keys.

When I joined the environmental movement on my return from military service in 1960, I was eager to join a number of the state's most prominent and aggressive nongovernmental organizations, including The Nature Conservancy. I was familiar with the Conservancy, as one of its first projects was to protect the Mianus River Gorge not far from our family's home in Greenwich, Connecticut. My father was fascinated by the potential of a land preservation organization and was an early supporter of the group.

The Florida branch of the Conservancy was made up of an astonishingly interesting group of women and men from every corner of Florida who recognized that unless major funding was made available, much of the "wonder areas" of Florida would disappear to intense development.

Regrettably, the state's mantra was "growth, at any cost, growth." Thousands of acres of state-owned lands were sold off at every Wednesday's state Cabinet meeting. Permits were issued to clear important mangrove jungles that provided nutrients to bays and estuaries and habitat for young fish and eggs from sport and commercial species. Bay bottoms were filled, creating islands. Dredge and fill permits were issued regularly for new waterfront developments after mangroves were ripped out.

The most pressing need – aside from a state commitment to preserve mangroves and end the long era of dredging and filling uplands and even shallow underwater flats to create artificial islands for intense development – was to compile an inventory of what was left of the best of Florida.

"We the people" needed to ignite public interest that would make land preservation a political issue. I was fascinated by the potential of a crusade to raise the level of excitement among our citizens and save examples of Florida's very best.

Leaders of the nascent state branch of The Nature Conservancy had agreed on a list of "critically important acquisitions." These leaders had approached members of the state park advisory board and land experts within the Department of Natural Resources' state parks division to discuss priorities for potential

Photo courtesy Capt. Samantha Zeher

purchases.

Following Claude Kirk's election as governor in 1966, my position as environmental advisor afforded me "broad responsibilities" focusing on the vast water pollution of Florida's waters from untreated sewage and toxic industrial wastes. Provided with an office, a secretary and not much more, I was determined to halt the sale of so-called "submerged land" that for years had created waterside housing. Land acquisition, management and preservation were all priorities: These were potential land development proposals that should not have been permitted.

I met with a small delegation of Nature Conservancy leaders, who stressed that an emergency existed and only the governor could defeat a terrible proposal. The specific subject at hand was Lignumvitae Key, a longtime dream of preservation by the Conservancy and the state Park Board.

The situation was simple: Monroe County had passed a bond issue that was to be matched with state road funds to upgrade the island's roads and allow what the proponents called "improvements" for land development.

A syndicate of well-known, politically well-placed investors had acquired Lignumvitae Key and proposed that matching funds be used to construct a bridge from U.S. 1 to the island or build a causeway by dredging the bottom of Florida Bay.

I was appalled by both alternatives. I asked the governor what I should do to prevent Monroe County and the state from allowing access to this most botanically rare treasure that was surrounded by some of the finest bonefish flats in the Keys. He listened carefully and asked his secretary to hook him up with Chairman Jay Brown of state Department of Transportation.

A minute or so later, the governor told Brown that his key environmental aide, a fellow named Nathaniel Reed, needed to see him right away about a problem in the Keys that was solvable and that he hoped would be worked out "as soon as possible." He asked Brown if he was free and the response, naturally, was that he looked forward to my visit. The governor replied, "He is coming down to you now in a state police car," our early form of staff transportation.

Off to the Burns Building the officer and I went. The officer asked me what the "deal is all about" and I replied simply, "Wish me luck." I was ushered into Chairman Jay Brown's opulent office. He rose from behind an immaculate desk that obviously had been cleaned moments before my arrival.

After pleasantries, he asked what he could do for me and the governor. I explained the problem we had with either a bridge or a causeway to Lignumvitae Key. He asked his secretary to bring in the list of projects that Monroe County had submitted for approval for matching state road funds.

There, carefully typed in order of priority, was the project, a bridge or causeway to the Key. It was ranked No. 3. I stated our objections and, within a moment, Brown reached for an impressive desk pen and swiped out the project! No causeway and, he added, no bridge would be allowed to be built.

He remarked, "It should never have been so far up this list. It is incredible that the department would ever consider bridging to the island or dredging up a causeway for a private development." He ended by saying, "Do come and see me when you see grave errors or potential mistakes that either county or even state road engineers come up with. The state is growing rapidly and we need to spend our dollars on important traffic projects, but we want them to be environmentally sound."

I stood, shook his hand and bolted for the door. When I was in the state police car, the officer asked, "How did it go?" I pondered for a moment and replied, "I think my days in Tallahassee may be very rewarding."

I called representatives of The Nature Conservancy and reported that neither a bridge nor causeway would be approved as a part of the Monroe County road improvement plan. There was great rejoicing!

Lignumvitae Key, photo © Peter W. Cross

Of course, the developers were enraged and swore vengeance. They attempted to finance a causeway, without success. The permits needed to cross one of the Keys' most famous bonefish flats would not have been approved, regardless of the owners' political influence.

When the causeway proposal was vetoed, the developers notified the Conservancy and the state Department of Natural Resources that a sale was in everyone's best interests. Ney Landrum, director of the Division of Recreation and Parks for DNR, worked with a team from the Conservancy and, with my input, realized that the only way to ensure permanent protection of the island's natural features would be acquisition by a sympathetic entity.

The Nature Conservancy, still in its infancy, recognized the magnitude of the undertaking and appealed for assistance from the state of Florida. In late 1969, the Florida Department of Natural Resources referred the matter to its Division of Recreation and Parks for review and recommendation.

On the basis of its evaluation, the Division of Recreation and Parks concluded that acquisition of Lignumvitae Key, concurrently with acquisition of Indian Key on the opposite side of U.S. 1, would be fully justified as desirable additions to the Florida State Park System. Negotiations with the owners of each property were initiated on March 3, 1970.

I briefed Gov. Kirk on the incredible potential acquisition of this unique island. He sent word to the director of the Department of Natural Resources that acquisition should be consummated quickly. I contacted the Cabinet aides and they all were enthusiastic supporters of the proposal. Negotiations eventually were successful in both instances, and a staff recommendation for the lands' purchase was approved by the Board of Natural Resources. Gov. Kirk led the Cabinet in a unanimous vote to ratify the deal on December 8, 1970.

Tedious negotiations finally led to closings for both properties on March 3, 1971. The purchase price for Lignumvitae Key, including nearby Shell Key, a smaller, adjacent island, was $1.85 million. Of that, $1.65 million came from the State Land Acquisition Trust Fund using documentary stamp proceeds, and $200,000 came from The Nature Conservancy.

Although delighted to have the property under state ownership, a consortium of university scientists that for some time had used Lignumvitae Key for research purposes, expressed concern about seeing it managed as a state park. Having no intention of converting this rare and fragile resource into an amusement park, Ney Landrum readily accepted a recommendation by the Conservancy to include language in the deeds restricting the property for use "...as a nature preserve for the controlled recreational enjoyment of the public, and for related and compatible scientific, educational and esthetic purposes."

Now, whenever I visit, and as my bonefish guide races west from Islamorada past Lignumvitae Key, I must admit that I have a great sense of satisfaction knowing that a swipe of a pen can change history – and conserve our natural resources.

Earth Day: A Catalyst of Change

"It's just a bunch of kids."

The creation of Earth Day in 1970 served as the spark of a national awakening and led to a generally accepted consensus that environmental degradation was a daily and unacceptable fact of life across America.

In many ways, everything that follows in this book and in my life – our work in Florida, in Washington, and around the nation and the world – flows from the environmental awareness created and magnified by that first Earth Day.

Pete McCloskey, back then a Republican congressman from California, played a key role in recognizing the importance of Earth Day. He also was a major sponsor of some of the landmark environmental protection laws that were passed by Congress during the remarkable early 1970s, among them the Clean Air Act, the Clean Water Act and the Endangered Species Act.

Pete was the all-time greatest pain in President Richard Nixon's rear end. He even ran as a presidential candidate attempting to embarrass Nixon and to end the Vietnam War.

We were not close friends (though we later became so), but Pete worked with me on the final drafts of our submissions of the Clean Water Act and especially on the Endangered Species Act. The assigned House committee consisted of strong, environmentally conscious members. I remember that Pete was the leading Republican and Rep. John Dingell of Michigan was the leading Democrat, both of whom crushed opposition and guided the bill to passage in the House.

Pete was intemperate, but great fun to work with as he believed in the impossible and often was proven right. Here are some of his memories regarding Earth Day and the environmental movement that led to it and emerged from it:

> "Sen. Gaylord Nelson had attended San Jose State in his college days, hiked in the high Sierras and grown to love the weather of California as compared with that of his home state, Wisconsin. And so it was that sometime in January 1970, I got a call from Gaylord asking if I would join him in the bi-partisan sponsorship of an Earth Day to be held on April 22, 1970 at colleges and high schools all across the country.
>
> Would I? Damn right. We met and he introduced me to [conservationist] Sid Howe, who had pledged to raise $100,000. Gaylord had asked Stanford's most recent student body president, Denis Hayes, to chair the event and put together a staff with a D.C. office. The staff were mostly teenagers or in their early 20s, and this was a constructive and happy thought at a time of increasing student unrest over Nixon's continuation of the war.

Hayes and his folks somehow got a list of some 2,000 colleges and 10,000 high schools and sent out a form letter: 'Dear Student Body President, would you be interested in holding an Earth Day on your campus on April 22, 1970? If so, we would be pleased to send you information on air pollution, water pollution, protection of the land, oceans and wildlife habitat, etc.'

The response was overwhelming. The day was to be a day of study, ideally with a 45-minute session on one of the four major environmental issues, and a fifth session on whatever the local problem was.

I remember that Mayor John Lindsay of New York set up a mammoth Earth Day celebration in New York City, and that my daughter, Nancy, reported a wonderful sunny afternoon on a grassy hillside at her college in California.

April 22nd was a Sunday, the first day of spring and with college campuses in a turmoil of revolt against Nixon and the Vietnam War. Nixon asked [aide John] Ehrlichman to have the FBI monitor all of the events and report back to him, anticipating that Earth Day would turn into anti-war outbursts. The weather turned out beautiful in most cases and the demonstrations were peaceful.

A couple of days after Earth Day, Ehrlichman called me, laughing as hard as I had ever heard him laugh. We had been friends since law school, and he and his wife looked after my wife and child when I went to Korea in 1951. John had flown 26 missions in B-24s over Europe.

John said, 'Pete, you won't believe this. I have just gotten the FBI's report, which I have to give Nixon tomorrow. Let me read you a couple of paragraphs.'

He then read how the various FBI agents, observing through field glasses, had seen a bunch of young girls with flowers in their hair, sitting in the grass petting their dogs, listening to some guy on a hilltop talking through a microphone about air and water pollution. There had been no protests of the war; the girls wore no more than a T-shirt and shorts, were barefoot and may have participated in smoking a little pot, drinking a little beer, and perhaps some lovemaking in the bushes."

Right here, I should mention that John Ehrlichman, later deeply implicated in the Nixon's Watergate scandal, had been a well-respected land-use attorney in Seattle and was a covert "green" within the White House. As readers soon shall see in coming essays, he was a reliable supporter of our environmental protection policies and activities. His deputy, John Whitaker, also was a great partner.

As for my own activities, during my early days of working for Florida Gov. Claude Kirk, I received notice that Earth Day celebrations were in the planning process around the state. I sought permission from the governor to speak at rallies at many of the Florida universities.

Governor Kirk became enthusiastic. I was prepared to privately charter a plane, but he deemed the opportunity of such importance that he assigned me a state plane – a rather aged twin-engine plane with a rather aged pilot. He ordered his scheduling staff to coordinate with the presidents of five state universities that were organizing Earth Day events.

I remember starting the day by being flown to Pensacola for a 9 a.m. rally on a beautiful green grass area within the university grounds surrounded by a large crowd of enthusiastic students. The school's president introduced me and appeared terrified as to what the event might turn into.

I spoke of the polluted bays, the industrial wastes pouring into the waters surrounding the universities. I spoke about proper stewardship of our resources and quoted Teddy Roosevelt, and then departed among cheers and through some antiwar demonstrators who took Earth Day as an opportunity to express opposition to the Vietnam War and President Nixon.

I also was flown to Tampa for two appearances, one at the University of South Florida, the other at the University of Tampa. Then, off to Gainesville. I always was met by a state police officer who was briefed to take me to a great green lawn.

The lawn at the University of Florida was covered with students all revved up by a previous speaker. I gave a brief but rousing talk, urging them to get involved. Only they could change a course that would lead inevitably to environmental disaster.

Next, I was flown to South Florida in a splendid twin Cessna owned by the South Florida Water Management District. I was rushed to the University of Miami, where President Henry King Stanford, an old friend, warmly greeted me. Once again, an outdoor arena was jammed with youth. There were many signs demanding a halt to pollution and to the Vietnam War.

When I concluded my remarks – I remember they were pretty harsh as Miami Dade's record of pollution and land deals was constantly being exposed by the *Miami Herald* – I urged youthful involvement. "Only you can change the reckless course of action that is destroying this state if not the country," I told them. Anyway, my talk roused them and created a scene of near hysteria.

There also was a curious odor in the air that I did not recognize. I asked the provost what it was and his reply was clear. "It's pot! They are all high as kites and enjoying this Earth Day enormously!"

Since then, I have spoken at a number of Earth Day celebrations, but none rivaled the first Earth Day. I became an ardent supporter of the League of Conservation Voters and, at times, a major contributor to campaigns intended to unseat congressmen and others hostile to our movement.

In fact, particularly on the national level, the significance of that first Earth Day in 1970 cannot be overstated.

Congress had just passed the National Environmental Policy Act of 1969 (NEPA) and, as required by that act, the White House had created the Council on Environmental Quality (CEQ), but Earth Day and the activism it unleashed turbocharged the federal government's environmental protection efforts.

President Nixon appointed Russell Train as the first CEQ chairman and added Robert Cahn, a Pulitzer Prize-winning author and a correspondent of the *Christian Science Monitor.* Cahn was an expert on the National Park System and on land use issues. Dr. Gordon MacDonald had been vice chancellor of the University of California-Santa Cruz and was an expert on geophysics and the environment. They were a team, but Train was the unquestioned leader.

In enacting NEPA, Congress recognized that nearly all federal activities affect the environment in some way and mandated that federal agencies, during their planning and decision-making processes, must consider the environmental affects of their actions.

CEQ would become a small but high-energy committee of experts who would oversee significant differences between federal agencies that were loathe to discuss their pet projects with other federal agencies that might object. The major protagonists were the Corps of Army Engineers, the Bureau of Reclamation, the Forest Service and the Department of Transportation, all of which had ignored years of environmental objections from the Fish and Wildlife Service and the Federal Water Pollution Agency (both located in the Department of Interior).

The new requirement that a constructing agency had to prepare a legally sufficient Environmental Impact Statement came as a shock to the development minded federal agencies that, previously, merely had needed congressional approval of their projects.

Although the Nixon Administration had sent a bland annual environmental report to Congress,

Train and his brilliant staff prepared four annual presidential messages regarding the nation's environmental challenges. The CEQ reports were superbly illustrated and printed. They contained a series of recommendations, including legislative proposals supported by sound science and budget realities that led to a series of executive orders, budget changes and significant opposition to ill-conceived so-called "public works" projects.

The new laws and procedures provided ample opportunity to challenge the supposed benefits of new projects. They also provided the basis for newly founded environmental advocacy groups to challenge the environmental impacts of a vast range of proposed projects.

For instance, the Natural Resources Defense Council and the Environmental Defense Fund swiftly took legal action against a host of congressionally approved construction projects; canals, dams and highways, on the grounds that their NEPA statements inadequately described the environmental consequences of their proposed actions. In addition, the League of Conservation Voters was created by the charismatic David Brower and dedicated itself to pressuring lawmakers on behalf of the environment.

Taken together, this was an unprecedented effort to engage the administration, Congress and the American people in the need for serious environmental reform.

Among other things, the CEQ urged creation of the Environmental Protection Agency (EPA), consolidating governmental agency efforts to control pollution. Democratic Sen. Ed Muskie of Maine, a potential presidential candidate, was working on such a plan. President Nixon, always recognizing political threats, proposed creation of the EPA before the Muskie effort was completed.

Still, not everyone in Washington got the message.

Pete McCloskey recalls that a youth group targeted 12 members of the House of Representatives and dubbed them "the Dirty Dozen." One of his colleagues dismissed the threat, saying it came from just "a bunch of kids."

"But those kids changed the world," McCloskey says now. Two Democrats promptly lost primary elections, five of 10 Republicans lost their seats in November, and others hostile to the environmental movement began to run scared.

"This, in turn, led to at least two-thirds of the House and Senate declaring themselves 'environmentalists.'"

Astonishingly, during one year alone – 1972 – we saw creation of the Clean Water Act, the Marine Mammal Act and the Magnuson-Stevens Fisheries Act. We also prepared the final draft of the Endangered Species Act, which passed in 1973.

Much good work was done by all of us as this bipartisan cooperation lasted for 24 years, until Newt Gingrich came to power and categorized Democrats as enemies.

Today, Earth Day is observed each year in the United States and 191 other countries, with more than 1 billion people taking part in the activities, according to the Earth Day Network.

The League of Conservation Voters remains a major factor, especially in House of Representative races but also in Senate and gubernatorial contests, and it still publishes an electorally effective list of the current Dirty Dozen.

Unfortunately though, the pendulum has swung the other way and coming elections well may determine whether environmental protection policy goes the way of the passenger pigeon.

We must find a way to overcome this near-hopeless division of interests and parties that ill performs its duties to the American people – and to our progeny.

I hope that these next essays can help us find that way.

Less is More: Defeating the Miami Jetport, Creating a National Preserve

"One of the high-water marks in my environmental career."

Despite the enormity of the cost of the Vietnam War and the pain of a national recession, Florida experienced an era of explosive growth during the 1960s. Investors from Central and South America, often worried about exorbitant taxes or unstable governments, flocked to the state, sheltering funds in Miami banks and investing in land developments that ranged from high-rise condominiums and office buildings to golf courses and tourist hotels.

Sleepy downtown Miami was transformed into an international destination.

Arthur Godfrey, America's favorite morning radio and, later, television host, proclaimed that sunshine, white beaches, warm ocean, fine hotels and restaurants offered investment opportunities from Miami to Key West. The era was highlighted by the credo: "Growth, any kind of growth, was desirable."

Out of this credo came a frenzy of proposed developments aimed at improving international trans-jportation and, therefore, enabling more investments from other countries.

One idea that emerged during this period was the construction of a supersonic jetport with almost six miles of runways deep in the Florida Everglades. Now, we are desperately trying to save this land through the largest restoration effort in the world at a cost that will exceed $8 billion. But, historically, these massive wetlands that once reached across the southern tip of Florida have been the scene of many schemes, frauds, and attempts to "improve" the land – ultimately leading to environmental crises.

And so it was with the jetport, proposed in the 1960s to aid in expanding Miami's air traffic capacity, which was hemmed in by the borders of the city's airport. Local officials, under the leadership of the Dade Count Port Authority, decided that the best place for a new jetport that could handle a new generation of supersonic and subsonic jets would be the Big Cypress area, located northwest of Everglades National Park. There, they could build up to six runways – with two up to 30,000 feet long – and position the jetport as an international hub.

Author Luther J. Carter wrote that county and port authority officials "entertained the dream that this jetport would ultimately become one of the world's largest, and divert international passengers from airports in New York and elsewhere." [1]

These aspirations, which would have been heralded as a great cause across the county a century earlier, initially seemed like a done deal, especially given the fact that "many people still were not sufficiently aware of either the value or the fragility of the Everglades and the Big Cypress..." noted Carter.

However, this was a new era in which a series of crises was awakening Americans to the value of preserving natural resources and systems. The jetport project became a focus of one of the nation's most important environmental battles of the twentieth century and, after an enormous effort by local, state, and national advocates – I am proud that I was one of them – led to the creation of Big Cypress National Preserve, a gem in the national park system. [2]

The defeat of this "jetport of the future," coupled with the acquisition of 547,000 acres of the Big Cypress in southwest Florida, also was the occasion for a curious crossing of two lives intimately involved in both efforts. Joe Browder and I were young men cast by fate to have our life journeys intersect at the Big Cypress.

As I've mentioned, following overseas military service, I returned to Florida, where I was outraged by the incredible changes that were damaging my vision of what the state meant to me. I joined the Florida Audubon Society, The Nature Conservancy, and "Friends" groups of every known effort to save a river, beach, lake, or unique landscape. I made friends throughout the state who were equally outraged by the all-too-rapid, thoughtless development.

Equally galling were the congressionally authorized drainage projects that were converting vitally important wetlands and water recharge areas into ill-conceived housing developments or pastures for the great cattle ranches. Until the latter part of the twentieth century, draining Florida's wetlands and Everglades was viewed as a desirable goal. Politicians were elected on promises of accomplishing just that, pledging that newer and newer technology would get the job done in order to "control" nature – never a good idea in the long run.

Those in authority did not care about the resulting pollution that flowed into the Indian River Lagoon, Lake Okeechobee or the west coast receiving waters. Despite valiant opposition to these projects by a group of committed, educated men and women who fearlessly challenged every U.S. Army Corps of Engineers proposal for more drainage, Florida became ground zero for a number of proposed engineering "feats," including the Cross State Barge Canal that would have bisected the state as well as dredging, filling and channelizing parts of Biscayne Bay to create an oil refinery complex and an unneeded waterfront resort community.

I found allies, attended countless meetings and spoke at dozens of rallies around the state, protesting plans by the state and our congressional delegations for more drainage, more sales of state-owned lands, and more Corps projects that were of dubious value, except to produce work for the Corps and its contractors.

Importantly, I made the acquaintance of Dr. Arthur Marshall, who became not only a great friend but also a wise, brilliant mentor. Marshall was recognized as one of the most thoughtful ecologists in our state's history. He trained a generation of young activists to understand the brilliant analysis of America's great ecologist, Aldo Leopold that every action has a connection that must be carefully considered. Marshall was a philosopher of science who understood that healthy human societies could not exist without respecting the integrity of natural ecosystems.

In 1965-66, when I campaigned with Governor Claude Kirk during his successful gubernatorial race, he often would be asked to describe his position on an environmental issue. His standard reply: "Nathaniel is writing a 'white paper' on that very subject!" He won by a landslide and I became his environmental assistant during his single term.

My "white papers" stressed the need to end the era of pumping raw sewage into the ocean from Palm Beach to Key West, and from Sarasota southward. Of equal concern was the sale of state-owned submerged lands, the clearing of thousands of acres of mangrove forests fringing the state's

southern estuaries, and the deposit of dredged material to underlie major waterfront developments. The condition of the Everglades, now considered a valuable natural resource, also was of great concern.

Although I had visited Everglades National Park many times and fished throughout Florida Bay, I was not knowledgeable about the Big Cypress, including its importance as the watershed of the westernmost part of the park and its importance as a great nursery of saltwater fisheries. I soon was to be educated as a result of the proposed construction of the Dade County Jetport, widely proclaimed to be the "supersonic jetport of the future."

Marjory Stoneman Douglas, the grand lady of the Everglades ecosystem whose seminal 1947 book *The Everglades: River of Grass* had awakened the nation to the Everglades' biological richness, called me one day. She said, "You have got to get to know Joe Browder. He is National Audubon's man and he is going to help me restore the Everglades." Browder had just persuaded Douglas to get involved in the brewing fight to stop the jetport; to do so, he encouraged her to use her fame and many connections to establish Friends of the Everglades, a support group that continues today long after her death.

Browder's American father joined the Royal Canadian Air Force in 1939 to help win the Battle of Britain. Following the Japanese attack on Pearl Harbor on December 7, 1941, American pilots were assigned to the U.S. Army Air Corps and Browder's father was assigned to military duty in Miami, where the Everglades Hotel had been taken by the Army as a post for officers awaiting further orders. Curiously,

my father was sent to the same hotel a year later, prior to his final assignment with the Special Services at Washington and Lee University in Lexington, Virginia.

Browder's mother took him for long walks along Miami's Bayfront Park, where he became fascinated by the natural world and especially the world of birds. He remembers getting hooked on birding by a teacher who used Junior Audubon bird identification flash cards.

The Browder family travelled extensively after the war, including a stay of many years in Cuba and Mexico where he became absorbed with nature. Browder returned to Florida in early 1961 as a young journalist with a family of his own to produce television news for the Miami NBC affiliate. His fascination with nature was noted by the distinguished Tropical Audubon Society leader Alice Wainwright of the Coconut Grove neighborhood, who served as vice mayor of Miami. She recruited Browder to lead tours for the Tropical Audubon Society in Everglades National Park.

As an Audubon officer and strategist determined to protect Biscayne Bay and the Everglades, Browder made waves.

In 1967, he was asked by the National Audubon Society to become Audubon's first regional U.S. field representative, working on environmental issues throughout the south. Browder begged to be assigned to Miami, "where," he said, "the action is." He persuaded Audubon's New York executives not to require him to operate from Atlanta, but instead to allow him to stay in Miami, where he could focus on protecting nature in South Florida at a time of unrelenting perils. And there were many.

There were threats to Biscayne Bay, including the prospect of dredging and filling the bay's islands to produce a Miami Beach-type development to be known as "Islandia." There was the threat of a potentially huge oil refinery to be constructed south of Miami, destroying thousands of acres of wetlands and mangrove forests. The refinery's construction also would require square miles of the bay to be dredged for deepwater access, devastating fragile coral reefs. At the same time, the Florida Keys were undergoing a siege from developers digging illegal canals and transforming mangrove jungles and tropical forests into subdivisions.

Overall, South Florida was in the grip of an explosive period of thoughtless, under-regulated growth.

As a television news reporter, Brower had learned about environmental politics from leaders of these fights, particularly Tropical Audubon's Wainwright, author/activist Polly Redford and Lloyd Miller, the latter of whom was a leader of the local Isaak Walton League. While still a Tropical Audubon volunteer, Browder had begun working to stop the Dade County Port Authority's jetport plan and was determined that the forthcoming debate over the future of the Big Cypress should become a priority issue of the National Audubon Society.

In every way, Browder was the representative of the National Audubon Society, working from a tiny office with one administrative assistant. He

Dade County's preliminary runway in the Big Cypress

was unfazed.

Browder quickly recognized that development of a major jetport in the middle of the Big Cypress would doom any opportunity to maintain natural water flow to the western portion of Everglades National Park and it would destroy the Big Cypress wilderness, a virtual second home of a vast group of outdoorsmen who could find relief from crowds in eastern Dade and Broward counties.

They could hunt deer and hogs, or just meander through miles of the great wet wilderness in their airboats and high four-wheel-drive "swamp buggies." Browder fit in well with these unique characters, who included small landowners, hunters, poachers and moonshiners. They were a tough crowd, united only in the belief that the Big Cypress was their territory, where they could and should be left in peace.

I met Browder in 1968 through my work for Gov. Kirk. Although my leading concern at the time was stopping the daily discharge of millions of gallons of raw sewage through long pipes off Miami's beaches, Browder intrigued me with a list of his own priorities that soon became mine. Our chemistry clicked. Browder had more missions than could possibly be solved by one man, but he was a tireless worker and he knew how to attract media attention.

Somehow, I had missed the first chapter of the potential environmental and fiscal disaster that the "Boomer" Mayor of Dade County, Charles "Chuck" Hall, had sold his fellow commissioners, who also served as the Dade County Port Authority. I never will know exactly who promoted the deal that resulted in Dade County acquiring substantial land within the Big Cypress wilderness, passing

a bond issue, and building a full-length runway, complete with a control tower capable of handling jet traffic.

Bob Padrick, my great friend and chairman of the Central and Southern Florida Flood Control District – the predecessor of the South Florida Water Management District – called me in October 1968 and said Gov. Kirk had attended a brief dedication ceremony the previous month and was "ecstatic" about the prospects of a major airport in the Big Cypress.

The groundbreaking ceremony had been a big production. "Colorful, hand-sewn jackets were worn not only by the Miccosukee Indian leaders who were present but also by officials of the Port Authority as well," Luther Carter wrote. The jetport site, ironically, was to be built on the sacred site of the tribe's Green Corn Dance, but for now the tribe was supporting the project – something it would later come to oppose.

The ceremony included a proclamation of praise from Gov. Kirk and a blast of dynamite that hurled "muck and pieces of limestone into the air." It was the typical kickoff of a major federal public works project – one that a later analysis estimated could exceed $1 billion in cost. A variety of federal agencies, including the U.S. Department of Transportation (USDOT) and the Federal Aviation Administration (FAA) were gung-ho supporters, as well. [3]

To my consternation, the governor did not discuss with me, his environmental adviser, his trip or his overt support for construction of the jetport's first runway. My only explanation is that I had begun seemingly endless meetings with mayors and county commissioners to forge agreements on how to finance and acquire needed land and build miles of sewage pipelines along with regional wastewater treatment plants.

I was determined to force the southeast counties and cities in Palm Beach, Broward and Dade Counties to treat all sewage to a secondary level before sending it to the sea through long pipelines. The disgrace of having millions of gallons a day of raw sewage sent to sea was my first priority. I was totally preoccupied by three things: sewage, halting the sale of submerged state-owned lands, and curtailing the clearing, dredging and filling of mangrove forests. Somehow, the jetport never made it onto my radar.

Padrick, a Fort Pierce automobile dealer, urged me to fly down to take a close look at the proposed jetport site because he thought a major jetport would pollute the air and water, create budget problems, and corrupt land-use principles. To reach the site from Miami, officials planned to build infrastructure to cross the most important water conservation area that supplied water to Everglades National Park. The water conservation areas were responsible for refreshing and recharging the Biscayne Aquifer, which supplied all drinking water for the ever-growing populations of the southern three counties and Florida Keys. It was the last great remnant of the "river of grass" that Douglas so poignantly described in her epic book.

By late 1967, Browder, who had been alerted by Dan Paul, a Dade County attorney and civic leader, about that county's secret purchases of land in Collier County just north of Everglades National Park, was already on the case. A year later, he researched the topic while recruiting scientists and business leaders to his cause and organizing student and environmental groups. He persuaded National Parks Advisory Board Chair Frank Masland to start the Everglades Coalition and helped mobilize the unique fellows who lived in the swamp or used the swamp to give their wives and children an Everglades camping experience while the men hunted.

This group sought to escape the ever-growing consequences of the misguided effort to lure millions of unsuspecting people to metropolitan Dade and Broward counties. Browder used his annual telephone budget up in one month. Browder's jetport challenge was universally agreed to be an all-out effort to prevent the construction of the proposed jetport and "save" the Big Cypress. His initial supporters were a small but vocal group, and they were given little attention by the powers that controlled Dade County. "Growth was God" to them even it was to be on the west side of the Everglades, in the middle of the vast Big Cypress watershed, far from downtown Miami. It should be noted that this largely had been the state's mantra about development throughout the peninsula and it had rarely been challenged on a large scale – until now.

Obviously, supporters counted on the potential development of a jetport in the middle of nowhere to ignite a land boom. Land sales at exorbitant prices had begun. Any hydrologist or conservationist could easily understand that development of a huge international airport in a swamp would require a major drainage system that would decimate the natural watershed of the southwestern Everglades ecosystem. A cursory review of the anticipated costs indicated that development of the proposed jetport would result in fiscal ruination to the county. Why the taxpayers, the newspapers and bankers didn't scream bloody murder over the costs and the annual expenses of developing a jetport in a wilderness swamp without access remains a mystery.

I flew down from Tallahassee in an ancient state plane for a flyover of the training field of the proposed jetport and Big Cypress. One long look was sufficient – an environmental disaster was imminent.

The most obvious first questions were: How would the airport be served? How would the passengers and their baggage get to the airport to catch their flights? How would they return to Miami? The obvious answer was to cross the Everglades – the most important water conservation area serving Dade County, and the largest segment of the historic Everglades – with high-speed trains and roads.

The Port Authority maintained that a system of high-speed trains would "whoosh" passengers to and from the jetport on tracks perched above the Everglades marsh – ecological and financial madness! Imagine the miles of pipeline needed

An editorial cartoon from Audubon Magazine shows the conflicts between airplanes and wildlife that the jetport would produce.

to carry fuel. Imagine an elevated high-speed train departing each way every 15 minutes. The problem of baggage was not considered to be a problem by the Port Authority minions.

The business community was firmly aligned with what I considered the snake oil salesmen. The traditional Florida land peddlers saw a golden opportunity to drain the Big Cypress and carve up hundreds of thousands of acres of land into saleable lots for industry, farming, cattle, and citrus – you name it. The "Good Ol' Boy" network that led the Florida boom of the 1920s was re-energized and ready for suckers.

My questions continued: What about a conveyer system for cargo? What about the hundreds of airport workers? What about customs and immigration? It was obvious the entire scheme was typical of an era of irresponsibility that only the then-Dade County mayor and fellow commissioners could have cooked up. The rest of the story unfolded in waves. Browder roared. The conservation community of South Florida joined forces to support Browder and fight the proposed jetport.

I quietly convinced Gov. Kirk to change his position and, to his lasting credit, he quickly realized that he had been taken in by an impossible dream cooked up by schemers and land peddlers.

What to do? I persuaded Gov. Kirk to inform Mayor Hall and Allan Stewart, director of the county's Port Authority, that far more information was needed before the state could relax its environmental standards and allow the jetport to proceed.

The mayor replied in late 1968: "Furnish us with a list of questions on the possible impact of the potential jetport and we will answer them all to your satisfaction." Browder and I assembled a team under Marshall comprised of federal and state experts on a wide variety of subjects, including hydrology, wildlife impacts, noise intrusion, pollution of surface and subsurface water, the potential of dramatically increased development within the Big Cypress that would be needed to house employees and store petroleum, and the countless chemicals – all of which are toxic and can contaminate ground and surface water – that are needed to clean high-speed jet engines.

The team of experts took two months to frame 110 questions that, when peer reviewed, were deemed to be "honest questions" that needed answers. Gov. Kirk informed the mayor that the task force had prepared the most important questions that needed to be addressed. He sent copies of the list to the mayor's office, other commissioners, and Stewart and his staff at the Dade County Port Authority.

To our surprise, the mayor responded that they were prepared to answer the long list of questions on February 28, 1969, only 45 days later. The mayor leased a ballroom in a hotel on the north side of the Dade County Airfield. Some 60 experts assembled the night before the hearing, all dumbfounded by the speed with which the airport consultants had seemingly been able to answer the extensive list of questions.

Promptly at 9 a.m., a crowd of state and federal scientists, interested spectators and an assemblage of newspaper correspondents from every corner of the state, plus national newsmen and TV cameras, waited for the presentation. Mayor Hall and Stewart took to the podium. The mayor dressed always in white: white suit, tie, socks and shoes. He announced that he expected the audience to be courteous and respectful, as the jetport was to become the "Gateway for Supersonic Aircraft" into North America: a bonanza for Dade County and the State of Florida.

Browder and I sat next to each other in the front row, accompanied by Marshall and then-Everglades National Park Superintendent John Raftery. Stewart stood before the microphone, read the first full question and then said, "Question Number One is under study." He continued on, reading each question and providing the same response: "This question is under study."

At question No. 9, I stood up and stated, "If this is going to be the same routine for the over 100 valid questions that you have received, and you are now preparing to give the identical answer that the question is 'under study,' you are wasting all of our time! In my view, this meeting is adjourned!"

Browder jumped to his feet and said: "I knew it! It's a 'fix.' You cannot answer those questions now or ever, because you have made a bad bet on locating a proposed major jetport in the middle of a wilderness swamp!"

The mayor screamed at both of us, shaking his fists. "You two are nothing but a pair of white militants!" he shouted.

Stewart, flushed and shaking, stated, "Reed, I hear you like butterflies. We'll build you a greenhouse, fill it with butterflies so you can use a butterfly net to your heart's content." The room exploded. Pandemonium broke out. People shook their fists at the mayor and Stewart. Dade County police surrounded the pair as they hastily departed through a convenient back door.

I called Gov. Kirk and explained what had happened. His response was, "The project just died. Return to Tallahassee as soon as possible and help me figure out how I get myself out of the jam I am in having supported the opening of the runway." We spent several hours together that evening and, with his public relations expert, worked out a statement calling for answers to the "pertinent questions that his panel had raised far beyond a training runway." We called for all construction to be halted until the questions could be answered to the satisfaction of expert reviewers.

As the jetport issue began to attract national attention, U.S. Secretary of Interior Walter Hickel's chief of staff called me and asked if I would meet with Hickel at Everglades National Park in March 1969 to discuss the proposed jetport and the continuing issues surrounding lack of adequate flows of water entering the park. He mentioned that Hickel, new to the job, wanted "personal time with me" and said that the meeting was to be private.

I replied that I was working for Gov. Kirk and would not damage our relationship by meeting with the secretary without the governor's presence or approval.

A few days later, Hickel called me with the following proposition: "Meet me at park headquarters. Fly with me over the park, the Big Cypress, the sugar plantations, and then we will meet the governor who will join us at Everglades City. The park has made arrangements for a comfortable boat to be secured within the Shark River. We will have ample skiffs. We will travel down the internal maze of saltwater rivers, then out into the Gulf of Mexico where we will inspect the mangrove fringes and finally arrive at the boat that has ample room for all of us to spend the night. There will be stone crabs, Florida lobsters and plenty of beer!"

It took only moments for the governor to agree and commandeer a state plane to take him to the Everglades City airport.

I drove to the park in time to meet Hickel, who had landed at Homestead Air Force Base just east of the park. We took the world-famous walk over the marsh near park headquarters, watched an alligator seize an unsuspecting raccoon, discussed a potential position for me on his staff, and then made the flight. I explained that I was not ready for a Washington assignment and I had a full agenda and the governor's support.

He graciously replied: "Perhaps later."

We met Gov. Kirk at the Everglades field and were promptly taken by skiffs down the twisting saltwater "rivers" and then briefly out into the Gulf before arriving at a very comfortable houseboat.

Hickel and Gov. Kirk knew each other from governors' meetings (Hickel resigned as governor of Alaska to take the Cabinet job) and it did not take a second beer before they were enjoying outrageously funny stories of their stewardship of their states. We gorged on cold native stone crab claws; Hickel ruled them "second best to Alaskan Dungeness crabs."

Cold lobsters were a second choice. The dessert was a masterfully baked key lime pie – a real Florida feast that Hickel and Gov. Kirk washed down with cans of cold beer.

At 9 p.m., although exhausted and full of beer, Gov. Kirk asked one of the chief park rangers to take them up the Shark River, a freshwater waterway in the heart of the Everglades, to see really big alligators. He assured Hickel that he was an expert at making the male alligator mating call, which surely would produce a large reptile for them to see.

Off they went into the night. The park superintendent and I followed by boat several hundred yards behind. As the "river" narrowed, Gov. Kirk began to make the most extraordinary calls. The ranger added a very realistic call. I thought their calls guaranteed that no knowledgeable alligator would come anywhere near them, but I was wrong. Suddenly, a 12-foot alligator splashed into the water and began a swift swim toward their skiff.

Gov. Kirk was beyond happy. "You see how I can call 'em! I bet you can't call any of your Alaskan beasts like that!" he declared.

The alligator was closing in for a closer inspection when the ranger ordered the two unsteady governors to sit down; they boated back to the houseboat.

Gov. Kirk and Hickel slept in late, before skiffs took them back to Everglades City the next day. They hugged and Hickel bellowed: "Claude, what an adventure! I owe you one in Alaska!"

"Wally," he responded, "let's work on how we can deliver more water to the park and settle this dispute over the proposed jetport together. It is obvious that it is a proposal that is in the wrong place."

Hickel left for Homestead in a helicopter. Gov. Kirk returned to Tallahassee and I went on to discuss other Everglades issues with the park's scientific staff – all of us quite exhausted.

Before long, President Richard Nixon and Hickel were calling for an end to the project.

Nixon, a Republican like Gov. Kirk, had been told by his close friends in the Miami area that the whole scheme was the work of the "hated Democrats" and speculators representing Dade County. Nixon immediately understood the political ramifications of cancelling all federal funding and declaring the scheme dead on arrival. There were problems, as the USDOT had paid for a certain amount of infrastructure for the runway and tower and the FAA had certified the strip as a training site.

Hickel called and asked me to recommend a science leader who could quickly amass the work that had been completed by the Leopold committee in a form that complied with NEPA. I recommended that the study, to be taken seriously, had to be undertaken by scientists from all federal and state agencies with expertise in the complex web of habitats and water relationships that shape South Florida's ecosystems. He agreed and on November 19, 1969, issued a directive not just to all of the DOI land and management agencies, but also to the Federal Water Quality Administration (FWQA), the DOI agency that Nixon later combined with the small air quality staff in the Department of Health, Education and Welfare to create the Environmental Protection Agency (EPA).

In May 1970, the FWQA produced *A Synoptic Survey of the Limnological Characteristics of the Big Cypress Swamp, Florida.* The report defined present and proposed drainage threats to the Big Cypress and proposed recommendations to restore natural water flows for it and for Everglades National Park. That same month, the U.S. Senate's Public Works Committee held a hearing and issued a report demanding that the state of Florida and the Corps uphold their responsibility to deliver adequate water supplies to the national park.

On June 2, 1969, Hickel, not to be outdone, established a Department of Interior (DOI) committee to investigate the ecological impact of the jetport. Dr. Luna Leopold, world-renowned chief of the United States Geological Survey (USGS), led the effort. Under Leopold's direction, Marshall formed a working team that included Jim Hartwell, Murph Kolipinski, Manny Morris, Rod Pegues and other experts from USGS, Everglades National Park, U.S. Fish and Wildlife Service (FWS), Florida Fish and Wildlife Commission (FWC), and others with specific knowledge on every conceivable subject.

They met for months at the U.S. Fish and Wildlife or Geological Survey offices in Vero Beach and Miami, and with Browder in the Coconut Grove home of Dr. Henry Field. My

environmental aide, George Gardner, frequently joined them as they discussed how to arrange the report and include all pertinent information on the Big Cypress ecosystem and its importance to the western watershed of Everglades National Park, the Ten Thousand Islands and Florida Bay.

Marshall was the leader and editor of the findings, but it was his team effort that produced the *Leopold Report – the Environmental Impact of the Big Cypress Swamp Jetport* in September 1969. Leopold was in constant contact with the Marshall working group, and he was adamant that the report that would bear his name would be "scientifically accurate and unchallengeable."

A highly respected author added fuel to the fire on September. 5, 1969, when *Life* magazine, a widely circulated national magazine, published an article condemning the jetport. John D. MacDonald, a Florida author who had published more than 50 best-selling mystery books, pleaded that the project would sound the death knell for the beloved national park. In his article "Last Chance to Save the Everglades," MacDonald wrote:

> "The commercial-political-financial establishments of Dade, Collier and Monroe counties are sweaty with excitement of a new boom, huge profits, and explosive growth. Every bit of this silent wilderness land around the jetport site is privately owned, and much of it has already changed hands in heavy-risk commitments. One Miami real estate agent has assembled a package almost as big as the jetport itself for a single corporate buyer. Collier County leaders have stated in Naples that they intend to make the jetport area the largest industrial center in Florida, and boosters are already talking about such projects as cutting a deep-water canal from the Gulf to the jetport to barge in the jet fuel and construction materials, and getting the authorized extension of Interstate 75 from Tampa to Miami officially realigned to bisect the jetport, with a thousand-foot right-of-way from the Gulf to the Atlantic. [4]

MacDonald added: "It is the entire complex that will finish the park, mostly by dramatically altering the volume and characteristics of the essential water flow. [5]

Protection of the national park and of Big Cypress became a central focus of the anti-jetport effort and Marshall shaped it in many ways. Powerful Dade and Collier real estate interests began a campaign to move the route of Interstate 75 so the only modern freeway connecting southeast and southwest Florida would follow the route of the Tamiami Trail instead of the Naples-to-Fort Lauderdale route of Alligator Alley. Marshall presented such a strong environmental case for keeping I-75 on the Alligator Alley alignment that he killed the Collier and Dade speculators' last hopes for turning the Trail into a development-stimulating super highway.

In one last desperate effort to protect the value of the lands that developers and real estate "gamblers" had made, they combined forces and engaged the services of Stewart Udall, the highly respected former Secretary of Interior under the Kennedy-Johnson administrations, to cook up an "attractive alternative" to full acquisition. Time was running out. The Udall proposal, "Beyond the Impasse," was released in December 1969 but fell on deaf ears, never fully being considered. Leopold called me and stated, "The train had left the station. Good going and best of luck pulling it off."

Authors Robert Gilmour and John McCauley wrote this fascinating chronology in *Political Science Quarterly*, Vol. 90, No. 4:

> "During June of 1969, three separate groups began intensive studies of environmental problems posed by the new airport. In early September the Department of Interior released its report, "The Environmental Impact of the Big Cypress Swamp Jetport" which was prepared under the direction of Dr. Luna Leopold and scientists associated with the U.S. Geological Survey. A few days later, a study of even larger scope, supported by private foundations, was issued by the National Academy of Sciences and the National Academy of Engineering, which treated the jetport as only one of the Environmental Problems of South Florida. A final report, "Beyond the Impasse" released in December, was commissioned by the Dade County Port Authority and conducted by Overview, a newly organized private consulting group headed by Steward Udall, a former Secretary of Interior. Although no one questioned Udall's credentials, it was generally regarded as difficult to maintain an uncompromised position while relying on financing from a vigorous developmental interest such as the Dade County Port Authority.

Editorials of The Tribune

Jetport Is Everybody's Concern

WEST COAST residents have a larger stake in the current controversy over the location of Dade County's jetport than just their choice of sides between people vs. alligators.

For upon the site of the mammoth airport could hinge the location of some mighty important highways — and the spending of a lot of highway money.

It is not beyond the realm of possibility that if Governor Claude Kirk and the conservationists allied with him get the site changed, the route of the Interstate 75 extension between Tampa and Miami might be changed with it.

And even if the I-75 route remain where it is, a change of the jetport site to areas mentioned by the Governor means some major roads, which wouldn't be needed if the site weren't changed, are going to have to be built—with Florida gasoline tax money which otherwise might be spent elsewhere.

* * *

THE PRESENT site lies near the convergence of the Dade, Monroe and Broward County lines. Work is nearly completed on the huge jet training runway which was the original purpose of the facility, and which will relieve Miami International Airport of 500 training flight operations a day. Some $13 million has already been invested there, and the jet runway is slated to go into operation Nov. 15.

Conservationists have said they can "live with" the jet training operations. Their great fear is that full-fledged commercial use of the airport would attract such a large population on the periphery as to endanger the water movement in the Everglades and ruin the nearby Everglades National Park.

Whether the just-proposed buffer zone to retard commercial and residential development around the airport would be acceptable to Secretary of the Interior Walter Hickel and other opponents of the present site remains to be seen.

What can be seen (on the accompanying map) is that if in seven years, as is highly possible, the jetport becomes a regional international airport, the proposed Interstate 75 extension paralleling the Tamiami Trail will be available to serve as its major vehicular traffic route.

Moving the jetport to Broward or Palm Beach Counties, as Governor Kirk has proposed, takes it off of I-75. It then would be much closer to the Alligator Alley tollway—which could revive efforts to route I-75 over the toll facility.

Congressman William C. Cramer of St. Petersburg, chief proponent of the I-75 extension, told The Tribune in Washington yesterday, "The jetport location has nothing to do with the bypass (around Tampa on I-75) and the I-75 extension to Fort Myers."

Beyond Fort Myers, he added "I don't know that the facts have changed for a new I-75 location. I would be surprised if the route is changed."

Nevertheless, considering Governor Kirk's previous fervid endorsement of the present jetport site and his sudden switch from it, a change in his position — and that of the State Department of Transportation — to favor rerouting I-75 would be less surprising than alarming.

But if I-75 is not the major access to the jetport, what will be? Depending upon the exact location of the new site, it would have to be either U.S. Highway 27 or Alligator Alley, or both.

If it is U.S. 27 alone, the improvement of it to handle the jetport traffic would have to be on the 50-50 basis for primary road improvement, half Federal money and half state. If Alligator Alley were included, there would be two choices. The state could spend $18 million of gasoline tax money to buy it out and make it a freeway, and then four-lane or six-lane it with primary money. Else, Alligator Alley would have to remain a toll facility, with toll money going to improvements. Paying a toll for access to Florida's major airport would not endear the state to its visitors.

* * *

MIAMIANS for the most part are girded for battle to defend the present site of the jetport. Other Floridians, even those who may never emplane or deplane there, should make it their battle, too.

The ramifications to road programs throughout Florida if the jetport location be changed are so considerable that the site is everybody's concern.

THE TAMPA TRIBUNE

Published by THE TRIBUNE COMPANY, Kennedy Blvd. and Morgan St., Tampa, Fla.

TAMPA, FLORIDA, SUNDAY, SEPTEMBER 14, 1969

"All of these studies agreed that the threat of full-scale development of training, cargo and commercial facilities might lead to serious and probably disastrous environmental consequences. The Leopold Report put the case most plainly: 'Regardless of the efforts for land-use regulations, the result will be the destruction of the South Florida ecosystem. Estimates of lesser damage are not to be realistic.' After the first two reports were issued, Secretary of Interior Hickel and Secretary of Transportation Volpe, in consultation, concluded that the impact of a commercial jetport at the present site, together with the development that would follow on adjacent land area, could destroy the Everglades National Park and the ecology of South Florida."

In response to the jetport controversy, Nixon called a meeting at the White House on Monday, September 8, 1969, at 10 a.m. Gov. Kirk and I flew to Washington a day in advance of the conference. We met with DOI Under Secretary Russell Train at his home. I sat on the living room floor and spread out aerial photographs of the white strip of runway in the midst of the Big Cypress. I had hydrological maps that showed the drainage into the western reaches of Everglades National Park and the Ten Thousand Islands, one of the great saltwater fishing areas and nurseries left in the greater Everglades system.

Following my briefing, during which Train asked dozens of questions, he called John Ehrlichman, one of Nixon's most important aides and advisors at the White House. Train wanted to alert the president that the proposal for the jetport was what he called a "sham." Ehrlichman called for an evening meeting at the White House. Nixon had been briefed and was agitated that USDOT Secretary John A. Volpe had made legal commitments to Dade County for the possible development of a jetport of which Nixon and his Cabinet were unaware.

Although I was not present at the Sunday late afternoon meeting at the White House, I am aware that Ehrlichman sternly informed all members of the Cabinet involved with the jetport decisions that Nixon had decided to "pull the federal plug and was opposed to further federal investment in the proposed jetport." Volpe spent the rest of the evening reaching his key USDOT and FAA staff members, informing them that a decision to cancel federal involvement was coming on Monday, and they must be prepared to break any legal commitments or financial contracts early in the week.

While Train was briefing Ehrlichman and the U.S. Justice Department staff on possible scenarios at the White House, DOI Secretary Hickel was informed of the decision and recognized that this was the opportunity of a lifetime to earn his "green spurs" by demanding that the jetport project be halted. He realized that when the federal government pulled the plug, the ongoing land boom would collapse and the administration would gain time to decide what to do about the Big Cypress watershed.

Gov. Kirk and I met in the White House the next morning. Ehrlichman ran the meeting. Volpe looked very nervous, as his agency had given the proposal a green light for a training site. The USDOT already had invested millions in the project.

Ehrlichman began the conference by stating that the jetport proposal had not undergone the type of environmental or fiscal impact review necessary to ensure that the Big Cypress watershed would be protected from unwanted growth.

After due consideration, Nixon had decided the project was to be cancelled – no further federal funds would go to it. The administration was simply going to state that the project was in the wrong place, would be far too costly, and would unleash unexpected impacts downstream in the remaining unblemished Everglades ecosystem.

Hickel announced that the DOI had spent a number of weeks investigating the potential impact of the project and found that a fully developed jetport would permanently damage the Everglades ecosystem and that he could not support the proposed jetport. He assured Ehrlichman that he supported the presidential decision and would back it up with sound science.

Gov. Kirk chimed in, stating that the jetport training field had been built in secrecy. Furthermore, he said, although he had been there for its groundbreaking, he had been assured that its future was to be only a training field. He believed it would replace the "touch and go" training sessions at the Miami International Airport, which involved real danger to downtown Miami in the event of an aircraft engine failure or pilot error. The governor fully supported the presidential decision and spoke warmly about his joint concerns expressed by Hickel. Ehrlichman mentioned that water delivery issues surrounding Everglades National Park had surfaced again and the president had shown an interest in having Hickel and Gov. Kirk work together to end the bickering over water flows into the park.

Volpe, a former Massachusetts governor known for his explosive temper, had turned red in the face but managed to speak about his problems. He would have to break a "legal contract" with Dade County and stop promised federal funding. He also would have to stop the FAA from providing further assistance to the training field. Volpe stated that he needed time to coordinate with his senior staff and prepare them to work with Dade County commissioners to implement the presidential decision.

Ehrlichman agreed that timing was of the essence. Volpe needed sufficient time to quietly pull the USDOT and FAA plugs, as there were legalities that had to be handled, preferably swiftly but, above

Gov. Kirk Joins Fight to Block Building of Everglades Jetport

By CHRISTOPHER LYDON
Special to The New York Times

WASHINGTON, Sept. 4—Gov. Claude R. Kirk Jr. of Florida has joined the effort to halt the construction of a jetport in Big Cypress Swamp that conservationists have warned could destroy the wildlife of the Florida Everglades.

According to Nat Reed, Mr. Kirk's chief adviser on environmental issues, the Governor will offer next week to have the airport relocated on state-owned land.

Until now, Governor Kirk had maintaned a careful neutrality on the battle betwen the Dade County Port Authority, which has already started work on the 39-square-mile development, and conservationists.

Governor Kirk's decision was the second major blow to the airport project in the last week and suggested that the conservationists might be approaching a decisive victory.

Administration sources confirmed last weekend that a report, commissioned by the Transportation and Interior Departments, had confirmed fears about the airport's destructive impact on the natural balance in the swamplands of southwestern Florida.

The unpublished report, by Luna Leopold, a senior Interior Department research scientist, warned that the jetport and the new city planned around it would permanently change the flow of water in the region and eventually extinguish the wildlife that now thrives there.

Secretary of the Interior, Walter J. Hickel, who chose Mr. Leopold to review the matter, has not commented on the Leopold Report.

It is understood tnat Secretary of Transportation, John A. Volpe, has not yet seen the report. He had indicated earlier that he would be guided bv Mr. Leopold's work.

An aide to Mr. Volpe said tonight: "There's been unanimity all along on the one point that, if it came down to a choice between saving the Everglades and building the jetport, the jetport must go. The Everglades must be preserved. The question has always been, can we have both?"

Before Mr. Leopold began his study, the Department of Transportation had made a $700,000 commitment to the airport project—$500,000 toward construction of the first pilot-training runway and $200,000 for development of rail and road links to Miami and the west coast of Florida.

all, quietly. We were instructed rather firmly to keep the news of the presidential decision quiet until Nixon conducted a press conference the following Monday, during which he would announce the jetport cancellation

Ehrlichman added, "Give me your oaths – no leaks. I mean it – no leaks! John must have time to break contracts and smooth feathers." The future of the Big Cypress was not discussed or seriously considered at that meeting.

Hickel, Gov. Kirk and I left the White House together. The secretary asked the governor how we were returning to the private jet facility at Washington National, where a friend of the governor's had lent us his jet for the day. Hickel insisted that the three of us ride in his official limousine to the airport.

We had hardly driven out of the White House gate when Hickel pulled out his address book and said to the governor, "Who wants to make the first call?" Gov. Kirk replied, "You have the phone and seniority."

I was sitting on the jump seat of the limousine and turned as the secretary picked up the car phone and began to dial a number. I said calmly but firmly, "Please don't disregard the presidential order for silence for a few days." They laughed. Hickel said, "Reed, you must learn to seize opportunities."

Hickel then proceeded to give a full briefing on the event to *The New York Times* environmental correspondent. Gov. Kirk followed by stating how Hickel had "aced" Volpe and what a triumph for the environment had been made by their joint efforts. I nearly died after their third or fourth telephone call to a bevy of environmental journalists.

The next morning, I was in my little office in the governor's suite in the old Capitol building at 7 a.m. The switchboard operator called and informed me that some "irate gentleman from the White House was on the phone wishing to talk to me."

I picked up the phone and held it seven inches from my ear, as I received a tongue lashing from Ehrlichman. The results of the meeting were on the front page of *The New York Times* and the *Miami Herald*. He asked: "Who was guilty?" I tried to fake it but finally blurted out that Hickel had made the first three calls and was supported by Gov. Kirk. Ehrlichman shouted, "I knew the so-and-so's couldn't keep a secret! They have destroyed the opportunity for the president to hold a press conference extolling his conservation credentials, and put John Volpe in an impossible position."

What could I say but, "You are right, but they could not resist."

He replied, "Damn them both!" and hung up.

The White House staff supported the president's halt of funding for the jetport, citing the Leopold Report as the reason.

On January 16, 1970, the U.S. government, State of Florida and Dade County signed a formal contract, the "Everglades Jetport Pact," in which Dade County agreed never to develop a commercial airport at the Big Cypress site. In return, the state and federal governments pledged to help Dade County look for alternative sites for a new Miami airport. Much to the benefit of Dade County's economy, no alternate site was ever agreed to and instead, a modernized Miami International Airport is one of the world's great aviation centers.

In November 1970, following the May 4 shooting of college students at Kent State University by the Ohio National Guard, Hickel wrote a personal letter to Nixon urging him to give more respect to the views of young people critical of the Vietnam War. Typical of Hickel, he sent copies of his letter to the Washington press corps prior to having it delivered to the White House, and was promptly fired by the president. Nixon then appointed U.S. Rep. Rogers of Maryland, to the post of secretary of interior in January 1971. Rogers was a much-admired member of Congress. His brother, Thurston, was a U.S. senator from Kentucky. Rogers was well liked by both sides of the aisle and, as chairman of the Republican Party, he was quickly confirmed.

At about the same time, in November 1970, after state Sen. Reubin Askew defeated Gov. Kirk decisively in the race for Florida's highest post, Gov. Kirk and I ended our four-year efforts with tears, mutual thanks and gratitude. We had made significant progress towards ending the environmental abuses that had been considered "normal" prior to his election. He was a remarkable man, with a combination of strengths and weaknesses, but his support for my efforts had been steadfast. As one knowledgeable Tallahassee journalist reported, "No one had a better time as governor of Florida as did Gov. Claude Kirk."

As I was preparing to return to Jupiter Island, Governor-elect Askew asked to see me. He urged me to stay on until he could find a suitable successor. As I've mentioned, I agreed and continued to work on sewage and industrial waste problems, which needed constant attention. By then, the state was selling very few submerged lands and issuing few dredge-and-fill permits, but Askew ended the practice for good.

I was in Jacksonville chairing an air-and water-quality hearing in February 1971 when my wife reached me with that message from the White House regarding a tour of the Everglades and Big Cypress with Secretary and Anne Morton, the Secretary's wife.

I was flown home in a state plane and, at dawn, ferried to the helicopter site where I said joyfully, "Good morning, Anne and Mr. Secretary." I had known them for several years and we had become friends due to mutual interests in wildlife management on the eastern shore of Maryland, the secretary's home territory.

We were accompanied by Joe Brown, superintendent of Everglades National Park, and Sonny Bass, the lead park interpreter. I examined the proposed route and insisted that the helicopters fly over the Everglades agricultural area at an altitude that would give the secretary some idea of the size of the nearby subsidized sugarcane crop and the complexities of delivering sufficient water to Everglades National Park. The helicopter tour took hours. We flew from the agricultural area to the Tamiami Trail, on to Florida Bay, and then backtracked and flew from the road known as "Alligator Alley" to the Ten Thousand Islands. The sheer size of the unprotected Big Cypress astonished Morton and, frankly, me.

We lunched at Everglades City, refueled, and continued the tour. Exhaustion began to show on everyone's face. Finally, we landed at Miami International Airport, where the secretary and I conducted a brief press conference, discussing the park's need for additional water and the gash the training runway had inflicted on the Big Cypress,

one of the last great South Florida wildernesses. The future of the Big Cypress was not discussed in any detail.

Morton and I went upstairs to the airport hotel bar for a cold beer. He passed me a note from Nixon, cosigned by him, that requested my service as Assistant Secretary of Interior for Fish, Wildlife and National Parks, the best assignment in the Department of Interior. I flew home to discuss the offer with my wife, who was highly supportive. Alita had seen me growing increasingly frustrated and exhausted after weeks and months of handling multiple pollution-control permits. She thought I would be renewed working on parks, refuges and land-use problems. I accepted the appointment the next day, excited that I would be an assistant to Rogers, a man whom I admired and became a close personal friend.

I flew to Tallahassee, and met with Governor Askew who received my news with grace.

He accepted my decision with regret, but typical of the great man, he wished me 'God Speed' and sincere thanks for the period of my service for Governor Kirk and our state. Saying goodbye to members of my staff and many of the cabinet staff members was tough, as I had a working relationship with many of the key future leaders of our state. The thought of working with the leadership of the U.S. Fish and Wildlife and the National Park Service was a dream come true!

I swiftly moved to a small suite at the Jefferson Hotel within walking distance of the Interior building. As usual Alita sent a car loaded with clothing and personal effects to the hotel, flew up and arranged the two rooms perfectly. I was busy on the Hill meeting the key members of the Senate and House leadership, especially the interested members of the leadership of the key Interior committees. Except for a 'chilly meeting' with Chairman Wayne Aspinall which was expected as he was a well-known 'Curmudgeon,' I was warmly greeted and made immediate friends with a number of the keen environmentally concerned members of congress who served on the key sub committees and full committees that had jurisdiction over the department's many responsibilities.

A confirmation date was set. I was flanked by Senator Spessard Holland, Florida's beloved former governor and one of the most respected members of the United States Senate and newly elected republican Edward John Gurney who both read flattering supportive statements. I was confirmed by unanimous vote although several western senators mentioned their concerns that the Department of Interior might be 'over influenced by easterners who might not understand the genuine concerns of the western states.' It was useful that Senator Holland mentioned the fact that my Grandfather Reed was a major figure in the development of western gold, silver, oil and local irrigation projects and had owned a splendid ranch near Sheridan, Wyoming.

I asked Rogers to swear me into office. I was surrounded by family and friends. It was an awesome experience!

Alita travelled back and forth in search of a suitable home. Recognizing that I was a hopeless work addict she insisted that we would live in Washington within minutes of the Department. After a series of visits that included hours of inspecting potential homes, she found and persuaded me to acquire a home on Woodland Drive. The drive to the office was less than 20 minutes down Rock Creek Drive. Nearby we made 'life friends.' Russell and Aileen Train lived just up the street. There were numerous small embassy dwellings all protected by the Federal Service. We walked in the evenings joined by friends with our dogs, safe from the light traffic. The house needed to be 'transformed'; so the interior and other corrections were not completed until the July 4th joyous evening.

The house turned into a wonderful happy home that was perfectly situated for the children's schools, the Mall and the Washington Zoo.

The first order of business was to attract a highly skilled, experienced staff that shared my conviction that the national mood would support major improvements in the basic environmental laws.

Within days of my confirmation, John Ehrlichman called with a date to meet with President Nixon.

The meeting was 'pleasant' although President Nixon made it abundantly clear that his priorities did not include personal interests in 'environmental issues or problems.' He quietly commanded me to: "Work with Rogers, Russ Train, Bill Ruckelshaus and other members of the administration that had 'environmental interests'." He stated that he wanted a fine environmental record, but hoped that the working groups would not produce too much legislation that would be controversial.

He commented on my request that I would have the 'ability' to select my own staff by joking: "I bet they will be all democrats!" I responded: "No, Mr. President, they will all be experts who will bequeath you a superb environmental record!"

He concluded: "Keep in close contact with John Ehrlichman," his trusted assistant who had a grasp of the many areas of environmental 'problems and crisis's' that had been growing due to years of neglect.

In May 1971, I was sworn in. Within days of my confirmation, Ehrlichman called me requesting a simple statement for a scheduled presidential briefing. He wanted "facts in the simplest form on why the administration had cancelled funding for the proposed Everglades Jetport."

George Gardner, who had accompanied me to Washington, and I, took quotes from the Leopold report, and the White House staff called our briefing paper "well done." Gardner had begun working for me in Tallahassee after his graduation from the University of Florida. His assignment was to monitor the study and assist Marshall. Browder assigned himself to Marshall. We asserted that the question of potential federal financing of "acquisition within the Big Cypress was under study." That statement sufficed until the Nixon Administration saw the opportunity for a "green coup."

Almost immediately, the administration turned to me to focus on the long-range future of the Big Cypress. The key question was: What was the federal interest in the future of the Big Cypress? The first directive on the path towards an answer was: "Reed, prepare a major study of the potential alternatives, from land purchases to limited development." I assigned Gardner to organize a working group of experts who had served on the Leopold committee.

The National Environmental Policy Act (NEPA) was passed in 1970 and required all federal agencies to prepare an Environmental Impact Statement discussing a full range of options and alternatives before making final decisions on projects with environmental significance. For the first time in

U.S. history, large-scale federal public works projects now had to consider and tally their environmental impacts – something that would figure largely in many coming environmental crises.

It took until April 1971 for all the federal science agencies to produce the study Hickel had requested – *The Big Cypress Watershed* – and deliver it to Hickel's successor, Morton. When adapted into an environmental impact statement, the study report could survive a legal challenge. It is a remarkable document whose preferred option torpedoed once and for all any prospect of building a "super jetport" in the Big Cypress Swamp. When the final report was completed, I ordered 100 copies to be secured in my Interior office while I awaited direction from the White House. A senior White House staff member who knew I had a complete set of the Environmental Impact Statements with a series of "preferred alternatives" simply told me to keep it "secluded."

Morton took one long look at the list of alternatives and stated calmly, "The best solution is to buy the whole damn watershed! I am sick about the constant confrontations with the state over the amount of water allowed to flow into Everglades National Park because they own the headwaters. When we select land for retention in national parks and refuges in Alaska when the Alaska Lands Bill passes, make sure to secure complete watersheds."

Despite the federal support, there were local problems to overcome. Cal Stone, president of the Florida Wildlife Federation, was skeptical of the management plan that was to be administered by the National Park Service (NPS). He would have been an influential voice opposing creation of the proposed national preserve.

Luckily for the supporters, Johnny Jones, a plumber by trade but also an ardent hunter and conservationist with a superb record of opposing environmental outrages, was elected vice president of the Florida Wildlife Federation. He recognized, and was supported by his wife, Marianna – a strong, well-connected conservationist in her own right – that the opportunity to save nearly 600,000 acres of "wild land" in southwest Florida would never come again. He was supported by Franklin Adams, a member of the federation board and a widely recognized expert environmentalist who had known the Big Cypress landscape since he was a boy.

Browder also was busy trying to protect the Big Cypress. He worked closely with Jones and they persuaded many of the land's users to support preservation, despite continued nervousness about how the NPS would manage the site. For decades, local residents had used the land whenever and however they wanted, regardless of the damage their swamp buggies inflicted on the wetlands. In some cases, the huge four-wheel-drive vehicles left scars that would take years to heal, and some feared the federal government's rules would limit their freedom.

A few outspoken opponents didn't want the federal government managing what essentially was a free zone, where they could hunt deer and wild hogs, camp, or just travel on their swamp buggies. It was the place to escape and marvel at the great stands of cypress trees and the incredible variety of plants, bromeliads and orchids. Browder and Jones had to convince them to support legislation to secure the Big Cypress or lose it forever. Many were leery of the idea, and especially of the thought that the NPS would be managing all activities in the Big Cypress if it were acquired by the federal government. The federation leadership was undecided but, due to the influence of Johnny and Marianna Jones, Adams and Browder, a majority realized the importance of preserving the wild, wonderful, last great part of native Florida.

Florida conservationists who championed the purchase of the region had previously been physically threatened while touring the swamp area. Some of the swampland real estate speculators warned that, if federal or state officials began to inspect "their land," they could not assure the officials' safe passage when they entered the great

Senator Bob Graham

swamp wilderness. One group of real estate promoters actually put up reward posters suggesting that environmentally-inclined state Sen. Bob Graham, Browder and I be shot for the crime of proposing federal protection of the Big Cypress.

Weeks went by and then, as the 1972 presidential election loomed, a White House senior staff member inquired whether I had finished the Environmental Impact Statement (EIS). I stated, "It is ready to go for final review at the Office of Management and Budget." The White House response was, "Forget OMB. Hold onto it – tightly." I had no cost figures for the various options, including limited development, pod development, major development or acquisition of the entire Big Cypress.

U.S. Sen. Lawton Chiles of Florida, a Democrat, announced that he was going to ask U.S. Sen. Henry 'Scoop' Jackson of Washington, also a Democrat, to hold a hearing in Miami to discuss the future of the Big Cypress. The Florida newspapers and all the national and state conservation organizations were highly supportive of full acquisition. The local sportsmen and back-country advocates remained ill at ease, as they still were concerned about federal control over their playground.

Jackson, chairman of the Senate Interior Committee and an ardent conservationist, would be the principal speaker, and would announce his own Big Cypress solution. The White House learned that Jackson supported full acquisition, as "the Big Cypress was a national treasure." It was becoming clear that Jackson – a social moderate, but a very conservative supporter of the military who advocated a tough line versus the Soviet Union – might make a formidable challenge to Nixon in the 1976 election. He already was credited with helping to author NEPA. As chairman of the key Interior Committee, he had presided over many decisions creating national wildlife refuges and national parks. Nixon's political advisors warned that if Jackson seized the leadership on saving the Everglades' most endangered watershed, he also might capture the votes of people who cared about nature and wild lands in America.

Nixon's team seemingly could not decide how to proceed. Congressional hearings were scheduled. At a Senate hearing in the spring of 1971 and in other public statements, I was ordered to give a very bland statement and evasive answers to questions about what the administration's final recommendation on the preservation of the Big Cypress would be. I was criticized by the green community, but the administration had not made a firm decision on what alternative it would support.

On November 16, 1971, Jackson announced that his hearing on Big Cypress and the Everglades would be held on November 30th. Finally, I received a telephone call from a White House staffer who asked the following questions: "Where are the completed Environmental Impact Statements? Is there a preferred option supporting the full acquisition of the Big Cypress?"

I answered: "The documents are here. There are 100 copies available. We prepared impact statements for each of the options, including full purchase."

The staffer's reply made me jump out of my chair. "Reed, it is the president's decision that the complete acquisition of the Big Cypress is the preferred option. Make whatever additions are needed to support this decision and have the reports delivered to the West Gate as quickly as possible. It's a go!"

Big Cypress was finally going to be saved for good. It was the right decision, certainly spurred by political finagling, but it was the right decision!

I called Gardner, who was ecstatic. We quickly arranged the option cover to support full acquisition.

Big Cypress Politics

Guided by a delegation of Miccouskee Indians, Julie Nixon Eisenhower and Secretary of Interior Rogers Morton had a look at Florida's Big Cypress Swamp — or at least part of it — and decided to buy it.

The pair — along with Floridian Nat Reed, an assistant secretary of interior and the state's former pollution control chief — were "out in front" of an administration campaign for passage of a bill to buy 567,000 acres of the vital watershed for an estimated $150 million.

Purchase of at least part of Big Cypress will be a key factor in assuring the needed freshwater balance for marine ecosystems in the Ten Thousand Islands area, protection of portions of Everglades National Park and assurance of drinking water for the state's west coast cities. Besides, it's a beautiful natural area crying for protection from the ditch-and-build housing developers.

The Nixon administration's goals in urging acquisition of Big Cypress are clearly laudable. But curiously, while specifics of the administration bill have not yet been made public, they apparently do not differ substantially from a Senate bill on which public hearings already have started. If that's the case, why does President Nixon seem to be mounting so elaborate a campaign for passage of the administration bill? Turning out his daughter and the Interior secretary to tout a bill that has not yet been introduced seems to portend a more vigorous campaign — a more publicity-centered campaign — than the circumstances require.

In fact, the Senate bill is co-sponsored by two Democratic senators, Florida's Lawton Chiles and presidential hopeful Henry Jackson. The situation suggests that Mr. Nixon wants to polish his image as a conservationist before election time and that he specifically doesn't want a major environmental bill passed with Sen. Jackson's name attached to it.

It also suggests that if the Big Cypress issue turns into nothing more than a political scramble between presidential contenders, both bills are liable to go down the drain. And that would be a real loss.

Julie Nixon Eisenhower, Rogers C. B. Morton (Foreground); Nat Reed (Right Rear) Deep in Swamp

Wading in the Big Cypress

My loyal driver, Garfield Lawrence, took the 100 copies to the White House and we waited in silence.

I received a call from Nixon's office that he would announce his plan to acquire all of the Big Cypress – the preferred option of the Environmental Impact Statement.

We had a "rejoicing party" in my office that evening with telephone calls to and from Browder, Marshall, Jones, Leopold and many members of the team that prepared the EIS. The only sour note was a statement the director of the National Park Service, George Hartzog, dropped like a small bomb: "You have saved the western Everglades and a great swamp, but you have created management headaches for the future superintendents that will last a very long time." Nevertheless, Morton arrived with a splendid bottle of bourbon, which we sipped while rejoicing.

There was still much work to be done. Recognizing the importance of the Big Cypress to the future of the southwestern Everglades ecosystem and the fishery of the entire southwest coast, including the Ten Thousand Islands, we knew compromises among traditional users and preservationists would have to be hammered out and become part of the legislation and legislative history.

One week before the Jackson/Chiles scheduled hearing, on November 23, 1971, Interior Secretary Morton announced at a White House press conference that Nixon would propose legislation to acquire the Big Cypress in full, thereby undercutting the hearing. Presidential support for "saving" the Big Cypress made front-page news across the country.

To gain support for the president's decision, I urged Julie Nixon Eisenhower, the president's daughter, to join us on an airboat ride and a swamp wade in the Big Cypress. She was more than willing. On January 6, 1972, I had the pleasure of escorting her on a jaunt through the Big Cypress, sometimes waist-deep in wetland sloughs, much to the alarm of a swarm of Secret Service agents. I promised them that if a water moccasin was near, I would let it bite me rather than the first daughter.

There was little need to worry though, as Browder had arranged for the Secret Service to pay famous alligator hunter Gator Bill to wade the route earlier and remove any water moccasins nearby. Well-known snake hunter Bruce Warren

Joe Browder in the swamp. Photo by Patricia Caulfield.

The congressional acquisition legislation authorized spending $117 million over a 10-year period. Florida Gov. Askew had promised an advance payment of $40 million from state funds, a noble act by a noble man. The vast majority of the land would be acquired from "willing sellers," but Congress authorized condemnation, if necessary. President Gerald Ford signed the bill into law on October 11, 1974.

Management problems began almost immediately after substantial land acquisitions were under way. They included how to use the preserve's vast wilderness without damaging it by misuse or overuse; the use of off-road swamp buggies became, and continues to be, controversial.

A simple road system has been built to protect the extensive wetlands from being crisscrossed by tracked vehicles. The real lovers of the Big Cypress are the hunters and back-country users who are careful not to damage this environmental jewel.

The Big Cypress is one of the greatest, most magical places in all of Florida, if not the world. It was a key component of the original plans for Everglades National Park until Congress removed it from the national park's boundaries in 1954. Big Cypress is biologically and hydrologically essential to the integrity of much of Everglades National Park and the Ten Thousand Islands. It remains one of the few areas in South Florida that is not crisscrossed with drainage canals and dikes, a fate that sadly befell much of the Everglades system.

It took time to trace the land ownership, acquire the land from willing sellers and complete "taking" from unwilling land owners. Many land owners made provisions for "life use" at a reduced land value.

The creation of the Big Cypress Preserve has been one of the high-water marks in my environ-

also accompanied us. Julie Eisenhower was a great sport, totally unafraid, and she thoroughly enjoyed her day in the Big Cypress. She generated great press by stating, "What an extraordinary part of America! I hope it will be preserved."

In May 1973, I testified before congressional committees in favor of the acquisition of 576,000 acres of the Big Cypress as a national preserve, including holdings and specific uses such as sport hunting and vehicular travel. I assured the American people the preserve was intended to protect unique areas and allow for recreation while preventing damage to the land. It was important that the permitted uses conform to the traditional uses by the Miccosukee Indians, who had rights that were historically and ethically superior to any other use. Former Miccosukee Tribal Chair Buffalo Tiger had been instrumental in helping stop the jetport, and both the Miccosukee and Seminole tribes supported establishment of Big Cypress National Preserve. I am particularly pleased that, decades later, Chairman Colley Billie was present at the celebration of the opening of the Big Cypress Visitors' Center as evidence of his tribe's genuine concerns for the preserve's management.

mental career. Browder and I have been asked repeatedly, "If the jetport training field had not been built and the propaganda for developing the site into a major supersonic jetport had not raised the environmental issues at a time in our nation's history when environmental issues were national news, would Congress have supported any effort to acquire the Big Cypress and create the Big Cypress Preserve?" The answer is an emphatic "No."

Every member of our office – Buff Bohlen, Douglas Wheeler, Jim Ruch, Dick Curry, Cleo Clayton, and especially George Gardner – deserves thanks for their assistance in guiding the studies and seeing that the conclusions were codified into legislation.

Browder was a critically important contributor to the final decision. He knew how to make waves that produced results.

Gov. Kirk and I had a special relationship built on friendship and trust. He could have sabotaged the jetport's cancellation by maintaining his initial support, but he didn't. His change of heart was very important to the eventual creation of the national preserve.

Nixon wanted to demonize the Dade County commissioners but then realized that a great environmental victory could help him get re-elected and translate into a positive environmental legacy. All of these pieces and many more came together and propelled the salvation of this great landscape forever.

'Who Ate Tomorrow?'

Reed: We Must Cope With Growth

By PAT CULLEN
Post Staff Writer

In the destructive quest to take profits from the land, people have "always assumed there were more resources over the next hill," says Assistant Interior Secretary Nathaniel Reed.

"Unfortunately, when we get to the next hill, we meet a fellow coming up the other side with the same idea."

The former Florida official said people must "face the fact that there is no next forest, no next marsh, no next bay."

Disregard for the land, as history silently testifies, has left several civilizations in waste, he said. And abuse of resources continues to threaten man.

In South Florida, Reed said, "People must recognize that they have a finite water supply.

"Already, Palm Beach, Broward, Dade and Lee counties are in direct competition from time to time for the same water supply in Lake Okeechobee.

"Last year drought carried the region to the brink of disaster. The rains came in the nick of time. But the region's population must not be allowed to breathe a sigh of relief and complacently assume that the crisis is over. It isn't."

The drought, which followed a period of record rainfall in early 1970, brought water rationing to urban South Florida.

Reed said it represented "a sample of things to come . . . unless we stop our headlong race to outgrow the other fellow.

"We must change the kind of thinking that leads us to exult over being the largest or fastest-growing city or county," said Reed, who was chairman of the Florida Pollution Control Board and conservation adviser to two state governors.

In the picture at left Nathaniel P. Reed sits behind his boss, Interior Secretary Rogers Morton, on a tour of the Big Cypress Swamp.

Browder and I made up an unlikely team, but we knew how to work together.

Each of us had a specific role. I doubt whether the Big Cypress National Preserve would be a major feature of the natural western Everglades ecosystem without this curious crossing of two lives that became intimately involved in a major land preservation effort.

We are equally proud to be part of the Big Cypress National Preserve's creation.

Notes – Less is More: Defeating the Miami Jetport, Creating a National Preserve

[1] Luther J. Carter, *The Florida Experience: Land and water policy in a growth state* (Baltimore: Johns Hopkins University Press, 1974), 189.

[2] Ibid., 187.

[3] Ibid., 194; Leslie Kemp Poole, *Saving Florida: Women's Fight for the Environment in the Twentieth Century* (Gainesville: University Press of Florida, 2015) 144-145.

[4] John D. MacDonald, "Last Chance to Save the Everglades?" *Life*, Sept. 5, 1969, 61. Accessed July 25, 2015 at https://books.google.com/ books?id=FU8EAAAAMBAJ&pg=PA58&source=gbs_toc_&cad=2#v=onepage&q&f=false

[5] Ibid., 63.

Support for our Big Cypress acquisition

The Additional Lands of the Big Cypress National Preserve

The headwaters of the Big Cypress remain in private hands, within the vast holdings of the Barron Collier family. Barron Collier acquired hundreds of thousands of acres in southwest Florida, developed the sleepy gulf-side town of Naples and used his own money to build the Tamiami Trail, connecting Miami and Naples. We now know that the road made from muck, sand and gravel interrupted the natural flow of water to Everglades National Park, which was established in 1934 and dedicated in 1947.

Culverts under the newly built Tamiami Trail were inadequate to allow sheet flow into the park and thence into Florida Bay. In its initial years, the highway was overtopped by heavy seasonal rainfall or wet hurricanes that dropped many inches of water upstream in the "glades" and the Big Cypress. As Naples developed, the Tamiami Trail was raised in height; additional culverts were installed but were inadequate and poorly placed, causing the highway to form a dike that prevented flow to the park and Florida Bay.

Battles were fought from the 1950s through the 1970s over the amount of water that was being stopped from flowing into the park, and those in authority did not fully understand the topic. Unquestionably, the South Florida Water Management District (SFWMD) withheld many millions of acre-feet of water north of the Tamiami Trail to benefit the shallow Biscayne Aquifer, which supported the water utilities of Palm Beach, Broward, Dade (now Miami-Dade) and Monroe counties. It also aided the profitable winter crop plantations on the sand lands from western Palm Beach County to south of Homestead. Winter crops were a vital part of Florida's agricultural economy and were reliant on drainage and ample supplies of fresh water.

In the mid-1980s, representatives of the Barron Collier family contacted Secretary of Interior Bruce Babbitt, suggesting a trade of 130,000 acres of the Big Cypress watershed for approximately 68 acres of prime property in downtown Phoenix, Arizona. The federal Bureau of Indian Affairs planned to close the Phoenix Indian School in downtown Phoenix and the Collier family had learned of the federal government's impending land surplus. The family saw this as an opportunity to make a big trade, although it proved to be a tough battle. Some members of the Arizona congressional delegation were upset at the idea of losing "their" land to the Everglades in Florida. They felt the federal government should offer the land to an Arizona company like the Bartram Land and Gas Company and, more importantly, give some to the city of Phoenix.

The other interesting development at this time was the expansion of State Road 84 – which crossed the Everglades and was affectionately known as Alligator Alley – giving it the designation of Interstate 75. This large transportation project was already initiated and moving forward, requiring the acquisition of land in the Big Cypress basin. Congress and the state realized this was an opportune time to expand the Big Cypress National Preserve to protect panther habitat and restore water flows to the western basin of the Everglades. People questioned whether the federal government should pay to acquire land for park expansion and the Reagan administration, represented in large part by Assistant Secretary Bill Horn, was opposed to that idea.

As the negotiations commenced, Florida Gov. Bob Graham played a critical role in ensuring the trade's success. As usual, however, environmental protection in Florida required not only Florida champions – including U.S. Senator Lawton Chiles and U.S. Rep. Tom Lewis – but also champions from outside Florida. Enter Morris "Mo" Udall from Arizona, who was a key legislator given his position as chairman of the U.S. House of Representatives Interior Committee. Udall was a champion of the Alaska National Interest Lands Conservation Act of 1980, which added more than 104 million acres of land to federal management, mostly as national parks and wildlife refuges.

Udall latched onto the controversial bill to conduct the land exchange and united the House Democrats to support it. The Reagan administration's threat of veto was not a deterrent. It passed both branches easily and eventually was signed by President Reagan. The transfer of more than 130,000 acres to be preserved was a big deal. Indeed, neither the NPS nor any other federal land agency has received as large a land trade since then.

The addition of these critical lands to the Big Cypress National Preserve was arguably for a different purpose than the original creation of the preserve. While Chiles tried to mandate that recreational use of the Collier land, such as hunting, fishing and trapping, be "promoted and encouraged," (H.R. 4090, at 5, 1986), the attempt failed in Congress. The committee said it "wishes to note the specific deletion of language that would have required the National Park Service to promote recreational uses, including hunting, fishing and trapping" (H.R. Rep. 99-692, at 5, 1986). The committee reiterated the land was preserved to protect the Big Cypress and restore the greater Everglades ecosystem.

The original preserve's recreational uses were very clearly protected by the incredibly hard work of off-road vehicle and hunting interests. The lands added by the Collier exchange were the headwaters of the vast watershed for water protection purposes, without the assumption that off-road and hunting activities would occur. The newly acquired land would restore water flow through the Big Cypress basin to Everglades National Park, particularly the Ten Thousand Islands area.

Once the smoke cleared from the legislation, an agreement signed May 12, 1988, detailed the actual exchange procedures. The deal included a number of other components that were debated for years after the bill passed. The federal government and the state of Florida would pay the Collier Enterprise $43 million for the land and, in turn, Collier Enterprises would deposit $35 million into the Indian education trust fund. The city of Phoenix would get 20 acres of land for a park and for development, the U.S. Veteran's Administration would get 10 acres, and Arizona would get five acres for a state veterans' nursing home.

Despite the political support at the federal level, the bill's passage and the Indian tribes' agreement, the city of Phoenix continued to protest the trade in the summer of 1991 in an effort to secure more land. In the end, the political pressure from those other entities, particularly the Indian tribes, resulted in Phoenix agreeing to the original trade.

The Indian Trust Fund Agreement was signed on December 18, 1992, between the United States and the Barron Collier Company. It added roughly 108,000 acres to the federal holdings in Big Cypress National Preserve, set aside 19,000 acres to create the Ten Thousand Islands National Wildlife Refuge, and expanded the Florida National Panther Refuge by about 5,000 acres.

It was an extraordinarily controversial deal but one that added vitally important land for Florida and the nation.

Biscayne National Monument Park: Preserving Our Precious Bays

"Something had to be done to save them. Nuts to dirty industry."

The world is filled with beautiful bays. They are hallmarks of almost every country that has access to the world's oceans. Some are surrounded by great cities: San Francisco, Melbourne, Tampa, Hong Kong and Sydney. Others are highly productive estuaries that act as nurseries and fishing grounds, such as the Chesapeake, Delaware and Apalachicola and the countless bays from northern California to Alaska whose entry rivers are the gateways of millions of Pacific salmon and steelhead trout.

The list is seemingly endless. Some extend into the far north, such as Alaska's Glacier Bay and Norway's great system of fjords. There are incomparable sights: South America and southern Africa enjoy spectacular bays, some remote and some surrounded by development. They are all priceless.

I never cease to be amazed by the importance of bays such as San Francisco and Sydney; they are integral to the lives of their nearby inhabitants. At 5 p.m. as if a whistle had blown, hundreds of sailboats of all sizes are manned and set sail, simply for the joy of feeling the wind and in a sense of freedom from the daily humdrum of work. Freedom: Let the wind take care of any problems.

During the twentieth century, it was undeniable that many of the world's bays had become despoiled by man's sewage and industrial wastes and the refuse from abattoirs and tons of manure from working horses that were deposited in waterways that flowed into the bays. The majority of the world's bays were treated as receptacles of unpleasant refuse in hope that dilution would handle the pollution.

As humans began to recognize the beauty of bays, the value of real estate lining them and the worth of seafood produced in them, it became apparent that something had to be done to save and restore them.

I will never forget sitting on the porch of a great Canadian friend's patio looking over St. Andrews Bay in New Brunswick: the utter tranquility, the successful effort to control unwanted development, the presence of shining clear, clean water. Just a half hour of sitting, looking and listening to the melody of an incoming tide reinforced my conviction that bays needed protection for many reasons. I worked tirelessly in my role as advisor to two Florida governors to combat water pollution and I'm proud that we made a real difference by stopping the flow of raw sewage and industrial wastes into the state's waterways.

Enormous progress in controlling human and agricultural pollutants has occurred worldwide. Recognizing that each bay is a jewel, the surrounding populations have fought to improve their bay's water quality and to control excessive development in favor of environmental quality; the joy of living adjacent to a bay now is recognized as part of its intrinsic value. In every land, groups are ready to fight

Photo courtesy National Park Service

to clean up estuaries such as the Chesapeake and Tampa bays. Protection also extends to stopping inappropriate development or industrial facilities. Great environmental skirmishes have been waged as a result.

Such a battle occurred in the 1960s in beautiful Biscayne Bay, an aquamarine jewel southeast of Miami. Two proposed projects – the construction and operation of a waterfront oil refinery and the development of barrier islands into a resort city to rival Miami Beach – set local conservationists into a flurry of action. Initially, it looked like a losing battle for bay lovers – after all, who would argue with projects that might boost jobs, tourism and the local economy? But the group's brilliant arsenal of facts, publicity and persistence, as well as a change in the political landscape, led to the 1968 creation of Biscayne National Monument, which later became a national park with the largest marine-scape in the United States. Now, it will be saved for future generations.

Biscayne Bay (Bahia Vizcaina in Spanish) stretches 35 miles from Key Largo in the south to a northern lagoon between Miami and Miami Beach, the latter of which was damaged in the last century by sewage discharges, dredging, storm water and agricultural runoff, and the creation and development of artificial and barrier islands. In its heyday, the development of Miami Beach led to its moniker as a "billion-dollar sandbar." Indeed, it originally was not much more than shallow stands of mangrove bushes – before the dredges arrived to suck up sand to fill in the island.

The northern part of the bay, adjacent to Miami, was always the center of modern human activities – the parties, millionaires, vacation homes, high-rise hotels, and a few scandals, as well. However, the central and southern parts of the bay remained largely untouched by modern development. There, human history stretches back centuries to the occupation by Native peoples.

By the 1500s, Spanish explorers in search mainly of treasure with which to stuff their pockets and royal coffers, had visited the area but were generally disappointed by its lack of riches. However, they couldn't avoid Florida's southeast coast since the nearby northward flowing Gulf Stream current was the fastest route for Spanish ships loaded with New World booty to return to the mother country. The current's changing location, nearby coral reefs, pirates and dangerous storms such as hurricanes made this a perilous voyage at times, and the remains of many ships now can be found ocean-ward of the bay's barrier islands.

By the early 20th century, a string of islands along the eastern part of the central bay was occupied by a handful of residents and farmers, with a few isles serving as weekend getaways for the wealthy. Disconnected from the mainland and with no utilities, these islands offered little opportunity for development, although they remained excellent hiding spots for pirates, wreckers, drug runners and Caribbean refugees.

Improvements in technology and in human scheming, however, made the bay and its islands a target for development by mid-century. One frequent proposal was to connect the islands to the mainland through a variety of causeway roads and bridges. Another included dredging the bay bottom to create artificial islands, each 4,000 feet wide, that would be home to massive high-rise hotels. This was the type of development that had created Miami Beach and was occurring throughout Florida – an effort to create waterfront property in a state that was booming with new residents who wanted watery access and beach views. Indeed, Miami had grown from 1,681 residents at the dawn of the century to 172,000 people by 1950. And most had come for sunshine, boating and sparkling waters.

Many of these proposals came and went until 1959 when Daniel K. Ludwig, an internationally known oil man of great wealth, bought 18,000 acres along the shore of Biscayne Bay. At first, he touted the property as a real estate development, but within two years the real plan became public: a port and industrial development near Homestead that included an oil refinery. The refinery would require a 30-foot-deep channel across the bay and a 40-foot-deep port. [6]

At the same time, plans for Islandia, a resort development on 30 barrier islands began to pick up steam. Some 300 landowners, at the nod of Metro-Dade commissioners, incorporated Islandia into a city in 1961 despite a lack of roads, electricity or infrastructure. However, Islandia now could issue municipal bonds to build the much-needed cause-way connection to the mainland that would make construction and tourism feasible. It also might end public access from the last undeveloped coast in the county. [7]

Local government and business officials, along with local newspapers known for their boosterism, were thrilled at the economic prospects the projects offered. In 1962, Metro-Dade commissioners approved Ludwig's Seadade Realty, Inc., project (hereafter referred to as Seadade). A handful of dissenters, many of them members of the local Izaak Walton League, a prominent national conservation group, quickly joined ranks and created an organization to fight the proposals. They called themselves the Safe Progress Association (SPA) and, despite an initial budget of only $11.05, decided to take on the establishment. [8]

SPA's leader was Lloyd Miller, a Pan American Airways employee in Miami and founder of the local Mangrove Chapter of the Izaak Walton League. Although other groups would join SPA in the

Biscayne effort, in my opinion, Miller was the real leader of the battle. He was unstoppable. And before it finally ended, Miller's dog was poisoned, his car was damaged when he was shot at, and some people tried to get him fired from his job. But he never gave up, never wavered in his belief that the bay was too valuable to be sacrificed to the gods of industry. [9]

Others working with Miller were author Polly Redford and her husband. Jim, who would go onto serve on the Metro-Dade commission; journalist Juanita Greene, whose persistence and writing slowly changed the stance of her employer, the *Miami Herald*; Belle Scheffel, who had great contacts with environmental and garden clubs; attorney Ed Corlett; and Lain Guthrie, an Eastern Airlines pilot. Guthrie had publicized the bay's problems with a very creative demonstration – he flushed orange colored peanuts down the local power plant's toilets to prove (as they floated up) that the plant wasn't treating its sewage before dumping it into the bay. In support, SPA distributed a bumper sticker that featured a bright orange peanut and the slogan "NUTS to Dirty Industry." [10]

SPA members spoke before any community group that would have them, arguing that the refinery project would bring air pollution and unavoidable oil spills into the bay – problems that would affect the quality of life and tourism. Dredging a deep-access channel would change the Bay forever. Even a report by the Miami city manager about a refinery in Hawaii that showed large levels of "noxious pollutants" (and Seadade would be twice its size) didn't sway commissioners. Miller recalls that Seadade took a group of "local industry leaders" to see a refinery in Anacortes, Washington; the Miamians came back speaking "glowingly" of the plant. Of course, Seadade failed to mention that the refinery "five years earlier had spilled 20,000 gallons of crude into Puget Sound when someone turned the wrong valve," Miller recalled. SPA also learned that Ludwig proposals for oil refineries had been turned down in Savannah, Jacksonville and West Palm Beach. [11]

The economics, however, had won over the Miami business community; Seadade promised to employ 18,540 people at an annual payroll of $130 million. That made SPA walk a careful tightrope. Polly Redford best said it in 1964 when she wrote that SPA wasn't against industry, just that which was "dirty." With the associated infrastructure needed for a refinery, she warned: "Miamians, then, had reason to fear several square miles of stack industry on south bay just where prevailing winds and currents would spread its effluents over most of Dade County." [12]

As the arguments dragged on and SPA attacked both projects from many angles, one idea took hold: seeking federal protection for the central and southern bay. It would halt development now and forever. And this is where I eventually got involved in bay protection.

In the summer of 1962, several members of the community met with Miller to discuss how to save the bay and its islands. The state and county, as Miller recalled, seem to have no interest in this angle, so "we wondered if we could interest the federal government." The next day, Miller called Joe Penfold, national conservation director for the Izaak Walton League, and told him about the unfolding situation. Penfold suggested that the only permanent win for the bay might be federal protection – perhaps as a national monument or a national park. Using his contacts, Penfold got the idea to U.S. Secretary of the Interior Stewart Udall, who sent a department team to study the environmental features of the bay. At the same time, Udall sent a letter to Secretary of the Army Cyrus Vance asking that the Seadade permit be withheld until the federal government could be assured that the nearby Everglades National Park (which came under Udall's authority and protection) and the John Pennekamp Coral Reef Preserve (now a state park) wouldn't be damaged by refinery pollution. [13]

What the team found was astounding; even local residents and SPA members didn't realize the value of the bay's natural resources. The bay was home

to the northern portion of the Florida coral reef; "luxuriant turtle grass beds;" tropical hardwood trees on the islands; and a treasure trove of wildlife. Udall's team decided the biota was of "national significance" and deserved protection.

In a November 1963 visit to the area, Udall confirmed his support for designating the area a national monument – at the time, it was too small to be a national park. When Polly Redford asked Udall for advice about how and if conservation groups should keep up the battle against industrial and agricultural interests, Udall replied: "We are losing the battle to keep America beautiful. You must band together more to make a stronger fight for conservation. It is not cheap, it's not easy but I say to you – persist, work hard, work together." As Miller noted, Udall's "answer is just as compelling today as it was then." [14]

The gears quickly went in motion to put together a national monument. Although the president can designate already held federal lands to be national monuments, using the 1906 Antiquities Act, that would not be the case in Biscayne. The monument would include islands in private ownership – including the mythical Islandia project. They would have to be federally purchased, so Congress would have to approve the monument and fund it. U.S. Rep. Dante Fascell, who represented the Biscayne area, became a tireless promoter of the monument, repeatedly introducing legislation, beginning in 1966, to make it a reality. Another great supporter was Herbert Hoover, Jr., of the same-named vacuum company, who pledged $100,000 toward island purchases if the monument were approved.

Islandia owners, however, tried to thwart preservation plans and lobbied vigorously to get their development approved. Their strategy was to get a four-lane causeway highway built to and through the islands, even a toll road, knowing full well that Udall considered such work incompatible with a national monument. Miller, of SPA, fought this project, noting that the work "would destroy 50 percent of the marine biology and choke off 200 square miles of bay bottom." The state's conservation director, Randolph Hodges, had estimated those "fish breeding grounds in the area were worth at least $500 per acre." Thankfully, the causeways were never approved. [15]

Another player in the project was the state of Florida, which held title to the bay bottom and would have to transfer 92,000 acres of it to the federal government for a monument. During his 1966 campaign, Florida Gov. Claude Kirk opposed Biscayne protection, siding with corporate interests who viewed it as a federal land grab. However, Gov. Kirk was an interesting character whose mind could be swayed when confronted with strong facts. And, in this case, a trip into the bay.

Before he and I ever set up shop in Tallahassee, I had a chance to persuade Gov. Kirk to change his mind about the Biscayne monument.

I loved the bay – still do. Alita and I have spent many wonderful hours there fishing, especially for large bonefish that swim in its sparkling waters. I had made friends with many captains and a Florida Marine Patrol officer that worked in the Keys area. It was a contact that would prove invaluable.

After the election ended, Gov. Kirk told me that he planned to take a multi-day sailboat cruise on Biscayne Bay with the lovely "Madame X," whom he later married. Her real name was Erika Mattfeld, but Gov. Kirk told the press her name was Madame X and they ate it up. At the time, I said, "Governor, are you really capable of sailing a 38-foot boat alone?" I pointed out the area's treacherous tides, shoals and reefs that could be troublesome. When he admitted that he might need some help, I set him up with a Marine Patrol friend. I advised the Marine Patrol officer, Lt. Little, that at some point "you're going to find time to explain to the governor how uniquely beautiful the islands are and how incredibly productive the bay is; both within minutes of a major city." I had told Gov. Kirk about the issues in the bay, particularly the island development scheme, which I called "the mythical land of Islandia," hoping to get him to change his mind on the issue. He liked to see things in black and white, in good versus evil, so I tried to frame the Islandia controversy in this way.

As expected, the governor and his lady friend became bored after a couple of days and managed to run the boat hard aground as they tried to navigate Card Sound. There was nothing to do but wait for three hours for the tide to rise; Madame X went down below and Gov. Kirk sat down and drank beer with the officer.

Lt. Little took this opportunity to inform him about the bay and its beauty and wildlife and the threats that would come from dredges, causeways and refineries. The governor came to believe that an evil empire was behind the potential destruction of this chain of pearls. When he came back on land, he accused me of setting it all up – I laughed – and then we launched a state/federal effort to protect the bay. This effort included the state denying any permits for causeways or dredging – the very things that Islandia developers needed. Gov. Kirk's change of heart was critical, and now Islandia was sunk. He was completely on board with saving the bay, wondering, "How could those greedy so-and-so's want to create another Miami Beach? They don't realize they will destroy one of the most beautiful bays in the world. Let's get going and save Biscayne Bay!"

A change in local government also ensured the death of Seadade and Islandia. Two bay preservers were elected in 1964 to the Metro-Dade Commission, whose approval was necessary for various issues, including a building permit for Ludwig and Seadade. That same year Seadade withdrew its refinery plans, instead proposing an

Stiltsville in Biscayne Bay

industrial seaport for the waterfront site in the southern bay. A year later, the commission decided to support the national monument project and oppose any causeway; Udall had warned that a causeway or similar access would end national monument consideration.

It was a new environmental era in Miami. Even the angry landowners on Elliott Key, which would have been central to the Islandia development, couldn't stop it. They plowed a 100-foot-wide, seven-mile-long road down the middle of the island, destroying much of its flora, in hopes that it would no longer be desirable for protection. They were wrong and today that road, known as "Spite Highway" is slowing filling back in with native vegetation. [16]

I'm proud to say that, on October 18, 1968, Congress approved Biscayne National Monument. President Lyndon B. Johnson signed it into law that same day. It certainly helped that Johnson had fished in Biscayne Bay and visited the Cocolobo Club, then a private holding on Adams Key. The new monument preserved 96,300 acres, including sites for two visitor centers. Its enacting legislation states that the monument was created "in order to preserve and protect for the education, inspiration, recreation and enjoyment of present and future generations a rare combination of terrestrial, marine, and amphibious life in a tropical setting of great natural beauty…." [17]

There have been two expansions of the monument. In 1974 there was another effort to expand the monument north including the Ragged Keys, the shallow prime bonefish flats and Stiltsville. I testified in favor of the addition with enthusiasm, but did not favor taking on Federal responsibility for Stiltsville. However, the Congress voted to include the structures and added 8,738 acres. In 1980, Congress declared it to be Biscayne National Park to which the state gave an additional 72,861 acres in 1985, mostly Bay bottom. [18]

The first person to sell property to the federal government for the new monument was Lancelot Jones, a well-known fishing guide who grew up on Porgy Key. His father, an ex-slave, had raised a family and farmed on three barrier islands, growing limes, vegetables and pineapples, as many people in the area did in those days. Although many of his neighbors hoped to get rich by developing the keys into Islandia, Jones spurned the idea and endorsed bay preservation.

I once asked Jones whether the potential of vast income was worth sacrificing his beloved tract of land.

He quietly replied, "No, I thought so months ago, but wanted a land-to-sea legacy for others to enjoy."

Jones received a life estate in the land deal so he could enjoy the rest of his years on Porgy Key; he stopped living there after Hurricane Andrew destroyed all its structures in 1992. Jones died five years later at age 99. The Jones homestead has been nominated to the National Register of Historic Places.

Today, Biscayne National Park is a unique gem in the National Park Service. It is the largest marine park in the country with 95 percent of its 173,000 acres underwater. More than half a million people each year visit to enjoy its beauty and recreational opportunities, including fishing, snorkeling, kayaking and diving.

It has many threats, mostly owing to its proximity to the booming Miami metropolitan area and all the problems that occur when a park borders an urban area. But thanks to Lloyd Miller, SPA and a cadre of people who decided to fight for a place they loved, there is no refinery. No Islandia high-rise resort. No channel across the shallow bay. It is a place where endangered manatees, bonefish, tarpon and butterflies can exist in subtropical wonder.

And it is a place where many generations to come will be able to see the raw splendor of Florida's precious Biscayne Bay. Perhaps they can look out at it as I have and be awed by a sunrise, and hook a bonefish or tarpon, and enjoy a day of peace on the water.

It is my hope for Florida's future.

Notes – Biscayne National Monument: Preserving Our Precious Bays

[6] Lloyd Miller, *Biscayne National Park: It Almost Wasn't*, (Redland, Fl: LEMDOT Publishing Col, 2008), 27-29.

[7] Ibid., 28-29.

[8] Jack E. Davis, *An Everglades Providence: Marjory Stoneman Douglas and the American Century* (Athens: University of Georgia Press, 2009), 441; Luther Carter, *The Florida Experience: Land and water policy in a growth state* (Baltimore: The Johns Hopkins University Press, 1974), 155; Polly Redford, "Small Rebellion in Miami," *Harper's*, February 1964, 96-97.

[9] Davis, *An Everglades Providence,* 444-445.

[10] Miller, *Biscayne National Park*, 25-16, 30, 32; Carter, *The Florida Experience*, 158-159.

[11] Miller, *Biscayne National Park*, 32-33.

[12] Davis, *An Everglades Providence*, 441; Redford, "Small Rebellion in Miami," 97, 101.

[13] Miller, *Biscayne National Park*, 38-39.

[14] Ibid, 46; Carter, *The Florida Experience*, 160-161.

[15] Miller, *Biscayne National Park*, 52.

[16] Ibid., 53; Carter, *The Florida Experience*, 161.

[17] "Enabling Legislation," Biscayne National Park website. Accessed June 4, 2015 at http://www.nps.gov/bisc/learn/management/enabling-legislation.htm

[18] Miller, *Biscayne National Park*, 154-155.

Saving the Magnificently Diverse Fakahatchee Strand

"The mysterious swamp man; a vision of what could be."

The years I spent working for Gov. Claude Kirk were some of the longest, toughest and most controversial years I have ever experienced in government. It started when I became chairman of the Florida Pollution Control Agency, replacing the ancient, ineffective State Board of Health doctors who did not believe in what they called "pollution control."

The environmental era had begun and the "Old Guard" that controlled the Florida legislature and state offices was not prepared to change its old ways. Although Gov. Kirk realized he would not win re-election, he nevertheless pursued an aggressive agenda that included giving me license to tackle every possible environmental challenge in our long state. This was exhausting but thrilling work – to change opinions, enlist constituents and make pollution control and land use central issues for future governors and ignorant county commissioners.

Despite working 12-hour days, often seven days a week, attempting to identify and bring under control the vast volume of under- or untreated human sewage and an incredible amount of industrial pollutants pumped into state waters, I never lost keen interest in land acquisition and management. I received numerous calls, notes and letters urging me to meet "Mel Finn." But who was Mel Finn and why did I have to leave the epicenter of action – the state Capitol and governor's office – and fly to Miami to meet him?

My newly appointed assistant, George Gardner, a recent graduate of the University of Florida's School of Forestry and Wildlife, produced a list of who had called or written me urging a meeting with Mel. It turned out that Mel had formed the Florida chapter of The Nature Conservancy in 1961 and, in 1962, the Conservancy had created the Fakahatchee Strand Committee, comprised of an incredible cast of well-known academic experts in many environmental areas, along with Dade County activists.

The list of callers included Joe Browder, Charles Lee and even Marjory Stoneman Douglas and a host of other acclaimed conservationists from Dade County. It was a call from conservationist Franklin Adams that finally piqued my curiosity enough to join him and Mel at the Fakahatchee Strand swamp. Adams had promised a strand of "unusual characteristics" – a wild, untamed swamp filled with indigenous orchids, bromeliads, ferns and recovering stands of previously cut giant cypress trees. It was, he said, a cornucopia of unique forms of botanical life, curiously different from the adjacent Big Cypress Swamp.

It was clear from Franklin's telephone call that I should bring associates who might be able to assist in the purchase of the Fakahatchee Strand. Although the state was receiving both federal Land and Water Conservation Funds and Environmental Land Bond Funds, it seemed improbable that we could

Ghost orchid

add the mysterious Fakahatchee Swamp to State Park System Director Ney Landrum's list of "must buys."

Franklin and I had met early in my tour in the governor's office and I immediately recognized that he was a truly significant environmentalist. He had incredible knowledge of the Big Cypress, having camped and hunted within its boundaries since childhood. Further, he was highly respected among the nascent southwestern Florida environmental community as a man who kept his word and could not be swayed by the omnipresent developers who traded in mangrove and swamp lands. He had opposed the destructive drainage plans of the "swamp peddlers" and fought permits that allowed drainage of thousands of acres of wetlands. He and his "band of brothers" urged Collier County and the state to halt the subdivisions of swamp land and the sale of small lots to unsuspecting buyers who could never develop their very wet lots lost in wilderness.

I persuaded the governor to authorize a group of us to meet Mel and Franklin and visit the Fakahatchee Strand. I confirmed a date, May 1, 1970. I was accompanied by Gardner, Landrum and Joel Kuperberg, a well-known Naples land manager who had vast knowledge and experience in southwest Florida's environmental issues. The governor assigned us a twin-engine state plane, and we landed at the Everglades City grass airfield. Franklin's mother's health was faltering, but he was waiting for us and we drove to Everglades City's aging but famous Rod and Gun Club for dinner and an overnight stay.

The mysterious Mel Finn met us. I immediately liked this energetic, dynamic, determined man. We sat in a screened-in porch for dinner and late into the night as he enthralled us with his tales of years of exploring "his discovery" – the Fakahatchee Strand. Mel no longer remained a "mysterious swamp man." In a matter of minutes, we all discovered that Mel was a fascinating fellow, a Miami attorney who hated practicing the law. He lived for the weekends to continue his years of exploring the Big Cypress wilderness and what became his life's passion – the Fakahatchee Strand. Mel encouraged the preservation of the Fakahatchee, even swaying Florida citizens who had never heard of or much less seen the swamp, but trusted the dream and excitement of a man who had a vision of what could be.

This is why he was so excited, so passionate, so committed to his cause:

- The Fakahatchee is the largest strand swamp in the world, extending 19 miles long and three to five miles wide. It is part of the Big Cypress Swamp physiographic region of the western Everglades. Its waters flow southwesterly into the Ten Thousand Islands and Everglades National Park.
- Its diversity makes the swamp unique, given its many species of plants and animals. The Fakahatchee is the royal palm capital of the United States, containing a population of 5,000 to 7,000 royal palms.
- It also is the orchid capital of the U.S., with 47 native species, eight of which are found only within the Fakahatchee. This is because the strand maintains higher water levels throughout the year, which produces a moist microclimate that limits fires that could kill the epiphytes. Put another way, it is a natural greenhouse.
- In addition, the Fakahatchee is the bromeliad capital of the U.S., with 14 native species, one of which, the Nodding Catopsis

Royal Palms © by Jay Staton

(*Catopsis nutans*), is found only there.

- The Fakahatchee has more species of Peperomia than anywhere else in the country. There are five native species, two of which – the Winged Peperomia (*Peperomia alata*) and Cypress Peperomia (*Peperomia glabella*) – are found nowhere else in the United States.
- The Fakahatchee contains two species of tropical ferns that are found nowhere else in the country. They are the Hanging clubmoss (*Huperzia dichotoma*) and Stately Maiden Fern (*Thelypteris grandis*).
- The Fakahatchee is home to the endangered Florida panther, black bear and Everglades mink, which is listed as threatened by the Florida Fish and Wildlife Conservation Commission. It is a refuge for many other mammals, birds and reptiles.
- The Fakahatchee preserves a remnant of old-growth cypress trees that were spared from the logging that took place between 1944 and 1954. The remaining trees cover 215 acres, the second largest patch of old-growth bald cypress remaining in Florida.

That first night, Mel gave me a thick folder containing hundreds of letters and newspaper articles describing the Strand and the incredible uniqueness of this relatively small area, which had been decimated by the logging of giant bald cypress trees that were more than 200 years old. Mel promised to show us the next day the incredible regeneration of the cypress trees from stumps and assured us recovery would continue over time. Mel said, "Mother Nature, combined with the tropics, can be quite forgiving."

He handed me a heartbreaking article to read – a January 26, 1966 *Miami Herald* story written by Tom Morgan describing the sale of 75,000 acres of the Fakahatchee to the Gulf American Land Corporation (GALC). It was sold by the Lee Tidewater Cypress Company, which had cut enough cypress logs to fill 36,000 train cars.

The article read, in part:

> "The 75,000-acre tract parallels the route of State Road 29 from Immokalee to Everglades City and would contact the present Everglades National Park at the park's northwest corner. Even the National Park Service was ignoring the fact that drainage from the Strand helps maintain park water levels in that area. The Strand is sought for preservation because it is considered a self-contained wilderness area which could preserve its wildlife if outside encroachment is prevented. The Strand is home to the world's largest stand of native royal palms. It has 38 species of orchids, including at least seven found nowhere else, plus 20 varieties of moss and 11 bromeliad species. Amid its bald cypress trees are alligator, panther, Florida mink, otter, deer and black bear."

Collier County commissioners were enthralled by the Gulf American Land Corporation's promises of thousands of new residents to reshape their economy and attract taxpayers. GALC was known for its highly suspect land-sales history. Collier County was governed by a commission that made development its priority. The commissioners cared not about the quality or even the legality of a developer's plans to cut, drain and fill.

They wanted development!

Mel produced a file that contained hundreds of letters, memorandums and newspaper clippings that Franklin and he had written to members of Congress, governors and the secretaries of interior, pleading to preserve this incredibly unique area. I woke at dawn and read through the file.

Mel was "possessed" – my kind of a guy. Mel and Franklin had written to every member of the Florida congressional delegation, every newspaper and every naturalist author for years urging acquisition of the Strand by the state or federal

Pond Apple Slough © photo by Jay Staton

government. The answers were always the same: "It seems like a very interesting proposal, but...."

Franklin's mother died overnight after our meeting, so regrettably he could not join us the following morning on an expedition led by Mel. After an early breakfast, we were picked up by a pair of Florida Highway Patrol officers who had been assigned by the governor who described us as VIPs and told the officers to keep an eye on us.

We followed Mel into the Strand along an old logging road that the county had taken over as a scenic drive. Despite the dry time of the year, the water was knee-deep in places and waist-deep on the route Mel used. We were outfitted with five-foot-long forked sticks that were useful in persuading water snakes and the occasional water moccasin to move quietly out of our way. George Gardner had brought along a machete. I had urged him to leave it with the state patrol officer, but he was last in line and could not resist the temptation of having a machete hanging from his hip.

The farther into the swamp we walked or waded, the more astonishing sights we experienced. The height and number of indigenous Florida royal palms was incredible. They thrust their trunks above the cypress and other tropical tree canopies. The cypress trees, many growing from stumps of trees cut for lumber 80 years before, had regrown into leafy towers. Their leaves were turning light green, a breathtaking sight.

The scent of the buds of numerous botanical specimens mingled with blooms of bromeliads and orchids. It was intoxicating. The royal palms reached 60 to 75 feet through the cypress trees; Joel insisted they were up to 100 feet high. Orchids and bromeliads were everywhere, growing with rare abandon, untouched by man.

We stopped frequently and Mel briefed us on some oddity, something special, or something we all found uniquely exciting. There were long periods of silence as the majesty of the excursion nearly overwhelmed us. Mel described what he called the "uniqueness of our surroundings," noting there was nothing like it even within the adjacent Big Cypress watershed.

As we began to return to the starting site, suddenly there was a cry from the rear of our troop. George had taken out his machete and swung it against a vine hanging from a cypress tree. The machete bounced off the tree and cut his leg very deeply. I helped apply a tight tourniquet and said, "George, you are too big to carry. You are simply going to have to be very brave and we will move as quickly as possible back to the road where we can get you a better tourniquet and get you to a hospital."

We mushed our way back to a waiting trooper's car and I sent George back to the airport with instructions to fly him to the nearest hospital. For reasons never fully explained, the pilot flew him to Marathon, where an ambulance took him to the area's tiny hospital. George survived despite the fact that he had to spend weeks battling all kinds of interesting infections.

Guzmania Garden © photo by Jay Staton

The rest of us huddled together, overcome by the sights of the Fakahatchee. We realized it would be difficult to acquire the swamp when the Rosen brothers, notorious land peddlers and owners of the Gulf American Land Corporation (GALC), had been permitted to plan a huge subdivision in the Strand. Their slick sales force already had sold hundreds of lots to unsuspecting buyers who thought they were purchasing property on the Gulf or land for small retirement settlements. What were the prospects of ending the land sales, acquiring the sold lots and then finding the funds to acquire the Strand and restore the vital water flow?

The proposed GALC Strand development plan was a perfect example of the outrageous lack of state regulations outlawing real estate sales of undevelopable lands.

Suddenly, an obvious rental car drove up and paused next to us. Two delightful ladies in their mid-50s inquired where they were. I answered that they were in the middle of the Fakahatchee Strand. "No, no," snapped one of them. "It's quite impossible! We have been paying monthly for land to retire on. We thought it was near the Gulf, certainly not within a very wet swamp! Our ranch, which we bought from the Gulf American Land Corporation, is right around here."

I had the unpleasant assignment of informing her that the Rosen brothers were facing both state and federal governmental legal actions as peddlers of swamp land all across southwest Florida. They exclaimed, "This is an outrage! How can Florida's governments allow such larceny? We are going back to their sales office and attempt to cancel our sale contract and never return to this hideous swamp!"

Before we were picked up by the police cruiser, we stood together and held our hands high and pledged that we would never give up until the Fakahatchee was preserved. We hugged Mel and informed him that we would work together to somehow realize his vision of a Fakahatchee state park that fascinated visitors with tour-guided explanations of its history, the devastation of the timbering period and the recovery of the Strand and its unique botanical mix.

Then, we departed having shared a memorable life experience.

What Happened Before and What Happened Next

Photo by Willard Culver, National Geographic Creative

In 1966, the Gulf American Land Corporation (GALC) purchased 75,000 acres of the Fakahatchee from the Lee-Tidewater Cypress Company, a subsidiary of the J. C. Turner Lumber Company, for about $100 per acre. (The Lee-Tidewater Cypress Company had logged the old-growth cypress from the Fakahatchee Strand beginning in 1944 and, by 1957, had cut all the towering cypress in the strand except for the Big Cypress Bend area.)

The sale was devastating news to Mel Finn and the Fakahatchee Strand Committee, both working tirelessly to have the state of Florida or the Department of Interior preserve and acquire the Fakahatchee Strand. The efforts of Jane Parks in Naples, who was chair of the Florida Federated Women's Clubs, prompted Congressman Paul Rogers to introduce a bill seeking to declare the Fakahatchee a National Wilderness Monument by the Department of Interior in 1966, the year it was sold to GALC.

That same year, Gulf American Land Corporation was cited for illegally dredging and filling land at its Cape Coral development in Lee County between 1959 and 1965. According to state officials, Gulf American had illegally dredged two to three million cubic yards of sovereign submerged lands at Cape Coral. Gulf American also was being investigated for unethical and fraudulent lands sales in Cape Coral, Remuda Ranch and Golden Gate Estates. It was charged with five counts of defrauding buyers and, in November 1967, pleaded guilty to all five counts.

Partly as a result, Gulf American was failing financially. The late 1960s was a time of environmental awakening and the state of Florida no longer was going to tolerate or overlook developers' destruction of publicly owned, submerged lands. The state pursued penalties against Gulf American.

To assist in resolving that litigation, GALC offered to pay damages by trading land in the Fakahatchee Strand.

Finally, in 1972, to satisfy state claims of illegal dredging and filling of public lands by GALC at Cape Coral, a settlement was reached. GALC would deed to the state of Florida 9,500 acres of salt marsh/mangrove lands south of the Fakahatchee Strand. In 1974, GALC agreed to sell the state 24,000 acres for $4.4 million. By 1998, approximately 44,000 acres had been acquired. This was the beginning of the major acquisition of the Fakahatchee.

The swamp peddling, unethical sales activities and illegal dredging and filling of publicly owned lands by the Gulf American Rosen brothers was no longer tolerated by the state of Florida and its residents. Florida and the state and federal environmental enforcement agencies adopted and enforced new permitting standards so another wetland violation similar to Cape Coral would never be allowed to happen.

(A case in point: The Mackle brothers acquired 24,962 acres on and around Marco Island in Florida. The majority of this land was classified as wetlands. Their plans to destroy significant mangrove wetlands resulted in the largest permitting fight ever, with both Florida and federal permitting agencies and a number of environmental groups becoming involved in litigation. The legal battle lasted several years, finally resulting in a settlement in 1982. There were nine separate lawsuits which, when settled, led to the preservation of significant wetlands that were protected from development.)

Back in the Fakahatchee, state parks Director Ney Landrum set about acquiring hundreds of properties in 1974. It took years of persistent effort to reach the owners of scattered private lands that had been sold, but not cleared, and in most cases they couldn't be clearly identified. The majority sold out for $100 an acre.

In 1972, the Florida Legislature passed and Gov. Reubin Askew signed the Endangered Land Program, one of Askew's greatest triumphs. Due to Landrum's persistence, the state bought the vast majority of the swamp's 57,297 acres, paying owners a total of $12,223,000. It was exhausting, time-consuming work requiring total dedication to the task.

Friends of the Fakahatchee and the citizens of Florida have much to be grateful for during Ney Landrum's incredible leadership of the state's park system, but one of the "greatest jewels" of his extraordinary land acquisitions is our Fakahatchee Swamp!

To date, the state has purchased 77,690 acres of the Fakahatchee Strand creating the Fakahatchee Strand State Preserve. The optimum boundaries desired in order to protect the watershed of the swamp strand add up to approximately 90,000 acres. Since 2000, the state has purchased 900 parcels from numerous owners and continues its acquisition.

With the passage of Amendment 1 in 2014, the state will – or should – have the money to acquire the remaining privately owned lands needed to complete the protection of one of Florida's most unique areas.

My last good deed in the Fakahatchee Swamp's preservation was being intimately involved in the acquisition of the Okaloacoochee Swamp, a major headwater of the Fakahatchee Strand. In time the Fakahatchee headwaters, the 13,000-acre Okaloacoochee Slough State Forest and surrounding high ground were also preserved, ensuring a continuous natural water supply.

Sadly, Mel had to have heart surgery in 1971 and complications took his life. Our pledges have stood the test of time. Mel Finn's spirit is still there.

We have lost Joel and the indomitable Mel, but the remaining three of us who gave our oaths are still living: never forgetting the incredible Mel Finn and our mutual pledge to save this precious gem.

In April 1999, Clyde Butcher, the world-famous photographer persuaded Joel, Ney, George, Franklin and me to pose for a photograph honoring our efforts to support and achieve Mel's vision of a protected Fakahatchee Strand. It graces my office wall. The photograph sums up what I cannot adequately express: the quiet satisfaction of success, the fellowship and the incredible leadership of Mel and Franklin, who would not give up and finally got the right players to the field of action.

I cannot over emphasize the importance of Franklin Adams to the history of a great experience which led to the improbable acquisition of the Fakahatchee Strand.

Finally, the swamp is ours. Ours, for the people of Florida; ours, for the American people, and ours, to be shared with hundreds of tourists from around the world who visit each year. One visit and the Fakahatchee is theirs, too.

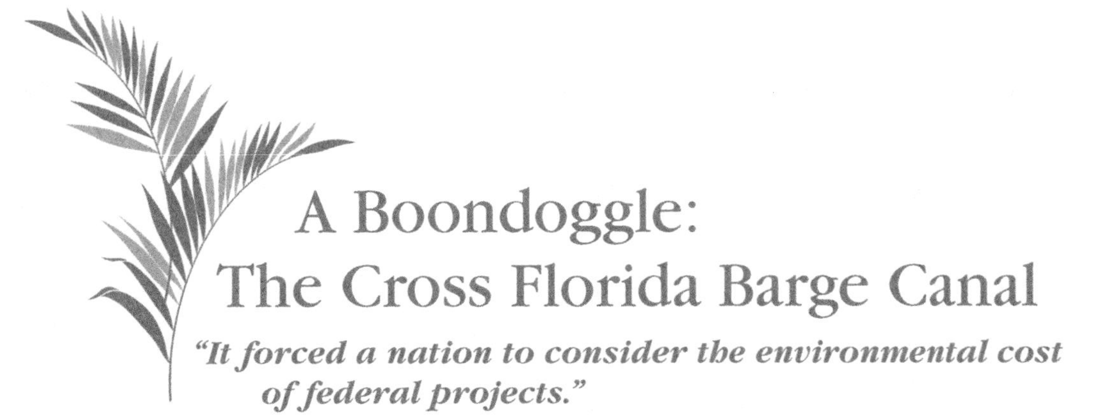

A Boondoggle: The Cross Florida Barge Canal

"It forced a nation to consider the environmental cost of federal projects."

It would have been the answer to the prayers of the earliest Spanish settlers and sailors – a water route across Florida's peninsula, far from the treacherous route between "La Florida" and Cuba that featured dangerous reefs, hurricanes and pirates. It would have allowed their wooden ships safer passage for transport of precious metals, rare china and other goods, assuring filled royal coffers and the conquest of the Americas.[19]

Many others shared this dream, but the closest it came to becoming a reality happened during the 1960s, when the federal government authorized construction of the Cross Florida Barge Canal. Nazi submarines that had roamed off the Florida coast during World War II helped spur the project, but so did an abundance of federal dollars, new technology that could accomplish the task, and the eternal hope that creating large public works projects would energize and satisfy the electorate.

The waterway was newly envisioned as a liquid conduit for cargo-carrying barges to head east from the Gulf Coast across to the St. Johns River, northward toward Jacksonville and then to the Atlantic Ocean. Its promoters were ecstatic about the riches it would bring – not gold and silver but jobs and promises of economic development, which regularly set aglow the hearts and minds of state politicians.

Ultimately, the barge canal proved to be an environmental disaster and economic boondoggle that was stopped by presidential edict. It set a national precedent and forced a nation to consider the environmental cost of federal projects. During my early environmental career, I encountered the project first as a protestor, then as a gubernatorial consultant.

But let's get back to the beginning of the story. At its onset, one of the canal project's main supporters (besides the businessmen and politicians from the small towns along the proposed canal route) was U.S. Senator George Smathers, D-Fl., and U.S. Rep. Claude Pepper, a staunch Democrat who represented the Miami area. During the 1960 presidential campaign, Smathers promised that he could get Florida's electoral votes for Democratic candidate John F. Kennedy, who was running against Republican Richard M. Nixon. In return, Kennedy offered Smathers any federal public works project that he wanted for the state.

Nixon carried Florida. But it was close and Kennedy was extremely well-received in the state. After his election, Kennedy made good on his promise and Smathers chose the construction of the Cross Florida Barge Canal as his compensation. Imagine if Smathers had asked for money to extend Everglades National Park or a greenway from Lake Okeechobee to the park. But, of all the things in the world to have picked – the barge canal?

It seemed like a done deal. All of Florida's top elected officials supported the project and the Florida delegation was the second or third most powerful in Congress. So, the money was funded and Kennedy's successor, Lyndon B. Johnson, came to Florida on a cold, gray February day in 1964. As historians, Steven Noll and David Tegeder noted, "Johnson stood in the pouring rain and gave birth to the dream of so many for so long." Johnson lauded the project and the need for humans to improve nature's waterways. Then, he pulled a switch that exploded the dynamite that heralded the project's launch. [20]

Soon, newspapers were filled with pictures of huge draglines and colossal machines that were digging canals for the Central and Southern Florida Flood Control Project, which would completely change the Everglades' water system. I would go to meetings and hear U.S. Army Corps of Engineers leaders speak, promoting more canals in Florida. And some residents were questioning the wisdom of this. Is this really what we wanted for the state?

A number of people, mostly in north central Florida, joined in that uncertainty and dismay regarding the proposed barge canal. They had pressured the Corps and the state government for information, of which they got very little. Finally, they demanded and were reluctantly granted a public hearing to air their concerns – a hearing set for January 25, 1966.

I believe it was Marjorie Carr who telephoned me to tell me about the hearing. Carr, a trained biologist whose husband was a well-respected sea turtle expert, was one of the leaders of the group that was trying to change the barge canal's route so it wouldn't damage the beautiful Ocklawaha River. Hearing about the project from a garden club friend, Carr urged the Alachua Audubon Society, which she helped found, to investigate the canal. To her horror, Carr discovered that the project would destroy much of her beloved Ocklawaha, a twisting spring-fed stream that had inspired poets and brought many tourists to Florida in the 1800s and 1920s. "Here, by God, was a piece of Florida, a lovely natural area right in my back yard, that was being threatened for no good reason," she said. [21]

The Tallahassee hearing was publicized around the state – and I heard that it was going to be rigged in favor of the canal project. Florida Secretary of State Tom Adams, who was there to applaud when LBJ detonated the dynamite, was going to chair the hearing and he had never seen a public works program that he didn't support. I was told, "If you really cared about your state's future, you had to be there." And I said, "By God, I'm going to go."

I rented a private airplane and pilot and, at the last minute, the weather turned bad in Tallahassee. With me was a great family friend and a member of the Jupiter Island Garden Club. We took off early in the morning and I was co-flying the airplane. As we got to Tallahassee, groping through rain and sodden skies, suddenly right there in front of us was the dome of the state Capitol building! We must have been four miles short of the airport. I am telling you, it would have been a fantastic arrival but instead we flew south to Cross City. At Cross City, we got out of the airplane and hugged each other, glad to be alive. After considering our options, we decided to try for Tallahassee and this time we made it to the right runway and caught a cab to the Capitol, where a real disaster was about to occur.

The hearing was rigged. Only proponents could speak during the morning and there was a huge luncheon the proponents had for themselves, which I went to by invitation of Gov. Haydon Burns. I went in and sat down and had my hors d'oeuvres and, as luncheon came, I put my hand up and was recognized.

Burns said, "Young man, do you want to say something?"

I said, "Gov. Burns, I just want to say as a citizen who's in Tallahassee for the first time of my life, I don't think this is the way a public works project should be presented. A lot of us have come a long, long way and it doesn't look like we're going to be able to speak in opposition to this project in any meaningful way."

"You're right," Burns replied. "Get him out of here," and I was strong-armed out of the room. That was the end of my luncheon.

At the hearing, where hundreds of patient opponents finally got to speak in the late afternoon, I met Carr, along with some of her team. Adams chaired the meeting, sitting at a huge podium and Burns came in and out and there was a whole cadre of generals who literally slept through the proceedings.

Adams challenged and quizzed canal detractors but never its supporters; some even described his confrontational behavior as bullying. The entire process infuriated canal opponents that day, and served to make us completely committed to the cause.

I remember flying home, fighting the airplane like I was grabbing those guys by the throat. This is not the American way, I thought. This is wrong. This is rigged. The Corps is involved. Of course, all the diggers were there – the guys who were going to make a ton of money on the project. They were the equipment salesmen, the maintenance people. The hearing in Tallahassee enlightened me. It was clear that state officials already had made up their minds to support the canal.

But it would backfire. As a result of Burns trying to ram the Cross Florida Barge Canal down the state's throat, the environmental movement coalesced, becoming a powerhouse force. The Florida "good ol' boys" establishment and the Corps did not see it coming. [22]

"We were so proud. We were so eloquent – my we were eloquent and very, very good," Carr later recalled of canal protestors who spoke at the public hearing. "And we stood up to Tom Adams badgering us. He was awful, just awful." The hearing went on until about 9 p.m. and the anti-canal forces drove home from Tallahassee "feeling quite smug," she recalled.

Then, as they drove, they heard a radio broadcast stating that the state's Water Resources Committee had met that morning and had voted to continue the barge canal on its original route. "They had made the decision before they had met with us," she said, calling the hearing a "watershed meeting." The ensuing anger inspired opponents and "woke up the press," Carr said. [23] Every key member of the growing Florida conservation movement was present. We met, hugged, and vowed not to 'lose our beloved state' to developing drainers and builders.

Carr and others soon moved from trying to re-route the canal project to trying to defeat it completely. She organized a number of experts, many from the University of Florida, to oppose the project on many fronts, including potential damage to the aquifer, the long history of the Ocklawaha River, and the sheer financial numbers of the project's cost and benefits to the community. The economics of it were shocking.

When you stopped to think that the plan was for ocean-going coal barges to be dragged from Alabama across the Gulf of Mexico, where they had to be offloaded onto smaller barges (the canal wasn't big enough for ocean-going barges) and then they would be hauled across Florida by small tugboats and offloaded again into ocean-going barges to go up the St. Johns River to Jacksonville and then onto Savannah and Charleston; it just didn't make any sense.

Marjorie Carr's opposition to it was utterly fantastic. She built her case on science and environmental action and reaction. I read all of her paperwork, and she churned it out in those days. She was young and filled with enthusiasm and vinegar, and she really believed. A lot of people began to really believe. They looked upon it as a slice across Florida that was going to destroy and pollute the great aquifer and do immeasurable damage at both ends, where there would be dams and pools of disaster.

Carr, who many wrongly dismissed as a

"Contrary to what you may have heard, there are some still interested in completing the Barge Canal."

"Micanopy housewife," eventually worked with others to create the grassroots organization, Florida Defenders of the Environment (FDE). They consulted with a number of people involved in different environmental battles and decided their strategy would be to develop an environmental impact statement for the project. In the 1960s, federal agencies weren't required to consider what damage their projects might do to the environment. But a series of environmental crises had left Americans clamoring for a greater examination and protection of the nation's natural resources. FDE and Carr understood this and worked from this angle, assembling facts, facts, facts to counter the Corps and canal supporters.

As I looked at it, there was no way of stopping it on those terms. Instead, I approached it from the political point of view. Florida's Congressional delegation long had been assured by the Corps that the project would be beneficial and economically sound. They looked at opponents as "crazies" and we did look a little crazy. This was a new way, new ground. I decided one way to oppose it was to characterize the canal as a Democratic pork-barrel project, as bareknuckle politics being rammed down the throat of rational Floridians by a bunch of Yellow Dog Democrats – the conservative state leadership that mostly hailed from North Florida and was also called the Pork Chop Gang.

As the barge canal fight waged, a funny thing happened in Tallahassee – this is when, as I've mentioned previously, Florida got its first Republican governor since Reconstruction, Claude Kirk. And I unexpectedly became his chief environmental consultant.

In the mid-twentieth century, Florida's population centers had begun to shift to urban and southern parts of the state. But its government was seized in a stranglehold by these northern politicians – a power base that shifted with the 1966 gubernatorial election. As Noll and Tegeder noted, "Though Tom Adams seemed pleased with himself for shouting down Marjorie Carr and her allies, pictures of a crew-cut Pork Chopper – complete with a seersucker suit and white socks – berating ordinary citizens, did not play well to the state's new constituency."

Kirk, who championed "modernization and democratic reform with a new constitution," personified a radical change in politics. This swing in politics gave Carr and other canal opponents hope that they would finally be heard. [24]

As I've mentioned, on the night he won the primary, Kirk came to dinner at my home in Hobe Sound. I had raised a significant amount of money for his campaign and it turned out that it was more than he anticipated.

We were having dinner with the state Republican chairman on the patio overlooking the beautiful Indian River Lagoon and celebrating the fact that we had engineered a reform movement within the state party. Kirk, smoking my best cigar and having drunk at least half a bottle of brandy, watched the election returns. He won the Republican primary and, surprisingly, Burns had been ousted in the Democratic primary by a Miami mayor. We all looked at each other and Kirk said, "You're looking at the next governor of Florida."

During the campaign I wrote Kirk's white papers on conservation. He liked to think of himself as against many entrenched issues and naturally would champion the environment because it was the poor stepchild of all state issues. I would make everything a clear good versus evil battle, simplifying the issue and pointing him in the right direction. He loved to make news and he would take on almost any issue – sales of submerged lands, which was a terrible policy by the state; the Cross Florida Barge Canal; the plight of the Everglades. You name it, Kirk would pick up the issue and run with it.

And I was at his side, at a salary of $1 a year. The work was terrific and I soon was swamped with water and air pollution issues, particularly with trying to get municipalities to adequately treat their wastewater before disposing of it in Florida's waterways. The federal government had passed a faulty non-enforceable Clean Water Act but even with limited vision and power, not a single industry or city in the state met its guidelines in 1967. We had to set up a whole new system of rules. It was grueling work and I was gone too often from my wife and family at hearing after hearing across our very lengthy state.

Kirk was from Jacksonville, which was heavily pro-canal, and he initially supported the project. However, after he was briefed about the canal's operations, particularly about the need to repeatedly offload and reload the barges to transport goods (mostly coal) across the state, Kirk came to believe that it made no economic sense.

Still caught up in the Cold War between the U.S. and the U.S.S.R, Congressman Pepper called Kirk and begged him to support the canal lest Russian submarines interfere with coal supplies around the state. It was a laughable moment during the controversy and an example of the kind of opposition we were facing from the elderly congressman and from others.

Subsequently, Kirk and I met quietly – and secretly – with canal opponents and he was briefed by experts who fueled his growing hostility about supporting appropriations to fund the project. He turned to me finally and quietly stated: "Let's see if we can enlist Nixon to end this Democratic boondoggle!"

During Kirk's campaign in autumn 1970, he made it clear that he thought the canal was Nixon's problem. As Noll and Tegeder write: "Facing pickets protesting canal completion at a rally in Clearwater, Nixon asked Kirk pointedly: 'They want to stop a canal. Are you building it?' Kirk answered, 'No, you are.'" [25]

Despite his environmental record, Kirk was defeated for reelection that fall by Reubin Askew, whose running mate was none other than Tom Adams. Despite Adams' long history of supporting the project, Askew had a different view, not favoring its completion. And although I was a moderate Republican, Askew asked me to stay on with his administration in order to fend off potential corruption in environmental regulation. [26]

Carr and FDE had been very busy battling the canal, gaining valuable media and public support. In September 1969, they worked with the Environmental Defense Fund, which sued the Corps in federal court, seeking to stop the canal project. It generated an enormous amount of publicity. In March 1970, FDE published its environmental impact statement, which attacked the project on multiple fronts, particularly the Corps' long-touted claims about its economic benefits. The recent 1969 passage of the National Environmental Policy Act (NEPA), which required environmental impact statements for all federal projects, also supported FDE's cause. On January 15, 1971, U.S. District Court Judge Barrington D. Parker issued a temporary injunction to stop the Cross Florida Barge Canal because the Corps lacked the NEPA-required environmental impact statement. [27]

There had been ongoing debate within the Nixon administration about the fate of the barge canal. Kirk appealed to the Republican presidential bureaucracy about how the canal controversy was hurting the state and Nixon had responded in a speech that he would not let any project be built that would affect the environment. The issue came to a head in early 1971 when, inconveniently, I was on vacation. [28]

Alita and I had planned a short vacation to fish for giant swordfish off the Ecuadorian coastline. My charter was for a 40-foot boat and a bilingual crew. On arrival, we discovered that my boat had been released and I was stuck with a 28-foot boat – and a captain and one crew member, neither of whom spoke English.

After two frustrating days taking three hours to reach the famed swordfish grounds, the hopelessness and real danger of the fishing expedition were all too clear. I saw a few swordfish sunning themselves, but never was confident that the crew could maneuver the boat so that the squid bait would pass directly in front of a sleepy swordfish. Further, the boat's tiny cabin was insecure. Tackle had to be returned to the lodge every evening.

We promptly suffered from "Ecuador stomach" and took a day off visiting a town high in the coastal hills.

On our return to the lodge, we were handed a telegram that was barely comprehensible.

We spread it out on a table to try to figure it out. It was from John Ehrlichman, Nixon's assistant for domestic affairs, and the best we could make out, it said, "The president has decided blank, blank Cross Florida Barge Canal. We need you here. Call the White House blank, blank on return. Very important that you be here." But as hard as we tried, the hotel couldn't get a telephone line back to the United States. We were exhausted and frustrated.

I was in a quandary: A giant swordfish caught on the surface was a lifetime dream.

Alita stated firmly, "Now listen. The odds of you catching a really big swordfish are minimal. And you've worked too many years on the Cross Florida Barge Canal. Something is about to happen. Let's go home!" She was insistent. "We have spent too much time, raised too much money from family and friends not to go to Washington if the president is really going to shut off the federal funding for the damnable canal!"

We sat up late into the night repacking rods, reels and boxes of fishing paraphernalia.

At 4 a.m. we loaded our car and headed for the Guayaquil Airport. Miraculously, there were two seats on an early morning flight to Miami. I was able to reach home and called the White House. Ehrlichman's remark was: "Where have you been? Can you fly up tomorrow?" Despite a groaning stomach, I was on the morning plane.

Once in Washington, D.C., I sped to the old

Executive Building where Russell Train (then chair of the Council on Environmental Quality), Nixon's White House staff, and the president's spokesman were composing the president's announcement; I was happy to participate.

Then history happened: on January 19, 1971, four days after Judge Parker's injunction ruling, Nixon announced that he was issuing an executive order halting the canal in order to save the Ocklawaha River and prevent environmental damage. It was the first time that an American president had stopped a project this far along; the "sunk cost" of the canal was estimated at $71-77 million.[29]

Historian Luther J. Carter noted that the "manner of the President's action in this case was extraordinarily ironic: Over the years, canal supporters had benefited from some undemocratic, high-handed, and devious or arbitrary actions by presidents and other politicians to further the project. Now, the project, though already partly completed, was being stopped by a presidential order" that was conceived in private, without consulting Florida congressional leaders.

Later, Train would recall that the important thing about the canal's presidential demise was not how it was arrived at but that it ever occurred. "The president was challenging the established practices and attitudes of the Corps of Engineers, the public works committees in Congress, and of state agencies such as the Florida Cabinet and Department of Natural Resources. More specifically, whether the President fully realized it or not, he was challenging their make-believe economics, their single-minded

12—B **Sentinel Star**
Tuesday, May 6, 1975

Canal Backers Want Reed Fired

PALATKA (UPI) President Ford has been asked by a group advocating the construction of the Cross Florida Barge Canal to remove from office an assistant interior secretary who called the canal project "a dead duck".

In a letter dated April 30 and released here Monday, the six-county Florida Canal Counties Association asked Ford to fire Assistant Secretary Nathaniel Reed "for his recent outburst and numerous other disservices" to the people of Northern Florida.

Reed

ACCORDING TO the association, Reed made the remark recently during an interview with Florida media on the future of the controversial canal project.

The Cross Florida Canal was halted by former President Richard M. Nixon in 1971 when it was 40 per cent completed.

With the "dead duck" remark, the association charged, Reed "prejudged" the Environmental Impact Study ordered by a federal judge to determine whether Nixon acted legally in impounding the funds for the project.

"Reed has been openly associated with people in Florida who continually attack and are avowed to destroy the canal project," the association wrote Ford. "He is identified with groups such as those who halted the Alaskan pipeline and not the taxpayers."

"**. . . AFTER MANY** times trying to look the other way and smile about Mr. Reed (the six counties represented by the association) ask for his removal as an assistant secretary of the interior.

concern for economic development and token regard for aesthetic values and biological diversity, and their habit of catering to narrow economic interests," Carter wrote. [30]

It also gave Nixon great pleasure to retaliate by slashing a Democratic pork-barrel project. Kennedy gave the canal to Florida, Smathers supported it, and now Nixon could take a shot at his long-time political opponents, those "damnable Democrats." Politics figured large in the decision, more than ecology, as far as Nixon was concerned. His staff was trying to formulate an ecological policy that played well among Florida voters but for Nixon it was long-simmering revenge. Remember, Kennedy's election was Nixon's defeat.

Anti-canal activists could hardly believe it was true. Many gathered at Carr's rural Micanopy home, setting in motion a "boisterous party that lasted long into the night" that included at least one burly biologist dancing on a kitchen table. [31]

It was a wonderful, hard-won victory but it is not over yet. Carr died without seeing her ultimate dream fulfilled: that the project be dismantled.

Parts of the canal project still stand today, including a dam that prevents the Ocklawaha from moving along its original path. The failure to remove the dam and restore the river's flow, which would lead to the recovery of an important riverine habitat, remains to be corrected.

Only then can we complete our assignment to stop the canal.

DAEN-CWP-E 24 February 1977
SUBJECT: Cross Florida Barge Canal

f. Funding. Because of the marginal economic justification and the absence of State support, the Administration should not seek further funding for this project other than may be necessary to assist Congress in reaching a decision and to maintain existing facilities in the interim.

In summary, I conclude that the Executive Branch should not support any further investment in the Cross Florida Barge Canal until such time as Congress has reviewed the thorough and exhaustive studies which have been completed in accordance with its instructions.

6. Recommendations.

Based on the foregoing conclusions, I recommend that Congress authorize and direct the Secretary of the Army, acting through the Chief of Engineers, to:

a. Terminate all activities leading toward the completion of a canal;

b. Undertake a supplemental study in cooperation with the Department of the Interior, Department of Agriculture, Environmental Protection Agency, and State of Florida to determine the best disposition and use of canal facilities and lands;

c. Operate and maintain completed facilities pending Congressional action.

J. W. MORRIS
Lieutenant General, USA
Chief of Engineers

2 Incl
1. Restudy Report
2. Memorandum

NOTES – A BOONDOGGLE: THE CROSS FLORIDA BARGE CANAL

[19] Wayne Flynt, "The Cross-Florida Canal and the Politics of Interest-Group Democracy," *Florida Historical Quarterly*, 87:1 (2008), 1.

[20] Steven Noll and David Tegeder, *Ditch of Dreams; The Cross Florida Barge Canal and the Struggle for Florida's Future* (Gainesville: University Press of Florida, 2009), 142-143.

[21] Flynt, "The Cross-Florida Canal and the Politics of Interest-Group Democracy," 13.

[22] Noll and Tegeder, *Ditch of Dreams*, 174-77.

[23] Marjorie Harris Carr interview with Leslie Kemp Poole, October 18, 1990, Gainesville, Florida.

[24] Noll and Tegeder, *Ditch of Dreams,* 179-180, 182.

[25] Ibid., 260.

[26] Ibid., 260-261.

[27] Leslie Kemp Poole, *Saving Florida: Women's Fight for the Environment in the Twentieth Century* (Gainesville: University Press of Florida, 2015), 94-95; Luther J. Carter, *The Florida Experience: Land and water policy in a growth state* (Baltimore: Johns Hopkins University Press, 1974), 298.

[28] Noll and Tegeder, *Ditch of Dreams*, 263-266.

[29] Ibid., 95; Noll and Tegeder, *Ditch of Dreams*, 266-267.

[30] Carter, *The Florida Experience*, 298-301.

[31] Noll and Tegeder, *Ditch of Dreams*, 267.

An Ongoing Battle to Save Southwest Florida

"Developers commonly made outrageous efforts to sell to unsuspecting buyers watery land."

The assault on Florida's east coast was reenacted on its southwest coast, which boasted wide, white beaches and a chain of unspoiled islands along the Gulf of Mexico that offered a breathtaking glimpse into the wild, fragrant Florida of yesteryear.

As Naples began to grow in the 1950s, more developers discovered the pristine coastline of southwest Florida and envisioned stately waterfront homes in place of sprawling mangroves and woodlands. By the end of the decade, three development firms had bought miles of mangrove coastline near Naples and dredged the bottom of adjacent waterways, using the displaced sediment to create residential building lots. These increasingly common dredge-and-fill activities wreaked havoc on sensitive estuaries, threatening plant and animal life, disrupting natural drainage flows and leaving the shoreline more vulnerable to storms.

Local conservationists began to take serious note of the development-at-all-cost frenzy in 1964, when Collier County commissioners were poised to allow construction of a road nearly 10 miles long across the pristine chain of Ten Thousand Islands. The road would have passed through Rookery Bay, an environmental gem, and crossed Gordon Pass into the pristine Ten Thousand Islands. In exchange for approving the road, which developers hoped would stretch from Naples to Marco Island, the county would receive 50 acres on Holloway Island for use as a park.

Residents of a nearby island accessible only by boat hired a lawyer and botanist to oppose the road, fearing its construction would bring a string of high-rises akin to those common in Miami Beach. With help from a local fisherman, the duo secured more than 2,000 petition signatures against the road and persuaded the county to postpone action.

It was the opening salvo in a years-long battle that would unite hundreds of like-minded conservationists in a quest to save Florida's shrinking wilderness from dredges and backhoes. Eventually, the group united as the Collier County Conservancy, later becoming the Conservancy of Southwest Florida. Members waged wars against many disastrous building projects on Florida's southwest coast, fighting developers lured there by a clean Gulf of Mexico, fine fishing and low land prices.

Early in the fight, I mentioned to the Conservancy's leadership that Russell Train, who had become chairman of the World Wildlife Fund, could be a valuable ally during the continuing battle over the unwanted, environmentally destructive development plans, particularly around Rookery Bay. I had known Train for many years, as he had built a lovely home on Jupiter Island, overlooking the Indian River. Our chemistry was excellent. During my years serving Gov. Claude Kirk and, later, Gov. Reubin

During my time in Washington, shortly after I denied his proposed land development proposal, I had a near-miss encounter with Frank Mackle that could have gone badly but mostly just resulted in widely shared – if somewhat embarrassing – amusement.

It was a lovely morning in early summer. The news that the Mackles would not be allowed a fill permit had reached Wall Street and the company's stock began a precipitous slide. The "property owners" who had bought bayside lots that now would not be available were restless, demanding an equivalent site or their deposits returned.

And, John Ehrlichman's secretary called to have me join him for a short visit in the White House. This was a bit worrisome.

I entered the South Gate and was walking slowly toward the White House when I saw Frank Mackle walking toward me, thankfully head down. Not welcoming a confrontation at that point, I stepped into the White House tennis court and waited until he passed. I needed to relieve myself (also known as a pee) and did so, not realizing the whole area was covered by security cameras.

When I walked to the entrance, my mind was in a dither. What if Mackle had "rolled" my decision to void his land sales? I made the decision that the importance of my actions were sufficient enough that I would have to resign.

When I entered the White House door, I was oddly at peace with my decision. Great howls of laughter greeted me from the internal security force, which had watched me relieving myself on the tennis court. I returned the laughter stating: "When nature calls even at the White House, action is needed!" That produced more laughter.

It turned out that the meeting with Ehrlichman was about a totally different subject. The Mackle permits were never raised. I have always wanted to know who Frank Mackle visited with, but it was not worth finding out.

Askew, I frequently sought Train's advice on a variety of land use issues.

As mentioned in the previous essay *Saving the Fakahatchee,* developers commonly made outrageous efforts to sell to unsuspecting buyers watery land in the Fakahatchee Strand and other wetlands. The Mackle brothers bought Marco Island, which should have been saved as a state park, and sold adjacent land that did not have development permits from the U.S. Army Corps of Engineers.

A call from me to Train, by that point U.S. Undersecretary of Interior, led to an epic but little-known letter signed by Army Secretary Stanley Resor to the chief of the Corps and Florida's district engineer, forbidding issuance of any permits to fill mangrove wetlands without express permission. Further, Resor ordered the Mackles to halt all sales of land that were below the bulkhead line or mean high-water line if there were no established bulkhead line. The Mackles had sold hundreds of thousands of dollars of waterfront property that consisted entirely of mangroves. The Resor letter was a blessing, as it essentially ended the sale of mangrove wetlands – statewide.

Still, the battle over the Mackle holdings raged for years, straight through and even beyond my 1971-1976 tenure as assistant U.S. Secretary of the Interior. At one point, I rejected an agreement reached by the Mackles and Gov. Askew that would have allowed the brothers to create some of the hundreds of housing sites they originally proposed. I must concede that I was shaken by this decision by Askew, whom I greatly respected, and it caused me some discomfort to play a role in scuttling his agreement and any development of the area.

Even the most determined developers now knew they could not count on receiving a dredge or fill permit from the Corps. Meanwhile, the federal Fish and Wildlife Service finally invoked the "Coordination Act" and insisted on being involved in all Corps permitting, even involving docks.

Despite that victory, many more battles were to be fought. The Conservancy of Southwest Florida expanded its scope across five counties in southwest Florida: Collier, Charlotte, Lee, Hendry and Glades. More attempts were made to build a bridge across Rookery Bay, but each time the Conservancy group presented overwhelming evidence why such a project would destroy the very attributes that made the bay so valuable. In the end, the road was never built.

Working on multiple fronts to preserve the land, the Conservancy finally succeeded in getting the National Audubon Society to seek designation of the bay as a National Estuarine Research Reserve. In 1978, more than 110,000 acres were set aside for research and preservation.

In its own words, the group says its members "maximize the combined forces of environmental policy, advocacy, research, education and wildlife rehabilitation to protect southwest Florida's natural treasures – our water, our land and our wildlife.

"Our goals have become more ambitious as even greater pressures are placed on our natural heritage," the group declares on its website. "We have concerns about our water. Will it be clean? Will we have enough? Over one million acres of rural lands are proposed for development. Will it be done in a way that protects lands vital to our survival – and to the 60 listed, endangered and threatened species in Florida? We are constantly working to find a sensible balance between the demands of a growing population and the preservation of our natural resources."

The group lists a few of its key milestones as follows:

- Conserving 55,000 acres of land in Southern Golden Gate Estates to help restore natural water flows to the Western Everglades.
- Monitoring existing species populations for the Western Everglades Restoration Project.
- Protecting more than 265,000 sea turtle hatchlings since 1982 through our Sea Turtle Monitoring and Protection Program.
- Treating over 3,200 animals per year and successfully releasing about half of them back into their native habitats.
- Helping to preserve our bays, their mangroves and sea life through various research, monitoring and restoration projects.
- Encouraging voters to protect environmentally sensitive land for conservation by assisting in the passage of conservation initiatives in Collier, Lee and Charlotte counties.
- Helping to negotiate the successful state purchase of 74,000 acres of environmentally sensitive land at Babcock Ranch, keeping all parties talking when the deal was threatened.
- Earning the "People's Choice" Award from the Naples Daily News five years in a row for our summer camps and environmental education programs.
- Reaching over 50,000 children and adults each year through public awareness and

community outreach programs.

- Assessing the state of our region's water quality and publishing our findings and recommendations in the Estuaries Report Card.

"The Conservancy is committed to helping citizens stay informed; assisting our government and business leaders with science-based research encouraging them to make growth decisions that keep the health, well-being, and the sustainability of our region in mind," the group says. "We, along with several other dynamic environmental organizations, have achieved a long list of accomplishments in this region."

I am proud of my long association with the Conservancy, standing by its side for the better part of six decades, as it has worked to preserve all that is best about southwest Florida.

For those with particular interest in the work of the Conservancy of Southwest Florida...

here are a few words from Robert Moher, the group's president and chief executive officer:

With the primary battle for the preservation of Rookery Bay now behind it, the Conservancy realized that pitched battles on the policy and land acquisition fronts were not enough – the Conservancy would need to strengthen its scientific capabilities to better understand the ecological value of the areas it had and was seeking to protect. Perhaps more importantly, the organization realized that education was the foundational pillar upon which truly sustaining the victories rested. In other words, saving Rookery Bay today, without educating the next generation that would be responsible for continuing the effort to protect it, was only a temporary victory.

The Conservancy set upon an aggressive phase of growth, building up its internal scientific team first directed by Dr. Bernie Yokel, and subsequently attracting a number of highly talented scientific experts. The Conservancy became a staunch advocate for the acquisition and restoration of the Picayune Strand State Forest – or, as it was known back in the 1970s, as the South Golden Gate Estates, which was proposed to be one of the largest residential subdivisions in the world.

The Nature Center and the first wildlife hospital were built in the early 1980s to accommodate the growing demand for environmental education and an urgent need for the treatment and release of native wildlife caught in the crosshairs of a rapidly growing region.

Subsequent presidents, starting with Dr. David Guggenheim, led the Conservancy of Southwest Florida through many tumultuous battles surrounding growth in the sensitive lands of the region and notably in eastern Collier County, home to most of the remaining primary habitat for the Florida panther, along with critical wetlands, sloughs and other environmentally delicate habitats.

Always leading with scientifically based and thoroughly researched policy positions, the Conservancy's credentials as an effective conservation organization grew through these efforts.

Its role as one of the principal advocates of the Western Everglades and the coastal estuaries is now well established. In the face of sustained proposed growth, and with the further intensifications of lands through mining, all of which dramatically threatened the region's core ecological assets (notably its water resources), the Conservancy's board of directors engaged in a two-year strategic planning effort to learn how best to prepare the organization for immediate and longer term challenges.

The result was a strategic vision that laid the foundation for what ultimately became a $38.8 million capital campaign completed in 2012. One of the largest fundraising efforts for conservation undertaken in the State of Florida, the campaign enabled a complete rebuilding of the organization's nature center, the acquisition of sensitive lands adjacent to the center for permanent conservation, the raising of over $8 million in new endowments to attract and retain the best and brightest conservation staff and millions in core programmatic investments to sustain the effort to meet the Conservancy's mission.

The campaign created dramatic new institutional visibility for the Conservancy and enhanced its reputation as an organization with first-rate philanthropic supporters willing to invest heavily in conservation for the region's benefit. The success no doubt has acted as an effective deterrent to those seeking to outlast or outspend the Conservancy when it comes to critical environmental matters. The Conservancy was even better positioned to stay the course on a wide variety of issues.

As the Conservancy moves into the future, I see a wide range of challenges for the region.

The cumulative impacts of mining, proposed fracking and related enhanced oil extraction activities, paired with hundreds of thousands of proposed new residents on lands well east of Interstate 75, threaten the Western Everglades and the habitat of over 47 already threatened and endangered species.

With active citizen engagement, we still have a chance to shape the patterns of development to protect remaining critical ecological assets of the region – assets that not only are essential to the beauty and functioning of our ecosystems, but assets that are the absolute foundation of our economic and social well-being in Southwest Florida.

These include land where our aquifers exist, the remaining vital shallow and deep wetlands that are so essential to water quality and flood control, and lands and plant communities that can help minimize the negative impact of the upstream treatment of multiple pollution sources that ultimately flow into our coastal estuaries – the basis of the multi-billion-dollar fishing and tourism industry in the State.

It will take a more centrist and balanced set of political actors, in particular at local and state levels, to help steer the inevitable development of Southwest Florida in a manner that protects the actual assets which have attracted so many before to our shores – the land, water and wildlife of our beautiful region.

Secretary Rogers Morton surrounded by the Reed and Weaver families.

The Most Extraordinary Day of My Life: Russian Polar Bears

"The last thing the president wants is a confrontation between American poachers and Soviet fighter jets."

Within five days of being sworn in as Assistant Secretary of the Department of the Interior, I relieved all of the appointed staff members of their duties and began working to hire responsible, highly qualified and dedicated staff. I wanted people who recognized the opportunities of the "American environmental renaissance" to join me. I had learned from my five years working for two Florida governors that there is no substitute for a committed, energized and competent staff.

Until I was able to identify staff assistants, I worked with a selection of trusted senior staff members from the three agencies that reported to me: the Bureau of Outdoor Recreation, the U.S. Fish and Wildlife Service and the National Park Service. I learned firsthand their expertise, knowledge and ability to handle much of the mail and messages flowing into my office. I was briefed on issues and problems, given sound advice and, contrary to politicians who rail against federal employees, I found my designee assistants to be among the finest advisors and confidants with whom I have ever worked. I was and am profoundly proud of the men and women who work for the Department of Interior.

The problems that confronted me because of the abrupt firing of the previous assistant secretary were quite staggering. Following my awesome swearing-in ceremony, my wife returned to our Florida home and planned to return in a month to Washington to seek a home for us and our three children. Alita arranged for a small suite at the Jefferson Hotel, within easy walking distance of the Department. I had time to work and learn late into the evening, but nothing could have adequately prepared me for what would become the most memorable day of my life.

It was in the late afternoon, perhaps two weeks after taking my oath of office, I was reading files of potential staff members when my marvelous senior secretary, Nori Uchida, came into the office stating that Ambassador Anatoly Dobrynin, ambassador of the Soviet Union, was on the line. I had known Ambassador Dobrynin for a number of years, as he was an annual guest of Averill Harriman during the winter season on Jupiter Island.

The Ambassador was a fanatical "birder." I had guided him toward many new birds in the Everglades and on Lake Okeechobee, all added to his exhaustive life list. He actually had an elevated bird blind in a national wildlife refuge near Washington where, under heavy guard, he spent many Saturdays or Sundays in the spring, summer, fall and even winter keeping track of waterfowl and the vast number of migrating birds that used the refuge as a feeding and rest stop.

I answered the call and heard the ambassador's booming voice: "Nathaniel, congratulations on your confirmation. Please come by the embassy this evening at 6:30 p.m., as I want to discuss a serious problem with you."

Secretary Morton was on a field trip, so without any guidance I arrived at the embassy, where my car was parked by a member of the embassy staff and I was escorted inside by two huge men. The ambassador welcomed me warmly from the top of a curving staircase. "Nathaniel, congratulations on being confirmed by Congress! You have the post that is perfectly suited for you. I will be able to call on you to add to my bird list. Come upstairs, I need to talk to you."

The embassy was a curious combination of Rococo-style interior decoration, complete with the most garish examples of "new wealth." The combination of marble floors, a gilt banister leading to the second floor and a ceiling painted with small, winged, flying angels shooting arrows at what appeared to be Venus seemed incongruous for a Soviet residence. I asked as I walked up the steps to join the Ambassador, "What the devil is the history of this extraordinary building?" The Ambassador replied, "It was built by Mr. Pullman of Pullman Company railroad sleeping cars. It is a bit over the top, but incredibly comfortable. We must have a glass of vodka to wish you great success in your new position."

A butler appeared and we downed icy cold, small glasses of Imperial Vodka. We moved into a study where, on a large table, were six oversized photographs of men skinning polar bears. The men were adjacent to two single-engine planes mounted with snow skis, with the Russian headlands in the background.

"Nathaniel, your government has allowed the overhunting of polar bears while we ended all polar bear hunting 10 years ago," Ambassador Dobrynin said. "We need to have this illegal hunting stopped before we have an international incident when one of our fighter planes shoots the illegal hunters and their guides. Seriously, someone's ass is going to get shot off!"

I swallowed hard, enjoyed another round of vodka and stumbled across the street to my temporary quarters in the Jefferson Hotel, where I spent a restless night – before a hectic day.

At 8 a.m. the following morning, I called an emergency meeting with U.S. Fish and Wildlife Service Director Spencer Smith and Chuck Lawrence, the well-known chief of the wildlife service's law enforcement agency. I showed them the photographs and explained the Ambassador's concerns.

"Chuck, what is going on," I asked, "and why haven't your agents stopped this illegal hunting?"

He reported that a small cadre of pilots had been enlisted by a world-renowned, big-game outfitter and taxidermist whose firm was among the best taxidermists in the country. Wildlife service agents could identify the pilots and had a list of the successful hunters, but once the pelts were flown back to the Eskimo village of Kotzebue – where they were carefully treated for safe travel – they "disappeared" and were conveyed through Canada by unknown methods, probably to the famous taxidermists located in Seattle. Without proof that a taxidermist's pelt came from a polar bear killed on Soviet ice, it was doubtful that a federal charge would hold up in court. That's because polar bears legally could be killed on Norwegian ice, making it difficult to identify pelts illegally imported to the taxidermist's headquarters from Russia through Canada.

At 9 a.m. my secretary announced that I had two visitors who identified themselves as members of the Federal Bureau of Investigation. I welcomed them into my office.

After brief pleasantries, one asked me in a very authoritarian voice, "What were you doing at the

Photo by Joel Sartore, National Geographic Creative

Soviet Embassy last evening between 6 p.m. and 6:45 p.m.?" I showed them the photographs and explained that the Ambassador had called me to visit and see evidence of Americans poaching polar bears on Soviet ice. They informed me that I should have been briefed and given a telephone number to report my entry into the Soviet Embassy or any other building that the embassy controlled. All visitors were required to draft a memorandum of the purpose of their meetings. I assured the two FBI agents that I had never been briefed on the prerequisites for a Soviet visit and would dutifully dictate a short memorandum detailing my visit. They were satisfied and departed.

At 9:45 a.m. I thought it would be wise to inform John Ehrlichman at the White House of my meeting with Ambassador Dobrynin, the visit by the two FBI agents and my early morning meeting with the director and chief of enforcement of the Fish and Wildlife Service. I described the meeting and the potential of a serious confrontation on Soviet ice. Ehrlichman stated, "Nathaniel, this is now your highest priority. Stop the flights, stop the killing of Russian polar bears and report to me on progress or problems."

Within minutes, my secretary came into the office and announced that Secretary of State William Rogers was on the line. I had the pleasure of knowing the secretary previously as he, too, was a winter visitor to Jupiter Island. "Nathaniel, can you come to my office now!" he asked urgently. "Yes, Mr. Secretary, my car and driver are ready," I replied.

I was met on the steps of the State Department

and ushered into Rogers' office. I spread the incriminating photographs on a side table and described the meeting with the ambassador. "For God's sake, Nathaniel, let's get this stopped before someone has their 'ass' shot off!" I said as I repeated the line the ambassador had used.

The secretary stepped to his desk and called Attorney General John Mitchell. "John, you may have heard of Reed's encounter with Ambassador Dobrynin last evening. You need to see him now. You should have senior FBI agents with you."

Thirty minutes later, I was driven to the Justice Department and escorted into the attorney general's office, still clutching the incriminating photographs.

Mitchell looked at the photographs with interest and turned to two senior, serious-looking FBI agents and said, "Work with the chief of the Fish and Wildlife Enforcement Service and Secretary Reed and end this potentially serious problem within the shortest time possible, before we have an international incident. I think the Wildlife's Service enforcement staff needs FBI support. Reed, inform the director and Lawrence that the FBI will call for a full briefing this afternoon. We need to get on this outrageous poaching problem before someone's ass does get shot off and we have an international incident. We will need this set of photographs. I will have another set sent to you after these pictures are further blown up to obtain the aircraft numbers so we can positively identify the pilots."

I returned to Interior and briefed Secretary Morton on a long-distance call. He said, "Nathaniel, get this situation under control starting now!"

Within minutes I received a call from Henry Kissinger. In his most formidable German accent he demanded, "Nathaniel, what the hell is going on with Dobrynin and you?" I described the meeting and offered to bring him copies of the photographs. "No, I don't want to see them. I believe Anatoly and you. Just clean this situation up starting now! The last thing the president wants is a confrontation between American poachers and Soviet fighter jets. This could lead to a confrontation neither country wants." My only appropriate response: "Yes sir."

The rest of my day was spent reviewing reports, problems and interviewing what was to become the best staff in the Interior Department, if not the Nixon administration.

As I drifted off to sleep that night I couldn't help but wonder whether this was going to be a "normal day" in my new position as Assistant Secretary of Interior for Fish, Wildlife and National Parks.

During the next several weeks, I met with agents from the Fish and Wildlife Service and FBI. They had devised a plan to "invent" a young FBI agent and transform him into the young recipient of a major bequest from a spinster aunt. Now an idle youth, he had a huge bank account and a record of over-shooting waterfowl and doves over baited fields. He had always stated publicly that he wanted to become a famous big-game hunter.

The decoy made contact with the unscrupulous, world-famous outfitter and after a very careful background check, the outfitter offered him two dream hunts – a polar bear and a major bull elk.

I interviewed the undercover agent quietly in my office before the hunt. My admonition was simple: "Be careful, if you are discovered, you will die in a 'hunting accident.' "

The agent shot a polar bear on Russian ice and marked it with an invisible chemical that would glitter when a black light was shined on the pelt. Flown in by helicopter, he killed a giant bull elk on the Crow Indian Reservation out of season and again marked it with the invisible chemical.

To top things off, he was offered and accepted the opportunity to be secretly let into a southwestern national wildlife refuge that was home to highly endangered desert sheep. He called me from a pay station asking whether he should miss, considering the importance of the remaining herd. I told him to shoot the oldest ram and mark it.

Weeks later a paid informer notified Lawrence

and the FBI agents that the three animals' skins and heads were at the suspected taxidermist's headquarters. Wildlife service agents, backed up by a team of U.S. Marshalls, obtained a legal search warrant and raided the large taxidermy center. Afterwards, a search discovered a secret room filled with illegal trophies from around the world. The three marked animals were there.

The pertinent guides were arrested. The pilots lost their licenses. The owners of the taxidermy shop pleaded guilty, paid a record fine and signed a legally binding agreement to allow wildlife service agents to inspect their "trophies" and record books.

That ended the gruesome hunts of the polar bears. Testimony showed that bears were spotted by one of the two planes and hounded until exhausted. The plane carrying the "hunter" then landed and the second plane drove the exhausted bear to within rifle range. It was very expensive, but there seemed to be no end to the so-called "big-game hunters" who wanted a polar bear mounted in a standing position, its mouth open and claws extended as if on the verge of attack.

Due to enforcement of the Endangered Species Act, polar bears are now breeding and producing cubs on Alaskan ice. The numbers of both Russian and American polar bears have increased dramatically but continue to be threatened by the loss of Arctic ice on which they need to hunt their major prey – seals that bask on ice flows.

Their future as the largest of all bears will have to be closely monitored to determine whether they can adapt to a changing world.

The Saga of the Presidential Order Banning 1080: One of the World's Most Dreadful Poisons

"Mr. President, it should have been banned long ago."

My swearing-in ceremony as Assistant Secretary of Interior for Fish, Wildlife and Parks was memorable. Interior Secretary Rogers Morton swore me in. I was surrounded by my wife, our eldest son, my parents, brothers and close friends.

It was an unforgettable occasion.

The next day, I had an early morning appointment with the secretary in his private office. He informed me that I was authorized to select my own staff, but he had two members of the Hickel team who needed to be interviewed first. I met Buff Bohlen and Douglas Wheeler and we meshed perfectly. They both agreed to serve with me. I emphasized that it would be a team effort. I told them that, despite serving five years in two governors' administrations, I had much to learn and I knew that a brilliant, committed staff would "rub off" not only on us, but also on the department.

I had notified the existing members of the former assistant secretary that they had served with distinction and would receive a letter of commendation from President Nixon.

Following that duty, Morton said, I was to call John Ehrlichman at the White House, so we might become "working friends." Morton noted that I had inherited one of the department's greatest senior service secretaries, Nori Uchida – a truly wonderful human being who went on to serve me with great distinction. I also had the privilege to work with Cleo Layton, a senior service employee of the U.S. Fish and Wildlife Service, who turned out to be a gift from God. He was respected throughout the Interior Department and had many contacts on the committee staffs on the Hill.

Cleo and I formed a tight relationship, although we were quite unalike. He was a quiet, unassuming worker compared to my more determined, often hasty demeanor, as an innovative thinker and doer.

Soon, I met with three directors: Spencer Smith, who directed the Fish and Wildlife Service; George Hartzog, director of the National Park Service; and Jim Watt, who directed the Bureau of Outdoor Recreation.

Our offices were on the third floor of the department, within easy walking distance of one another. It also was an easy walk or an elevator ride upstairs to the sixth floor, where the secretary of interior's vast offices were located.

My office was huge. Designed under the watchful eye of former Secretary Walter Ickes and built in the 1930s, each of the assistant secretaries' offices had a functioning bathroom with a shower.

The furniture was standard government-issue, but Cleo knew members of the staff who were in charge of such things and we changed the room around to fit my taste. My desk was imposing, but there was an area furnished with easy chairs and a sofa, a place where we could have informal discussions. My father loaned me an extraordinary group of "Americana" – lithographs of the Capitol during the stages of its construction, fascinating, hand-colored prints of the former presidents, and a marvelous, large World War I poster.

I added photographs of my wife and three young children.

After three days of settling in, I called John Ehrlichman. He welcomed me and made a date at 3 p.m. to meet with him and perhaps visit with the president.

I had not received my official White House pass, but I was expected by the Secret Service officers at the gate and an aide led me to Ehrlichman's office.

I liked him immediately. He had been a prominent land-use attorney in the Seattle region and was well versed in the beginnings of the "environmental revolution" that was sweeping the nation and gathering support in Congress. He stressed that Russell Train, an old friend of mine who was chairman of the President's Council of Environmental Quality, was what Ehrlichman called "the real quarterback" of the Nixon administration's effort to produce meaningful changes to our basic environmental laws without causing too much trouble with Republicans on the Hill.

We discussed my interest in keeping a small staff. He promised that he would prevent the Republican National Committee from demanding positions for the sons of wealthy donors.

His secretary came in the door and announced that President Nixon wanted to visit with me.

I must admit a feeling of acute nervousness walking into the Oval Office. The president stood and shook hands with me. He laughed at concerns that some friends had shown over my nomination and said Beebe Reboso, his close Florida friend, "says you get things done!"

He asked what my major priorities were. I stated that freedom to select my own staff was the most important priority. The president laughed and said, "I bet they will be Democrats!" I promptly replied, "No, Mr. President, they will all be knowledgeable and determined to work for changes that will produce a record that no other president can match."

"Well, young Mr. Reed, what are your next three priorities?" he queried. I answered, "Mr. President, I will organize a committee of experts to examine the misuse of a dreadful poison used in the Rocky Mountains west by owners of sheep flocks, ostensibly to kill predatory coyotes, but in reality they want their subsidized public land-grazing leases to be devoid of all coyotes whether the dead coyote had even killed one of their sheep. The poison, called 1080, is a terrible one. The animal that eats the poisoned bait dies slowly, in great pain. Then, even worse, its body is a killer for any other animal or bird of prey that feasts on it. It kills that creature slowly, gruesomely. It should have been banned long ago."

The president showed interest by replying, "Pat has mentioned that she has read reports on the misuse of this poison." I responded, "I'll produce a peer-reviewed Executive Order for you to sign, accompanied by an Environmental Impact Statement that will withstand legal challenge."

"What's next?" the president asked.

"I'll gather expert reports on the harmful impact DDT is having on normal egg thickness, which damages the birds' ability to reproduce, and I'll have the experts ready for another Executive Order banning this chemical, which by now is in every corner of the earth and even in the oceans and in the bodies of all Americans at sub-lethal levels," I replied.

"Enough," said the president. "Keep in close contact with John. Let him work with you as he does with Russ Train. I really don't have time for environmental issues, but I want a record that is memorable. Meet the other members of the Cabinet so they know who you are. Give my best to Rogers, and for heaven's sake don't get caught up with the Georgetown cocktail and dinner group that members of my administration seemingly cannot resist. They're all Democrats down there. Stay away from them!"

I replied that I had three young children and took the post to work, not to dine in Georgetown. He roared with laughter and gave me a parting handshake before I followed Ehrlichman out of the Oval Office. I admit that I was perspiring. Ehrlichman said, "You made a good impression. The 1080 issue is already under litigation and I like the idea of a Presidential Executive Order for the banning of 1080 and maybe even for DDT."

I stumbled back to the gate where Garfield Lawrence, my faithful driver, was waiting. He asked, "How did it go?" I answered, "I am still shaking, but I think I was met with approval. We shall see. The Vietnam War, the Soviet Union, disorder all over the world, and our nation's economy will be his highest priorities. It will be up to Chairman Train, his staff and the Interior staff to produce the effort and results that are so desperately needed."

So, one of my first operational priorities was to ban 1080, the brand name of sodium fluoroacetate, a rodenticide that had been in use since the 1940s. Luckily for me, I met with Dr. Stanley Cain several weeks after being sworn in. He had been selected by the University of Michigan to found its Department of Conservation.

He had served as assistant secretary during the Johnson Administration and was a widely acclaimed, eminent ecologist. He visited me frequently, briefing me on ongoing problems that had been left to me to solve. He said that one of his greatest regrets was his inability to ban 1080, as it was killing thousands of "non-target" animals annually. He assured me that the Animal Control agency under the supervision of the U.S. Fish and Wildlife Service, both in the regions and at the Washington level, was unable to control the application of poisoned baits due to political pressure.

Loss of sheep grazing on leased public lands was a problem, but it was not being solved by attempting to limit the number of coyotes in a given grazing area, most of which had never killed a sheep. Dr. Cain strongly advised the formation of a review committee of the foremost ecologists familiar with western grazing sheep, especially on public lands. We discussed potential members of the committee. I wanted ecologists who could not be challenged due to their backgrounds and reputation.

I called Dr. Starker Leopold, one of the nation's most respected ecologists, and told him, "You are a natural to chair the committee," but he was determined to oversee a task force that had made significant progress in convincing the leadership of the National Park System to make a strong science program an NPS priority.

But Leopold did agree to serve on the committee because he had seen the impact of 1080 on non-target animals and believed it was being grossly misused. I looked Dr. Cain in the eye and stated, "Stan, you are the perfect choice for chairman of this committee. You know the problems. You know who should serve on the committee. I will hire an excellent ecologist and wildlife expert as a member of our staff to assist the committee. You will have time to give him oversight as he prepares the Environmental Impact Statement and the Executive Order banning 1080."

Without hesitation, he accepted the challenge and went to work selecting highly qualified and respected members of what became known as the "Cain Committee." The panel was soon filled with exceptional ecologists and experts on grazing and animal control.

I was able to attract James Ruch, a young biologist who was working for the National Wildlife Federation, to join our office's team. I assigned him to work with the committee members and travel to locations where 1080-laced "baits" were being used to control real or perceived coyote depredations. Field staff would place the baits – usually stillborn sheep or calves or deer, or animals killed in traffic – in areas where sheep herders were complaining about losses. His investigation and verbal reports from the animal control managers and field staff members of the program were eye-opening.

The field workers maintained that twice as many baits were in the field than reported by management teams. Furthermore, the field workers were urged to place multiple devices named a "coyote-getter" – a pipe pushed into the ground that contained an explosive charge. It was activated by an attraction bait and a "trigger" that delivered cyanide into an animal's mouth, killing it nearly instantly. Numerous privately owned dogs died as a result each year.

Owners were paid for the loss of their pet from a fund. Field workers said political pressure from the local congressman, a friend of the sheep owners, made it nearly impossible to make sound decisions to kill a specific coyote that was killing sheep. They admitted that the evidence indicated that a few coyotes were responsible for the vast majority of the sheep kills, but said the sheep owners insisted that all coyotes be killed in their grazing leases, much of it on public lands owned by the National Forest Service or the Bureau of Land Management.

The field workers also questioned monthly reports on the number of "non-target" animals and birds of prey that were killed by ingesting bait meat or the residual left by a dying coyote. The coyote carcass became a lethal target for any predator, including eagles, bears and wolverines. The field workers maintained that for every coyote killed by 1080, more than 20 non-target animals or eagles perished.

The committee worked through the summer and fall, and I stayed in close contact with Chairman Train's scientists at the Council on Environmental Quality (CEQ) and experts from the Justice Department. We knew the presidential decision to ban 1080 would be legally challenged if the proposed Executive Order, required under the Environmental Policy Act, wasn't legally sufficient.

In early December, the committee's report was completed and the Environmental Impact Statement was considered "sound" by experts at CEQ and the Justice Department.

Director Spencer Smith of the Fish and Wildlife Service, a long-time believer that animal control should be transferred to the Department of Agriculture because the use of 1080 was an "impossible task" for his agency to manage, signed off with distinct pleasure.

Jim Ruch was commended by Secretary Morton, who despised the program and called 1080 "the most ghastly poison ever created."

The Cain Committee members all signed on to the report except for one noted professor whose university position would have been in jeopardy if he agreed to sign the recommendation.

Ehrlichman, who was kept apprised of the committee's work, kept his promise. He took the final products – the Executive Order prepared by the Justice Department, the Cain Committee report and the voluminous Environmental Impact Statement – to the president.

In January 1972, President Nixon used his authority to ban the use of 1080 on all public lands. The chemical was banned from production and use even on privately owned land enforced by the Environmental Protection Agency. Every state agency was required to relinquish their supplies of 1080 for disposal.

Experiments with live, captured coyotes indicated that only a small percentage of coyotes in the wild were responsible for the vast majority of the predation. We continued to develop plans to kill offending coyotes. Coyotes near sheep herds were shot from the air. A poisoned sheep collar was developed but did not succeed. A variety of large dogs developed in the Caucasus and Asia were imported, as they had shown great success in minimizing losses of their country's sheep to predators such as wolves and bears. Alas, only a very few sheep owners attempted to control depredations by the use of guard dogs.

Meanwhile, the American wool subsidy was under attack by fiscal conservatives who questioned the expenditure of federal funds to subsidize wool and lamb that were being produced in excess worldwide. Lamb and mutton were falling out of favor with young diners and foreign wool competition drove many sheep owners out of business. Many of the nation's environmental organizations had filed suit against the use of 1080 and the Justice Department's attorneys questioned, "Why was this program allowed to develop for such a comparatively few beneficiaries?"

Russ Train and I suffered through several congressional oversight hearings before members of Congress, who were infuriated by the Executive Order. But, even after a legal challenge, the Executive Order withstood the tests.

Dr. Cain, the committee members and James Ruch are all owed a permanent "thank you" for a successful effort that has saved the lives of thousands of non-target animals. Jim became an invaluable member of our staff. Following President Ford's defeat, he continued on with a brilliant career in wildlife management.

Among the threatening notes and letters from sheep owners was a positive one from Dr. Maurice Hornocker, Director of the University of Idaho's Department of Wildlife Resources. Dr. Hornocker was one of the world's greatest experts on the world of "cats," from mountain lions to African lions, tigers, leopards and the vast variety of the world's small wild cats. Widely respected throughout the Rocky Mountains west, his support was welcome.

He wrote, "The misuse of 1080 had 'eliminated the wolverine population,' as they live partly on carrion. The elimination of 1080 was long overdue." He added: "Thanks to the Presidential Executive Order banning 1080, thousands of non-target animals will live."

Two years later, he called me with the news that two of his student field biologists had radio-tagged a pair of wolverines in northern Idaho and that additional wolverines were bound to repopulate the western mountain states.

The banning of 1080 by President Nixon due to the well-staffed Cain Committee, resulting in a Presidential Order and an Environmental Impact Statement that easily survived legal tests, was one of the greatest highlights of my first year in office.

Cumberland Island National Seashore: An Enduring Controversy

"The mysterious swamp man; a vision of what could be."

During my five years as Assistant Secretary of the Department of Interior, I was involved in some extraordinary land preservation efforts, including the basic plan that created over 150 million acres of national parks and national wildlife refuges as a part of the Alaskan Land legislation.

The most difficult addition to the National Park System, for many reasons, commenced with being invited to Paul Mellon's private suite in the National Gallery of Art for luncheon.

Mr. Mellon and his sister were heirs of one of America's greatest fortunes. They had developed a long relationship with the growing National Gallery, and their incredible generosity included the donation of a new gallery wing. Mr. Mellon was the institution's longest-serving chairman and, after relinquishing his tenure, he continued to serve on the board. The siblings' donations included some of the world's finest paintings that their father had acquired. I had known Mr. Mellon due to his friendship with my parents, but I was surprised by the invitation.

My driver dropped me at a private entrance to the museum, where I was escorted to his executive suite. Paul Mellon was short, handsome and immaculately dressed and welcomed me with good humor. He asked many questions about my parents and their careful development of Jupiter Island. He mentioned the "balance" between my fathers' development of Jupiter Island compared to the rest of the coastal islands flanking not only Florida's coastlines, but the many islands off the rest of America's east coast.

Mellon expressed delight that The Nature Conservancy and the U.S. Fish and Wildlife Service were working to preserve many remaining undeveloped islands into national wildlife refuges. He made a memorable observation: "There are just so many undeveloped islands off our coastlines that are all extraordinary, whether they be rocky islets or islands of size. Nathaniel, buy what you can. You will be running against the tide."

Mr. Mellon related that his previous donation was of fundamental importance to the creation of Cape Hatteras National Seashore in 1937. His major, last-minute donation broke the deadlock over the details of how the state and federal governments' share of the costs was to be handled. Years of failed negotiations were settled by his critically important "investment," which led to the final acquisition of this extraordinary national seashore park.

Over dessert, he quietly announced that he was not trying to duplicate the Rockefellers' amazing land donations to our country, but he had bought out Charles Fraser's land holdings on Cumberland Island – in the southeastern corner of Georgia – and planned to donate the holdings to the National Park System.

This was a major opportunity for the park system.

Mr. Fraser had developed the famous Hilton Head Golf Course surrounded by major home sites and had hoped to duplicate his success on Cumberland Island. He had made an unwise investment and turned to Mr. Mellon, seeking to be bought out of his Cumberland Island venture.

The National Park Service had spent years studying potential national seashore areas and produced a report titled "Our Vanishing Shoreline" in June 1955. In the report, the park service attempted to identify the nation's "seashore jewels" for recreation and preservation. Cumberland Island – rich in history, with significant habitats and miles of beachfront – had been selected as the second most important priority, after Cape Cod. But the project had stalled, foiled by politics, local opposition and monetary considerations.

Mr. Mellon advised me that a percentage of his $6 million donation to the National Park Foundation had allowed acquisition of Fraser's one-fifth portion of Cumberland Island and that he had given the newly formed foundation permission to spend the remainder to acquire the majority of the privately owned land. He hoped the purchases could be made through a combination of significant payments and "some retained rights" for the current landholders.

Mr. Mellon described the potentially difficult relationship any federal or state agency would have with members of the Carnegie family, the major landowners and, most importantly, the aging Mrs. Lucy Ferguson. She had served as the "Queen Bee" of the family and wise steward of all her family's land holdings for more than 80 years.

Mr. Mellon described the years of "peace," when no land could be sold due to a trust established by Mrs. Thomas Lucy Carnegie, Lucy Ferguson's grandmother. The matriarch had sought to control land sales and any divisions of land until her last heir died. Following her mother's death, Lucy Ferguson became the supervisor of the Carnegie land holdings on Cumberland Island.

The Carnegie offspring grew up without land management or financial cares: Miss Lucy was the matriarch who saw to their every comfort and, along with other friendly landowners, controlled the island with an iron grip.

Florence Carnegie Perkins, the last Carnegie heir, died on August 15, 1962, ending the trust's restrictions and allowing the sale of the heirs' land. Foreseeing the end of the trust's provisions, the Carnegie heirs had split the Carnegie land holdings five ways. Each branch of the Thomas M. Carnegie family received an equal share. The sale to Charles Fraser was consummated rapidly by one branch of the family.

I was stunned by Mr. Mellon's donation and by his statement that, at points after 1962, many acres from various land owners had been acquired by the National Park System in fee and with life tenancy and, in some cases, multiple lifetime tenancies prior to congressional action or review by the department.

National Parks Director George Hartzog had been involved from the start and had a vision of how the island could accommodate 10,000 visitors a day. Mr. Mellon warned me that it would take years to acquire the last of the privately owned homesteads on the island. He foresaw difficulties in the creation of an "acceptable master plan" that would satisfy congressional committees, the emerging influence of the environmental community and the remaining landowners.

He ended his briefing by stating: "I think the development of Cumberland Island as a national seashore should not follow the pattern of existing state and federal seashores that maximized recreation. There are simply too many assets on the island to allow it to be developed as Jekyll Island State Park or even as a Cape Hatteras. I am advising you and the secretary not to be in a rush. The creation of Cumberland Island as a part of the National Park System is going to take time and has the potential of being highly controversial."

That statement proved to be incredibly accurate.

Mr. Mellon asked me for two promises. First, he wanted a personal letter signed by President

Nixon that accepted his land and cash donation to create Cumberland National Seashore. Second, he asked me to promise that I would guide the enabling legislation through the congressional committees. In addition, I would be responsible for the final land use management agreement that would protect the natural and historic importance of the island.

I departed without full recognition that the saga of Cumberland Island would test my patience and require valuable time when our office was confronted with so many other extraordinary opportunities and challenges.

When I returned to the Department of Interior, I called Secretary Rogers Morton and informed him about the meeting with Mr. Mellon. He promptly arranged for an appropriate letter to be signed by President Nixon gratefully accepting the donation of the Fraser property and the funds that could create Cumberland Island National Seashore. It was delivered that afternoon.

Secretary Morton also called National Parks Director Hartzog and requested a full-scale briefing on the island and its potential development under the National Park Service.

The following afternoon, Hartzog and a senior staff member spent more than 90 minutes describing Cumberland Island, the largest sea island in the southeastern United States and part of Camden County, Ga. The island is approximately 17 miles long and half a mile to three miles wide. It consists of 36,415 acres, including 16,850 acres of marsh, mud flats and tidal creeks. The highest elevation at several points is 55 feet. There was no bridge to the island, which sits about 500 feet off the mainland.

Following disputes with his brother, the imperious Andrew, Thomas Morrison Carnegie sold his interests in their partnership and retired from active business life. Thomas and his wife, Lucy Carnegie, visited Cumberland Island and fell in love with its tranquility, miles of beachfront, woods, and above all, privacy. Here they could raise their family and forget the tempestuous years when the Carnegies created one of the world's great fortunes.

Thomas' share made him among the wealthiest of all Americans. The Carnegies set to work acquiring the vast majority of the island and constructing beautiful homes and a "village" to house 200 servants needed to maintain their lifestyles. The Carnegies produced nine children who grew up on the island each spring and fall.

The children eventually married, and their children shared their parents' lifestyles and love of adventures in an idyllic setting. The Carnegies were examples of an era when the very rich indulged in a lifestyle that only the European kings could emulate. It took the multitude of 200 servants to care for the buildings, prepare their meals, laundry, household cleaning, gardens, swimming pools, etc. Additional segregated dormitories were built with appropriate dining facilities. There was a church and grave site for the black employees who had been used during a period of cultivation that required hundreds of slaves.

The Chandlers, heirs to the Coca-Cola fortune, had acquired 2,200 acres at the northern end of the island in 1928 and built their own comfortable, rustic homes and support buildings, in contrast to the opulent Carnegie estate.

The two families became close friends. Their children played together, swam and picnicked together, and played tennis and golf. Every conceivable Carnegie "wish" was accomplished regardless of cost of construction and maintenance. It was a lifestyle that did not survive the Great Depression.

Twenty-five other landowners, including members of the Rockefeller family, also shared a passion for the island. Since childhood, many had grown up every spring, summer and fall on the island. The community's adults, children and grandchildren explored every inch of the island, had exciting adventures with feral horses and pigs and watched great sea turtles swim ashore to lay their eggs. They walked, rode horseback, swam, and fished along the 17-mile beach. And, through it all, Lucy

Ferguson saw to every detail of how the island was to be managed.

We were shown countless photographs of the island's historical buildings, ruins, slave grave sites and existing homes, including Greyfield Inn and its adjacent farm named "Serendipity" – also the domain of Lucy Ferguson. She had fallen in love with the island as a three-year-old and decided to spend most of her life there.

We saw many photographs of miles of beaches, unique habitats and overgrown palmetto jungles. The north-south road and the pictures of existing estates that had been acquired from the Carnegie family solidified our joint initial recognition that any management plan would not satisfy the existing owners of this beloved land. It also was obvious from the briefers that the National Park Service had studied Cumberland Island for years, including a number of visits by Director Hartzog, members of Congress and former Secretary of Interior Stewart Udall.

Hartzog explained his vision of a Cumberland Island National Seashore, complete with multiple ferries requiring extensive dock construction, trails, overnight facilities and jitneys to carrying tourists to the many beaches and historic structures. Headquarters would be located on the mainland at St. Mary's. It would include a major orientation center and, obviously, acres of parking would be required. There had to be provisions for staff housing.

Every portion of the island would be used for recreation or historic preservation. His briefing was received by the secretary and me with incredulity bordering on disbelief.

We wanted something much more modest, much more protective of the island's wilderness and historic importance, and also much less expensive.

Also, there were no responsible cost estimates for buying the remaining thousands of acres of the island or realizing Hertzog's development vision. The authorizing congressional legislation had been prepared without review by the Interior Departments or the Office of Management and Budget. It became clear that Hartzog had briefed the leaders of the authorizing and appropriations committees in the House and Senate without following rigorous departmental procedures.

Morton asked the director and his aides to leave the briefing room. He sat calmly and stated to his personal assistant, Bob Hite, and me in a very firm voice, "Nathaniel, you haven't had time to attract that 'world class staff' that you persuaded the president to allow you to select. You need time to attract the expert staff that we both want.

"There are so many issues left unsettled since Secretary Hickel's firing, we must think long and hard about what our priorities are going to be, as the options and opportunities for real environmental progress is here now.

"At this very moment Russell Train, chairman of the Council on Environmental Quality, has formed teams to prepare a Clean Water Act, an Endangered Species Act, a Marine Mammal Act and a Fisheries Act that will expand our nation's ocean fisheries boundaries to 300 miles offshore. There is an opportunity to create new land and forest management acts.

"There is a distinct possibility that your office will be delegated the fantastic opportunity to prepare for me a selection of 80-million acres plus, of the very best of Alaska for permanent protection as national parks and national wildlife refuges. We have a full deck.

"We can lose the department's influence if we get bogged down in what I perceive to be a long, drawn out, intense battle with no winners in sight for years to come. Let's go ahead and schedule two more meetings with Hartzog and his staff. I want a half-hour briefing on the history of the island, followed by a 30-minute briefing on the Hartzog-proposed management plan.

"Further, I will personally reach the senior members of the congressional authorization and appropriation committees. I want to know what promises have been made if we support the creation of the seashore. I refuse to be locked into the Hartzog vision of a huge investment in turning Cumberland Island into another Jekyll Island."

The following day, a group from the Interior leadership sat with me while two park historians briefed us on the island's lengthy history, which was fascinating.

Paleo Indians ventured onto what is now Cumberland Island in search of food approximately 13,000 years ago. Intensive use of the area began around 4,000 years ago. The people of Cumberland Island referred to themselves as the "Tacatacura."

The Spanish and English battled for ownership of the island in a long history of conflicts that is worth interpreting. Nothing is left from the years of English ownership except stumps of once-huge oak trees that were cut and said to be among the best ship's timber in the American colonies.

The history briefing revealed years of multiple ownership and the construction of major buildings, including an imposing Dungeness mansion which was uninhabitable by the 1880s. One of the only productive crops was Sea Island cotton. During its peak production, the coveted and expensive "fine and silky cotton" was much desired for luxurious fabrics.

During this period, Cumberland Island supported a population of 65 whites and 455 slaves. Following the Civil War, the freed slaves insisted on being paid for their labor. The cotton planters claimed they couldn't afford it, so the new freemen left the island for mainland farms and paying jobs.

The once productive fields lay fallow. Cumberland Island slept.

The combination of the Great Depression and a dramatic rise in income taxes forced the Carnegie family to seriously consider their options in 1962 after the trust's dissolution. The $1.55 million sale of one of the five family units to Charles Fraser for intense development forced the remaining family units to seriously consider the National Park Service's offer to acquire their interests and create Cumberland Island National Seashore.

Despite numerous efforts by park service planners and appraisers to work with the local landowners, they remained suspicious of the service's involvement with their beloved island. It took time before they became reluctant supporters of a national seashore, but they continued to have many reservations about its development.

Some residents supported creation of the seashore and sold their properties at below appraised value to the newly formed National Park Foundation while retaining rights of use for a lifetime or multiple lifetimes. The freedom they enjoyed led to a common agreement on a unified plan to preserve Cumberland Island from major development – with a view toward forming a private conservancy or a state park or by forming an alliance with the National Park Service. Following the purchase of Fraser's one-fifth of the island and subsequent acquisition of lands owned by the Carnegie family, many remaining owners agreed to support creation of Cumberland Island National Seashore, but with reservations. Their participation was contingent on the drafting of an acceptable master plan.

As a result, Secretary Morton and I met with Sen. Allen Bible, chairman of the Senate's subcommittee on national parks, and the irascible Rep. Wayne Aspinall, chairman of the House subcommittee on national parks and recreation. We also met with the "gentle lady from Oregon," Rep. Julia Butler Hanson, chair of the House subcommittee on park service appropriations.

They all were aghast at the Hartzog vision that was teed up for authorization, even as the service's manpower numbers and operating budget were being reduced by President Nixon as an example of "fiscal responsibility" during an election year.

The Cumberland Island National Seashore creation bill was signed into law on October 23, 1972 by President Nixon – two weeks before the election in which he thoroughly defeated Democrat

George McGovern. We still did not have, however, an approved management plan.

Recognizing that she had lost her power of veto on the sale of all Carnegie land, Lucy Ferguson decided to support the designation of the national seashore and sold part of her land to the National Park Service. However, for as long as she lived, she waged a continuing battle over the park's authorizing law, management plans and its wilderness proposals. She became a vocal critic of every management decision as the park service prepared plans for initial low-intensity use.

I once commented to her that, despite the fact that the majority of Cumberland Island was now owned and would be managed for the American people, she still clung to her vision: "My way or no way." She laughed and said: "You are damn right!"

At one point, she visited Secretary Morton and was rude and demanding. He gave orders that she was never again welcome in his office. I received the assignment to meet with her and suffered through agonizingly long tirades about the service's treachery and its efforts to control damage from her livestock, feral horses and pigs. I remained calm and allowed her numerous long hours on several occasions to rant and rave.

When she died at the age of 89 in 1989, she retained 1,300 acres, including the Greyfield Inn and Serendipity Farm. She had lived on the island since she was 3 years old – a total of 86 years. She was survived by two sons, two daughters, 17 grand-children and 19 great-grandchildren. I respected Lucy Ferguson for her abiding love of "her" island and her frustration over the changes that were inevitable with the creation of any new addition to the National Park System.

I also met with other landowners. Some under-stood the changes that were bound to occur and accepted the fact that the secretary and my visions for the development of the park bore no resemblance to the rumors of a mass park service recreational com-plex. The only disappointment was a very rude if not angry meeting with a Rockefeller heiress who I had known since first grade. I was astonished when she charged me with 'perfidy' and being 'an accomplice and agent of unwanted change' on their land.

An astute park service land use expert who had worked on many national park proposed master plans and was an invaluable source of information commented, "Congress is often asked to consider the establishment of a new unit of the National Park System. When it does, it asks the director: If we created this new unit, what would you do with it? How would it be developed for use and preservation? Director Hartzog's response to this question about Cumberland was based on a superficial knowledge of the island. He did not know where the resilient areas were that might be suitable for visitor support facilities like restrooms that would require septic drain fields and dune-crossing boardwalks. Nor did he know where the fragile areas with special habitats or archaeological features were. The lack of detailed knowledge was all too apparent."

Buff Bohlen, my deputy assistant secretary, urged the Hartzog team to go back to the beginning and base its development plans on comprehensive knowledge of the island. Initially, Buff's admonition was forwarded to the Denver Service Center, which handled all management plans for new parks, and was met by fierce resistance. Seni or staff had their orders from Hartzog and "they were experts who didn't need outside advice or an intense review of the island's ecosystem," Bohlen said.

The public's reaction to the service's first hearing on a proposed master plan was met by a tsunami of outrage. The Denver Service Center managers began a serious look at how the island's master plan could be balanced between "the Hartzog vision" and the leadership's determination to "preserve and protect" the island's natural and historic qualities.

Every slight or even significant modification of the original master plan was met with increasingly fierce opposition. Proposed daily visitation was reduced to 1,400 from 10,000 visitors. An influential reporter for the Atlanta Constitution, infuriated by the proposal of even 1,400 visitors per day, urged citizen reaction. The National Park Service regional director received more than 4,000 letters sternly recommending to "Leave Cumberland Island alone!"

Secretary Morton and I stood aside and let the Denver Service Center's series of proposed master plans die by outraged constituents. It now sounds cowardly but, in reality, it was the most successful way of defeating the Hartzog vision and promoting a master plan that would be based on respect for this incredible asset destined to be permanently protected by the National Park Service.

Finally, I had one last crack at the Denver Service Center's master land use planners. They showed me yet another rendition that they said "was acceptable to Director Hartzog." I must admit I lost my cool and told the dispirited trio never to reenter my office: "Go and never appear with another Cumberland Island Master Plan such as the one you have attempted to gain my support."

Hartzog was beside himself. He stated that no other assistant secretary had ever treated his staff in such a brusque manner. He came close to hinting that a 38-year-old assistant secretary with a lack of congressional support should not dare to dismiss the service center's plan that was being opposed solely by "preservationists." I paid him no heed.

The final congressional authorizing language emphasized environmental protection over mass recreation. I am confident that Rogers' extraordinary influence with the members of Congress was responsible for the preserve and protect language in the enabling act.

Alas, the Cumberland Island saga continues to this day.

Following the creation of the national seashore over the next decade, land acquisition would become vastly more complicated. The number of landowners swelled by more than 100 as the Carnegie heirs sold off acreage to developers. Six housing subdivisions would be authorized by county commissioners.

The National Park Foundation, the organization initially charged with acquiring land for the future park with money donated by Mellon funds prior to federal funding, set a precedent by granting liberal and highly variable and complex retained-estate deeds to the original owners. When the National Park Service assumed negotiations, both large and small landowners drastically raised their prices and demanded generous retained rights.

I recognize that, as assistant secretary, I could have spent my five-year tenure working daily on the incredible battles over the management plans that were modified almost semiannually, if not monthly. Members of my personal staff and the more perceptive members of the National Park Service staff who recognized that our moderated vision – a mixture of wilderness and historic importance for the future public use of Cumberland Island National Seashore – was the only one that was acceptable are to be forever thanked. It was, in most ways, a team effort.

Unfortunately, my relationship with Director Hartzog disintegrated over his continued efforts to undermine the secretary and our concept of a tightly controlled management plan: The situation became nearly impossible as he attempted to galvanize congressional support for his vision of something akin to a Disneyland complex.

We finally met and I quietly but firmly stated that if he continued to attempt to sabotage the developing vision of protection and limited use, I would relieve him as director of his beloved National Park Service. With that admonition, Hartzog divorced himself from all decisions regarding the island's master plan and wilderness acreage.

Both the master and wilderness plans took years to settle.

I cannot finish recounting my limited part in this saga without stating that I made three friends whose visions on how Cumberland Island should be developed were crucially important.

I honor Jane Hurt Yarn, Georgia Gov. Jimmy

Carter's keen advisor. When Governor Carter became president, he appointed Jane to become the Council on Environmental Quality. Her wise input was of critical importance to galvanizing opposition by Gov. Carter to the "Hartzog vision."

Secondly, there was Joe Tanner, Georgia's commissioner of the Department of Natural Resources, who was reluctant at first but later became a supporter of the seashore and a very limited development plan.

Thirdly, I salute Hans Neuhauser, leader of the Georgia Conservancy, who quietly and effectively pointed out flaws in numerous management and wilderness plans. He crafted the language of both the management and wilderness plans that a combination of local and national conservation organizations and island landowners could support.

After too many flawed efforts by the park service to produce acceptable management and wilderness plans, his work was accepted in 1984 by acting Park Service Director Ira Hutcheson. Due to Neuhauser's calm, astute, expert guidance, the final accepted plans created the foundation for present – and even perhaps the future – management of Cumberland Island.

I also thank The Atlanta Journal and Constitution for its editorial support of a low-key management plan and accurate, exemplary reporting of the difficulties we endured in reaching agreement on a sensible management and wilderness plan.

Now, the current plan promotes extraordinary experiences for a maximum of 300 visitors a day. Greyfield continues as a prized inn that provides accommodations and an excellent experience.

Still, there are many historic preservation problems remaining, especially the reconstruction and stabilization of important buildings. Adequate funding is always an issue. Management problems revolve around necessary controlled burning, the removal of feral pigs and questions regarding the "reserved rights" of previous landholders that conflict with both management and wilderness legislation.

There will never be peace and harmony until these reserved rights are extinguished by land sales or the deaths of existing private landowners. Managing 36,415 acres of the seashore with 9,886 acres of designated wilderness and 10,500 acres of "potential wilderness" is a mind-boggling assignment, especially with constant pressure from the 29 remaining landowners to protect their "rights."

Some time ago, I had the privilege of being asked by Mr. Mellon to deliver the 25th anniversary speech at St. Mary's High School ball field, complete with a local school band. Mr. Mellon was failing in health but transmitted his thanks for securing passage of the act and suffering through the predictable difficulties as the park service attempted to understand that the original plan for a huge, expensive development vision was not acceptable to Secretary Morton, me or the American people.

Mr. Mellon's message concluded: "Cumberland Island has unique values that need to be well managed by the National Park Service's superior staff – managed as one of Georgia's and America's island jewels."

In my anniversary speech, I thanked Mr. Mellon for his foresight and major donation that allowed the National Park Foundation to acquire Mr. Fraser's property and donate an additional 12,260 acres for the creation of the Cumberland Island Seashore. The American taxpayers are to be thanked, as Congress appropriated $28.3 million to acquire the vast majority of the island's acreage.

Special thanks to author Larry Dilsaver, whose book published in 2004 and titled *Cumberland Island National Seashore: A History of Conservation Conflict*, is the invaluable history of the arduous creation of Cumberland Island National Seashore.

Hacking Ospreys and Bald Eagles: A Story of Assisted Adoptions

"The New England bald eagle population was near total collapse."

With the controversy over the poison 1080 still reverberating, it didn't take long before a similar challenge emerged – this time, during my second year in office; this time, involving another perilous chemical and its harmful effect on another important species: ospreys. And soon, the magnificent bald eagle would be involved.

In 1972, Spencer Smith, director of the U.S. Fish and Wildlife Service (USFWS), joined me in my office and introduced me to a young man, who was concerned by evidence that the controversial insecticide DDT, still in use at the time, was contaminating osprey eggs and thinning the shells, endangering the species. The man, whose name I cannot recall, proposed that the service collect and relocate to impacted regions uncontaminated osprey eggs from sites such as the Ten Thousand Islands and other Florida areas where ospreys continued to nest and raise their young successfully.

It was known that ospreys that lost their eggs to storms or predators were capable of re-nesting successfully. I believe the first year's proposal was to collect 50 eggs from nests and move them within specially designed, lined and heated boxes to nests in Georgia, South Carolina and North Carolina where the nesting ospreys had already cracked their thin eggshells.

The program was so successful that the USFWS began moving 100 eggs per year all the way to Maine. There were wonderful stories from volunteer watchers, who reported that moved eggs often would hatch far sooner than the brooding ospreys seemed to expect. The sight of the parent "feeling" its hatching chick only days after brooding it apparently was quite amusing.

By now, the program has been so successful that ospreys are common throughout their range. But even back then, we were mindful of that success when another crisis presented itself.

One day during my tenure, I was going to give an evening speech in New York City and was asked by Congressman Brownie Reid representing Westchester, New York, and Pete Krindler, one of the owners of the famous "21," a New York landmark eating and drinking establishment, to join them for lunch. The pair had friends who had summer homes in the Finger Lakes area of upper New York State. They were delighted by the exciting news of the successful osprey egg transfer and wanted the service to continue its efforts. They insisted that the osprey egg transfer was apparently so successful that there should be no reason why bald eagle eggs could not be transferred to known nesting sites.

This was crucial because the New England bald eagle population was near total collapse.

Years of overuse of DDT on the vast acreage of apple trees and summer crops had migrated through

james kozan

to the food supply of the eagles. Blood samples of dead or dying bald eagles recovered by the service and the northeastern states departments of conservation indicated incredibly high levels of DDT.

Reid and Krindler made this point: It certainly seemed worthy to determine if Alaskan bald eagle eggs, still not subject to DDT contamination, could be transferred to nests in the upper regions of not only New York but also to eagle territories in New England, in the Midwest and even in California.

Upon my return to the Interior Department, I discussed the issue with Spencer Smith of the USFWS. He agreed that his senior science staff located at the Patuxent Wildlife Research Center would study the issue and see if what he called "a copycat operation" might be successful.

He felt confident that the New York Department of Conservation would become partners in the effort to locate indigenous eagles' nests so that egg transfers could be accomplished expeditiously. Further, members of the National Audubon and New York Audubon Society had enlisted numerous volunteers who had watched the osprey nests containing the transferred osprey eggs. Surely, they would coalesce around an eagle egg restoration effort.

Dr. Lucille F. Stickel, an outstanding scientist who managed the services' Patuxent Wildlife Research Center, which had an incredible record of success, was an enthusiastic supporter. Her assignment was to have appropriate staff members study the proposition and unravel any potential problems that would inhibit the transfer of Alaskan Bald eagle eggs to New York and to New England states.

After detailed examination of Alaskan eagle eggs and fragments of broken New England bald eagle eggs, she determined that there were only minute and inconsequential differences in the eggs' DNA.

The USFWS initiated discussions with the New York Conservation Commission and a counterpart in Alaska to determine the feasibility of moving Alaskan eggs to New York nesting sites. The New England conservation commissions were keen to copy a successful New York effort.

But, rather than use eggs, a decision was made to "hack" young eaglets. In short, the hacking process involves removing eagles, preferably six to eight weeks old, from their nests and relocating them into artificial nests on man-made towers in appropriate habitats. Then, the "adoption" of the eaglets by foster eagles is arranged.

Jack Hodges was in charge of the effort for the department. He reported that two eaglets, a brother and sister, probably from the Patuxent stock were successfully hacked in 1976. (They eventually returned to New York in 1980 as a mated pair and successfully hatched two eggs and fledged one.)

Between 1977 and 1980, with the assistance of the USFWS, New York continued its program and successfully hacked 21 more eaglets. The young birds came from Michigan, Minnesota, Wisconsin and the Patuxent breeding stock. The success rate of this effort was so encouraging that there was consensus that far more eaglets were needed to restore the bald eagle population in the lower 48 states.

The service made an announcement of its intention to move Alaskan bald eaglets to states that had diminished eagle populations in a carefully designed test to see if the indigenous eagles would accept Alaskan eaglets.

The USFWS contacted the leadership of the National Audubon Society and Audubon of New York plus other interested and concerned conservation organizations with a well-prepared proposal requesting critique and comment. The replies were uniform: "Go full speed ahead, as the eagle populations from New England to New Brunswick, Quebec, and the Mississippi River states were near collapse." Meanwhile, we received accurate reports of pelicans on the California coast laying yokes uncovered by a scrap of shell – more victims of DDT.

A well-drafted environmental statement was

painstakingly prepared. Alaskan State Wildlife officials were delighted to become partners in the proposed transfer. With the great salmon fishery at their front doors, the Alaskan eagle population numbered in the many thousands.

At the last possible moment, unfortunately, a lawsuit was filed by a recognized ornithological society claiming that the introduction of Alaskan eggs or eaglets into northeastern territories would "disrupt the gene pool." We were stunned by the thrust of the legal attack.

The case was well defended in front of a federal judge in a Washington federal court. Both the Justice Department attorneys and the spokesmen for the Patuxent scientists and non-governmental scientists, all experts on the impacts of DDT on nesting birds, answered the judge's questions effectively.

At one point, the judge leaned back into his chair and asked a simple question: "I, too, enjoy the sight of bald eagles. I want the experts from the Fish and Wildlife Service to answer one simple question: If the Alaskan eggs or eaglets are not moved to the northeastern territories, will my grandsons enjoy the sight of a soaring bald eagle?"

The answer was a simple: "No!"

The judge ruled in favor of the experiment, which soon began.

Alaskan eaglets were removed at great risk to the Fish and Wildlife Service climbers, who had to negotiate very tall fir trees to reach active bald eagle nests. The stories of the dedicated service staff members who climbed the trees to remove eaglets, under attack from the parent eagles illustrate a remarkable achievement.

Aside from that, however, there were no significant difficulties moving Alaskan eaglets to the northeastern states. Young eaglets could be removed from their Alaskan nests and successfully transferred to Patuxent to grow and strengthen and then be placed in foster bald eagle nests. These experiments showed that the foster parents, indeed, would tend to the newcomer.

Other experiments at the Patuxent Center with a group of caged bald eagles from the lower 48 showed that birds that had been wounded by hunters or had flown into power lines could be returned to good health. They formed a productive breeding group that led to recovery in many areas that were devoid of eagles.

Bald eagles, both young birds raised from 'captive eagles' and those that made the long trip from Alaska, have been successfully released and now breed in areas where they had either disappeared or were on the way to extinction due to their inability to produce an eggshell sufficiently strong enough to survive the 35 days of being shifted around in the nest by one of the parents.

The bald eagle population in the lower 48 has made remarkable recovery due to the newly introduced uncontaminated birds. Once on the Endangered Species List, the number of bald eagles in 2015 are estimated to be over 10,000 nesting pairs in the lower 48 states.

I am pleased to tell you that they no longer are considered endangered – and that we were instrumental in getting DDT banned from use in the United States. That, in itself, is quite a story, as you shall see next.

The Banning of DDT

"This not only was essential for wildlife but for mankind's health as well."

Following publication of Rachel Carson's book, *Silent Spring,* in 1962, much of the nation and the world realized that the pesticide industry had been writing, broadcasting and promoting pure fiction when it claimed that DDT was the most valuable, broad spectrum pesticide ever invented by man and that its use had no lasting consequences to wildlife.

Writing that "DDT is the most powerful pesticide the world has ever known," Carson proved through her extensive research that DDT contaminated the entire food chain and was capable of upsetting the natural order of the world's species. She did not advocate the outright ban of DDT, but she insisted that its use be curtailed and tightly controlled.

Incredibly, beginning as early as 1959, 1.3 billion pounds of DDT were used in our country on everything from farm crops to elm trees susceptible to Dutch elm disease.

Carson's book was serialized by the New Yorker and it produced howls of protest from major chemical manufacturers along with ugly personal attacks on her. Excerpts of her book also were published in Audubon Magazine, and *The New York Times* editorialized its view that the use of DDT had to be tightly restricted – if not prohibited.

In response, President Kennedy ordered his Science Advisory Committee to examine her book and its extensive bibliography. The panel supported her conclusions.

The problem with controlling pesticide use in the United States was that, for many years, such action came under the Department of Agriculture – and its close connections with pesticide manufacturers represented a national disgrace. The agency was obviously concerned over a frontal attack regarding its shabby record of controlling the misuse of many pesticides.

Finally, when the Environmental Protection Agency was formed in 1970, control of pesticides was transferred from the Department of Agriculture to the EPA through passage of the Insecticide, Fungicide and Rodenticide Act. The fate of DDT was now in independent, competent hands of experts of the newly formed EPA, headed by William "Bill" Ruckelshaus.

Russell Train, my colleague from the Council on Environmental Quality, and I were invited to visit with Bill to discuss his forthcoming decision on the proposed ban of DDT. The Environmental Defense Fund had begun a series of legal actions highlighted by a series of experts' analysis of eggshell thinning. Their case was well supported by sound science and their aggressive legal actions were having an important impact of Ruckelshaus' forthcoming decision to limit the use of DDT by regulation or ban its use.

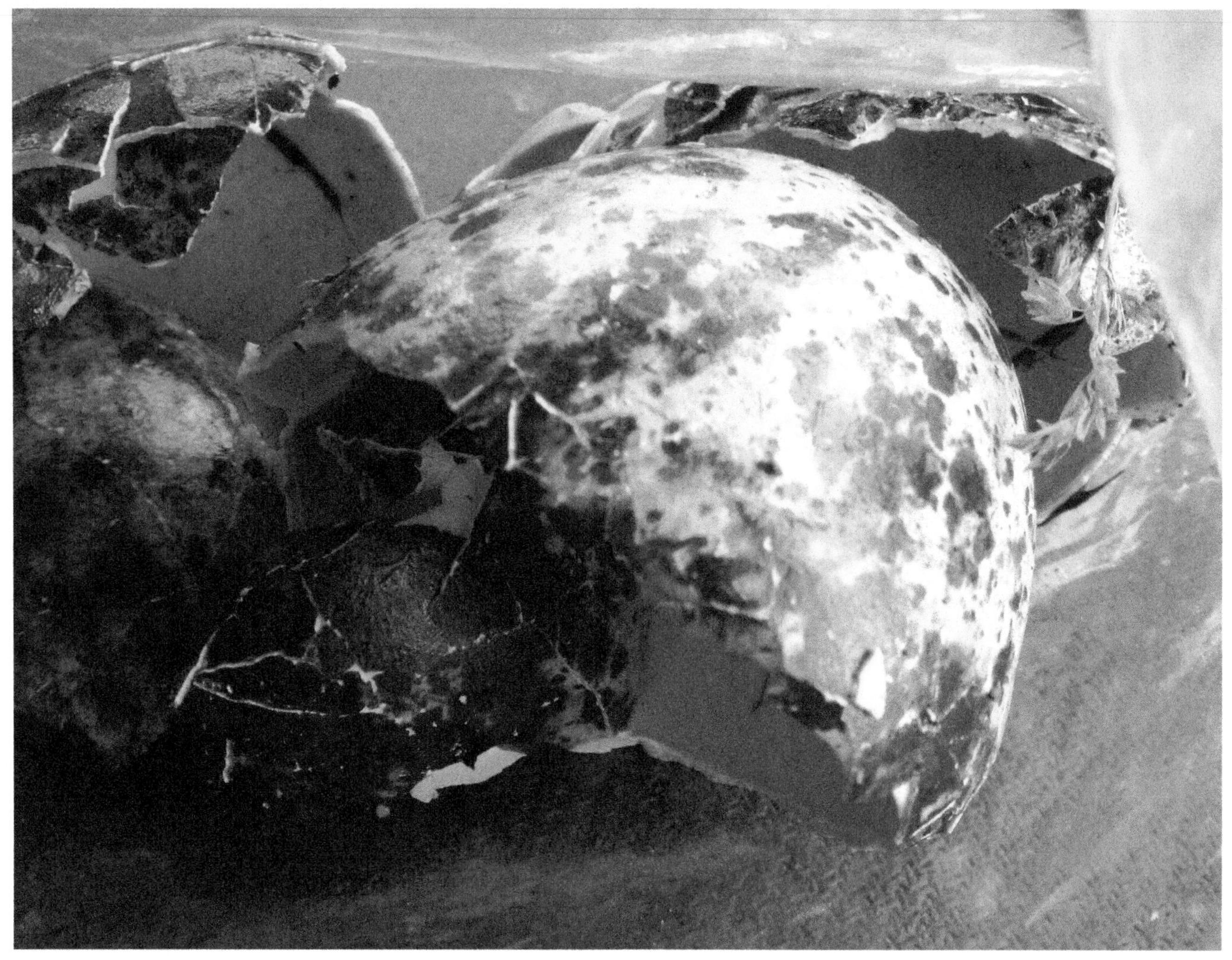

Osprey egg shells

I had a list of prospective experts who could be counted on to survive personal attacks from the chemical industry's attorneys, who were sure to challenge in court any decision by Ruckelshaus to control or ban DDT. When viewed in combination with the list of experts produced by EDF, we agreed that we had strong support for a total ban of the chemical.

The final chapter of the DDT debate began on June 14, 1972, with Ruckelshaus' decision to ban the pesticide. He wrote:

"Finally, I am persuaded that a preponderance of the evidence shows that DDT causes thinning of eggshells in certain bird species. The evidence presented included both laboratory data and observational data. Thus, results of feeding experiments were introduced to show that birds in the laboratory, when fed DDT, produced abnormally thin eggshells. In addition, researchers have also correlated thinning shells by comparing the thickness of eggs found in nature with that of eggs taken from museums. The museums eggs show little thinning, whereas eggs taken from the wild after DDT use had become extensive reveal reduced thickness. The evidence of record storage in man and magnification in the food chain is a warning to the prudent that man may be exposing himself to a substance that may ultimately have a serious effort on his health."

The order was effective on December 31, 1972.

The key witnesses on our team of experts were Dr. Robert Risebrough, associate ecologist, University of California at Berkeley; Dr. Joseph Hickey, professor of wildlife ecology at College of Agriculture, University of Wisconsin; and Dr. Cade, professor of zoology at Cornell and Research Director of Cornell Ornithology Laboratory.

They knew that their testimony in the legal action to overturn Ruckelshaus' decision was going to be fiercely contested by the manufacturers of DDT. These experts had spent years studying the impact of DDT on the eggs of a vast variety of birds and even mammals. They were gifted scientists, and they accepted that their credentials would be subject to legal attack.

I could not attend the first day of the federal hearing due to a conflict on the Hill. But, late in the afternoon, I received a call from Dr. Lucille Stickel at the Patuxent Wildlife Research Center, our partner on the bald eagle project. She said that our experts were furious over the lack of effective defense by members of the Justice Department. I was needed promptly at the laboratory to "buck up" our team.

Garfield Lawrence, my great driver, somehow wove through early evening traffic to the Patuxent headquarters. I found our witnesses enraged by the lack of effective defense by junior members of the Attorney General's staff who were no match against the powerful attorneys representing the DDT manufacturers.

I went to a private room, called the White House, asked for Attorney General John Mitchell and reached him within minutes. I relayed the pertinent information including the president's promise to ban DDT and the outstanding job Bill Ruckelshaus had done in ordering the DDT ban. I told him that this not only was essential for wildlife but for mankind's health, as well.

Mitchell replied very calmly but firmly: "Nathaniel, I promise you that there will be a highly trained group of attorneys from this department defending the decision and the witnesses tomorrow."

I returned to the meeting room and promised the staff and witnesses who had spent so many years investigating the adverse effects of DDT that a new team from Justice would be defending them in the morning. With that promise, the room relaxed and I had a drink with them before heading home.

The next morning, I was able to attend an hour of the hearing and the tone was far different. A new group from the attorney general's staff objected to questions posed to the DDT expert witnesses. The mood of the hearing was completely changed. Our witnesses' credentials and records of years of scientific study were brilliantly and aggressively defended.

The outcome was that the Administrator's decision to ban DDT was found to be consistent with the health of wildlife and man. The appeals process, of course, took years and it was not until December 13, 1974 that the Court of Appeals upheld all aspects of the cancellation order.

Tragically, during 30 years of intensive use in our country, 600,000 tons of DDT were used without knowledge of the consequences.

But it finally was banned.

Thanks go to Bill Ruckelshaus, John Mitchell, the expert witnesses and even President Nixon who made no effort to reverse the prohibition of the pesticide – even though he was begged by the industry to overrule the Ruckelshaus' decision.

The entire staff of the U.S. Fish and Wildlife Service under Director Spencer Smith and his successors' watchful eyes deserve kudos for restoring two iconic American birds – the osprey and the bald eagle – and for saving countless other lives, including those of many fellow Americans.

The Battle Over Tall Tree Corridor at Redwood National Park

"Seeds were placed there by foresters to try to fool me. That did it!"

The unrivaled and fascinating series of challenges and opportunities that appeared after my confirmation as assistant secretary in May 1971 included an exceedingly troubling environmental threat in northern California.

This was a crisis and legal battle that persisted for six years and involved several secretaries of the interior, three presidents of the United States and countless government officials, outside experts and timber industry figures.

It was quite a battle. It made for quite a saga. It produced quite a triumph.

It all began in mid-July of 1971, when Dr. Edgar Wayburn, one of the most respected leaders of the Sierra Club, requested a get-to-know-you meeting. At the time, legislation that would monumentally increase protected lands in Alaska was moving slowly through Congress. Wayburn and his wife, Peggy, had spent years during his long summer vacations inspecting our "Great Land," yearning for the possibility that landscapes could be preserved in national parks and wildlife refuges. They were acknowledged experts on the vast majority of prime Alaskan landscapes and scenic and wildlife areas.

I thought our visit would be focused on the possibility that the Alaskan Land Bill would present opportunities for major reservations of public lands as parks and refuges.

After a pleasant and informative initial discussion about his keen interest in working with our staff on issues important to the Sierra Club, Wayburn launched into a heated diatribe about the clear-cutting of hillsides above the Redwood National Park's Tall Tree Corridor in northern California. This extraordinary Redwood Creek Corridor of coastal redwoods was discovered in 1963 by a National Geographic Society research team. It led to prompt action by Congress, which created the 58,000-acre Redwood National Park in 1968. The inclusion of three state redwood parks into the national park increased its size to 131,983 acres.

These were considered to be some of the tallest trees in the world. One giant redwood was later calculated to be more than 367 feet high, and there were others that rivaled it. It was one of the great discoveries by the National Geographic Society during Gilbert Grosvenor's tour as president. Although it was difficult to reach the tallest tree on foot, it was worth the lengthy walk to see the spectacular sight. It was equally incredible when viewed from an overhead flight.

At our meeting, Wayburn produced several aerial photographs that showed extensive clear-cuts on

Photo (left) by Michael Nichols, National Geographic Creative

privately owned forests upstream of the park's boundary; it was clear that the logging was causing significant soil slippage. Further, tons of debris were sliding down the wet hillsides into the creek, blocking natural drainage. Wayburn made it very clear that the National Park Service (NPS) was, in his words, "ignoring a significant problem" that he maintained was imminent: That is, "the combination of soil erosion and debris could cause massive blockage of Redwood Creek." He believed a heavy rainfall would cause floodwaters to break through the dam, imperiling the tall trees located on the banks of Redwood Creek.

I immediately reached for my phone and asked George Hartzog, director of NPS, to join us. It was not an attractive or pleasant meeting.

Wayburn did not like Hartzog, as they had fought over NPS policies for years. Hartzog, who reported to me, maintained that the clear-cutting of privately owned forests upstream was the responsibility of the California Board of Forestry. He could not imagine that Congress or the U.S. Department of Justice (DOJ) would allow the NPS to halt the logging of millions of dollars' worth of valuable timber.

Hartzog maintained it was the Sierra Club's issue and recommended that the group sue the California Board of Forestry or convince California Gov. Ronald Reagan that the clear-cutting endangered the Redwood Creek Corridor of the Tall Trees.

Wayburn argued that it was the responsibility of NPS to protect a very expensive, unique addition to Redwood National Park. The meeting dissolved into name-calling and remembrances of former disputes. I called it off and agreed to fly out and view the scene. I briefed Secretary of the Interior Rogers Morton, that a serious problem existed upstream of Redwood National Park's Tall Tree Corridor and that I would need additional assistance.

On my staff was Dr. Richard "Dick" Curry,

who had been assigned to me by Morton. Curry had served as the American Political Science Association fellow to the Republican National Committee from August 1969 until March 1971. Morton, a former member of Congress, was chairman of the Republican National Committee when, in November 1970, he was nominated by President Richard Nixon to succeed Walter B. Hickel as secretary of the interior.

Shortly after his confirmation as secretary, Morton invited Curry to join him at the Department of Interior (DOI) as a special assistant. One of his duties was to serve as Morton's liaison with the NPS. Earlier in 1971, Curry had met with Wayburn and was familiar with his concerns about logging around Redwood National Park. It was a natural fit for me to assign Curry to this issue, as we always were on the same wavelength.

Curry had the background and knowledge to decide what DOI's role should be to protect the huge investment that had been made in creating Redwood National Park. The secretary immediately agreed and Curry welcomed the opportunity. In addition, I wanted Curry to work with Dr. Starker Leopold's task force, which recommended the NPS consider science more seriously when making individual park decisions.

Morton became increasingly concerned about my assessment that the tall trees were vulnerable and sent me a memorandum on September 24, 1971, after receiving a letter from the Sierra Club that reiterated our mutual concerns. The NPS finally seemed to wake up to the gravity of the situation and, in early November, it prepared a briefing recommending very few alternatives that concentrated on "buffer zones" along the creek.

My senior staff listened to the briefing and agreed it was insufficient to protect the tall trees. We all concurred that the NPS should concentrate on the Redwood Creek corridor as a critical area of concern. Further, I insisted that the NPS staff prepare a far more extensive "options paper," which was received in late November and again was unanimously found to be totally inadequate.

It took months for my trip to the forest to be arranged, as Congress was in session and I found that I was the busiest of all of Nixon's assistant secretaries when it came to Congressional hearings. This was the era of "Environmental Renaissance" and, in addition to legislation creating new parks and expanding the duties of the U.S. Fish and Wildlife Service (FWS), there were many major environmental initiatives that were assigned to my office.

Finally, in mid-January 1972, my visit to Redwoods country was arranged. Although I had donated to Save the Redwood League, a conservation group that had long been protecting these trees, I had never seen a redwood tree. After Curry and I landed in San Francisco, the NPS regional director drove us across the Golden Gate Bridge to nearby Muir Woods National Monument, the 10th monument created by President Theodore Roosevelt. Established in 1910, it honored preservationist John Muir and was the first monument created from a private donation. I changed into jeans and boots and walked down a trail amid a unique, small grove of coastal redwoods that receives incredible visitation each year. The trees were majestic in their height and elegance.

After a lengthy day reviewing a long list of problems and needs in the western region of national parks, Curry and I spent the night and flew the following morning in an NPS plane from Crissy Field, located below the Golden Gate Bridge. (The airfield was later removed after creation of Golden Gate National Recreation Area.) We flew up the coast to a field in redwoods country, where we were met by the superintendent. We toured various groves that were being managed by the NPS and state forest system or owned by Save the Redwood League.

The sight of these giant redwood stands was breathtaking.

We enjoyed a superb briefing from a park service

Photo by Michael Nichols, National Geographic Creative

expert on the Sequoia sempervirens, the scientific name for the coastal redwood tree. Many centuries ago, this tree dominated the northern hemisphere. The weather was warm and wet, perfect conditions for this spectacular tree. As our world's climate patterns changed, the coastal redwoods disappeared except from the forests along the California and Oregon coasts.

These trees needed to be "wet" to survive. They needed the warm, moist air flowing across the cold surface of the Pacific Ocean, which created fog banks that kept the trees moist, if not wet. They received between 25 and 122 inches of annual rainfall, but the near-daily fog was the special ingredient that made them grow into the tallest trees on Earth. The trees are estimated to have covered 2.1 million acres at one time. [32] But experts have calculated that the harvesting of redwood trees since the 1850s has reduced the size of the coastal redwood forests by 95 percent.

In the late morning, an NPS helicopter took me, Curry and an NPS forester to a site above Redwood Creek where we could observe clear-cutting in an area of "critical concern" on the steep banks. From an observation platform overlooking the Skunk Cabbage Creek watershed – from which Lady Bird Johnson, the former first lady, had dedicated the new park – a clear-cut logging operation, referred to as a "hole in the doughnut," was visible.

We flew over magnificent stands of protected redwood groves and suddenly emerged into what looked like a war zone. I had no idea how the combination of really tall redwoods and Douglas fir trees could be harvested from such steep slopes. I looked in near disbelief at the maze of roads that had been built, zigzagging along the slopes.

The NPS forester explained that redwood trees can splinter if they fall heavily. Logging companies had developed a system to build a soft landing cushion by bulldozing masses of topsoil into a wide, long "bed" where the trees could fall without breaking. Since each giant redwood and fir tree was

Photo by Paul Zal, National Geographic Creative

worth thousands of dollars, its landing bed was built with great care. It took a skilled sawyer to land a tree on the bed. Once the tree was felled, it was cut into giant lengths, loaded onto massive trucks and sent to a mill to be made into a vast variety of wood products.

The damage to the hillsides was unbelievable. Hundreds of acres of clear-cut slopes could be seen from the helicopter. Soil slippage and debris sliding down into Redwood Creek was obvious. A large sediment plume could be seen where Redwood Creek emptied into the ocean near the town of Orick. The creek's once-clear water was stained by the sloughed-off earth that had slipped down the steep hillsides.

It was a nightmare! I likened it to the French landscape after the last Battle of Verdun!

When we returned to Washington, D.C., we briefed Secretary Morton. He raged, "How could this be going on under Ronnie Reagan's stewardship and where is George Hartzog? I should have been briefed on this situation months ago!" I volunteered, "I am nearly overwhelmed with budget and Congressional testimony, plus the all-important assignment of oversight of the Alaska lands team. I am serving on four additional teams preparing legislation on critical issues from clean water to endangered species. I can only hope that I can depend on my brilliant staff members and that they can come to the fore, as the demands and opportunities are extraordinary."

By March 1972, Curry and I began an in-depth study of the redwoods (*Sequoia sempervirens*) rate of growth, and the previous forest management and mismanagement that led to formation of the Save the Redwood League in 1918. The NPS had only a few decent photographs of the logging activity, so Curry flew back to California and spent days visiting the privately owned groves that were being cut on flat coastal land and slopes above the Redwood Creek Corridor. Up to this point, one could not get access to the upslope logging operations, which were conducted on private land above the corridor.

Curry spent time with scientists familiar with the northern California ecology and the damage that had been allowed along many rivers once teeming with salmon and steelhead fish. He took a series of photographs that graphically depicted the harm that was being inflicted on the land and would in time destroy the Redwood Creek Corridor. We feared heavy rainfall and blockage of creek drainage would create a "blow-out" that would cause enormous floods of blocked rainwater to undercut the streamside redwoods, toppling trees even well back from the creek.

On his return to Washington, D.C., we asked for a private showing of Curry's slideshow, with only the secretary's personal assistant and undersecretary present.

Morton was shocked again asking, "How could this disgrace take place on my watch?" He decided to "sleep on this very upsetting briefing."

The next day, I joined the secretary in his office when he placed a call to Norman "Ike" Livermore, California's secretary of resources. Livermore was a superb human being and was of invaluable assistance as he tried to make sense of the many natural resource problems that confronted local and state government. The Livermores were "old-family" Californians. Ike's brother, "Put," was chairman of the California Coastal Commission.

The secretary and the Livermores were old friends. They chatted away before Morton told him of my experience in Redwood country and my concern that the corridor was endangered by ruthless forestry practices. Livermore said the governor appointed the California Board of Forestry and despite his repeated efforts to gain some control over logging throughout California, neither the governor nor the forest products industry allowed any reform measures to be introduced in the California Legislature.

He ended this sad tale by suggesting that I fly back out to Sacramento to visit with Governor Reagan and accept an invitation by Arcata Redwood, Simpson Timber and Georgia Pacific (now Louisiana Pacific) logging companies for an onsite inspection and opportunity to hear their side of the issue. Within days, we agreed upon a date. I was met by Livermore, who immediately became a friend. He was a simply marvelous, caring human being who knew every inch of his home state. He was concerned that the state's population was "eating up" more and more open space. The developers countered his vision of additional state and local parks by pointing out the 47 million acres of federal and state lands that already were in parks and wildlife refuges. They were not interested in open space, only more instant towns.

Livermore took me to the state Capitol. I visited his office and we discussed the Board of Forestry, which was made up of representatives of the major companies harvesting timber in northern California. He said, "Let's make an effort with the governor, but I do not hold out much hope." I was warmly met when we entered Governor Reagan's office. As a former aide to Florida's Gov. Claude Kirk, I had met Governor Reagan and discussed fishery issues with him during past governors' conferences.

Reagan obviously liked and admired Livermore.

The Redwood National Park superintendent had furnished me with recent photographs of the clear-cutting and soil in the creek that was causing barriers to natural creek flow in the park. One could easily see that construction of the extensive road system and "landing beds" was loosening tons of soil on the steep slopes and sending it cascading into the park's creeks.

The governor looked at the photographs but did not seem interested. He finally asked Livermore if he thought the situation called for a "review." Livermore stated unequivocally that the clear-cutting was far too extensive for the angle of the slopes and federal lands unquestionably were being damaged by activities that should have been controlled by the state.

The governor called his secretary to have the chief of the state forestry agency join us. That gave Livermore and me time to emphasize our concerns about the potential damage to one of the world's most unique areas. Reagan, however, seemed more interested in whether I was "getting on" with California Sen. George Murphy, a former actor and a close friend of the governor's. I had to admit I shook his hand once and never saw him again.

The chief arrived and the governor passed the photographs over and asked, "Is this type of clear-cutting permissible under the California rules?" The answer was, "Governor, the clear-cutting is legal and we have a handle on the downstream movement of the slipped soils that will be implemented in the near future."

The governor thanked him, turned to Ike and me and said, "Nathaniel, you can see that the situation is under control. Let's not worry about California's responsibility for good timber management. I have appointed an excellent board."

The governor told a couple of his "famous" jokes and indicated that the interview was over. I felt deep despair.

As I departed, Reagan called me back to his desk and asked if I would return for an on-site visit with logging representatives to discuss how their practices could be improved. I answered briskly, "I am so concerned that let's have us make that date in the near future, as I think time is an enemy."

Governor Reagan also made a final comment to Ike Livermore: "Ike, I really don't know why Nathaniel is so obsessed with these redwood trees. For heaven's sake, once you have seen a redwood tree you have seen them all!"

Livermore, bless him, replied: "Governor, this is an extraordinary grove of the tallest trees on earth – worth protecting."

Reagan simply shook his head.

Livermore knew my pain and, as a wise steward of California's unique national resources, he was embarrassed by the governor's obvious indifference.

On return to Washington, I briefed Morton, who called John Ehrlichman, Nixon's aide at the White House, and discussed my report. Ehrlichman recommended that I accept the invitation and visit with the representatives of the logging companies. Curry and I were in constant communication with Wayburn and Grosvenor, who were passionate about the National Geographic Society's discovery of the Redwood Creek Corridor.

Several weeks later, Ehrlichman invited Curry to bring his slide show to the Office of Management and Budget (OMB), where members of the White House Domestic Council and political experts would review the situation and make recommendations for action.

The slide show produced the expected outrage, as it showed the blatant costs of clear-cutting hundreds of acres of steep slopes on both sides of the creek. The amount of acreage that required protection was of concern, as OMB recognized potential major expenditures.

I met with Morton the next morning. He quietly said he had been in contact with Ehrlichman at the White House. It was a "tricky political environmental issue," he said. The agreement they reached was to conduct a scientific study that could genuinely prove that the clear-cutting of upper Redwood Creek was threatening the viability of the avenue of tall trees. The president was informed that "something had to be done," Morton said, and agreed that my small task force had to prepare an executive order to force change in the clear-cutting operation.

The problem centered around Reagan's political ambitions, program funding and presenting proof positive that logging practices were damaging the national park.

After a pause, the secretary reached for the phone and spoke to Dr. Luna Leopold, chief of the U.S. Geological Survey (USGS). The conversation was broadcast on a speaker phone. Leopold was Starker's brother and was considered one of the world's most brilliant hydrologists, with a vast range of expertise on water-related subjects. I had known him for years, as he had a summer cabin near Moose, Wyoming, and joined me for dinner on a number of occasions with the incomparable Mardy Murrie, one of Jackson Hole's great ladies. He was one of the most respected scientists in the federal government. I gave Leopold a brief outline of the problem. He was very knowledgeable about the issues. He accepted the challenge of proving that upstream logging practices were damaging the creek and threatening the integrity of the avenue of tall trees.

Leopold said, "Mr. Secretary, give me three days to select the most competent researcher who I can assign to this project. Nathaniel, I know you are anxious and in a rush, but to prove damage beyond doubt will take two to three years and a hefty budget."

The secretary replied, "Luna, you are our ace-in-the-hole card! You must get this research project underway to protect the corridor as rapidly as possible. Adequate funds will be made available."

Leopold called back with the name of Richard Janda, whom he described as young, brilliant, thorough and tough, and whose analysis would stand up if the situation called for legal action. Curry was to work with him on devising a scientifically sound report – on the impacts of the clear-cutting – that would survive legal challenge.

Dr. Janda, a geomorphologist, received a B.S. degree in 1960 from the Department of Geology and Mineralogy at Pennsylvania State University and a Ph.D. in 1966 from the Department of Geology and Geophysics at the University of California at Berkeley. During his employment with the USGS, Janda worked extensively in diverse forested terrains in California, Oregon, Washington and Hawaii. He also conducted intensive studies on the coastal ranges of northern California and southern Oregon.

In addition, he had casually visited the drainage basin of Redwood Creek twice prior to his involvement on our recently formed Redwood Task Force. In the spring of 1965, he inspected the flood plain near State Highway 299 and Orick as part of a regional reconnaissance of stream sedimentation related to the destructive flood of December 1964. In the late spring of 1969, he walked the channel of Redwood Creek from the mouth of Prairie Creek to the mouth of Bond Creek to inspect parts of the newly established addition to the Redwood National Park.

Janda served as part of the DOI-sponsored interdisciplinary professional team led by Curry to investigate the actual and potential impact of timber harvest adjacent to Redwood National Park. The initial visit of the team was March 20-23, 1972. It was evident from that initial visit that additional geomorphic data would be needed to help the NPS develop an effective means of dealing with processes that could threaten park resources.

Between April 1972 and September 1973, Janda spent about 45 days in the Redwood Creek Basin gaining background information needed to develop an effective study plan. From September 1973, when the USGS's intensive Redwood Creek studies commenced, until September 1975, he spent more than 200 days in the basin in all kinds of weather. In all, 17 reports germane to the protection of Redwood National Park served as the scientific basis that supported policies enacted to protect this invaluable national resource owned by the American people.

This was a classic example of science seizing the day and withstanding the assaults of pseudo-science, ensuring a solid outcome of the political process.

On January 30, 1973, the Sierra Club filed a Freedom of Information suit with the federal district court in San Francisco seeking release of the task force report on Redwood Creek.

In February 1973, a report titled Resource Management Actions Affecting Redwood Creek Corridor – Options Paper was completed and briefings were held within the Nixon administration. The preferred option was incredibly expensive, as it called for major expansion of the park far upstream of the Tall Tree Corridor.

The Office of Management and Budget rejected the proposed recommendations of extensive land purchase or even a "federal taking," emphasizing instead the "direct concern" of the state of California and private timber companies over logging practices. OMB insisted that protection was to be gained through cooperation and at no cost to the federal government.

By agreement, since the body of the report was supported unanimously by scientists on the task force and the recommendations were solely the responsibility of the preparer, the recommendations were removed and the body of the report was approved for release. Importantly, the report accurately reflected the task force's unanimous agreement that logging, past and present, was damaging the watershed in general and park resources in particular. This was a position from which the DOI never retreated.

As a result of the OMB position that we seek relief from the state of California and the timber companies, it fell to me to continue to meet with the Reagan administration to try to get regulatory relief and persuade the timber companies to harvest more sensitively.

In March 1973, Curry and I briefed Dr. David Joseph of the California North Coast Water Quality Board on the contents of the task force report. That state agency had been the most responsive to date in showing its concern for the impact of logging on water resources. Briefings on the report were given to the appropriate state agencies in Sacramento on March 10. Based on their comments it was evident that support from this group would not be forthcoming. State officials insisted that timber-harvesting practices were in compliance with state standards and that if water-quality standards were rigidly interpreted and enforced, the companies would be forced out of business. California Department of Fish and Game representatives said clear-cutting was beneficial to wildlife, and the state park director even suggested divestment of a state-owned section of the park along Redwood Creek.

The following day, March 11, a meeting with representatives of the timber industry was held in Arcata, California. The timber industry was advised that the policy decision was not to acquire more land to protect the park but to rely on such things as the modification of existing harvesting practices, a temporary moratorium on stream-bank harvesting, remedial work on the road network and further analysis of the watershed. It was agreed that further discussions would be held with each company separately. On March 12, the Sierra Club was briefed in San Francisco and expressed surprise that there were no additional recommendations. Its representatives were informed that this was a complete summary of the task force's findings but were not told that the recommendations had been stripped in order to secure release of the document. The briefing team consisted of Howard Chapman, NPS western regional director; Jack Davis, superintendent of Redwoods National Park; Janda and Curry.

Following these briefings, another field team was assembled on April 9 to develop harvesting guidelines. This team consisted of some members of the original task force and included personnel from the FWS and U.S. Forest Service familiar with timber harvesting in the Redwood Region. The task force toured the properties of Arcata Redwood, Simpson Timber and Louisiana-Pacific to examine their respective harvesting practices. Based on this inspection, prior on-site observations and data gathered since March 1972, the task force drafted guidelines for future harvesting and presented them to the industry in late April of 1973.

With the release of the Harvesting Guidelines – Redwood Creek Watershed, NPS and DOI pressure was mounting on several fronts. News articles began to focus on harvesting practices, and the California Division of Forestry released a report supporting the practice of clear-cutting or "clean logging." The state maintained that clear-cutting "is an extension of nature's method of perpetuating redwood as a forest type," while DOI concluded that clear-cutting and tractor-yarding were "producing more ground disturbance and vegetative cover damage than any other combination of practices heretofore employed or envisioned." In spite of that, the task force-designed harvesting guidelines were based on a composite of harvesting practices of the companies involved. The task force took the best practices of each as a starting point for developing a new standard.

After much back and forth between the NPS and timber companies, NPS pressed for more sensitive logging and access to company lands as part of the guidelines to make sure that mitigation actions, once agreed upon, were in fact being implemented. The companies responded that they would need compensation for harvesting in a manner that exceeded state regulations. After much correspondence between the companies and NPS, I wrote to all of the companies on August 10, making it clear that their demand for compensation for harvesting in a more sensitive manner was unacceptable. I also stated that DOI would seek protection using other options and did not feel bound to prior statements ruling out land acquisition. I also mentioned the potential of DOI seeking judicial relief. That got their attention.

It was in this context that late in 1973, leaders of the timber companies and my staff finally agreed to a firm date for us to meet on a slope overlooking Redwood Creek.

The timber companies suggested that I be picked up at a landing site near the park superintendent's headquarters and be flown in one of their helicopters to a luncheon site. They promised a full briefing by their foresters and experts on reclamation of clear-cut zones. Dutifully, I flew out and was transferred by the park service to the superintendent's quarters. We spent the afternoon touring the extensive groves. I saw my first Marbled Murret, an endangered bird that requires old-growth forests to survive. The battle over the little birds' existence was a major test of the Endangered Species Act and has had a major impact on Pacific forest management.

The next day, I flew in a helicopter to a site above the grove of giant trees for a picnic lunch. I was met by leaders of the concerned logging companies and their staffs. We walked down some yards of roads, examined the "beds," noted a small effort to control erosion and then returned to the site, where I received a long briefing by foresters who explained the value of the timber and the care it took to cut the huge trees successfully. Then the forest engineers took over, explaining that all clear-cutting looks "like hell," but with careful land reclamation the clear-cut acreage could be "reshaped" to prevent downhill erosion. They claimed the "beds" would be shoved back into the ground and the 800 miles of roads would disappear with new techniques of mitigation.

I explained to them quietly but firmly that time was not on the side of saving the avenue of tall trees. The amount of silt and earth was increasing dramatically and debris was moving down the slope after every heavy rainstorm. I informed them that the secretary, as "steward of the national parks," was alarmed enough to instruct the universally known Dr. Luna Leopold to study the impacts of their logging on the future of the creek and Redwood Creek Corridor. They seemed concerned and stated how much they would like to work with Leopold.

They stressed that they had decided to seed the clear-cut sites as soon as logging was completed. I told them that seeding the slopes would never work, as the rainfall was so great that the seeds would end up in the Pacific Ocean. The only possible mitigation would be to replant with thousands of tall redwood seedlings that they could acquire or grow in their nurseries. They said I was "overreacting" to a permissible method of clear-cutting steep slopes under California's forest regulations and reforestation.

There was no agreement to be made. I smoothed my hand across a giant redwood log upon which I was sitting and discovered that it was covered with redwood seeds that shouldn't have been there.

They had been placed there by foresters to try to fool me. That did it!

I stated that I would never expect any first-class companies to seed an area merely in an attempt to show concern. I asked to be flown back to the park ASAP. I promised them that the federal government would protect its investment in Redwood National Park. As I was walking to the waiting helicopter, I overheard one of the young foresters say, "I told you it was stupid to seed the area! For heaven's sake, he worked for Weyerhaeuser on rehabilitation projects."

I flew back to Washington, D.C., more convinced than ever that the Nixon team had to take steps to control the threat to one of the world's most unique areas. Nevertheless, we agreed to resume negotiations over harvesting practices and meet with each company separately.

A continuous release of data from the USGS demonstrated the need for more stringent logging practices and clearly confirmed that logging in Redwood Creek and other areas adjacent to the park was damaging park resources. In addition, the federal district court had postponed a decision on whether the DOI was adequately working to defend the park. We did not want to be painted with the same brush as the timber industry. I wrote Ike Livermore in August 1973, asking whether timber companies were complying with state laws related to timber harvesting, water quality standards, the Fish and Game Code and the Health and Safety Code. He reluctantly provided me with those assurances. We were on our own in regard to getting viable protection from the state.

In June, California Rep. Philip Burton introduced federal legislation to expand the park. No one expected anything to happen immediately, but the editor of the Del Norte Triplicate newspaper opined, "The Burton Brothers may not get very far with their bill to expand the Park. But, nobody should take anything for granted." [33]

In late 1974, before the redwood issue could be fully addressed by the Nixon Administration, the presidential resignation brought White House-level involvement in it to a complete halt. We were on our own.

In 1975, Morton changed positions and became Secretary of Commerce. Wyoming Governor Stanley Hathaway was confirmed as secretary of the interior after one of the most controversial confirmation hearings ever, highlighted by the governor's professed "pro-business actions versus environmental stewardship in the management of Wyoming's lands." He was confirmed, but was "blistered and bruised."

Hathaway asked for and received an update on all pertinent major issues that fell under his responsibility. Obviously, Curry's slide show was a highlight of his briefing schedule. He called Donald Rumsfeld, President Ford's chief of staff, and urged him to take the time to see the slide show and decide whether this issue might be useful for Ford's election campaign.

Rumsfeld recognized it as a very visible "green issue" that might be helpful during the 1976 presidential campaign. Following another round of briefings by Curry and me, the campaign directors decided that the issue was not national and that the "green vote" probably would go to Ford's Democratic opponent, Georgia Gov. Jimmy Carter, anyway. The political consensus was, why infuriate the timber companies, all major donors to the Ford campaign?

The saga was further complicated by the sudden unexpected resignation of Hathaway, who served only four months before being replaced by Tom Kleppe. Most of the DOI issues were far beyond Kleppe's experience or even his interest. He was appointed as a favor to the western senators who wanted to significantly curtail environmental efforts. I was deemed the major "responsible person in Interior," reporting to Rumsfeld. After Rumsfeld became secretary of defense, Richard Cheney became President Ford's chief of staff.

And Cheney was no fan of environmental causes.

After Curry and I prepared a memorandum and briefed new members of the presidential staff, Ford seemed genuinely interested and concerned about the issue. He accepted the science that outlined the grievous damage logging was inflicting on the creek and tree corridor. Janda's data was incontrovertible, and it seemed that political changes at the federal and state level would have a positive impact on the redwood cause.

In December 1974, I met with newly elected California Gov. Jerry Brown, a Democrat, for a box luncheon. We sat on the floor of a house that had been rented for him during the transition. There was no furniture in the room. We sat in lotus position and discussed redwood and California environmental issues. He was extremely well-briefed and knowledgeable and seemed committed to changing the era of "good ol' boys" to some semblance of ecological balance and stewardship. I pointed out that he had a great opportunity to dismiss the members of the California Forestry Board and tackle the problem of reforestation. He seemed genuinely fascinated by an unexpected opportunity.

After taking office in 1975, Brown appointed Claire Dedrick, a member of the Sierra Club, as secretary of natural resources – a sign of great change in the state's environmental attitude. In December, Dedrick declared she was engaged in "an honest attempt to bring environmental protection into the normal course of business." However, it took a couple of years before Brown was able to wrest the forestry board from the virtual control of the timber industry through the appointment process.

Of more immediate importance was the fact that a superior court judge from Mendocino County ruled that the California state forester was required to prepare and consider environmental impact reports when granting permits for timber operations. The state forester was transformed from a ministerial functionary to a key decision-maker in the logging plan approval process. The court's decision prompted the state forester to, in effect, cancel all existing approvals of logging plans in sensitive areas. Policy changes were being made in spite of intense resistance from the timber industry.

On the litigation front, DOI had to respond to the Sierra Club lawsuit, which alleged we were not protecting park resources from physical and aesthetic ruination. The group argued that the cooperative agreements to implement the harvesting guidelines were unenforceable and unable to provide the level of protection that the government's data showed was needed. I was the principal witness for the government and detailed what we had been doing to date.

Representatives from the timber companies took the stand in support of the cooperative agreements and said they were affecting actual practices in the field. We put Janda on the stand to describe study efforts that were under way. OMB insisted I should argue that more output from these studies was needed in order to develop and evaluate further actions required to protect the national park. We also argued that a lack of funds precluded the adoption of several of the recommendations we had previously made.

We had prepared a photo mosaic to show the court what we were up against. At the onset it worked to our disadvantage, but coupled with additional data presented by the USGS, it proved to be a powerful argument for even more rigorous action. The court found that we unreasonably, arbitrarily and in abuse of discretion had failed, refused and neglected to take steps to exercise and perform duties imposed upon us by the National Park

System Act and the Redwood National Park Act. The judge then left the case open and ordered the government to report back on December 15, 1975, as to what we intended to do to protect the park.

Although all of us who had been laboring intensively to get a viable resolution were embarrassed by the judge's harsh words, we quickly realized that the decision gave us ammunition to press the issue more vigorously.

We continued to push for better control over harvesting practices that were endangering the park. However, the companies continued to fight by producing a consultant's report denying that harvesting had any adverse impact on the park and claiming the threats to the park were a result of natural forces at work in the watershed.

Nevertheless, armed with a continuous stream of irrefutable data, the NPS pressed for a logging moratorium and changes in state regulation and endorsed a program for rehabilitation of cut-over lands in the watershed. This resulted in the timber companies bypassing me and setting up a meeting with Secretary Kleppe.

On October 31, 1975, the same day the companies were meeting with Kleppe, I was meeting with a group of industry representatives in San Francisco. That evening, Dedrick and I and our respective staffs met in San Francisco to promote closer coordination with the state.

Shortly thereafter, Dedrick posed three general questions in a meeting with the California Forestry Board. First, is there a need for additional mitigation measures for logging virgin redwood forests in the Redwood Creek Basin? If so, what would they be? Secondly, should further logging operations in certain areas be temporarily postponed until those portions of the watershed have had an opportunity to recover from prior natural and manmade occurrences? And thirdly, should there be a long-term rehabilitation program established to aid in the overall recovery of the drainage from past occurrences?

The California board was still under control of the timber industry, which was most evident at hearings November 17 and 18 and in the board's early 1976 decision to concur, in essence, with the industry's position. NPS answered all three of these questions in the affirmative and each time it met with the companies to discuss terms of a cooperative agreement, its position strengthened.

The board answered Dedrick's three questions on January 15, 1976, exactly the opposite of NPS's position. The board found it was inappropriate to adopt special forest practice rules for Redwood Creek drainage. It advised NPS to negotiate agreements with its neighbors as it had done in the past. The board also rejected a temporary moratorium and said it had insufficient information to deal with the need for a long-term rehabilitation program in the watershed.

It did, however, accept a recommendation that the state forester work with all parties and corporate special requirements in a site-specific logging plan which would then be enforceable by the state. The companies could appeal the forester's decision to the board.

The enhanced role of the state forester made the review of harvesting more meaningful and turned out to be an important tool in negotiations between the companies and government. In addition, the testimony by Clyde Wahrhaftig, a Brown Administration appointee and professor of geology at Berkeley, compared reports by the timber industry's consultant and the USGS. He endorsed the soundness of the USGS's methodology and data, which gave the government a strong measure of confidence in its data. That, in turn, supported increasing the level of protection in cooperative agreement negotiations.

I pushed to hold the companies to standards that would provide substantial protection to the national park and withstand the "reasonable man" test. With a flourish, the companies rejected the strengthened government guidelines and introduced their own set of self-imposed rules, saying they would seek no compensation as long as no further demands were placed on them.

Analyses showed that none of the major issues were addressed in the self-imposed standards, which were inadequate to achieve the needed protection. The companies not only continued to lobby the U.S. secretary of interior directly, but they also proceeded to go to OMB. They were successful at OMB in blocking my legislative proposal to impose guidelines by regulations, playing on the fear that it could lead to compensation to the companies. At my request, Peter Raynor from the U.S. Solicitor General's Office crafted a petition for injunctive relief seeking to prohibit logging in the buffer zone. This approach was ultimately rebuffed by the DOJ, which didn't believe DOI would prevail in court if it asked preemptively for relief by prohibiting logging in the buffer zone. The DOJ argued that once the damage was shown to occur, injunctive relief could be sought.

On June 7, federal Judge William Sweigert found that DOI was now acting in good faith a nd had, to the best of its ability, attempted to exercise its powers and perform its duties within the limitations placed upon it by Congress. I continued to press for greater state involvement and, if necessary, the pursuit of injunctive relief to protect the park. On June 25, I wrote a letter updating the appropriate congressional committee heads and informing them that we were seeking protection of the park in two ways.

I cited our efforts to utilize the injunctive process to restrict harmful timber practices and our efforts to participate in the state review process. I discussed the evolution of harvesting guidelines but noted that they were still insufficient to protect the park from the cumulative impact of many years of undisciplined timber practices. Among other things, I advised the committees of the court's ruling that the DOI had done all it could under existing authorities and that "Congress now has the primary responsibility to decide if new legislation should be passed to provide additional regulatory powers or funds for the protection of the Redwood National Park."

The timber industry was quick to respond to my letter, which in turn generated a detailed DOI response. In September, an oversight hearing was held in San Francisco by the U.S. House Committee on Government Operations. Testimony was presented by Curry, who was now associate director of the NPS for legislation, Janda of USGS – both of whom were on the Redwood Task Force – and Assistant Attorney General Peter Taft. In addition, Dedrick and the California Attorney General's office weighed in. Their appearances assured us that more pressure would be forthcoming from the state.

On November 17, a cooperative agreement was reached with all three companies. However, I advised Congress that there was still unfinished business regarding timber practices. As 1976 came to a close, the state was proceeding to take a more aggressive posture in using its regulatory authority on behalf of the park, pushing for rehabilitation in the watershed and seeking expansion of the park. Under my direction, a legislative proposal and a set of recommendations were prepared.

I remained committed to resolving the redwood issue. Unable to complete the mission before my tenure was up in late 1976, I submitted my observations to Secretary of the Interior-Designate Cecil Andrus and both the House and Senate committees that would handle any legislative proposals. I stressed the need for regulation, rehabilitation and land acquisition to protect the resources of Redwood National Park. I had hoped by doing so, that the transition between the Ford and Carter administrations would be equipped to provide a seamless continuation of focus on this critical issue.

To my delight, the new administration needed little prodding and Congress quickly began to take action. Curry was retained by the Carter administration and Peter Raynor, now an expert on the issues, was a career attorney in the solicitor general's office. The two of them were able to continue to staff the issue within the DOI and worked closely with Congressman Burton as he drafted and shepherded what would become an expanded park bill through the maze of the legislative process.

The Ryan Committee, an oversight congressional panel, had held a September 18, 1976, oversight hearing in San Francisco and released its report on March 23, 1977. It made six recommendations, including imposing a moratorium on timber harvesting in the basin to permit action on park legislation. It urged Congress to consider expanding the park an additional 21,500 to 74,000 acres and giving DOI the authority to regulate harvesting on adjacent lands, if necessary, to provide further protection for Redwood National Park.

On the first day of April, the 1977 harvesting season began. As it had done several times in the past, the Arcata Company began logging in a very conspicuous location close to the national park boundaries and well within the recommended park expansion zone. Among cries of outrage, calls for a moratorium were raised and the logging companies were accused of trying to force park expansion and rush the government into a hasty purchase at a high price.

The timber companies rejected all calls for a moratorium. Robert A. Ferris, Arcata's general counsel, admitted that the possible purchase of his company's land was a factor in its decision to begin logging. "The day we agree to a moratorium is the day they get their extra park land without paying for it," he said. "The timber company would lose its bargaining power if it did not hold on to its land."[34] The state of California was able, in effect, to establish a harvesting moratorium in Redwood Creek by rejecting timber plans not previously approved.

On April 22, the Carter Administration released its legislative proposal, which had three parts: a 48,000-acre addition to the national park; a $12 million rehabilitation program to repair logging damage; and a $40 million economic assistance package to ameliorate the impact on affected workers and the local economy. The plan was greeted with approval on the Hill. Most importantly, Burton was ready to join forces with the administration. Burton was one of the great champions of the national park system. A master of the art of the "possible," he and his brother were major figures in national park issues, not just in California but nationwide.

The pace was picking up rapidly and the timber companies, ostensibly opposed to land acquisition, continued to throw gasoline on the fire by cutting close to the park. In one case, Arcata even began harvesting in the scenic corridor, which was part of the original Redwood National Park Act. Andrus responded quickly by using a donation from Save the Redwood League. The money was deposited with the Court of Claims as part of a declaration of taking procedure, whereby the government was awarded title to the property. The final sales price would be decided in a subsequent proceeding. This action by Arcata prompted a stinging editorial rebuke of the company in the major local paper entitled, "Just Who Are the Area's Friends?"

The three logging companies – Arcata Redwood, Simpson Timber and Louisiana Pacific – owned most of the acreage comprised of old-growth redwoods. Congress has to approve all land appropriations for park expansions. Under normal authorizations, the government can back out if the price exceeds the authorized amount. If the authorization is in the form of a legislative taking, the process is different. With a legislative taking, when the president signs the bill with such a provision included, the property immediately transfers to the government. The cost is decided later in negotiations, which usually wind up in a judicial proceeding if there is an irreconcilable dispute over price.

Once the legislative outcome appears inevitable, property owners may opt to take some action to threaten the value of the land to be taken, which usually forces Congress to include legislative taking language. Historically, landowners get more money in this type of procedure. The owners get the court-determined value plus interest for the period of time between possession and final determination of value. This is what happened with the redwoods legislation and later in the acquisition of Congaree Swamp in South Carolina. In that case, the landowners received a payment of interest that was approximately the size of the Park Service's original estimate of the value of the land.

President Carter and Secretary Andrus took a long, hard look at the California forest rules and the destruction they allowed and supported the most expensive land condemnation act in America's history.

The Burton Bill included a legislative "taking" that was part of the original Redwood National Park Act. However, the companies were unhappy with a provision that authorized Andrus to regulate harvesting activities in the buffer zone. Pressure was building to get the bill enacted before the end of the Congressional session but, on November 5, 1977, Congress adjourned without enacting it.

Both House Speaker Phillip "Tip" O'Neill and Senator Robert Byrd promised early consideration in the next session of Congress. The House Rules Committee released the park bill on February 7, 1978, but the timber companies were able to lobby to eliminate the regulatory authority provision. Congress passed the legislation expanding the park on March 21, 1978, and on March 27, President Carter signed it into a law. Nearly a decade had passed since the original Redwood National Park was created and for more than six years I had been involved in the logging controversy.

Now a new chapter was about to begin.

The timber companies made no effort to remove any equipment from the property that NPS obtained in the park expansion. In fact, they dumped used equipment including bulldozers, huge cranes and timber trucks and just walked away. After years of judicial maneuvering, they received the largest amount of taxpayers' funds in our nation's history from a legislative land taking.

Congressman Ryan, chairman of the House Government Operations Committee, had been prescient in 1977 when he released the Government Accounting Office study of the cost of the original park purchase, noting, "The companies that fought the establishment of the Park and who are now opposing expansion of the Park have literally cried all the way to the bank." [35]

The final chapter of this story is fascinating.

Governor Brown followed through on his promise to assist the reforestation of Redwood Creek's slopes by opening a reform school for juvenile delinquents in one of the state forests. Under careful supervision, the inmates planted hundreds of thousands of seedlings of native northern California trees. Although I have yet to see the results, I have talked to successive park superintendents who report that the slopes are covered with redwoods and a mixture of other fir; the issue of soil movement is ending by the removal of 800 miles of roads and landing "beds." Thousands of seedlings will take another 50 years to dominate the slopes, but in 250 years, the hillsides will give visitors a semblance of the grandeur of what once were the redwood slopes.

The Redwood Expansion Act of 1978 authorized an appropriation of $33 million to the NPS with directions to restore the sloping, clear-cut areas and protect the Corridor of the Tall Trees. The magnitude of the restoration effort required painstaking research to avoid creating an even more difficult situation. Managing the forces of erosion and 36,000 acres of clear-cuts, removing the extensive road system and reforesting required expertise from many agencies, including the state of California.

A team of experts was formed and agreed on various methods of controlling erosion. They planned to stabilize the sloping hillsides, remove the "beds" that had been scraped up to soften the fall of giant redwood trees, get rid of the incredible skid tracks where the cut logs were dragged to a road side, and remove 415 abandoned miles of logging roads. The park's management team continues to improve techniques for restoration.

The continuing work requires expertise and an annual commitment of funds. The good news is that the rate of erosion has been minimized and the threat to the trees has been dramatically reduced. Thousands of redwood seedlings were planted by hand over the course of the first 15 years of restoration. There have been problems establishing redwood groves on the drier sites, but those sites have seen the recovery of native vegetation started mostly as herbaceous ground cover, progressing to shrubby vegetation; in time it is expected to become an overstory of redwoods and Douglas fir.

The seedling program was highly successful in the wetter areas of the slopes, but expensive. In the 1990s, park managers reviewed older sites for vegetative recovery and discovered that natural regeneration was more than adequate in restoring native vegetation, particularly trees such as redwoods and Douglas fir, to former road corridors. Natural regeneration has replaced expensive hand planting of seedlings. Work that has been accomplished has been so innovative that the techniques developed in the park have been applied extensively throughout the region in similar programs addressing legacy logging impacts on watersheds.

The critical importance of road removal is highlighted by additional appropriations that have allowed as many as six concurrent contracts employing heavy equipment to remove and reshape logging roads within the park.

Regrettably, there have been no congressional appropriations to continue plans to fully restore the upstream slopes or the remaining road mileage. Park personnel are preparing detailed assessments for developing cost estimates to remove the remaining roads and ski trails.

In summary, credit must be given to the Redwood National Park personnel past and present and their expert colleagues who were hired to restore a semblance of natural beauty to the great redwood forests that were desecrated by massive clear cuts.

The present challenge facing park managers is to secure additional funding to continue the work of removing the remaining 200 miles of logging roads, failing culverts and other infrastructure left from the logging era. Park staff requires adequate financial resources to remain alert and active so long as the elements continue to threaten the soaring redwood forests of Redwood National Park.

The legacy of those who fought so hard and so long to establish and expand this magnificent redwood park and world heritage site in perpetuity demands no other course of action.

This is a success story: a validation of President Carter's and Secretary Andrus' determination to request a "Congressional taking" of the land for the expansion of Redwood National Park, to seek appropriations, and to invest in expertise on how to plan and execute the restoration.

To achieve this, congressional appropriations for continuation of the great effort must be a priority.

None of this could have been achieved without the group efforts of Secretary Rogers Morton, Richard Curry, Dr. Luna Leopold, Dr. Richard Janda, Congressman Phil Burton, Peter Raynor, Congressman Leo Ryan and Secretary Cecil Andrus.

A special thanks goes to President Jimmy Carter and the members of Congress who collectively saved the Redwood Creek Corridor and expanded Redwood National Park.

Nine years after enactment in 1987, a federal court accepted the timber companies' appraisals of value, awarding them $688 million for their land and the broken-down equipment they intentionally left within the expanded boundaries of Redwood National Park. There were additional payments to smaller landowners plus interest payments.

Photo by Ted Spiegel, National Geographic Creative

The total cost of the expanded park was more than $1.4 billion, including $306 million spent on the original park, $120 million to help displaced timber workers and cushion the impact on the local economy, and $233 million to restore the acquired, clear-cut lands.

It proved to be the most expensive park in history. [36] Considering the inestimable value of forever saving Redwood National Park, protecting Redwood Creek Corridor and establishing a new redwood forest centuries in the making, it was, I believe, a small price to pay.

I believe the future is bright and our grandchildren will see not only the Tall Trees but also the upstream slopes covered with native plants and large redwood, Douglas fir and other native conifer and hardwood trees reaching for the sky.

Perhaps a visitor may not know the history of the effort to protect and reforest the steep slopes, but participants in the saga will know that they jointly saved a great natural resource and created a unique national park of extraordinary value.

NOTES – THE BATTLE OVER TALL TREE CORRIDOR AT REDWOOD NATIONAL PARK

[32] Wikipedia reference which I summarized on page 106: Before commercial logging and clearing began by the 1850s, this massive tree occurred naturally in an estimated 2,100,000 acres (8,500 km^2) along much of coastal California (excluding southern California, where rainfall is not sufficient) and the southwestern corner of coastal Oregon within the United States. An estimated 95% or more of the original old-growth redwood trees have been cut down (Kelly, D. and G. Braasch. 1988. *Secrets of the old growth forest.* Gibbs Smith, Layton, Utah: 1–99.)

[33] Editorial, "The Burton Brothers Will Make A Name for Themselves," *Del Norte Triplicate,* July 10, 1974.

[34] "California Redwood Being Felled on Private Land Near a Park," *The Washington Post* 4/8/77. A.4 Bill Richards.)

[35] Park Expenditures: "excessive," *Times Standard,* August 20, 1977.

[36] "What if they made a Park and Nobody Came: A New Park Saved the Tall Trees but at a High Cost to the Community." Edwin Kiester, Jr., *Smithsonian Magazine*, October, 1993, 42.

Stream Channelization and the Good Ol' Boys

"It was time to expose the outdated perk system."

I had been in office at the Interior Department only a few weeks when my assistant, George Gardner, transferred from my Tallahassee office to become a member of my Washington team. George was well-trained by brilliant staff members of the University of Florida and had a great sense of curiosity.

He scheduled an early morning appointment with senior members of the Fish and Wildlife Service (FWS) who wanted to disclose a serious problem that had been ignored by previous administrations and even the Office of Management and Budget (OMB).

The briefing led to a confrontation within the Department of Interior between the Bureau of Reclamation, the Army Corps of Engineers, the Tennessee Valley Authority and the Soil Conservation Service.

George had been briefed by expert FWS staff and told that miles of steams throughout the middle and southern states had been channelized under the guise of flood control. These vitally important natural areas had functioned as nature's drains, but farmers and federal lawmakers had pushed to widen and deepen the streams to prevent occasional flooding on private land.

The activity killed most living organisms in the streams and threatened waterfowl and other creatures dependent on the organisms. Farmers saw no reason to use natural drainage systems that had functioned independently of man's activities for eons. Man was to get his way, and that meant canalization and rapid draining of farmlands.

I called FWS Director Spencer Smith and arranged for a full staff meeting with his deputies. I included my two deputies who were experts on the "art of add-ons" to congressional appropriations acts. I questioned the group, asking why these projects hadn't been reviewed under the newly passed National Environmental Policy Act. Why weren't there mandatory Environmental Impact Statements that clearly showed the adverse consequences of large ditches and draglines being driven through very important wildlife corridors that flanked streams or small rivers? Why hadn't the OMB disapproved of the proposed projects and eliminated funding?

The answers were disquieting.

Long before passage of the National Environmental Policy Act (NEPA), the Soil Conservation Service and the Tennessee Valley Authority had become jealous of large, expensive water-related Corps and Bureau of Reclamation projects and decided to expand their "duties" to widespread drainage of small watersheds throughout the middle south. To obtain funding, the agencies attached "add-ons" to the annual Public Works Budget, circumventing OMB review. The costs were buried within the colossal Public Works Bill that passed by voice vote every year. Every member of Congress seemed to feel that they were entitled to having their drainage project considered by a small group of House representatives, mostly senior members of the Public Works Committee. If the applicant had voted for other members' pet projects, his project would be favorably considered.

The OMB was faced annually with a congressional budget proposal that far exceeded the President's request, but a veto was rare. President Eisenhower vetoed the most public works projects due to his dislike of millions of dollars of add-ons. President Johnson signed every annual Pork Barrel Bill to ensure Congress continued to support and fund the Vietnam War and the Great Society.

My problem was that I was "green," in the sense of new on the job, and unknown on the Hill. I recognized instantly the perils of opposing a long-standing practice that allowed members of Congress to help constituents regardless of the devastation to fish and other wildlife.

I called Secretary Morton and discussed the Gardner-Bureau findings. He asked to read the "finding," which showed unacceptable lawsuits to native forest, fish and wildlife, and immediately authorized my Deputy Douglas Wheeler for Congressional Affairs and the department's legislative counsel to translate the "findings memorandum" into congressional testimony.

It was obvious that the add on-system avoided review by the Office of Management and Budget and failed to obey the recently passed requirements of the National Environmental Policy Act which required accurate environmental review.

There were obvious violations of the then federal clean water rules. The major effort to create a new federal Clean Water Act was well underway as was the Endangered Species Act which both applied to the majority of the 'secretive' channelization projects.

When the testimony was completed and peer reviewed by the under secretary, it was sent to OMB for review and the standard system of sending all controversial testimony to the affected federal agencies for review and comment. All hell broke loose!

I was authorized to proceed and I distributed some of the proposed statements that afternoon. Leakage occurred. Congressional friends demanded a hearing to discuss my fact paper, which was being circulated and read within 48 hours by all the construction agencies.

Interior's Assistant Secretary for Water Projects, who oversaw activities of the Bureau of Reclamation, wrote a condemnation memorandum insisting that my fact paper should never see the light of day. Similar complaints were issued in mass by the Corps, the TVA and especially the Soil Conservation Service, which maintained it was the right of individual congressman to seek solutions from the service for damaging floods on productive farm lands.

The fact that the projects were ongoing, and many more miles of streams were slated for work according to planning documents Gardner uncovered, encouraged the Nixon Administration to clearly state that this old-fashioned pork-barrel system had been carefully constructed by the House of Representative's Public Works Committee to reward lawmakers at the expense of the environment. Most insiders agreed it was time to expose the outdated "perk system."

The assistant secretary for water continued to object, publicly calling me "a dangerous malcontent dedicated to opposing projects that really helped farmers nationwide."

The House governmental operations subcommittee was chaired by veteran lawmaker Henry Reuss, who disliked the perk system and was an acknowledged investigator of governmental misconduct.

Reuss was a mirthless power who rankled the "good ol' boys" by exposing countless add-ons to every budget and behind-the-scenes lobbying by governmental agencies for more work, whether it be ordering military equipment or digging out streams. He chaired a committee on banking, currency and housing. In that role, he could order investigative hearings at a moment's notice. He requested that I appear at 10 a.m. on June 3, 1971, to disclose our findings of "illegal activities by governmental agencies."

It was my first appearance before a congressional committee. Alita and I developed a formula prior to all of my extensive congressional hearings. She had a list of tough questions prepared by staff and we discussed not only an accurate answer, but also one that was easily understood.

I dutifully appeared as a young "whistle blower" and was treated humanely by the chairman and members of his hand-picked, reform-minded subcommittee, which believed that major budget reforms were needed. The questions were all "soft balls," and I was excused with thanks and commendation for exposing the continuing flood-control plans by the so-called public works agencies that had hidden from Congress the scope of their projects and the exorbitant monetary and environmental costs.

Most pleasing was that the Council on Environmental Quality (CEQ) accepted my recommendations and began forcing agencies to comply with NEPA, which required Environmental Impact Statements on all stream channelization projects ongoing and planned.

One of the most interesting oddities of this saga was a quiet meeting with the head of the Soil Conservation Service, who came to see me in my office to thank me for exposing his service's shady practices. He said he deeply regretted many of the destructive drainage projects that had been completed or commenced on his watch. He was going to seek immediate compliance with NEPA, which he assured me would halt most of the ongoing drainage plans and reduce future plans to only those that preserved the environmental quality of adjacent lands and required mitigation to balance the wildlife losses.

Furthermore, the Federal Coordination Act,

WILLIAM K. DUPONT
4 GREENVILLE CENTER
WILMINGTON, DELAWARE 19807

from the Wilmington Evening Journal

June 16, 1971

New Vigor for Interior

Conservationist Reed Takes Lead

By Stewart Udall

Capitol Hill veterans who followed the recent House hearings on stream channelization are agape over testimony by Nathaniel P. Reed, the Interior Department's new assistant secretary for Fish, Wildlife and Parks.

At congressional hearings bureaucrats usually "waffle" their comments, but the tall, thin Interior official came on like gangbusters. He accused the Soil Conservation Service and the U.S. Army Corps of Engineers of paying "nothing more than lip service" to good conservation. They were, he said, creating "the aquatic version of the dust bowl disaster" in their flood control, navigation and drainage projects.

As if that wasn't enough nonconformity for one day, Reed defied tradition on the issue of budget cuts. Most bureaucrats suffer in loyal silence when their fund requests are smothered by the imperious Office of Management and Budget (OMB). Not so Reed. He not only criticized the past shortchanging of Interior's Bureau of Sports Fisheries but promised to send Rep. Henry Reuss D-Wis., copies of the bureau's fund requests, Interior's revisions, and the final emasculations by OMB.

The episode left many old hands wondering just who Nathaniel P. Reed was and whether he could, indeed, survive in a town that has elevated double talk to a fine art. But Reed seems to be enjoying the flap immensely. Some conservationists compared him with Bill Ruckelshaus, whose tough talk won plaudits soon after he was named chief of the Environmental Protection Agency last December. There is a crucial difference between the two men, however. Ruckelshaus is an environmental novice, and his early bluntness has had a "look-at-me" quality designed to establish his credibility.

Reed needn't prove anything of the sort. He is the President's best environmental appointment to date, and comes to Washington after serving with distinction as the top conservation adviser to two Florida governors.

I talked with Reed a few days after his startling debut before the Reuss subcommittee. He was in a buoyant mood—partly because the Bureau of Sport Fisheries (BSF) had just been assigned over 150 new job slots after years of morale-killing cutbacks.

"Look," said the 37-year-old Interior aide, "I didn't come up here to play the maverick king. I'm on the team. But I also didn't come up here to condone the destruction of our rivers and streams. Channelization as now practiced is a disgrace. It must be stopped. I couldn't have testified otherwise."

Reed has wisely set himself a few priorities for the next few months, knowing that scatter-shooting would waste his administrative energies. With Interior Secretary Rogers C. B. Morton's backing, he has insisted that BSF biologists be heard early, loud and clear in watershed projects planned by the Soil Cons vation Service and the Engineers.

Reed has also served notice that he will tolerate the sloppy violations of Interio predator and control program, which is kill off wildlife throughout the West. Recent poi ings of bald and golden eagles in Wyom have strengthened his hand, and he announce stiff controls this October.

Just as emphatically, Reed has asked P Service and BSF officials to stop dawdling o the designation of their lands for the Natio Wilderness Preservation System.

Interior's new assistant secretary has gi President Nixon a slender new Reed of cre bility with conservationists—and he has grea strengthened Secretary Morton's environme tal credentials as well.

Los Angeles Times Syndicate

which required consultation with the U.S. Fish and Wildlife Service on public works projects, had not been enforced and became an intense issue for me. Within a year, all public works agencies were required to advise the Fish and Wildlife Service of their proposed projects and give the service time to modify or even veto projects before the agencies would waste millions of dollars preparing Environmental Impact Statements.

Although I never was accepted as anything more than a troublemaker by many of the construction agencies and the public works agencies, this was one of the high points during my first year in federal office.

To my surprise, the vast majority of my recommendations were enforced by OMB and CEQ.

OMB Director George Schultz actually called to thank me for disclosing what he called "the underground, expensive projects that had been able to avoid OMB's reviews and critical comments."

So, during my initial weeks in office, George Gardner and his brave team from the Fish and Wildlife Service won their first spurs with this exposé.

Wolves, Moose and a Frozen Adventure at Isle Royale National Park

"I begged for forgiveness but secretly rejoiced at surviving my adventure."

One of the most wonderful opportunities afforded me through my work as assistant interior secretary involved access to some of the nation's most important biological research. That is how I came to have a grand adventure with scientists, wolves and moose in the frigid wilds of northwest Michigan.

It was a fascinating, yet harrowing, experience that I cherish, especially now in my warm Florida home. I learned much about the web of life, about the interdependence that all species – including human beings – have on each other.

At the Department of Interior (DOI), I developed a firm friendship with Dr. Durward Allen of Purdue University that began when he visited Washington, D.C., as a member of the National Park Advisory Board. (Overseeing national parks was part of my duties.) He was in close contact with his great friend, scientist Starker Leopold, with whom I worked on numerous projects. They spent many happy times in my office and at dinner. One of their goals was to pressure National Park Service (NPS) Director George B. Hartzog, Jr., to dramatically increase the development of "sound science" in individual park operations. Sitting with these two great men, each with a keen sense of humor, was a genuine delight.

Allen was recognized by his peers as a wise sage of the many environmental and wildlife issues that confronted national park managers. His unique, long-term study of the wolf-moose relationship on Isle Royale National Park, a 45-mile-long island park in northwest Lake Superior in Michigan, was considered one of the most outstanding long-term scientific investigations of relationships between predator and prey – in this case between wolves and moose.

A century ago, it was common practice in many federally held lands to eliminate predators – including mountain lions and wolves in order to preserve and increase deer herds for human hunting. Just as land managers hoped, as the predators were extirpated the deer population irrupted. But the ecological damage the deer caused by their overgrazing was disastrous.

Famed ecologist and author Aldo Leopold (Starker Leopold's father), as a young forest service employee in the west, participated in wolf kills and witnessed the aftermath. He wrote about it in *A Sand County Almanac*, published in 1949 after his untimely death. Leopold told of how the increasing deer populations ate "every edible bush and seedling" and defoliated trees. Ultimately, too many deer with too little vegetation led to the starvation of many and the decline of the ecosystem. "I now suspect that just as a deer herd lives in mortal fear of its wolves, so does a mountain live in mortal fear of its deer," Leopold wrote. "And perhaps with better cause, for while a buck pulled down by wolves can be replaced in two or three years, a range pulled down by too many deer may fail of replacement in as many decades." Ultimately, Leopold concluded, predators were important to overall environmental health, something humans would understand if they learned to "think like a mountain." [37] It is wisdom that the NPS has come to embrace.

Allen's studies of wolf-moose relations at Isle Royale took him there in the dead of winter, where he stayed at the small NPS headquarters, assisted by Park Superintendent Hugh Beattie. They often were accompanied by a few graduate students and Don Murray, a superb pilot of a tiny aircraft fitted with skis that allowed aerial observation of the wolf packs. Critical information was gained on the wolves' strong sense of territory, and their innate ability to spot a vulnerable moose and kill it.

Killing a 900-pound moose is extraordinarily difficult for any predator. The moose defends itself by employing its hoofs: kicking, rising, and thumping downward. One hard hit on a wolf is sufficient to break bones and end its life. The moose has to be vulnerable to be successfully attacked. Allen's studies confirmed that, except for rare if not unique circumstances, the susceptible moose were elderly or "short-yearling" calves.

Once two years of age, the moose were physically too strong to be vulnerable. Allen's work revolved around two major areas: the constant conflict between wolf packs over territory, often ending in dead wolves, and the age and condition of the dead moose. The latter was determined by sawing the lower jawbone from the carcass.

The condition of the teeth was an all-important guide to the animal's health. The vast majority of the retrieved moose jawbones showed that their teeth were worn down and filled with cavities and abscesses from 12 to 14 years of chewing tough fir and other plant material. They were unable to effectively chew the needed plant material. In this state, their stomachs "growl" and they lose health. Following heavy snowfall or a long period of windy, extremely cold weather of 30 degrees or more below zero, they are significantly exhausted and vulnerable to attack.

Moose bone marrow, removed from carcass leg bones, was analyzed for fat content. Invariably, the dead moose were in very poor physical condition. The Allen Study was featured in National Geographic and was recognized by a large group of people who financially supported much of Allen's work, with NPS assistance. The major expenses were the costs of the all-important airplane, fuel, pilot and repairs. Without Don Murray, one of the most experienced and expert low-flying pilots, the study could not have been conducted over such a long period of time. It continues, to this day.

During one of our Washington, D.C., meetings, I begged Allen to let me join him on a short visit to Isle Royale. He issued an invitation with the warning that it was going to be one of the coldest experiences of my life and furnished me with a list of clothing needed to visit the arctic in mid-winter.

I flew on February 8, 1975, to Duluth, Minnesota, and landed in cold, low clouds. Beattie met me and drove to the take-off location in Ely, Minnesota, but said that it was too dangerous to fly that day to Isle Royale due to the low ceiling. I was to stay overnight at a nearby facility.

He urged me to put on my arctic clothing and join him to watch the start of an important dog sled race that began on a frozen lake. On arrival at the starting line, I could see perhaps a half-mile of the route ahead, as the path went straight across a frozen lake from the starting line and abruptly turned left. The dog teams then were hidden by dense forest as the trail continued on for miles over broken countryside. It was very exciting to watch the countdown and start, with the "musher" running behind until he had to jump on the sled's runners to guide the dogs and hang on for dear life.

I became so cold that I left for a warm meal and a nap after an hour. I had never seen dog sled racing in person and now admire both the men and women and, particularly, the dogs that train and appear to love the competition.

The next day, the weather was sufficiently clear to fly safely to the island where Allen was waiting. I met famed pilot Murray, whose tiny aircraft could carry just one passenger plus the pilot. I settled in, went over the clothing that Allen insisted I have and enjoyed lunch in a very warm, simple cabin that was the superintendent's winter headquarters and home of the Allen Study. I got an intense briefing and was warned that the weather patterns could change in minutes. In no case should anyone go out for a snowshoe walk without notifying someone of where he would be exploring. There was danger even on the frozen inlet of Lake Superior. Recognizing my love of adventure, Allen and Beattie begged me to follow the rules, saying my life might depend on my compliance.

Murray flew me that afternoon, cramped in the tiny plane not designed for a six-foot-four-inch passenger; almost immediately we spotted a frozen carcass of a thoroughly eaten moose perhaps a mile or two from the camp at the end of a Lake Superior inlet. Murray mentioned that the jawbone and leg had yet to be removed for the study of aging.

The next morning, we flew a longer route, seeing several packs of wolves that had eaten well and were either sleeping or playing. Finally, we flew directly over a pack on the hunt. The wolves paid no attention to the plane. I watched, fascinated by the approach of the wolf pack, led by the "alpha" lead male wolf, to a female moose feeding on low fir branches.

We circled and circled while the young wolves charged close to the moose, which backed up against a dead tree and repeatedly rose up and slammed her front feet down. After 10 minutes, the alpha male informed the pack that this particular moose was not on the day's kill list; they broke off and began a long trot looking for a vulnerable moose. We had to return to camp. I had leg cramps and was nearly frozen but rejoiced at the sight that Allen had so brilliantly described.

I had not realized that among Allen's incredible accomplishments was his ability as a camp cook. We ate like kings. He baked delicious bread, prepared meat and vegetable stews, and finished every dinner with a freshly baked pie or cake.

After a great night's sleep, aided by a touch of old single malt whiskey, I flew again with Murray for one hour, locating a kill that may have occurred the previous day. The carcass was still full of meat and the pack was sleeping in a semicircle around it. We flew to a nearby area where there had been territorial conflict between two packs of wolves. Allen wanted to know if a wolf had been killed. There was ample sign of a battle left in the snow, but no sign of blood or a dead wolf.

Upon our return, I begged to be able to get some exercise as the weather was perfect, so to speak, warming to 15 below zero. Beattie helped me select a proper fitting pair of snowshoes and we mushed along, giving me the feel of the botanical makeup of the island. It was vulnerable to being overgrazed by the very large herd of moose, which even the successful wolf packs were barely able to reduce to a "carrying capacity."

I saw a number of beaver lodges – huge pyramids of cut wood, carefully constructed. The beavers were deep in their dens as their young were about to be born. The animals had stacked piles of soft wood next to the den, frozen in ice, so they could burrow up and retrieve the nutritious wood without exposure to weather or wolves. I learned that, during the summer months, wolves watched the dens with care – one of their primary prey was beavers.

By midday, my legs were tired, a result of too

many hours spent behind my DOI desk.

We enjoyed an early lunch as Allen was also tired after flying, working on jawbone inspections, and a short walk on the frozen lake. He was going to fly with Murray again in the afternoon if the weather remained perfectly clear. We agreed to a nap time and then, depending on the weather, a visit to the dead moose and removal of its jawbone and leg.

I slept soundly for an hour in my separate building. The rest of the camp was quiet. The weather was superb: cold but clear. The snow sparkled. Temptation prompted me to disregard my earlier instructions, as I was determined to visit the carcass of the dead moose that I knew was at the end of the frozen inlet. I dressed in my arctic clothing and pulled on my snowshoes.

It was so surprisingly warm that after ten minutes of snowshoeing over the snow-topped ice, I shed the arctic jacket and wrapped it around my waist. I was tempted to remove a wind shirt that covered a thick, warm, woolen turtleneck sweater and a warm underwear top. Three-quarters of the way to the site I was perspiring, but thoroughly enjoying the walk on that glorious afternoon.

Before I reached the moose carcass, however, I stepped into a wet spot on what appeared to be a totally frozen lake, probably caused by a spring. The snowshoes' webbing froze and it was impossible to continue. I went slowly ashore and after some difficulty, removed the frozen leather straps that held the snowshoes to my legs. I beat the shoes against a tree, freeing the webbing from ice. I continued on the frozen lake toward the moose carcass.

I found the dead moose and unloaded from my small backpack a very sharp saw to remove its lower jaw and cut off one section of its legs. As I started to work, I heard an unforgettable noise that sounded like a runaway express train. Within minutes, the weather changed and a vicious storm roared in. The temperature plunged and the snow, driven by 25-mph-plus winds, made visibility just sufficient to follow my inbound tracks back towards camp.

I quickly put the arctic jacket on and hastily began following my trail before it became covered with fresh snow. Although I was aware of the soft spot in the ice, the combination of the violent wind and snow often kept my eyes closed and my forward visibility was restricted to just feet. I was careless and stepped again into the wet spot, instantly freezing the snowshoe webbing. I had to go ashore again, take off the snowshoes, and beat them to free them from ice.

I was now faced with the problem of reattaching the straps of the snowshoes. The leather attachments had frozen and my cold hands could not soften the laces sufficiently to reattach the shoes. For the first time, I realized that unless I made a gigantic effort, I could be in trouble, as the temperature was dropping and the snowfall was increasing. Although my hands felt frozen, by clasping the leather thongs in my mouth I softened them sufficiently to finally be able to attach the snowshoes to my boots. With a mighty determination, I rose, carefully avoiding the soft spot, and began the trek back to the camp. I could barely see my former path, as the snow and wind were covering my trail.

After 45 minutes of leaning into the wind and snow, I knew I was close to camp. I could hear the men starting snowmobiles and yelling instructions on what directions to take.

I yelled at the top of my voice, "I'm all right, just 300 yards away. Don't panic!" But of course they could not hear me.

I distinctly heard Beattie holler at Allen: "If we lose the assistant secretary, my career in the National Park Service will come to an abrupt end!"

Allen replied, "I would lose a friend and a key supporter of the study. We must find him."

Gratified by their concern, I increased my pace and arrived just before they headed out on snowmobiles to search for me. They were relieved if not overjoyed by my arrival, but most unhappy about my unannounced departure from camp during what was

designated as nap time. I begged for forgiveness but secretly rejoiced at surviving my adventure.

The storm persisted for two days, making flying impossible. We examined a collection of retrieved jawbones and carefully noted their condition. We played cards, read reports and novels, and watched television on Hockey Night in Canada. Again, we ate like kings. I allowed a very old fox into the dining area, completely against the rules in a national park; he shared three small meals with us every day. He had little time remaining, lived in warmth under the camp building, and was my welcomed guest. When I left, I made sure that he had a stash of extra food hidden from Beattie, whom I begged to continue to feed him. Later, Beattie informed me that the fox "passed" in the spring but enjoyed our company and had a full stomach per my instructions.

When I finally took off for one more flight with Murray, we almost immediately located a pack of wolves that was on the hunt after the terrible winter storm. Moose were everywhere and I'm confident the wolves had full stomachs that afternoon.

Boundless thanks go to Dr. Durward Allen, a real friend and great biologist, to Hugh Beattie, superintendent of Isle Royale National Park, and to Don Murray, a devoted pilot who made the study of the interactions between moose and wolves a continuing, unique wildlife study.

It was a great adventure and I'm glad I lived to tell it.

Note – Wolves, Moose and a Frozen Adventure at Isle Royale

[37] Aldo Leopold, *A Sand County Almanac* (New York: Ballantine Books, 1949, 1966), 137-140.

The Allen Study Continues to This Day (in 2016)...

Don Murray

The wolves weathered a serious reduction in their numbers because of parvovirus that may have been brought to the island by a visitor's dog. Inbreeding has been a real problem as no new wolf packs or individual wolves have been evident for many years. There are ample wolf packs adjacent to Isle Royale, but no new wolf packs have migrated to the island. The moose population continues to grow, threatening the island's botanical makeup.

There are two alternatives that seem viable, both supported by recognized experts:

- Alternative One: Add new blood. Release a wolf or two to revitalize the remaining eight or nine wolves.
- Alternative Two: Let nature take its course of action. Isle Royale is a national park, where nature's role is considered a major objective. If the surviving wolves are unable to produce pups, the pack seems doomed. One scientist believes it is better to start with a fresh pack or two.

Most authorities agree that without wolves, the foliage on Isle Royale (in the manner described by Aldo Leopold) will be significantly damaged by ever-increasing numbers of moose until they ultimately die off from lack of food. Some wilderness enthusiasts think that is acceptable, if that is what non-intervention brings.

Don Murray was the key to Allen's continuing, epic research effort. Born in 1928, he was on his own at the age of 12. He completed formal education through the eighth grade and became a truck driver at age 14. As a teenager, he leased small planes and barnstormed with friends. He volunteered as a soldier during the Korean War, earning three Bronze stars. Married in 1950, he and Helen produced seven children.

Don had an extraordinary ability to see animals in the field. His intuitive understanding of animal behavior and his ability to fly a very small aircraft proved indispensible to his annual work on Isle Royale, where he was the winter study pilot from 1959 to 1979.

No better pilot or man worked so diligently as the key to Dr. Durward Allen's unique study of the moose and wolves of Isle Royale.

The Yellowstone National Park Grizzly Bear Saga

"Once they find garbage, they will search for it the rest of their lives."

Our national parks mean many things to Americans. They are places of wonder, of wilderness, of recreation – and re-creation of the human soul. As our thinking about the parks has changed, so has our treatment of the natural resources and wildlife within them.

In the case of Yellowstone National Park, I became involved when park managers, guided by scientists, realized that the decades-long practice of feeding human garbage to the bears needed to stop. Bears – black bears and grizzly bears – were accustomed to eating our human food and therefore might end up in clashes with tourists that might become deadly.

By the 1930s, "bear feeding shows," for which hundreds of humans gathered in an amphitheater to watch bears rummage through garbage from the park's hotels, had become standard fare. One report noted that at least 75 animals showed up for one evening "bear cafeteria," in which a truck drove into a gated area and dumped garbage for the animals.[38]

Who wouldn't love a bear show? It guaranteed visitors a look at these massive, magnificent creatures, seemingly from a safe distance. Indeed, the spectacles were considered great recreation and compared to the gladiator fights of ancient Rome. Some visitors felt otherwise, stating that the bears looked sad and degenerate compared to their wild ancestors.[39]

Some bears were notorious for holding up traffic and demanding food from passing cars. After all, it is no coincidence that the cartoon creation, Yogi Bear, lived in "Jellystone Park." Tourists loved it.

By the 1960s, Yellowstone National Park maintained a minimum of five garbage dumps located near the park's major campgrounds and lodges. Garbage sites changed infrequently, but for years they operated near developments inside and outside park boundaries. Outside the park, a large garbage dump at West Yellowstone and a smaller one at Cooke City also attracted a number of grizzly bears.

Scientists, including Dr. Stanley Cain, eminent chair of the Department of Conservation at the University of Michigan, who served four years as Assistant Secretary of the Interior under Secretary Steward Udall, were concerned. Cain had spent time considering the impact of garbage-addicted grizzly bears on visitors and worried that the number of bear-tourist interactions and human deaths from these interactions was growing. Although Cain was concerned that forcing a change in the bears' diets could provoke more interaction with tourists, he decided that allowing the bears to seek human food posed a greater risk to their well-being and to tourists. He ordered the garbage dumps closed.

Within days of my joining the Department of the Interior (DOI), Cain came to see me and we covered many topics, including his past environmental victories and defeats. He concluded with a list of what he called "opportunities and serious problems" that he was turning over to me.

I was quite taken aback by the number of serious problems! And Yellowstone's bears were to become a major part of my concerns for many years.

Cain said that one of the most vexing issues that had bedeviled him was his decision to close the garbage dumps within Yellowstone National Park after all scientific evidence concluded that a garbage bear, in time, would become a dead bear.

The Craighead brothers, who had conducted a long-term grizzly bear study, financed in part by the National Geographic Society, concentrated on bears that were using the garbage dumps as principal sources of food, especially during the spring and early fall months. In the Craighead study, bears feeding in garbage dumps were easily tranquilized while they fitted them with radio collars and removed one tooth per bear to determine aging. Then, the bears were revived and released.

The study showed that as their dependence on human garbage grew, grizzly bears were losing their fear of man and becoming a significant danger to park visitors. Cain's data-based decision to close the garbage dumps and have all garbage removed from the park and sent to bear-proof disposal areas, definitely riled the popular Craigheads, who wanted to leave everything as it was. Cain warned that he was bequeathing to me the dubious distinction of having to make his decision permanent, even though it meant that a "number of bears" that had grown dependent on garbage would have to be "removed" from the population. That would make no one happy.

Cain continued his briefing by reviewing the attempt to increase the number and quality of scientists within the park system. He felt that the 1963 Advisory Committee to the National Park Service (NPS) study, chaired by Dr. Starker Leopold, was worth my study and implementation. He noted there was great reluctance and resistance by many senior NPS superintendents to having a strong science program or assigning highly qualified scientists to major national parks because they feared their extraordinary management authority could be challenged.

Dr. Starker Leopold

During a second session held the next day, Cain called Leopold at the University of California at Berkeley and together we enjoyed an hour-long telephone conference on far-ranging subjects.

Our chemistry was excellent. High on Leopold's list of priorities was "science in the national park system." He had chaired a high-level committee that was very critical of many decisions being made throughout the national parks without expert scientific review. The vast majority of major park superintendents considered themselves "lords of their domain." The thought that a young Ph.D. would question their decisions was abhorrent, especially if the scientist was female. Leopold had made arrangements at Berkeley to be able to return to Washington on a frequent basis to insist that NPS Director George Hartzog and the assistant secretary implement the Leopold Committee's recommendations.

Leopold, son of famed ecologist Aldo Leopold, made a date to visit with me in July 1971 to continue his campaign for a vigorous park science program. He also wanted to discuss the vast opportunities to expand the NPS in Alaska due to the pending passage of the Alaska Lands Act.

He urged me to fly to Yellowstone in July and meet park Superintendent Jack Anderson and a favorite former student, Dr. Mary Meagher, to discuss the issues of grizzly bear, elk and bison management.

I followed his advice and spent three days being briefed on the park's problems with a "contention in the scientific community" that the number of elk within the park was destroying a variety of habitats. Meagher briefed me on the perceived problems with the contagious brucellosis disease and Montana's request to corral all the Yellowstone bison and remove all that carried the disease lest they infect nearby cattle herds. As elk also carried the disease and were intermingled with cattle on the periphery of the park, it made no sense to pin the disease solely on the park's bison herd.

Leopold urged me to meet him for his annual fall inspection of Yellowstone, combining reports on wildlife issues with afternoon fly fishing. We agreed to meet at Yellowstone in September, when he stayed at the park's Mammoth Hot Springs to fish the adjacent rivers. I suggested we could develop a four-day meeting schedule – four mornings devoted to ecological threats to wildlife and the Yellowstone ecosystem and afternoons devoted to fishing. He thought that was a splendid idea and we held those sessions annually for the next five years.

I met with Anderson at park headquarters in July 1971. He was the personification of how a superintendent of the "Mother Park" should look and act. He was larger than life. We toured the park, dined together, fished together, and talked and talked. He described his encounters with the Craighead brothers and his conviction that they violated their research permits. He said they paid no attention to the NPS staff or visitors and did what they wanted to do. They acted as if Yellowstone was their park.

Anderson had voided the brothers' original research permits and a war of words had begun. He then ordered senior representatives from the NPS and U.S. Fish and Wildlife Service to redraft the research permits. The Craigheads found the revised permits unacceptable and decided on their own to end their research on garbage-dump bears within Yellowstone National Park.

Leopold gave credit to the brothers' astonishing "breakthrough" research using radio collars to track bears from spring awakening to the denning and the long winter's sleep. Leopold, Anderson and other highly respected wildlife experts were critical of the data, which they believed was tainted by bears that were habituated to human garbage. The Craigheads maintained the vast majority of Yellowstone bears needed human food and that the closure of the garbage dumps threatened their existence.

The Craigheads issued a series of comments critical of NPS regarding the closure of the garbage dumps and the loss of their research permits. Their scathing comments were carried in many Rocky Mountain area newspapers. I urged caution in responding, as the Craigheads were unquestionably recognized expert scientists, and had a large following due to the prominence that *National Geographic* magazine had given their work on Yellowstone's grizzly bears.

Leopold and I eagerly anticipated the September meeting. Anderson was devoted to Leopold and was beginning the metamorphosis of accepting recommendations from Glen Cole, Meagher, and the fishery biologists on management issues within the park. It was obvious that I needed staff assistance to handle the growing disputes on many issues concerning management of the park and, moreover, the application of research in our national parks.

I had a problem: My lead wildlife staffer, Jim Ruch, was deeply involved in preparing the Presidential Executive Order and Environmental Impact Statement banning the use of 1080, the dangerous pesticide discussed in the essay about banning 1080. These documents would be vital to our efforts to survive a legal challenge.

Another of my key aides, George Gardner, was an Everglades and water expert and was deeply involved with Leopold's brother, Dr. Luna Leopold, and Dr. Arthur Marshall with their epic study

of the potential impact of development within the Big Cypress wetlands in south Florida (see *Less is More: Defeating the Miami Jetport, Creating a National Preserve.*) With that assignment finished, Gardner became my lead grizzly bear staff person. He maintained contact with Anderson and Starker Leopold two or three times a week. His wise counsel was invaluable to me.

The grizzly bear news from Yellowstone in the fall of 1971 was not encouraging. A number of bears, accustomed to feeding on human garbage, had to be removed from the park. At first, they were tranquilized and flown at great expense to distant locations within the park far from a dump. Others were relocated to adjacent national forests, sent to zoos, or, as a last resort, destroyed and utilized as scientific specimens. In the 1960s, in a good faith move to protect the animals, marked Craighead research bears were relocated multiple times. Sadly, mother grizzly bears simply brought their cubs, once they were weaned, directly to where the nearest garbage dump had been.

Moving bears was a failure. Once hooked on garbage, they found their way back to the park and to a former or closed garbage dump, sometimes within a few days.

The Craigheads maintained a steady drumbeat that the superintendent and the park service, including NPS Director Hartzog and me, were allowing, if not encouraging, the destruction of grizzly bears in Yellowstone National Park. They urged a change that would reopen the garbage dumps and lessen the amount of garbage to be delivered daily and weekly. They maintained that it was possible to "wean" the bears off of garbage.

When Leopold, Anderson, and I met in September, we covered four days of informal but structured agenda items that were vital to the park's wildlife issues. The loss of a great number of bears was discussed carefully. Many were old and would not have been alive if not for garbage.

Unbeknownst to me, a research paper had been recently published describing the loss of numerous bear cubs to boar grizzlies when their mothers were distracted by feeding in the dumps. Leopold made and repeated the point: Bears that were allowed to feed on garbage were permanently imprinted. They would seek human garbage forever. They would "get in trouble, serious trouble," he said, and continue seeking human food from campgrounds and even trailers. There would be an increase in human deaths directly attributed to the bears' demands for human food. It was impossible to wean bears from garbage, he said. The only solution was to "tough it out."

We were unhappy that the park had not received adequate funding to completely "bear-proof" garbage containers within the campgrounds. I was dismayed to learn that quantities of Yellowstone trout were caught and killed daily from the lake, then photographed and discarded in the garbage containers.

Photographs of grizzly bears opening supposedly secure garbage containers and devouring human food infuriated me. I addressed this problem with the congressional appropriations committees on my return to Washington. I was so concerned about criticism of the park's grizzly bear program and personal attacks on me, the park's superintendent and scientists, that I urged DOI Secretary Rogers Morton to seek a review by the National Academy of Sciences, which subsequently created a Committee on Yellowstone Grizzly Bears.

The committee's conclusions regarding the negative role of garbage dumps were identical to those expressed by Drs. Leopold and Cain and supported by Dr. Durward Allen of Purdue, our nation's preeminent wolf expert. The committee's most important criticism was the failure of the park's managers to carefully document the removal of bears. That was corrected immediately.

Congressional oversight hearings were often confrontational. Leopold's assistance was invaluable as I prepared my testimony. Good staff work protected me on the toughest of questions and saved the day. Frankly, I often felt lonely, as the rest of the conservation-environmental community waited to see if the corner would be turned and the bear would slowly but surely make a comeback.

Dr. Gilbert Grosvenor, the well-known and respected leader of the National Geographic Society, had championed the Craigheads' research and made the two highly photogenic men national heroes. He would call me with a simple question: "Do you think you are right?" He was a great admirer of Leopold and liked me, and was willing to listen to our perspective. In the end, he shared many of our concerns.

However, reports of the continuing number of park grizzly bears that had to be destroyed made national news. I cannot begin to describe my personal feelings when a call would come in from the park detailing the removal of bears that had invaded campgrounds or torn up vehicles in search of human food. The Craigheads, confident that their position was scientifically sound, ran a highly efficient campaign denigrating Anderson and pointing out that I had "no qualifications" to support the judgment of senior park service officials. They criticized the park's determination to keep the garbage dumps closed.

Dr. John Craighead was a federal employee, a member of the U.S. Fish and Wildlife Service. The director of the U.S. Fish and Wildlife Service informed me that Craighead's constant criticisms had not been peer reviewed for their scientific basis and were in violation of federal rules.

I asked John Craighead to meet me at the Mammoth Springs Hotel to discuss the problem. I asked Gardner to join me to keep accurate track of the meeting. Craighead admitted that he felt so strongly that the grizzly bears were being "exterminated" by the Yellowstone staff that he did not feel bound by the federal rules of peer review. After a heated discussion, he agreed to follow federal procedures. Thereafter, as a workaround, he furnished his brother, Frank, who was not employed by the federal government, data and his interpretation of the data without peer review.

I was so concerned about the continuing loss of grizzly bears, especially after confrontations with herds of sheep allowed to graze within known grizzly bear territories in adjacent national forests that I agreed to place the bear on the Endangered Species list as "threatened" in 1975. This gave the Fish and Wildlife Service the opportunity to question the U.S. Forest Service's grazing allotments within known bear territories. In my mind it was counter-productive to lease grazing sites when the Forest Service's own biologists acknowledged that the areas would encourage conflict with grizzly bears. It took time for Forest Service leaders to free themselves of the political influences that permitted grazing leases and major timber harvesting in key grizzly bear territories.

An epic confrontation took place at the 1975 September meeting at Mammoth Hot Springs. The meetings had always been open to the public. Leopold and I invited several experts to deliver papers on a variety of subjects. For instance, Dr. Maurice Hornocker, who had become a friend, led a discussion on my view that mountain lions should be transferred from a "surplus population" in Idaho to the park to manage the size of the ever-increasing northern elk herd. He suggested that a study might prove that there were more lions within the park than were acknowledged.

His observation and recommendation for a mountain lion study was borne out by subsequent, excellent scientific field studies (funded in the 1990s by my former staffer, Amos Eno, and the National Fish and Wildlife Foundation). The only problem the mountain lions have is that they are successfully hunted and shot by supposed "big game hunters" when they exit the park's boundary.

Leopold, Dr. Durward Allen and Glen Cole enlightened me and the audience about the power of "replacement," the tendency of any species to compensate for extraordinary losses by accelerating birth rates. As bears died or were killed, space within the park opened and additional food supplies became available with less competition. Data suggested that surviving wild bears were beginning to show increased birth rates.

Suddenly, the Craighead brothers marched into the room. Frank declared that the meeting was "illegal" because notice had not been published in the Federal Register. I countered that the meeting was "informal" and that notice had been given to federal and state agencies, academia and the general public. As a matter of fact, half of the room was filled with curious citizens not affiliated with the government who were fascinated by the subjects discussed over the four mornings.

Frank Craighead asked for time to show a computer printout of his conclusions that the grizzly bear would be "exterminated" from the Yellowstone ecosystem by the mid-1980s. A long printout was displayed. Leopold asked a number of highly technical questions on how the data had been obtained and assembled and how the conclusions were reached. Frank was very emotional about his sincere belief that the bears were being 'exterminated' by the NPS with my support. He urged that the garbage dumps be reopened and the bears allowed to be "weaned from garbage."

Leopold answered that it was his opinion, shared by many other scientists, that animals, especially bears, cannot be weaned off garbage. "Once they find garbage, they will search for it the rest of their lives," he said. "Every cub that is taken to a garbage dump by its mother is forever imprinted on the delights of human garbage."

Frank responded that the Yellowstone grizzly bears were doomed without garbage. Leopold looked him in the eye and calmly stated, "Frank, between Yellowstone's 2,466,586 acres, surrounded by five national forests totaling nearly 12 million acres, you must admit that there are grizzly bears throughout the greater Yellowstone ecosystem that will repopulate the park in time without the need to be fed human garbage."

There was uncomfortable silence broken by

Dr. Charles Loveless, the chief of research for the U.S. Fish and Wildlife Service, who had examined the printout and, looking directly at the Craigheads, pronounced, "Frank and John, an old statistical rule: Garbage in produces garbage out!"

I called for an immediate recess to prevent bodily harm.

Later that evening, as he sat by the Yellowstone River, sipping aged bourbon, Leopold commented, "There are ample wild bears in this vast system that will reproduce without garbage. You will have to be patient, as it will take time, but it will happen."

Soon thereafter, I had the privilege of meeting and signing off on Yellowstone National Park's appointment of Dr. Richard Knight to lead grizzly bear research. I urged him on, and his high-quality research brought great credit to him personally and the park's management effort as it sought to understand the dynamics of the bear recovery program. I was able to gain significant funding for his efforts and the entire science program within the park.

One of my major disappointments was the length of time it took to close the garbage dumps outside the park that served West Yellowstone and Cooke City. The lack of leadership and cooperation by the town fathers of those two gateway communities still irritates me. I had to threaten them with penalties under the Endangered Species Act. They continued to keep a number of bears alive on garage so tourists could sit on the periphery of their respective dumps and photograph "garbage-dump bears."

The grizzly controversy effort took a toll on me personally as I had to withstand five-plus years of constant criticism, defend an unpopular program, and deal with an issue that for the majority of the American people was difficult to understand. The impact has been tempered by the fact that today the grizzly bear population is at record numbers. Bear populations have expanded from approximately 180 during the Craighead years to over 700 today. The grizzly population continues to grow and expand its range well beyond park boundaries and the Yellowstone ecosystem.

I have always regretted that the Craighead brothers were not able to embrace with enthusiasm the palpable recovery of bears not dependent upon garbage.

Frank Craighead continued his innovative work with a range of modern telemetry equipment, producing exceptional results for wildlife management, especially in Alaska.

Later, while serving on the board of the National Geographic Society, I had the pleasure of voting for the brothers to receive the Society's coveted John Oliver La Gorce medals in 1979 for their innovative work that has led to incredible advances in radio telemetry and LANDSAT satellite imagery.

I left office in 1976 with the strong feeling that the corner had been turned and the bears would make it. Most importantly, I left highly competent staff to continue the work of the Interagency Grizzly Bear Study Team.

Dr. Knight and Dr. Chris Servheen (appointed FWS grizzly recovery coordinator in 1981) formed a remarkably successful team. They were aided by former members of my staff: John Spinks had become FWS deputy regional director, and Amos Eno of the National Audubon Society and, after 1986, became executive director of the National Fish and Wildlife Foundation. As of 2014, the bear has recovered in every corner of the park and throughout the surrounding national forests.

I am forever grateful for the support of Dr. Starker Leopold, Dr. Stanley Cain, Dr. Durward Allen, Dr. Maurice Hornocker, Dr. Glen Cole and Dr. Mary Meagher. Each of them was important to me not only as a wise group of advisors, but as friends. I seriously doubt that any other assistant secretary in the history of the Interior Department ever sought and received advice from such a group of renowned and dedicated experts in land and wildlife management.

Staff members Amos Eno and John Spinks, who replaced Jim Ruch, deserve recognition for efforts in the 1980s and early 1990s to augment and coordinate vastly expanded intergovernmental grizzly recovery initiatives after the administration changed.

In 1985, Amos helped establish the Interagency Grizzly Bear Committee (IGBC), which included the five National Forests and states of Idaho, Montana and Wyoming as full partners in the grizzly recovery effort. The IGBC coordinated research and law enforcement patrols and mandated consistent management policies by all land management agencies. It also implemented bear-proof dumpsters and food-storage regulations throughout the bears' habitat.

Amos successfully worked with the IGBC to convince key members of Congress to secure additional funding for the IGBC's implementation of grizzly recovery throughout the bears' habitat and expanding range. John Spinks had the foresight and wisdom in 1981 to hire Dr. Christopher Servheen, who has led the recovery effort for the Yellowstone grizzly population and other subpopulations. Chris is still the grizzly bear recovery coordinator as I write this. His mission was extremely difficult as he had to coordinate all bear-related activities in five national forests, BLM lands surrounding Yellowstone National Park, and two FWS refuges, in addition to working with the NPS and state wildlife agencies.

During my tenure, I was unable to convince the leadership of the Forest Service that it should become partners in preserving the grizzly bear. The Forest Service land managers were "influenced" by members of Congress to increase timber harvesting and maintain grazing permits for sheep and cattle near the park's boundaries. They resisted innovative regulations that required careful consideration of all grazing permits within the national forests in grizzly bear territory.

Change is often very difficult, especially as the Forest Service, congressional delegations, governors and state wildlife agencies all had differing views on the need for change within known grizzly bear territories.

Servheen's remarkable success story is one of the reasons for the great bears' recovery and expansion of territory. His professional story is difficult to fully appreciate unless one recognizes the incredible problems of working within the confines of interagency bureaucracy. Despite this, he managed to protect the bears as their populations expanded far beyond the boundaries of Yellowstone National Park.

After my departure, the grizzly population in Yellowstone and surrounding areas slowly recovered, alleviating my anxiety about their future and the killing of garbage-habituated bears. Leopold would remind me that I was forced into the issue with my appointment at DOI and the need to close the dumps. He told me, "I know you cried when a sow and cubs had to be captured and sent to a zoo, but they had been ruined by the attraction of garbage. You will live long enough to see a remarkable recovery of this great bear – *Ursus Arctos Horribilis.*" And he was right.

Both Leopold and Cain repeatedly called and shared the good news about nature's power of replacement: more space, less competition, more food, less loss of cubs. In fact, the strong well-conditioned "wild bears" were producing twins, even triplets. It was worth the criticism to achieve the goal of a "wild bear" inhabiting a far larger ecosystem.

There are now wild grizzly bears in every one of the sites that experts selected to gauge the great bear's recovery. It took time and endless wrangling, even a bit of suffering and tears, but we stayed the course and the great bear has recovered. Though every year brings new challenges, it is hoped we soon can de-list the bear from the Endangered Species Act.

Interestingly, when wolves were reintroduced into Yellowstone National Park in 1995, the grizzlies discovered a new "friend." When they arise from their long winter hibernation, bears seek out the remains of wolf kills (in many cases, aged elk) or even follow wolf packs and steal their kills. The wolves often surrounded a bear that had taken over a freshly killed elk, howling in annoyance, but they are smart enough not to challenge the bear. Three to four hundred pounds of elk is a great way for a bear coming out of hibernation to regain its strength. Females with cubs are particularly grateful for an elk dinner.

"HE WANTS TO GET OUT OF THE NATIONAL PARK. TOO MANY PEOPLE!"

FOR NATHANIEL REED; WITH VERY BEST WISHES —

The bears still face many issues, many of them driven by human management of the environment.

One continuing dispute on the great bear's status concerns its dependence in late fall on the nuts of the high-altitude white bark pine. Disease and a century of forest mismanagement, which included the reluctance of setting controlled fires in a fire-adapted ecosystem, are impacting the pines, thus limiting the number of nuts. Bears favor them for adding an important final layer of fat before retiring to their hibernation den. The bears, like us, will have to adapt to changing habitat conditions and an array of traditional food sources. I am confident they will survive, if not continue to expand their ranges.

The Greater Yellowstone Coalition, made up of 3,000 members who live within a radius of the "Mother Park" and surrounding forests, reported in 2014 human fatalities occurred during 2011 and 2012. These tragic events occurred despite years of work with the Forest Service to "bear-safe" garbage bins and food storage containers, provide better signage and close or move campsites due to persistent encounters with grizzlies.

The coalition accelerated efforts to enhance its existing program of providing bear-proof bins to communities that were experiencing repeated human-bear conflicts. Although progress is being made, more needs to be accomplished. The leadership of the coalition acknowledges the fact that "a fed bear is a dead bear."

The group is concentrating on the entire 20 million acres, which includes five national forests and 164 developed campgrounds. In all, the project requires bear-safe containers throughout the vast ecosystem.

The Greater Yellowstone Coalition is committed to ending the necessity of killing a garbage-addicted grizzly bear – a worthy, long overdue goal that requires the Forest Service and the states to be active partners. They have been joined by the Yellowstone Association, of which I am one of the founders. Due to the incredible generosity of the board members and concerned citizens, vast improvements in visitor education and additional land acquisitions have become worthy goals.

Even experienced hikers must be prepared to meet grizzly bears. An unexpected encounter with a mother bear with cubs will always result in a serious confrontation. Bear spray and frequent noises to warn bears of human presence can minimize fatal conflicts, but the grizzly bear must be recognized as a very dangerous animal.

May the bear not only survive, but also continue to prosper.

About The Yellowstone Park Foundation

During the 1996 summer months, I received a telephone call from Michael Finley, superintendent of Yellowstone National Park. He was a close friend, as he was a major force in bringing federal litigation against the state of Florida for allowing highly polluted water to enter the Everglades system and threaten the integrity of the rich botanical diversity of Everglades National Park.

Michael was an impressive human being with an appetite for forceful decisions. He described a vision he had of creating a Yellowstone Foundation similar to the successful Yosemite National Park model that had made great strides in raising corporate, foundation and major private donations. These funds added features and repair infrastructure that congressional appropriators could not or would not include in the park service budget.

I was highly supportive of his Yellowstone initiative, as I had encouraged the creation of the Yosemite effort with my great friend Bill Lane, publisher of *Sunset* magazine.

A diverse group met at Mammoth Hot Springs. We shared our love of the "mother park" and our growing concern that important educational projects were inadequately funded. Further preservation of many buildings – and of objects that were included in the earliest days of the park's opening that were inadequately stored in an ancient warehouse and without attention – would be lost forever.

Within an hour of the start of the meeting, sitting around the Finley's dining room, we agreed to initiate the legal steps necessary to create the Yellowstone Park Foundation.

Included among the founders was my great friend, John Good, who had served with great distinction as superintendent of Everglades National Park. The group also included major land owners adjacent to the park, summer home owners who lived outside the park along the Yellowstone River and a coterie of Yellowstone Park lovers who recognized this opportunity to raise significant funds to enhance, improve and even construct a major visitor's educational center at Old Faithful, the most important tourist destination within the park. The list of needs and opportunities was long, well documented by Finley's staff and it encouraged us to combine our talents to solve an obvious major problem of national if not international importance.

Thanks to a member with an extensive legal background, the foundation was legally formed within months. The board consisted of an amazing number of retired successful businessmen and concerned women who had vast contacts with the philanthropic and corporate worlds.

Our mission was clearly stated:

The Yellowstone Park Foundation is dedicated to ensuring that America's Park endures for generations. As the official fundraising partner of Yellowstone National Park, the Foundation is committed to raising funds and resources to provide a margin of excellence for Yellowstone and its visitors' experiences.

Federal appropriations provide Yellowstone's basic, day-to-day operations. However, these funds do not cover additional needs, including, for example, long-term wildlife research, preservation of historic documents and artifacts, and educational exhibits.

Grants and in-kind contributions from the Yellowstone Park Foundation help fund such projects, as well as innovative new programs and facilities that help enhance visitor experiences associated with the Park.

The Yellowstone Park Foundation is the official fundraising partner of Yellowstone National Park, and is a nonprofit. The Foundation receives no annual government funding; it relies instead upon the generous support of private citizens, foundations, and corporations to ensure that Yellowstone's great gifts to the world will never diminish.

The list of projects that the Foundation has financially supported is long and truly impressive. Highlights are many, but actions being taken to preserve the largest concentration of Yellowstone cutthroat trout, the construction of the Old Faithful Visitor Education Center, and creation of the new visitor's site overlooking Artist Point are just a few examples of the incredible generosity and foresight employed to create and attract a world-class board of directors to the Yellowstone Foundation.

The Yellowstone Park Foundation continues its incredible support for high-priority programs that cannot be funded through the National Park Service. In the midst of the Foundation's Yellowstone Forever Campaign – a $40 million, five-year effort, these priorities include:

- Preserving the resources and history of Yellowstone and connecting with future stewards and advocates of Yellowstone and parks throughout the country.
- Restoring and making accessible the trails and overlooks within the Grand Canyon of the Yellowstone.
- Restoring historic museums, built in the 1920s, such as Fishing Bridge, Norris, Madison and more.
- Transforming the historic north entrance (Roosevelt Arch landscape) to meet today's transportation needs and provide a safe entrance to the park.
- Creating a new Yellowstone Youth Campus that will double the number of students learning in an environment that will teach us how to live in a more sustainable way.
- Funding vital youth education programs to develop future stewards and leaders for our national parks.
- Funding ongoing wildlife research and funding wildlife and visitors safety programs to preserve these incredible resources.

I am honored to be a founding member. It is a remarkable feature of the American people – a small group dedicated to a purpose can yield wonders.

My love of the Mother Park is becoming a national love affair, thanks to The Yellowstone Park Foundation and superb management of the world's first national park can produce miracles.

Notes – The Yellowstone National Park Grizzly Bear Saga

[38] Alfred Runte, *National Parks: The American Experience* (Lincoln, NE: University of Nebraska Press, 1979), 168.

[39] Ibid., 169.

National Elk Refuge, photo © Tony Hough

Bison and Butz

"Damn you, I have given my word!"

A few days before I was to make my first official visit to Yellowstone National Park, Superintendent Jack Anderson called to inform me that a tourist had been gored to death by a bison.

The rangers' report indicated that a pair of tourists from New Jersey stopped their car next to an aging bison that was lying asleep in soft grass near the road. The tourists walked up to the bison and the husband took several photographs at ever-decreasing distances. Dissatisfied by the sleeping bison's failure to stand up, the man's wife dropped a large rock on the bison's rear end, rangers reported. The bison woke with a start, moved forward and "hooked" the photographer in his stomach with its horn, tossing him out of its way as it proceeded to join other males resting nearby. The tourist died.

Two days later, U.S. Sen. Harrison Williams of New Jersey called and demanded that I have what he called "the offending bison" killed. I had the unhappy experience of attempting to explain to the senator that there was no way the bison could possibly be identified and, furthermore, the so-called "accident" had been caused by one of his constituents. The phone call ended abruptly with a warning, "I'd be more concerned about tourists than dangerous wildlife if you want to last in government!" I thought to myself, "Welcome to the problems managers face in our national parks!"

On arrival at West Yellowstone airport, I was met by the superintendent. Anderson and I discussed the bison and bear issues and agreed on the outline of a one-page flyer that would warn tourists that wildlife was dangerous and should not to be approached. Furthermore, the flier would say, food was an "attractant" that encouraged bears to enter campgrounds or attempt to force their way into recreational vehicles. Human food had to be tightly secured.

Anderson had prepared a series of briefings on the major issues confronting wildlife management at what we considered the "Mother Park."

The grizzly bear confrontations had begun as the park's garbage dumps had been closed and some bears were struggling to survive by invading campgrounds and attempting to enter recreational vehicles.

Glen Cole, the park's highly regarded supervisory research biologist, briefed me on the issue of elk herd management, in which park managers were being criticized for encouraging the herd to expand and cause significant changes in vegetation. The ongoing disputes included the proposition that the supposed excessive number of elk living within the park needed to be reduced by sport hunting.

With thousands of acres of Forest Service land and other public lands in Idaho, Montana and Wyoming, it was clear that an increased effort by state wildlife managers in scheduling sport hunting seasons could reduce the numbers of elk dramatically without breaking the concept of what a national park is supposed to be.

On my second day of briefings, I learned about an ongoing dispute with the park's three adjacent state departments of agriculture over the problem of controlling brucellosis, an infectious disease endemic in elk and bison. The disease can cause abortion of fetuses. The ranching communities of the neighboring states wanted their herds to be certified to be brucellosis-free to increase the value of breeding stock. There is little evidence that brucellosis is a serious problem in the herds of cattle, elk or bison. Nevertheless, the USDA has made a concerted effort to eliminate brucellosis nationwide.

Dr. Mary Meagher, who started her National Park career as a seasonal interpreter at Zion National Park, gave the briefing. Disregarding the advice of the "Old Guard" superintendents and park scientists, who clearly believed that females would never fit into the park science system, she pursued her dream to become a research biologist, completing her Ph.D. at the University of California at Berkley. Her mentor, Starker Leopold, was often quoted as saying that Mary was his most intelligent student, with a vast range of interests that covered many aspects of managing a national park as complex as Yellowstone.

Mary is short, wiry, incredibly intense, outspoken and fascinated about not only bison, but also the whole range of environmental and ecological challenges in managing our most illustrious national park – one that often is called our "Mother Park." She worked well with her fellow scientists and was obviously a favorite of Anderson's, who was among the first superintendents to satisfy a mandate to increase the use of science in making management decisions.

Contrary to the stuffy "Old Guard" mentality, Mary was one of the first female senior scientists to work with male scientists. Together, they gave the superintendent factual information on which to base important management decisions. She became fascinated with bison and published her first book titled, "The Bison of Yellowstone National Park."

I interrupted her briefing often, as I knew absolutely nothing about brucellosis except that one of our family's great friends became seriously ill from drinking raw milk from his herd of milk cows, which must have been infected.

Not only did I know nothing about brucellosis, but my knowledge of bison was limited to the history books, which gave epic descriptions of the great nomadic herds that travelled from southern Canada to the Mexican border in search of grass and water.

They died by the thousands when they faced droughts that diminished both food and water supplies. They were nomadic creatures that could survive the coldest of winters by drifting down-wind for miles, digging through snow to find nutritious grass. Bison was the staple food of the Native American plains tribes that, after acquiring horses from Spanish explorers, became masters of the buffalo hunt. Imagine the skill of riding through a large herd of racing buffalo, no saddles, and spearing or killing the young with lances or bow and arrows. Later, the destruction of the nomadic bison herds by buffalo hide hunters ended forever the annual migration of the many Native American tribes that depended on the buffalo migrations.

Mary once told an interviewer, "Bison are curious. For many people, they are an icon, a wonderful symbol, but the reality is we humans have so taken over the earth that we really don't want to live with them except when they are tidy and fenced in preserves. We are going to have a tough time allowing the processes that bison represent because they are nomadic. They are always on the move. If they could adapt to new winter ranges outside the park, they would be home free. But we have man-made boundaries and the modern world doesn't want the free-ranging bison outside the park."

She continued, "As I think about what the

present bison population is, it has been teaching me about this truly nomadic species, always on the move – take a bite, take a step and I read historical accounts, thousands drowning in the Missouri River and so on; I suspect that a feature of the species is to increase at biological maximum, and climatic events, not predators, knock them down."

She went on, "They are very habituated to vehicle traffic, to the normal patterns that people use. You're much safer if one moves toward you while you are sitting there than if you violate its space and walk up with your camera and shove it up against the animal's nose. As we have more bison and more tourists, we have an increasing injury rate. It's not because anything has changed with the bison."

We discussed the Secretary of Interior's decision in the early 1960s to join with the USDA to round up most of the park's bison, test them for brucellosis and send any that tested positive off to be slaughtered. Unfortunately, many who showed no sign of the disease also were killed to deliberately reduce the numbers within the park.

When Europeans arrived several centuries ago, bringing cattle with them, they also brought brucellosis, which eventually infected both wild elk and bison. Cattle calves are vaccinated within the greater Yellowstone Surveillance Area. Moreover, brucellosis has essentially been eradicated in U.S. cattle. There are so few cases overall of cattle being infected that one could only say, "It happens now and then."

The problem is not with bison, but with elk migrations beyond the park's boundaries. The elk share state and federal winter feed lots with bison. They meet cattle on ranchers' feed lots. They are artificially attracted to supplemental hay, where the disease is easily transmitted.

There are no known ways of treating the thousands of elk that inhabit various drainage areas in the park and migrate out of the park during a cold winter. But the numbers of infections are small: only 20 cases of infected cattle between 2002-13, all resulting from interaction with infected elk.

The telling point of Mary's fascinating briefing was that, in the three surrounding states, there has never been a case of brucellosis in cattle that could be attributed to Yellowstone National Park bison. Cases of brucellosis that can be traced to interaction with elk have occurred in all three states.

I returned to Washington impressed by Supt. Anderson and his staff. I shared my concern over the increasing visitation by snowmobiles and the expense of grooming the roads for people who rode them. I had not understood that the bison quickly learned that groomed trails made migration through the park far easier than prowling though feet of snow.

Snowmobiling within certain areas of the park had become big business, far exceeding Anderson's initial projections. Tourists yearned to see the magic of a snow-filled park. The consequences of grooming the roads for easy travel, allowing bison to move wherever they wished to go, would become a greater problem.

This brings us to Earl Butz, who was the Nixon-appointed Secretary of Agriculture.

Butz was well qualified for the position, having graduated from Purdue University with a Ph.D. In 1957, he became dean of agriculture at his alma mater. He performed admirably and was promoted to dean and vice president of the university's research foundation. He was appointed by President Eisenhower as Assistant Secretary of Agriculture.

A champion of corporate farming, he dramatically reduced the New Deal's programs designed to assist the small farmer, and he had a singular failing: He had the longest list of off-color jokes ready for all occasions.

We spent time together, as he was upset by my continuing, often bitter, battles with Ed Cliff, chief of the Forest Service, which is managed by the Department of Agriculture. I would send Cliff photographs of massive clear-cuts, serious drainage problems caused by ill-designed construction of extensive forest road systems and, worst of all, the clearing of old growth adjacent to some of America's former most productive salmon, steelhead and trout rivers.

The chief, who had to report to me for his annual appropriation for recreation within the vast National Forest system, invariably would complain that the photographs "obviously had been doctored." I would respond by giving the location of the timbering, the dates of the clear-cutting and the damage the road system was inflicting on some of our most once-productive rivers, destroying land that had the potential for re-growth.

We did not enjoy our meetings!

In late summer 1976, Butz called and asked if he could see me in my office. We agreed upon a date. We sat in two easy chairs and discussed the forthcoming election and the possible effect President Ford's pardon of former President Nixon would have on the result. He stated that "we should do everything in our power to assist President Ford."

Suddenly, ever so firmly, Butz said, "Nathaniel, I have given my word to the secretaries of agriculture of the three states bordering Yellowstone National Park that the entire park's bison would be rounded up and tested for brucellosis. I want your assistance."

I leaned forward, looked him in the eye and stated, "Earl, first urge the governors and state game managers of the three states surrounding Yellowstone National Park to round up every elk and kill those that indicate they have brucellosis. I will work on the phony bison issue once the elk are certified clear of the disease."

"Damn you, I have given my word!" he replied. "I am taking your reply to the president. We know perfectly well that elk cannot be rounded up, nor can infected elk be tested and, if found positive, destroyed. The only positive move would be to isolate the disease in bison."

I replied, "Earl, don't you understand? The elk that carry the disease are attempting to locate supplemental food on ranches and on winter feed areas designed to limit their deaths. The charge that it is a bison-transmitted disease is a smoke screen. With your background you should know that it is elk and not bison that is an unsolvable problem."

Butz stood up and, without another word, departed.

He was forced to resign a few months later after one of his most miserable and racist jokes was leaked to the press.

Before moving on, I want to note that Dr. Meagher never has been acknowledged for the excellence of her work. Perhaps her inability to suffer fools has kept her from the recognition she richly deserves as not only the most important expert on the parks' bison, but also on a whole range of environmental insights she has developed over the years she has lived in the park. Her expertise was a perfect example of what Starker Leopold and his committee wanted: a strong science program that could give park managers the tools to prevent foolish political decisions.

Alita and I have visited Yellowstone National Park frequently and always look forward to our time spent with Dr. Meagher. She has become a life friend.

One Box of Cigars: The Great Dismal Swamp

"The [one] condition is that I will never have the pleasure of ever seeing you again."

In the spring of 1972, Pat Noonan, the dynamic leader of The Nature Conservancy, called and asked for an appointment to discuss "an opportunity of a lifetime." He said he would be accompanied by Alexander "Sox" Calder, chairman and chief executive officer of the Union Camp Corporation, to discuss the potential donation of "a significant amount of land" within the Great Dismal Swamp in Virginia.

Aerial view of Lake Drummond and the Great Dismal Swamp,

Frankly, I knew nothing about the Great Dismal Swamp, which once covered more than a million acres. I called the director of the Fish and Wildlife Service (FWS) and asked for a briefing on the swamp and its apparent importance to eastern migratory birds and role as a nesting site for rare and endangered birds. The briefing was fascinating.

The experts reported that the Great Dismal was one of the most treasured North American swamps, covering more than one million acres of muddy land. It was the perfect example of a "southern swamp," one of many that existed along the Atlantic east coast. Other examples include the Everglades, the Fakahatchee swamp, the Okefenokee Swamp in Georgia and the Congaree and Four Corners swamps in South Carolina. The most common trait of these great swamps is a guaranteed supply of freshwater, producing a wide range of native vegetative communities and varied wildlife species.

I obviously was overwhelmed by the magnitude of the opportunity. After Pat Noonan and I set a firm date to meet, I convened a meeting of ornithological experts from the FWS, the National Audubon Society and the Smithsonian Institute.

The meeting of experts lasted only one hour, but they clearly were excited and nearly overwhelmed by the potential of a national wildlife refuge comprised of 50,000 acres of the Dismal Swamp. It was considered by some experts as a treasure trove for migrating birds flying north and south. The remaining acreage in the Great Dismal Swamp was considered to be one of the most critical breeding areas for the rare prothonotary warbler.

Any effort to log the swamp, which would require the installation of drainage ditches and roads, would be considered an environmental disaster.

I also asked for a briefing on the Union Camp Corporation and, again, found the information fascinating.

The Union Bag and Paper Company dates back to 1881, when it began as the Union Paper Bag Machine Company in Bethlehem, Pa., under the Calder family. In the late 1920s, the company built a major mill, one of the largest in the world, in Savannah, Ga. The company had a major impact on Savannah politics and employment, and it was highly respected for insulating Savannah from many of the severe effects of the Great Depression. The company grew and prospered.

The Camp Manufacturing Company was founded in 1887 by three Camp brothers who bought a small sawmill on the outskirts of Franklin, Virginia. The brothers began expanding the sawmill and, during the next 20 years, it experienced rapid growth. With the onset of World War I, the increased demand for lumber brought the company a period of financial success. With the stimulated economy, Franklin became a "booming wartime village."[40]

In 1925, with the passing of the first-generation Camp owners, the company was passed to the second generation. This new generation brought the company into the paper production industry, starting with brown packaging paper in 1938 and eventually producing specialty bleached paper in the 1950s. Under Dr. Jim Jordan, the firm prospered and steadily increased its sales. By 1949, it utilized four log trucks, each with several times the load capacity of earlier models.[41]

By the mid-1950s, industry competition was growing fierce, and extensive mergers occurred within the industry. Reluctant to forfeit its control and become a publicly traded company, the Camp family looked for other avenues to expand. A merger with the Union Company was consummated in 1956 and the Union Camp Corporation was created.[42]

The briefing I initially received about the history and ecological value of the Great Dismal Swamp made me more than satisfied that the Union Camp's 50,000 acres could lead to the acquisition of a much larger area within this extraordinary region.

The excitement was contagious, as experts from both Fish and Wildlife and the National Park Service commented to me that the proposed deal was an incredible opportunity.

On a beautiful spring day, "Sox" Calder, Noonan and I met in my office. Calder was a gentleman and had a keen wit and sense of purpose.

He indicated that Union Camp had a significant problem. The company wished to receive an advance appraisal from the Internal Revenue Service of its land holdings that it wished to donate to The Nature Conservancy to become a national wildlife refuge. If consummated, Union Camp could use the tax deduction to acquire major forestland in the Carolinas for the immense amount of wood needed to supply its ever-expanding series of mills.

This advance appraisal was important to the Union Camp board members and stockholders.

I promised to do my best to obtain the needed appraisal so The Nature Conservancy could acquire the Great Swamp and consummate a deal with the U.S. Fish and Wildlife Service to create the Great Dismal Swamp National Wildlife Refuge.

I was new to my position and could not see any impediment to requesting an advance appraisal, especially for such an ecologically and environmentally important acreage.

I had met several highly placed members of the Treasury Department and immediately called one of them and asked how an advanced appraisal could be considered. I was shaken when he replied with a laugh, "The commissioner of the Internal Revenue Service is the only man who makes a decision on advanced appraisals and he is opposed to them."

I begged for the opportunity to brief Com-

Great Dismal Swamp, photo © Rebecca Wynn

missioner Johnnie Walters, citing the history of the swamp. George Washington once attempted to survey, drain and farm this great wilderness, without success, and it was vitally important to eastern migrating birds and rare birds that nested there.

The Treasury agent laughed and replied, "No one from Treasury enters the door of the commissioner. It is considered improper for any member of the Treasury staff to 'touch' an issue such as a request for an advanced appraisal."

But then, he offered a spark of hope: "I understand you still have a cache of pre-Castro cigars. If I am able to arrange a meeting it will cost you a box of Montecristos."

A full month later, my wonderful secretary reported that after negotiations between secretaries, a meeting time and date had been established.

Pat Noonan furnished me with an aerial map of the 50,000 acres outlined in red ink. We went over the salient speaking points, emphasizing the uniqueness of the area and its importance to wildlife.

I was not informed that David Morine, one of The Nature Conservancy's most talented negotiators, had tried to obtain an advance appraisal but was unable to visit and convince Commissioner Walters of the need for one.

On arrival at the Internal Revenue Service's stately building at 111 Constitutional Avenue, my associate walked me through security, shook my hand and wished me luck. I was met by a member of the commissioner's staff and led to his imposing office. Seated behind a huge mahogany desk sat the commissioner of an extremely powerful government agency, the Internal Revenue Service.

Walters waved me to a chair placed closely to the side of his desk. He inquired cautiously, "What can I do for you, Mr. Secretary?" I explained my mission and unrolled the aerial photograph, at which he glanced. I gave him a six- or seven-minute briefing and explained the importance of the Great Dismal Swamp, George Washington's involvement and the failure of various drainage projects. I described the need for an advanced appraisal so Union Camp could donate its land to The Nature Conservancy, which would act as a "go between" with the U.S. Fish and Wildlife Service's refuge system.

Commissioner Walters looked me in the eye, paused and stated with a very firm voice, "I don't like advanced appraisals of property. If the recipients of the advanced appraisal disagree with the very strict appraisal rules of the Internal Revenue Service, they contest the ruling or they simply don't make the land donation. It costs the taxpayers plenty and, if the appraisal is not acceptable to the potential donor, valuable staff time and money is wasted."

I stared back and replied, "This is an opportunity that comes once in a lifetime. The Dismal Swamp is too important to lose as a national wildlife refuge. There will be years of litigation under the Clean Water Act and the Endangered Species Act if Union Camp sells its ownership to a timber or farming company that attempts to drain land and build roads to reach the valuable timber or, worse, clears the land and attempts to farm it. Union Camp recognizes the significant difficulty of timbering this property and has selected upland forests that they can acquire if they receive a fair appraisal to satisfy their board and stockholders."

Walters sank back into his immense chair. Twisting a pencil in his hand, he looked at the ceiling and finally gave me his decision.

"Secretary Reed, I have stated that the IRS does not like advance appraisals for the reasons I have stated, but I will allow an advance appraisal under one condition," he said. "The condition is that I will never have the pleasure of ever seeing you again."

I stood up, leaned over, shook his hand and stated affirmatively, "Commissioner, you have a deal!" I literally ran out of his office and called Pat Noonan.

The advance appraisal was slightly less than Union Camp's appraisal, as the value was affected by the ravages of Hurricane Agnes, which dropped 12 inches of rain and ended any possibility of a sale to a potential farming or timbering company.

Calder persuaded his board and the vast majority of the corporation's stockholders that the trade should be completed. David Morine, the Conservancy's expert land purchaser, took over. He worked with Walter McAllister, Fish and Wildlife Service's chief of land acquisition, and with Union Camp's legal and tax experts to speedily finalize the deal.

Calder, Noonan and the refuge land officials at Interior were thrilled.

The U.S. Fish and Wildlife Service sought and received administration permission to seek funding from Congress to create the Great Dismal Swamp National Wildlife Refuge.

The Great Dismal Swamp has 50,000 acres that is protected forever. It will remain a sanctuary for thousands of migrating birds and as a site for birders who travel from around the world to see the prothonotary warbler and the incredible numbers of other breeding birds.

With great foresight, Congress in 1974 added 112,000 acres to the Union Camp donation, including the 3,100-acre Lake Drummond, one of the largest natural lakes in Virginia. Outside the boundary of the refuge, the state of North Carolina has preserved and protected an additional 22 square miles (14,080 acres) of forested wetlands as the Great Dismal Swamp State Park.

My donation of a box of Montecristo cigars was well worth the effort!

NOTES – ONE BOX OF CIGARS: THE GREAT DISMAL SWAMP

[40] *Wikipedia*, s.v. "Union Camp Corporation", last modified 31 Aug. 2016, https://en.wikipedia.org/wiki/Union_Camp_Corporation.

[41] Ibid.

[42] Ibid.

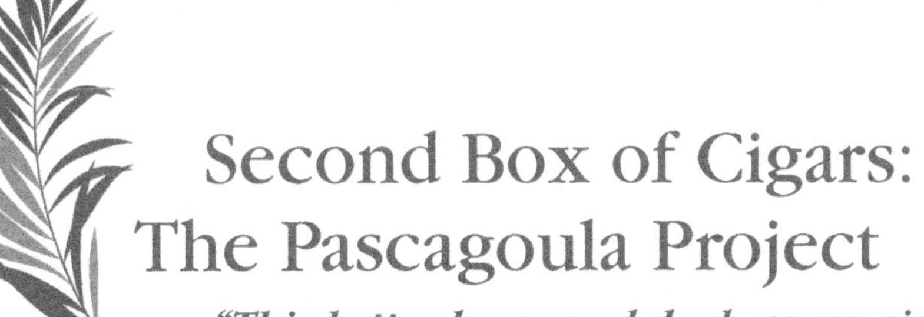

Second Box of Cigars: The Pascagoula Project

"This better be a good deal, as my cigar reserve has about run out."

During my tenure as Assistant Secretary of Interior, I'd come to appreciate how aggressive and intense Pat Noonan and his staff at The Nature Conservancy (TNC) were in their efforts to protect America's most significant natural areas. However, I was unaware of the complexity of some of the projects they were acquiring.

Pat's staff was dominated by young MBAs who were constantly pushing the edge of the envelope, especially when it came to showing land owners how working with the Conservancy could not only save their land, but also lower their taxes. As Pat and David Morine, his director of land acquisition, liked to point out, "The largest single donors to land conservation in America are the foundations and the U.S. tax code."

Of course, during our work to save the Great Dismal Swamp (as discussed in the previous essay), I'd seen firsthand the after-tax advantage of making a charitable gift of land to TNC. Plus, that's when I learned that asking the IRS to grant an advance ruling is like asking the Pope to grant a divorce. It is not something the IRS believes in, and for that reason, I'd sworn to IRS Commissioner Johnnie Walters that if he ruled just that once on the value of the Union Camp donation, I'd never darken his door again – and I never did.

In July 1976, I was at the Triangle X Dude Ranch in the heart of the Tetons vacationing with my wife and our three children when I got another call from Pat Noonan. "Nathaniel," he said in his usual cheerful and upbeat voice, "I'm sorry to bother you on your vacation, but I just want to bring you up to date on this very important project we're working on along the Pascagoula River in Mississippi."

I knew about the Pascagoula from my efforts three years earlier helping to create the Mississippi Sandhill Crane National Wildlife Refuge, which is just down highway I-10 from the Pascagoula bottom lands. I was sure this project was important, but why would he be calling me in Wyoming? Our vacation was just winding down and I was scheduled to be back in the office on Monday. Couldn't this update wait until then? There must be something wrong, as my two expert deputies Buff Bohlen and Doug Wheeler were covering the office and they could handle most any problem Pat had.

I began to suspect something had gone drastically wrong and he was hoping I could bail him out. "Pat," I said, "I'm quite familiar with the Pascagoula. It's near where I had that problem with the interchange DOT wanted to put in the middle of the Sandhill Crane Refuge." He replied, "Remember? Nathaniel, how could I forget?

"The Conservancy has bought hundreds of additional acres for the refuge and intend to acquire even more land. Now, imagine protecting 32,000 acres of the finest bottom land forest left in America right next to it!" Pat continued, still dancing around why he really called.

"Pat, it sounds like a superb project. Is there anything I can do to help?"

"Funny you should ask," he said, finally getting to the point. "We've run into a little problem with the IRS. It seems the project can't go ahead without an advanced ruling from the IRS that the dissolution of the company for the land will be a tax-free transaction."

"Oh no!" I moaned into the phone. "Pat, don't you remember the Union Camp Deal? I swore to Commissioner Walters he'd never see me again."

"Nat," Pat said very calmly and quietly, like he was asking for something very simple, "Dave Morine has spent three years working on this deal. He's gotten the state of Mississippi to appropriate $15 million for the purchase of the land. That's the largest appropriation for the creation of a state wildlife management area in the history of America.

"He's gotten over a hundred individual stockholders to tender 75 percent of the Pascagoula Hardwood Company's stock at a bargain-sale price, which translates into a $3.4 million donation to the project. He's gotten the state and the family members who won't sell their 25 percent stake in the company to agree on an equitable division of the 43,500 acres. Most importantly, he's figured out a way to dissolve the corporation so the family that's getting the land won't have to pay any taxes, and that's the key to the whole transaction.

"The old patriarch of that family is adamant that he won't do the deal without an advance ruling and we just learned that the two peons in the bowels of the IRS who were assigned this case have decided they won't even hear a request for an advance ruling. Nathaniel, we have to get upstairs to somebody who's not afraid to make a decision and, by the way, there is a new IRS commissioner."

"Pat," I said, "that would have to be the Commissioner Donald Alexander."

"I guess so," Pat said. "Nathaniel, you're our ace in the hole. Can you do it?"

Once again, he had me. He knew it, and I knew it. As Assistant Secretary for Fish and Wildlife and Parks, how could I possibly say "no" to a request to help save one of the finest bottomland hardwood swamps left in America? "All right," I said, "I'll give it a shot. You and Dave be in my office first thing Monday morning to brief me on the details, but you know, I don't feel comfortable about breaking my previous promise."

Pat and Dave were sitting in my office waiting for me when I arrived on Monday morning. They presented me with an aerial photograph of the Pascagoula Project and a briefing paper highlighting all the salient points of the deal. With this material, I could make a strong pitch for an advance ruling.

My wife, Alita, and I had become casual friends with several assistant secretaries of the Treasury we'd met at dinner parties. Cigars were in vogue after dinner in the vast majority of embassies and homes during that period and one of the Treasury men had always admired the #3 or #4 pre-Castro Montecristo cigars that I smoked after the ladies had departed to the sitting room. He had made the date for the successful Union Camp Advance Ruling.

I called him and told him The Nature Conservancy was in dire need of an advance ruling. Speed was essential. I admitted that I knew the IRS did not approve of spending taxpayers' time on advance rulings, but the Union Camp advance ruling led the way to formation of the Great Dismal Swamp National Wildlife Refuge. Then, I confessed that I'd given my solemn word to the former commissioner that if he helped us out back then, as he did, I never would ask for another advance ruling. Was there anything he could do?

My contact at the Treasury remarked: "Nathaniel, you burned your bridge the last time.

I don't think there has been another advance ruling since the successful effort for Union Camp to accept their valuation and proceeded with their donation of 50,000 acres of the Great Dismal Swamp to the refuge system. It was a great victory for Union Camp, The Nature Conservancy and the refuge system."

I agreed that the "deal" was a spectacular success, saving a property that had such great value to so many thousands of birds and was a summer home for the rare prothonotary warbler.

"I have another really important property that The Nature Conservancy has been working on for three years," I told him. "It is the greatest of the southern bottom lands that have been preserved in remarkably good condition. The multiple owners must have an advance ruling [appraisal] to establish value. It's a very complicated deal that needs expert oversight by your best team from the IRS appraisal unit."

"Let me check it out," he said. "If I obtain a meeting date for you, remember our past agreement!"

Much to my surprise, he called back the next day. "The commissioner will see you tomorrow at 2 p.m." He added: "But Reed, this appointment will cost you another box of 25 Montecristo No. 3s." I swallowed hard. My Montecristo cache had just been greatly diminished. I thought to myself, "Pat Noonan, this better be a good deal, as my cigar reserve has about run out."

At the appointed hour, my Treasury contact again was waiting at the entrance of 111 Constitution Avenue. He ushered me in the door and shook hands and stated: "Go for broke, you just might bat 100 percent. Good luck! Remember my box of cigars."

I again was led to the office of the commissioner, and I walked in. The visitor's chair was in a similar position to where it had been placed during my previous meeting. Commissioner Alexander glanced at me and inquired: "Mr. Secretary, do you keep your promises?"

Obviously, my previous request for an advance ruling to consummate the Union Camp donation and my subsequent promise were well known within the agency. I replied, "It would be a very rare occurrence that I would negate a promise, but I have another totally extraordinary property that could be saved in perpetuity if only an advance ruling is granted."

He looked up and said a bit sarcastically, "I suppose, in your opinion, it truly is a vitally important property or you wouldn't break your word. Quickly, brief me and I will make a decision."

I unfurled the aerial map Pat and Morine had given me and started my spiel. "Sir, with its ancient trees, oxbow lakes, sandbars, and marshes the Pascagoula Swamp is without question one of the greatest bottomland hardwood forests left in North America.

"It is an important habitat for rare and endangered species ranging from the American alligator to the magnificent swallow-tailed kite and a vital staging and resting area for migratory birds such as warblers, tanagers, and vireos making their way to and from South and Central America across the Gulf. In addition, this swamp is the source of millions of gallons of clean, freshwater that flows into the Gulf every minute, which in turn creates the conditions needed for a healthy coastal fishery. If lost, it is a natural resource that can never be replaced."

Then, I briefly emphasized how the state of Mississippi already had appropriated $15 million for the purchase and how over a hundred people had tendered their stock at below fair market price. In essence, I concluded, the people of Mississippi were totally behind this project and realized this was their best chance to preserve one of America's most significant natural areas. I added, "Drainage and timbering have crisscrossed Mississippi. This is the last great bottomland swamp left that is in superb condition."

That was it. The entire presentation had lasted less than six minutes, but I'd given it my best shot. Alexander sighed and with a strong voice said, "Reed, here is my decision: I will grant the request for an advance ruling, but I warn you, the tax-free transfer of land for stock in the dissolution of the corporation has to meet all the regulations set forth in the code so the owners' lawyers better know what they're doing. More importantly, from here on out I want to be sure you remember your promises. In short, I never want to see you again!"

I stood, shook his hand, and departed with a sense of deliverance.

Naturally, Pat and Morine were ecstatic when I delivered the good news. With the Commissioner's blessing, the two peons in the bowels of the IRS were able to view the advance ruling in a new and very favorable light.

On September 22, 1976, with the advance ruling in hand, TNC dissolved the Pascagoula Hardwood Company and took title to the 32,000 acres that would become the Pascagoula Wildlife Management Area, but the impact of this project went far beyond Mississippi.

When other states saw that Mississippi, which historically had been just about last in everything, was now No. 1 in land conservation, they were quick to get on board. With TNC's help, State Heritage Programs designed to protect national treasures like the Pascagoula River began popping up all over the country.

This big jump forward for land conservation in America had cost me a second box of classic Montecristo No. 3s, but it just goes to show, "You can't beat a good cigar."

Let's Take A Swim!

Pat Noonan invited me to join the board of The Nature Conservancy very soon after my Interior days ended in 1976. The first board meetings consisted of reports of fascinating projects that were complicated but so environmentally important that the staff was ready to bring back to the board costly propositions.

The board decided to meet at a resort in Georgia or Texas. David Smith, who was in charge of organizing the board meetings, faced a rather major problem. After being assured that a rather splendid resort had sufficient rooms for the board and staff, managers called and said they were sold out. Dave Morine hugged a shaken Smith and said, "David, it's all right. We will go to Mississippi."

International Paper was in the process of donating 3,000 acres along the Black and Red Rivers, which flow into the preserved Pascagoula tract. Johnny Vaught, the great head football coach at the University of Mississippi, was chairman of the Wildlife Heritage Committee and made sure a simple but comfortable Howard Johnson hotel on the beach was made available. He also guaranteed a huge fish fry at the end of our meetings.

Key to the visit was a float trip in canoes down the Pascagoula River. The state game and fish officers were assigned to the canoes and we departed from a landing for an eight-mile float down the river that had been "saved" by Morine and two boxes of my Montecristos.

The governor was considered a "black sheep" by supporters of the Mississippi Nature Conservancy and was not invited to the festivities.

It was one of those memorable spring days: warm but not hot. The sky was filled with soft clouds. The river was crystal clear and felt cool to one's hand. Pat and I were last off, sharing a canoe with an expert stern guide and each of us taking turns as the bow paddler.

It was peaceful and so memorable. We had only one more act to celebrate – the successful acquisition of this great southern bottomland. Let's take a swim!

Off came our clothes and to the hilarious laughter of our guide, we jumped into the Pascagoula. It was cool and there was sufficient flow to relax on one's back and drift downstream.

After 30 delightful minutes, the guide's radio crackled, "Where are you? The rest of the gang is involved in a canoe race to the landing. Better catch up!"

Our paddler beached the canoe, we dressed soaking wet and paddled furiously, arriving at the exit landing last.

To everyone's surprise, there was the uninvited governor dressed entirely in white: white Stetson, suit, shirt, tie, socks and shoes. He was surrounded by state policemen. He spoke at length about the importance of working together to preserve not only the Pascagoula, but also other areas in Mississippi.

He ended his oratory by saying, "If I could get my hands on that damn Assistant Secretary of Interior who nearly stopped I-10 for a bunch of sandhill cranes, I would strangle him right here and now." [For more information about the sandhill crane, see the essay, *Saga of the Mississippi Sandhill Crane National Wildlife Refuge.*]

As he turned to leave, Pat Noonan, always ready for any rebuttal called out in a loud voice: "Governor that 'damn' assistant secretary is standing right here!" Thankfully the governor and his entourage had headed back to his fleet of state police cars and the governor's limousine.

That evening, the Conservancy, with the governor's assistance, orchestrated the most fantastic cookout of shrimp, oysters, sweet corn and cases of beer in front of Jefferson Davis' mansion.

A memorable day!

The Mormons, the Sandhill Cranes and Gray's Lake

"Promise me that we never had this conversation."

A new challenge arose one day when Spencer Smith, director of the Fish and Wildlife Service, made a date to see me along with Lynn Greenwalt, director of the National Refuge System, and Walter McAllister, director of Refuge Realty. It turned out to be a challenge that reminded me – and, all of us, really – of the value of flexibility and compromise.

The group explained that some residents who surrounded the Gray's Lake National Wildlife Refuge in Idaho wanted to move southwest to join other members of The Church of Jesus Christ of Latter-day Saints. The long winters and meager financial return from the sale of their cattle and sheep led the younger members of a group of Mormon families to agree to sell their homesteads. They wanted to move to a new location where opportunities for their young and for financial reward were far greater than the snowbound Gray's Lake.

The problem: For starters, I had never heard of Gray's Lake or the refuge or the new controversy. In short, a cooperative agreement with surrounding landowners had been developed, but now, the refuge needed to be expanded on behalf of an important population of sandhill cranes and other species.

The refuge had a series of impoundments intended to manage water levels to benefit a very large nesting colony of sandhill cranes and abundant waterfowl. The high mountain valley "lake" is actually a large, shallow marsh containing the largest concentration of bulrush in North America, mixed with cattails. It is surrounded by grasslands that are superb grazing areas for domestic animals and wildlife. The area is a breeding oasis for more than 200 species of mammals, birds and fish.

In the early 1970s, the service decided to abandon construction and maintenance of dikes and impoundments, and it proposed a significant refuge boundary expansion above the lakebed meander line.

Meanwhile, Rod Drewin, one of the service's most knowledgeable whooping crane experts, had proposed an experiment – raising a second flock of whooping cranes in case disaster struck the wild flock that migrated to and from Canada's Northwest Territory and the Aransas National Wildlife Refuge on the Texas coastline. The perils of this long migration are obvious. A terrible storm, collision with a plane or with high-tension wires, or human poaching could put the future of this extraordinary species in doubt. A second breeding colony presumably could guarantee a significant defense against potential extinction.

So, the refuge needed expansion, as it was truly a most unique area.

In that context, Greenwalt informed me that the Mormon leadership at Gray's Lake had significant problems with the National Refuge Service's desire to acquire major upland areas around the lake. Their leaders asked for me by name through the regional director's office in Soda Springs, Idaho. They urged me to visit with them and hear their expectations and desires on if and how to proceed with land sales and with provisions for those members who wished to stay.

How they knew my name remains one of those mysteries that have never been revealed.

Being young and delighted by an offbeat assignment, I asked Secretary Morton for permission to fly to Jackson and meet with the elders of The Church of Jesus Christ of Latter-day Saints at their homestead adjacent to the lake. He urged me to accept their invitation to visit the Gray's Lake refuge, located a little less than two hours from Jackson, Wyoming, on the west side of the Grand Tetons. It consisted of a 13,000-acre marsh owned by the federal government as it was "un-deeded."

The final arrangements were confirmed. I flew to Jackson, spent the night with friends and, the following morning, was driven by a service enforcement agent up and over the pass to reach Idaho.

The drive was spectacular! It was late spring, but snow fields covered the Grand Tetons. As many times as I had been to the Grand Teton National Park, I had never seen the western side of the incredible mountain chain. It was equally beautiful. The grass was brilliant green and the fields were covered with spring flowers, including a tall plant with a large yellow bloom.

We arrived at the refuge. It was stunningly beautiful! Sandhill cranes were feeding in the shallows. This unique flock nested at Gray's Lake rather than the Canadian provinces, yet wintered together in Texas. The waterfowl, far more numerous than I expected, were feeding with their young. There was a small group of simple houses, and I decided the largest building must be the residents' meeting hall. I entered to find a semicircle of rugged-looking men of all ages sitting around a single chair.

I nodded to the man I presumed to be "the elder" and took the seat. I was met by a lengthy silence. Uncertain as to when I was to speak, I finally blurted out that I was Nathaniel Reed, Assistant Secretary of Interior, and had accepted their invitation to discuss their problems and find solutions.

At the four-minute mark, the presumed elder welcomed me and explained that a number of residents of the valley were willing to sell their land to the service in order to enlarge the refuge, while other members had departed due to the long, cold winters. Their children wanted to "see more of the world," he said. Another group of Mormons had found a property in Arizona and reported that the mild winters and availability of irrigation water made for a far more productive situation.

A rift had developed between among those who wanted to join them and those who wanted to stay.

A few members of the leadership spoke about what they claimed was an intrusion by members of the service onto private lands to secure potential acquisition rights. They were a tight-knit group and had agreed on two terms that had to be met if the service was to acquire significant amounts of land to enlarge the refuge.

First, no federal official would enter the area, aside from working on/or within the marsh, without pre-clearance. I thought that sounded reasonable and agreed with that request.

Second, all appraisals would be conducted by service appraisal officials who were members of The Church of Jesus Christ of Latter-day Saints. I thought about this request during a very long pause. I answered, "I do not know if the service's region has land appraisers who are members of the church. It is a delicate subject that is covered by federal rules on confidentiality."

the majority are willing sellers, but they have one absolutely binding request: No federal appraiser will begin negotiations with landowners unless he or she is a member of The Church of Jesus Christ of Latter-day Saints."

I could hear a pin drop. In a very low voice, the regional director stated, "Mr. Secretary, you know that a question on religious affiliation is a 'no-no'." I answered, "Go ever so quietly to your chief of appraisers and take him outside and tell him that the Gray's Lake real estate acquisition depends on whether there is an appraiser who is a member of The Church of Jesus Christ of Latter-day Saints and can be quietly selected to become the official appraiser for the land that is willing to be sold."

There was another long pause, followed by, "Hold the line!"

Moments later, he was back on the phone with a cheerful voice, replying, "The chief is a member of The Church of Jesus Christ of Latter-day Saints and we have three additional appraisers who are all highly qualified to accept the assignment. Promise me that we never had this conversation."

I replied, "You are the greatest! I am going to share the news with the elders. Go through the manager at Soda Springs to make contact with the leadership and have your appraiser, who they recognize as a 'godly man,' start the process."

I was driven back to Gray's Lake and stood

The elder replied, "This point is non-negotiable. How can you discover whether the region has qualified appraisers who are members of our church?"

I answered, "I will have to be driven to Soda Springs [to find a telephone] and reach the regional director and, if possible, obtain an answer to your stipulation. You know the rules on federal appraisals. There would be absolutely no difference between the estimate of an appraiser of your faith than from a member of a different religion." The reply was, "We insist on disclosing what we believe the value of our land and associated improvements are with a member of our faith."

I said I would be driven to Soda Springs and make a telephone call to the regional headquarters and would return with an answer to their request.

Off the agent and I went. My mind was spinning. I called ahead on the agent's radio to the refuge manager at Soda Springs and had him prepare the regional director in Oregon for my call.

I was welcomed, a room was set up for me, the door closed and the regional director was on the line. I had appointed him to his post and we had a firm friendship.

I told him, "Here is the problem at Gray's Lake. The director wants to dramatically expand Gray's Lake National Wildlife Refuge. It appears to me that

Antelope Flats, Grand Tetons, photo © Bobby Harrison

by "my chair" and gave them the good news. I informed them that contact would be made through the Soda Springs office. They could expect the assignment of a competent, honest appraiser in a short period of time.

They stood as one and thanked me for coming and assuring them that their concerns were answered. I shook hands with these hardy pioneers and left them with my telephone number.

On my return to Washington, Spencer and Walter gave the authority to initiate appraisals from willing sellers.

As of 2014, the refuge has been enlarged by the acquisition of 4,600 acres, bringing it to a total size of 22,000 acres.

However, there have been problems. The federal government's claim to ownership of the marsh has been challenged and needs to be adjudicated. Additional land needs to be acquired to protect the unique high mountain valley.

The refuge has a permanent manager. The headquarters for the southeast Idaho National Wildlife Refuges is now in Pocatello, Idaho, where four of the six Rocky Mountain National Wildlife Refuges are managed, including Gray's Lake, Bear Lake and Camas and Minidoka Refuges.

Regrettably, Rod Drewin, aided by experts, failed to succeed in "hacking" the eggs of whooping cranes under sandhill crane parents. The young birds were permanently bonded to their foster parents and did not realize that they were whooping cranes, not sandhill cranes. There were losses to coyote predation, sudden heavy rainstorms, power-line accidents and avian tuberculosis, forcing experts to abandon the well-intended project.

I am going to return to Gray's Lake, as my memory of that unique high mountain marsh remains indelible. It is a national wildlife refuge of unique beauty. It has become a major stopping area for the northern migration of sandhill cranes, which forage in the marsh and grasslands to add weight for their next long northern flight. It is an extremely valuable nesting site for cranes and waterfowl.

It simply is one of the most majestic national wildlife refuges in the lower 48 states. My visit there was a magical experience that I treasure.

The Wyoming Eagle Case

"I'm the man who protects his sheep by killing eagles. You think they're a pretty bird. I hate them! Damn you!"

The May 1, 1971 discovery of a dead bald eagle by two 18-year-old hikers trekking through rugged Wyoming countryside led to a fascinating chapter of my career. The dead eagle was found in prime eagle habitat about 10 miles southwest of Casper. Both bald and golden eagles made this rugged country a stopover during spring and fall migrations. There also was a significant resident population of both eagles.

The two young men were avid birders and were surprised to find the bald eagle carcass. It had been washed downstream from the spring runoff and "was wrapped around a tree," they reported. Its bald head was easily recognized.

The men walked a few more yards and discovered another dead eagle. They fanned out and discovered five more dead eagles. This was troubling.

They reported their discovery to leaders of the Murie Chapter of the National Audubon Society, whose members began an intensive search of the area. They discovered 22 eagle carcasses, half bald and half golden.

The bald eagle, a symbol of our country, is protected by federal wildlife law. Bart and Liz Rea were leading members of the chapter and immediately recognized that the eagles had been killed by poison, probably from a carcass of a stillborn lamb, calf or an illegally killed animal.

Bart Rea, a prominent geologist, lived in a region that was dominated by stockmen – ranchers of sheep and cattle. There was a common "mantra" in the Rocky Mountains west that eagles killed lambs. Producers of lamb depended largely on low wages for sheep herders, federal subsidies for wool, and low-cost grazing rights on federal land.

Experienced Spanish Basque shepherds received visas to come to Wyoming, Colorado and Montana in the spring to manage sheep herds until the fall "harvest" – sales or slaughter. They moved flocks of sheep onto leased public lands when the young animals were able to graze. Sheep owners eagerly sought to lease thousands of acres of federally owned grasslands either in national forests or Bureau of Land Management public lands for their flocks. The shepherds were responsible for as many as 600-plus sheep, which they guided to grazing sites and water and guarded from predators such as coyotes, bears and – the stockmen maintained – eagles.

The ranchers used political power to obtain what they called "coyote control" from federal employees. Their objective was a "clear range," with no loss of cattle or, most importantly, sheep to coyotes or any other predator, including eagles.

Poisoned eagles in bags

It was within this political environment that Bart Rea recognized that the dead eagles were too valuable to be turned over to Wyoming authorities, who were influenced by Old West stockmen who paid little attention to many state or federal laws. He organized a group to retrieve the carcasses from the canyon. Bart's young son, Dan, was an able assistant.

Bart and Dan took a number of the best preserved eagles and attached them to poles to ease the rigorous task of retrieving the still-heavy bird carcasses. Then, they placed the dead eagles in bags and secretly stowed them in Bart's freezer.

He notified a U.S. Fish and Wildlife Service (FWS) enforcement agent that he had the dead eagles. Chuck Lawrence, chief of the service's Enforcement Bureau, flew to Casper to meet the Reas. He also held a private conference with members of the Rocky Mountain federal enforcement staff and a few knowledgeable, retired stockmen who were outraged by the consistent killing of eagles and other wildlife by indiscriminate misuse of a variety of poisons.

Within days, Lawrence arranged for the dead eagles to be retrieved from Bart's freezer and shipped in dry ice to the Patuxent Wildlife Research Center near Washington, D.C. Necropsies bore out the suspicion that the eagles had been poisoned. They had ingested lethal amounts of a deadly poison called thallium sulfate.

Lawrence immediately transferred additional enforcement agents to the area. They discovered that a number of local ranchers had killed antelope and laced their bodies with poison. One report indicated that baited carcasses retrieved contained enough thallium sulfate to "kill every animal in the state."

The prime offender was found to be Van Irvine, former president of the Wyoming Stock Growers Association. After months of indecision, the federal attorney allowed Van Irvine to plead guilty before a justice of the peace to violating a number of state statutes, including one that banned the use of game animals for bait. Irvine paid $675 in fines. Other co-conspirators paid similarly low fines.

I received a written account of the eagles' deaths, Bart Rea's actions, the results of the necropsies, and the ridiculously low fines levied. I also received a very troubling letter from Wyoming Gov. Stan Hathaway, who accused the FWS of "stealing" the dead eagles from the state. He declared himself "outraged" by federal intervention in what he claimed was a "simple Wyoming issue of protecting stock from predators."

Secretary Morton insisted that I call Governor Hathaway and explain that the transfer of the eagle carcasses was not an attempt to preclude the state from completing its own autopsies. I told the governor that, since both types of dead eagles were protected by federal law, it was our duty to discover what killed them. The telephone conversation was short. The governor claimed that the "heavy hand of the federal government had stolen Wyoming's eagles without his personal approval."

I tried to explain that the state had control of a number of other recovered eagle carcasses and it would be helpful if their experts confirmed the type and strength of any poison that was present. The governor seemed more concerned over the national press accounts of the number of dead eagles killed by poison in his state than responding to my request.

He said, "Reed, you are giving Wyoming a bad name." I replied, "Governor, the men who poisoned those eagles are responsible for the bad press. Your wildlife officers should have halted the misuse of whatever poison was used." The conversation then ended with the governor's final tart remark, which I overlooked.

I set up a couple of hours for briefings by FWS Director Spencer Smith, Chuck Lawrence and other enforcement staff. I learned that the bald eagle was protected by the Bald Eagle Protection Act of 1940 and a 1962 amendment granted a lesser protection for golden eagles, which could be taken to protect livestock only with written permission from the Department of Interior.

Lawrence emphasized that the vast majority of state agencies and livestock owners obeyed the laws. They demanded coyote control, but universally felt that the loss of calves or lambs to golden eagles was grossly over estimated. The bald eagle was a carrion eater, a bird that sought and lived on other dead animals and was adept at catching fish. It was never a killer of livestock. The golden eagle can and will kill a lamb, especially a newborn lamb, but feeds mostly on a wide variety of native animals.

As an interesting side note, a number of highly respected bird watchers and even ranchers who did not "run sheep" informed our agents that there was a discernable reduction of both eagles' populations in Wyoming.

Secretary Morton was astonished by my report of the dead eagle discovery. I informed him that rumors persisted that far more eagles were being killed by aerial gunners. He arranged for Director Smith, Lawrence and I to meet with appropriate members of the U.S. attorney general's staff.

Lawrence needed help to uncover the facts surrounding rumors that eagles may have been shot from single-engine airplanes and helicopters. The decision that came out of the meeting was to insert an undercover federal agent into a ranch suspected of arranging or supervising the eagle killings. The agent would come from the FBI or from a new crop of field agents that had been enlisted into the Fish and Wildlife Enforcement staff.

Bart Rea and son

I called Bart Rea and thanked him for his invaluable assistance. We discussed the possibility that eagles were being shot from aircraft without his knowledge. He agreed that the numbers of resident golden and bald eagles had dropped significantly and that the rumor mill might just be accurate.

The number of bald eagles had dwindled to between 400 and 500 breeding pairs. The estimated population of golden eagles in the United States was between 12,000 and 15,000. (These figures do not include populations figures for the state of Alaska.) More eagles had been killed in Wyoming than were thought to exist in the state.

The most likely suspect was Herman Werner, one of Wyoming's largest landowners and owner of major herds of cattle and flocks of sheep. He leased thousands of acres of federal lands for grazing. He was known as a man who demanded to go his own way regardless of laws. He was a major donor to good causes and Republican political campaigns and was considered the dean of Wyoming's stockmen.

Bart and I ended our conversation. It was one of those "life moments" when your approach is identical to that of the person you have met or talked to about a mutual concern. It is a feeling of friendship that is overwhelming.

Within days, Lawrence whispered into my ear,

"We have an agent ready to go." I never learned who the agent was or exactly for whom he worked. Lawrence said simply, "He is a real cowboy, from a ranching family, with cow manure on his boots. He will fit right in with Werner's ranch hands, as there is a considerable turnover at the Werner Ranch."

Our young cowboy was hired immediately. Living in the bunkhouse with his fellow hands, he heard them discuss openly in front of him loads of dead eagles that had been dumped in a corral within the ranch. A backhoe operator reportedly dug a pit and the dead eagles were thrown in and covered with a chemical to speed up their decomposition and then covered with soil.

Rumors persisted in Wyoming that an air taxi company headquartered in the town of Buffalo was making itself available for eagle extermination. Supposedly its biggest customer was none other than Herman Werner.

Our young informer notified Lawrence that there was no doubt several dead eagles had been deposited in an open, very wide ranch corral, but his affidavit was insufficient evidence to obtain a federal search warrant. Incredibly, Bart Rea and one of his Audubon colleagues were at the Casper airport taking custody of yet another dead eagle when they noticed a man working on a helicopter in which they could see shotguns and spent shells. Rea and his colleague walked over to the helicopter and took a snapshot. The pilot, aware that he had been photographed, apparently began to worry about the fact that he had been flying most of the helicopters and single-engine planes carrying gunners to shoot innumerable eagles.

Rea called me. I informed Lawrence that we needed to find the pilot, who would be key to any prosecution of Herman Werner. In the meantime, the Western press of the Rocky Mountains began to carry stories of dead eagles and pinpointed Wyoming as the center of eagle killing.

Governor Hathaway again expressed in a letter his frustration that the federal Department of Interior was overriding states' rights. He insisted that the Wyoming Game and Fish enforcement officers were able to protect any state or federally protected bird or animal. Furthermore, the now widely published accounts of eagle killing made national news. He added, "This is not the kind of publicity that a state that relies heavily on tourist income wants or deserves." That ended the conversation. I wanted to add, "Why haven't your wardens discovered dead eagles?"

I looked at my schedule for the following day and remarked to my secretary that the 9 a.m. appointment with Generals Smith and Jones was an obvious mistake, as their names were obviously fictitious and why would they want to visit with me?

She replied that the office of the Secretary of the Air Force called and made the appointment. I could hardly wait until the following morning.

Nori opened my office door, and in walked two very young brigadier generals who I made comfortable and asked what I could do for them.

They replied, "It is not what you can do for us but it is what we can do for you." I said nothing, other than "Please, what can you do for me?"

They said they were responsible for a biweekly training flight from an undisclosed location to the tip of Alaska and back in a "vehicle" that had a superb array of cameras. They had read about the problems I was having determining the number of grizzly bears in the Yellowstone ecosystem and offered their assistance to photograph the vast, multi-million-acre area. They offered to fly Alaska's arctic coastline to determine the size of the Porcupine and Central caribou herds.

I stated that it would be very difficult to pinpoint in Yellowstone what animal their cameras would capture, as elk, grizzly bears, black bears and moose are among the large mixture of animals that inhabited the Yellowstone ecosystem. They agreed it might be difficult but said it was a "challenge." I urged them on. I knew that the service would be delighted to receive information on the size of the

Arctic Porcupine and Central caribou herds.

Suddenly I thought, "What about Mr. Werner's ranch?" I rang for Chuck Lawrence, who joined us. I said "Chuck, would you take these two generals into my conference room and give them the co-ordinates of the main Werner Ranch in Wyoming where we suspect the dead eagles are buried?" Thirty minutes later, one of the generals stuck his head back inside my office and said, "We will fly over the ranch with our infrared cameras and see you in a week."

Frankly, I was unaware of a federal statute that forbids military aircraft to be used to assist in making a felony case within our country. Nevertheless, a week later, the generals were back with a roll of film that the "vehicle's" cameras had taken of the Arctic Porcupine and Central caribou herds, which had begun their long summer migration.

More to the point, there also was a series of infrared photographs of the Werner main ranch corral. There was a highly visible red spot in the main ranch coral. "That's where the eagles are buried," said the general.

I gave him a proper salute and never found out which of America's high-speed vehicles had given us such important information, which verified the work of the young FBI-trained cowboy. But we couldn't use the photographs to obtain a federal search warrant, and we still needed the pilot.

I conducted a series of interviews to the Denver Post and the Rocky Mountain News, explaining the potential number of eagles we feared had been shot from an airplane or helicopter. I was seeking that pilot.

As weeks went by, we waited for the name of the man who could make our case. On a very warm day, my secretary came into my office and announced that there was a very nervous gentleman sitting in a chair in my lobby who kept mumbling, "I'm the man. I'm the man who the secretary is looking for."

I buzzed for Chuck Lawrence to join me and then walked out and stood before a large man who was literally shaking. I said, "Who are you?" He said, "My name is James Vogan and I'm the man you're looking for."

I asked, "Why am I looking for you?" He said that he flew a helicopter and the planes from which sharpshooters firing shotguns were responsible for downing more than 500 bald and golden eagles over Wyoming and Colorado. Cowboys retrieved eagles on the ground that were killed or wounded and picked them up, following the client's instructions, he said.

I asked him to stop talking. Chuck Lawrence was approaching rapidly. I asked Chuck to read him his rights, as Mr. Vogan was "the man" – the pilot we have been seeking. Mr. Werner was his principal client, Vogan said.

Chuck quickly read him his rights. Vogan burst into tears and said, "If I am convicted of illegally flying sharpshooters who killed federally protected eagles, I think I will lose my pilot's license. I have no other way to provide for myself or my family. What will happen to me?"

I told him, "If your testimony holds up under tough interrogation by Mr. Lawrence and Mr. Werner's highly capable defense lawyers, I promise you immunity so that you will not lose your pilot's license."

Lawrence led Mr. Vogan away. I returned to my desk and called Secretary Morton. I brought him up to speed and he said, "This is a case that could end the indiscriminate killings of bald and golden eagles everywhere in the country. It is up to you to see that the full force of the federal government is used to convict Mr. Werner."

The Justice Department obtained a valid search warrant and, accompanied by federal wildlife enforcement officers and federal marshals, arrived at Werner's main ranch.

The Werner cow hands wisely disappeared when the heavily armed federal agents entered the ranch. Equipped with backhoes, they dug the contents of the deep pit to the surface. They found a stinking mess of dead eagles. The marshals and agents

'NOW, THIS'N HERE IS THE BALD EAGLE, OUR NATIONAL BIRD AND SYMBOL — I WANT YOU TO KILL EVERY ONE OF THE VARMINTS YOU SEE!'

collected hundreds of pairs of eagle talons and took countless photographs.

At last, the evidence was sufficient to bring charges against Werner on numerous federal violations. There was a pause while the U.S. attorney in Casper considered the evidence before formally indicting Werner.

Charles Callison was the National Audubon Society's best Washington representative who ever lived. He was widely respected on the Hill by both Republicans and Democrats and throughout the federal bureaucracy. He was a "straight shooter" – scientifically sound, straightforward, with determined insistence, fearless, and, in my opinion, the finest wildlife lobbyist in the capital.

He was an old friend, as I had met him at the Audubon Center in Greenwich, Connecticut, prior to my governmental service. He was fully briefed on the Werner case and wanted to know how National Audubon could help see that Werner was prosecuted.

Armed with pilot Vogan's testimony, Chuck and I met with appropriate members of the Justice Department, who laid out to the U.S. attorney in Cheyenne, Wyo., how the case would be prosecuted. The Justice Department sent that U.S. attorney a complete recapitulation of the evidence and the statutes that had been broken and asked him to prepare a case against Werner in Casper.

This story made *The New York Times, The Washington Post,* even *The Palm Beach Post* along with *Time, Life* and *Newsweek* magazines. Bart Rea was interviewed and was quoted as saying, "These were systematic, orchestrated killings."

Vogan verified our report by testifying that on Werner's ranch, he'd seen 65 dead eagles piled as high as a haystack. Pat Oliphant, the great cartoonist, drew a ghastly cartoon that he presented to me. It depicted a rancher holding a dead eagle with outstretched wings and the rancher bragging to his son, "That's a bald eagle, the symbol of our country. We kill every one of them."

The U.S. attorney reviewed the Justice Department's outline of the prosecution's case to file criminal charges against Herman Werner, but he resisted filing charges and setting a trial date. Charlie Callison came to my office and forcefully urged me to call the U.S. attorney and demand prosecution.

I began making a weekly Wednesday morning telephone call to the U.S. attorney, who initially stated that he had a number of other cases of greater importance that he was trying to prosecute. After three telephone calls, he finally said there was no jury in Wyoming that would convict Herman Werner of killing eagles. I responded that this case was of national importance and failure to prosecute would allow continuation of both poisoning and shooting eagles indiscriminately from the Southwest through the Rocky Mountains.

I told him he had to bring the case to trial even if the verdict was uncertain. Another two weeks went by with the same response: "No Wyoming jury will convict Herman Werner of paying to have eagles killed on his ranches." The calls usually ended by the U.S. attorney hanging up on me.

In those days the Department of Interior, along with most federal buildings, had no security system. Anyone could and did come in without authority. To my best recollection, it was a warm day and suddenly a wiry man dressed in a Western suit and

Rocky Mountain News

A Scripps-Howard Newspaper

Reg. U.S. Pat. Off.

Colorado's First Newspaper—Founded in 1859

113TH YEAR, NO. 42

Published every morning by Denver Publishing Co
Second class postage paid at Denver, Colorado

DENVER, COLORADO 80201, THURSDAY, JUNE 3, 1971

HOME EDITION ★★★★

FORECAST: Partly cloudy

10¢

112 PAGES

UPI TELEPHOTO

Circumstances surrounding the deaths of nearly 50 bald and golden eagles in Wyoming are the subject of U.S. Senate appropriations subcommittee hearing. Examining mounted specimens of the eagle species are, from left, Sen. Gale McGee, D-Wyo., subcommittee chairman; Nathaniel Reed, assistant interior secretary, and William Ruckelshaus, head of the Environmental Protection Agency. Ruckelshaus said more eagles will die unless action is taken.

Poison linked to eagles' deaths meant for rodents

a Stetson, pushed open my office door.

He pointed his finger at me and said, "I am going to get you!" My secretary pushed the button for Chuck Lawrence or another armed agent to appear as rapidly as possible. I said quietly, "Before you get me, please tell me who you are."

In a very loud voice he answered, "I am Herman Werner. I'm the man who protects his sheep by killing eagles. You don't know anything about the loss of lambs to eagles. You think they're a pretty bird. I hate them! I'll do anything to protect my animals. Damn you! I am the most important rancher in Wyoming. You haven't a chance of convicting me of anything. I do what I want to do to protect my sheep."

I rose to my full six-foot-four frame and walked toward him. "Mr. Werner, get out of my office now," I demanded. "I never speak to alleged felons and that means you. Get out. I'll see you in court!"

Shaking his fist, Werner backed slowly out of the door as two enforcement agents surrounded him.

During that time, I received considerable assistance from veteran newscaster Walter Cronkite, who ended his evening commentary at least once a week by mentioning the killing of eagles, the discovery of dead eagles, the case against Herman Werner and concern that the killing of eagles was far more widespread than the public knew about.

Weeks went by. I became very impatient, especially when that wonderful alternative newspaper, the High Country News, complained that justice was not being served as long as "the central figure in the whole matter, Herman Werner, jokingly and smugly walks the street in Casper unprosecuted and unruffled."

I asked Secretary Morton for assistance. He called Attorney General Elliot Richardson, who made a date to see me the next day. I had known General Richardson for a number of years. I considered him a friend and one of the most highly ethical, intelligent members of the Nixon administration.

When I joined him in his spacious office, he was accompanied by two senior members of his staff from the lands division. I sat next to Richardson and explained the reluctance of the U.S. attorney in Casper to bring the case to trial. Elliot was appalled. He asked his assistants what the problem was. They answered that all legal procedural work had been accomplished. Werner had been indicted and the reluctance of the U.S. attorney to bring the case to court was "disturbing," they said.

Richardson called his secretary and asked to be placed on a conference call with the U.S. attorney in Casper. Their conversation went as follows:

Richardson: "How do you like your role as U.S. attorney in Wyoming?"

The attorney: "General Richardson, this is the finest position I could ever hope for. I have found it very challenging. I have a fine staff. I have made some very important prosecutions and won. Seriously, when my term is over, I may seek a federal judgeship."

General Richardson quizzically inquired as to the status of the Herman Werner-eagle case. There was a long pause by the U.S. attorney.

Finally he replied, "Is Secretary Reed with you now?"

Richardson: "He is sitting next to me on the speaker phone. He has briefed me, as have my senior staff and we are dumbfounded that you have not brought the Werner case to trial."

The attorney: "General, there is no Wyoming jury that I could select that would find Mr. Werner guilty of killing eagles, even though they are a protected bird."

Richardson, very quietly: "Your job is not to be a member of a jury. You are a federal prosecutor sworn to enforce our nation's laws. The evidence is overwhelming. You will bring the case to trial. I will assign one of my deputies to be in contact with you in order to assure me that the proper procedures are followed and the case will be brought as rapidly as possible. Do you understand?

Palm Beach Post, Thursday, June 3, 1971

Reed Calls for Ban on Poison That Killed Wyoming Eagles

From Post Wire Services

WASHINGTON — Assistant Secretary of the Interior Nathaniel P. Reed said yesterday he has asked the Environmental Protection Agency (EPA) to ban from interstate shipment the poison thallium sulphate, which has been pinpointed as a killer of 22 eagles in Wyoming.

He pledged to try to find out who is reponsible for the deaths of the eagles, found last month in a rugged canyon near Casper, and prosecute them.

William O. Ruckelshaus, EPA administrator, asserted he is powerless to halt further accidental poisonings of rare and endangered species of wildlife unless Congress strengthens pesticide-control laws.

"We can't control the use of these pesticides," Ruckelshaus told a Senate subcommittee investigating the deaths of 48 golden and bald eagles in Wyoming.

Of the 48 dead eagles, Ruckelshaus said, 22 were killed by thallium sulfate poisoning. The remainder died of electrocution from high tension lines or from gunshot wounds.

Reed said action "will be started immediately to identify other toxic compounds used in animal damage control which should be similarly banned." In addition, he is encouraging states "to take appropriate action on local control of toxic chemicals."

Reed, assistant secretary for fish and wildlife and parks, announced his actions in testimony prepared for the hearing by Sen. Dale McGee's agricultural and environmental agencies subcommittee.

Reed also discussed the department's widely criticized predator control program by some prominent national conservation organizations," he said.

He reported the Interior Department and President Nixon's Council on Environmental Quality last month began "a broad overview" of the predator program. Reed said a non-governmental task force will conduct "an intensive revaluation of all existing animal damage control programs and make recommendations for any needed program changes or modifications."

That is an order!"

The attorney, after a pause: "General, I will proceed as ordered."

Richardson: "I think that ends this conversation."

He turned to me and said, "Nathaniel, I apologize for the U.S. Justice Department. You should've come to me earlier but the wheels of justice sometimes turn far too slowly. Mr. Werner is going to be brought to trial and I am going to have oversight of the procedures and ensure you that the Justice Department will do everything in our power to convict this man of reckless disregard of federal laws."

On August 3, 1971, I and Bill Ruckelshaus, the recently confirmed administrator of the newly created Environmental Protection Agency, were summoned by Sen. Gale McGee of Wyoming to testify before the Senate subcommittee on interior affairs. We were joined by Vogan, the pilot, to testify about the extraordinary case of the killing of more than 500 bald and golden eagles over Wyoming and Colorado.

As I headed for the first hearing, I suddenly had a "flash." I called Dillon Ripley, secretary of the Smithsonian Institution, and asked if he could have a stuffed bald eagle and a golden eagle at his front door in eight minutes. He said, "It will be my pleasure." I picked up the two birds and placed them on the table where Vogan, Ruckelshaus and I testified before the subcommittee.

The flashes of cameras and lights from the TV cameras almost blinded us. Senators held the dead and stuffed birds in their arms. It was quite a show of solidarity that even Western senators would no longer tolerate the indiscriminate killing of bald and golden eagles.

Vogan explained that Doyle Vaughn, president of the Buffalo Flying Service, had employed him to fly a chopper or a single-engine plane while sharpshooters fired automatic shotguns, bringing down those hundreds of bald and golden eagles. His testimony was so devastating that it reinvigorated national news of the travesty.

Bill Ruckelshaus testified that "more eagles will die unless action is taken." He further stated that he was "powerless to ban the sale and use of thallium sulfate" and a number of other highly toxic chemicals that were been misused in many parts of our country. He added he could not promise that rare and endangered species would not be poisoned unless Congress strengthened its outdated pesticide laws. He urged Congress to give him the authority to ban "killer pesticides."

Almost immediately, a bill was introduced to increase the fine for killing a bald eagle from $1,000 to $10,000 and the golden eagle was given further protection.

Widely read environmental writer Michael Frome referred to the poisoners and airplane killers as "the Wyoming monsters."

Curiously, a federal judge had fined Vaughn, the air service president, a paltry $500 after he pleaded guilty to 75 counts of assisting in the eagle massacre.

As promised, pilot James Vogan received immunity from prosecution, but his flying days in Wyoming were coming to an end. A former president of the Wyoming Wool Growers Association took a swing at him in the association's magazine: "He is a prime candidate for the liar of the year award."

Vogan sued for libel, seeking $1.2 million in actual damages and another $1 million in punitive damage. In 1974, a jury awarded him $55,000, but the judge declared the amount excessive and directed Vogan to accept $10,000. Vogan demanded a new trial but eventually settled for an undisclosed amount.

And Walter Cronkite gave a thrilling commentary on the conclusion of finally getting Werner to trial.

Before the trial could go forward on August 6, 1973, Herman Werner died from injuries sustained in a two-car collision in Rawlins, Wyo. Slowly but surely, the Wyoming establishment came around during the height of the controversy. Governor Hathaway admitted that "eagles were never really a threat to livestock."

Today, discounting Alaska and Hawaii, the national eagle population stands at more than 7,000 nesting pairs, a turnaround so dramatic that many conservation groups, Audubon included, embraced the birds' complete removal from the endangered species list.

On June 28, 2007, both golden and bald eagles were removed from the list. Greg Buscher, Audubon's director of bird conservation, said, "The bald eagle has recovered throughout its range. The bird is still protected by the National Bald Eagle Act and the important thing now is to make sure that the law is interpreted correctly. The law makes it illegal to disturb or bother and not just taking or killing. The act has been responsible for maintaining a sustained number of both eagles throughout their range."

Bart Rea agreed that the climate in his home state had changed: "There has been an immense amount of public education since the '70s," he said, "including an emphasis on the bald eagle being primarily a scavenger and only secondarily as a predator."

A sign of the esteem in which the Wyomingites now hold eagles can be found on the state's visitor's bureau's website. On its tabs, wildlife watching is highlighted as an activity that tourists can enjoy.

To make this point, the site has a photo of a bald eagle.

After I left office, my friendship with Liz and Bart Rea intensified when we both became members of the board of the National Audubon Society. We often sat next to each other at board meetings and board dinners. We enjoyed the field trips. It is a friendship based on the same ethical principle of our moral responsibilities as stewards of America's wildlife. Liz and Bart have become life friends. It is a curious fact that unexpected events in our life journeys can lead to the development of life friendships.

This extraordinary experience was just another fascinating part of my Department of Interior career.

Outrage Over Pollution: The Clean Water Act

"We were quietly in awe of our joint responsibilities – we honestly believed it to be the opportunity of a lifetime."

Webster defines a "*Saga: as 1: a prose narrative recorded in Iceland in the 12th and 13th centuries of historic or legendary figures and events of the heroic age of Norway and Iceland; 2: a modern heroic narrative resembling the Icelandic saga.*"

Shortly after I was sworn into office, Secretary Morton assigned me the responsibility to represent the Department of Interior's participation in the administration's effort to compile a Clean Water Act. The main participants were William Ruckelshaus, the newly appointed administrator of the newly created Environmental Protection Agency and Russell Train, the president's Chairman of the Council on Environmental Quality. Ruckelshaus was a graduate of Princeton University and Harvard Law School. Bill was an engaging, determined attorney who had served as Indiana's deputy attorney general. He had been assigned to the Board of Health and counsel to the state's Stream Pollution Control Board. Shortly after he was sworn in and well before a final congressional bill was passed he issued a challenge.

Ruckelshaus announced that, "the EPA will insist with the authority Congress has provided and with all the powers of persuasion at our command, that all existing authorities for controlling pollution will be applied, across the board, in every city and town and to every industry in this country." This announcement caused responses from dozens of mayors of cities as large as Detroit and Atlanta, to small communities that simply did not have the tax base to be required to mount an effective campaign to clean their citizen's sewage without major federal support. The congress listened.

My two deputies both 'Buff' Bohlen and Douglas Wheeler had been participants in a series of working groups organized by Train in an effort to have input with the Congressional effort to produce an effective Clean Water Act. The Secretary arranged for me to meet with Senator Edmund Muskie who had become chairman of a special subcommittee on air and water protection in 1963. His passion on the two subjects has left an incredible mark on the foundation of America's environmental law. Florida was the beneficiary of the Water Quality Act of 1965. The regional administrators of the newly formed Federal Water Pollution Control Administration gave me vital assistance in strengthening the proposed Florida water quality standards. Although many 'state's rights' members of the Florida legislature and the politically powerful 'Old Guard of the usual suspects' demanded that Governor Kirk should prevent me from working with 'the feds', my rejoinder was, "We need all the assistance possible, as our state is befouled by raw sewage and untreated industrial waste and even toxic wastes being released from military bases."

Construction grants for municipal wastewater plants were dramatically increased. Florida's share of the then limited federal sewage construction funds increased dramatically, as numerous cities began to resolve differences and begin a cooperative effort to create multi-municipality projects. Senator Muskie and the pertinent House congressional committees held a series of hearings on the shortcomings of the 1965 Clean Water Act and the 1966 amendments. No new legislation was produced but the hearings were well attended. Newspapers and television accounts of the ill-treated sewage and industrial untreated or undertreated wastes were headed for legal show downs. The catastrophic oil spill off Santa Barbara which killed thousands of birds and spoiled beaches as far south as Mexico and the Cuyahoga River catching on fire twice within a short period of time made national news.

When Senator Muskie and I met, I was delighted to learn that he was well aware of my near 5 years of frustrations attempting to end the "polluted paradise-the State of Florida." We discussed my experiences in Florida, the desperate need to increase the funding for the sewage facilities in our nation's national parks system and pollution problems at the national fish hatcheries. I added the impasse that I faced as I left Florida that without far greater federal financing the cities and counties might agree on certain aspects of how to create regional sewage treatment plants and end raw sewage discharges to the Atlantic and the Gulf, but progress based on legal enforcement would be slow if achievable. Senator Muskie stated that he was quietly working with both Ruckelshaus and Train, but there were forces within the Nixon Administration that were not convinced that a major clean water proposal would be a priority considering the cost of the Vietnam War and the ever increasing costs of the "Great Society's programs." The Senator wished that the Ruckelshaus and Train 'water quality team' would work closely with his expert staff so that differences in the Senate's Bill and the Administration's Bill would be minimalized. I left his office mentioning my wife's family had summer homes in Winter Harbor, Maine, and every time I crossed the Penobscot River there was visible pollution from the Bangor municipal sewage plant and the upstream paper companies. He smiled grimly and stated: "Passage of a strong water quality act will know no boundaries. It will be a national effort."

On return to Interior I scheduled myself to have an extensive briefing by both my two deputies and Russ Train and his working group that in a short period of time would become Bill Ruckelshaus' major assignment. We met frequently and were in close contact with Muskie's key advisors: Tom Jorling and Leon Billings. They were convinced that any waste discharged into our nation's watershed had to be treated or otherwise meet specific water quality criteria that considered overall ecosystem health. The fallacy of the old belief that dilution was the cure for pollution was now finally ended.

I testified twice before Senator Muskie's subcommittee on Interior's position urging the final bill to recognize the environmental damage that pollution was causing fisheries and waterfowl habitat. The plight of the park and refuge service's budgets was causing a financial crunch that was eliminating other capital investments of major importance.

During one of my appearances before the house subcommittee discussing the needs for additional sewage control financing within many of our national parks, Congressman Henry Reuss elicited from me more information and personal feelings about my role starting what became Florida's Department of Environmental Protection. The congressmen quizzed me on my problems initiating a full-scale cleanup of raw sewage and untreated industrial and military waste. I gave the committee my honest appraisal of what was needed. A strong federal partnership willing to hopefully force compliance of strength and water quality rules and most importantly adequate federal funding to encourage – yes, even force, reluctant municipalities

Penobscot River, Maine

and industries to engage the services of our nation's engineering firms combined with time schedules for compliance. I added enforcement is critical. Time schedules are vital, but if the nation was really going to make the Clean Water Act truly effective, there was no alternative to significant federal funding.

A couple of days later the Secretary called and informed me that the leadership in the White House and OMB felt I had overstated the administration's position to control spending and dramatically reduce the Senate's version of the Clean Water Bill.

I simply shrugged and replied to Roger Morton: "Rog, yes I got a bit carried away, but I told the committee the truth – so help me God!"

Shortly thereafter, Ruckelshaus, Train, his staff, Senator Morton and me and my staff were curtly informed by Bob Haldeman that the president was dissatisfied by our efforts to reduce the financial commitments and the federal takeover of what should be a state's responsibility. The president remained in a very fiscally conservative posture. He simply did not believe the state of nationwide pollution problems required a major federal investment.

After months of meetings to finalize language and coordinate with the Muskie team, the leadership of the Office of Management and Budget informed Ruckelshaus and Train that President Nixon was concerned – deeply concerned over the size of the grants to construct wastewater treatment facilities. The Muskie draft proposal dramatically increased the grants far beyond the administration's budget requests.

Nixon was determined to fight the Muskie bill in the House of Representatives. Ruckelshaus, Train and Secretary Morton and me were warned by Haldeman to be very careful in public testimony and in private meetings on the hill with members of the Public Works Committee. The impact of the League of Conservation Voters 'Dirty Dozen' campaign had members of the prominent anti-environmental congressmen deeply concerned about their forthcoming reelection campaigns. That fact combined with the growing support of a vast variety of organizations from the Garden Club of America, the Federated Garden Clubs of America, the League of Women Voters and the old line conservation organizations plus the newly powerful, legally impatient environmental activists' organizations made Chairman Blatnik nervous. He was acutely aware that the newly passed 18-Year-Old Voting Act would encourage thousands of "green votes". Combined with the coalition of so many interests pressing for a strong Clean Water Act, House members were concerned that no act or a weak act would cost them critically important votes.

He wanted a strong clean water bill, but was uncertain as to the merits of the amount of federal fiscal commitment included in the Muskie Bill. He was determined to avoid production of a competitive Clean Water Bill that would be radically different from the Senate's version. Regrettably Congressman Blatnik suffered a heart attack. That removed him from the emerging potential confrontation.

In March 1972, after endless debates Chairman Muskie released his committee's version of the Clean Water Act. Some supporters of the Senate Bill were deeply troubled by many changes that they felt weakened the lofty goals of the initial bill. Congressmen John Dingell and Henry Reuss sponsored a series of amendments to the House bill designed to strengthen what they perceived were weaknesses that could be cured. Their amendments failed, but incredibly were included in the final bill. The House bill was passed by an astonishing margin of 380 to 14.

A conference committee was convened in May 1972. The conferees met 39 times. Incredibly the conferees feeling significant public pressure in the election year raised the Senate's recommended $14 billion grant proposal up to $20 billion. Sewage control grants were authorized for 60% of cost and 70% if the municipalities or state added significant funds.

Weeks went by. Members of Congress wanted to head home to campaign. Finally, exhaustion took hold of the House Public Works Committee. On October 5th the House Speaker called the Conference Bill to the floor. The bill passed 366-11. The Senate followed by passing the Conference Bill by a vote of 74-0.

President Nixon declared his intention to veto the Act as an example of 'conservative fiscal management' prior to the presidential campaign. He waited taking almost every moment of the ten days before the mandatory deadline for presidential action until 11:45 p.m. and vetoed the bill. Congress had not adjourned fearing his 'pocket veto'. The Senate convened within two hours of the veto message and voted 52-14 to override his veto. Within hours the Housed met and voted 247-33 to override the veto and went home.

The Clean Water Act of 1972 became law on October 18th, 1972.

Dr. N. William Hines whose incredibly detailed history of the pollution control efforts was a most valuable reference for me in concluding this personal history of the "inside stories" of how the congress finally faced up to the gross pollution of our nation's waters and estuaries concluded at the Act's 40th birthday: "Taking stock of the 1972 CWA's birthday, the nation has not come close to attaining the 'no discharge goal', only about half of our nation's waters are fishable and swimmable, and far too many toxic chemicals are still finding their way into our waterways. To idealists, this is disappointing, but to realists it is not all surprising. Achieving heroic water pollution gains in a country as geographically diverse and economically active as the United States is truly difficult work and requires great patience and perseverance. So, should we celebrate or mourn the still problematic quality of many of our waters? One way to think about this question is to ask: what would have happened in the absence of the establishment of these highly ambitious goals and the change in regulatory authority philosophy initiated by the 1972 CWA? One can only speculate, but my best guess is without the philosophical commitment to the proposition that no one has the right to use public waters to dispose of their wastes, enforced by progressively stricter effluent standards, our waters would be less clean today."

In finality he observed: "Although the 1972 CWA has sparked much improvement in many waterways, it has not lived up to its own lofty aspirations over the past 40 years. It will probably never do so until the commitment to high quality water resources nationwide regains the same level of public support it enjoyed during the unique decade of environmental reforms leading up to the adoption of the 1972 Act."

All great sagas have peculiar endings. So it was with the 1972 Clean Water Act. Despite widespread support for 'getting going', President Nixon was determined to have his way: specifically opposing the $18 billion increase in the cost of the bill associated with the construction of wastewater treatment facilities. He had his list of grievances with the act and the members of congress that had voted down a number of his legislative 'must list'. Nixon decided to defy congress by the use of the Impoundment Act of 1974 and ordered Russell Train, Ruckelshaus' successor of Administrator of the Environmental Protection Agency, to not disperse funds allocated in the 1972 Act. These funds were intended to be used to construct municipal sewers and water treatment facilities in several cities including New York City. This disagreement went to the Supreme Court in the 1975 case *Train v. City of New York* and the Court ruled in favor of Congress, noting that "the president cannot frustrate the will of Congress by killing a program through impoundment."

From my personal perspective the hours, days, years spent 'in the trenches' both in Florida and as assistant secretary, the nation needs a continuing federal government major infusion of funds on a matching system combined with truly effective enforcement programs both at the federal and state level. It is the only way we can achieve much higher standards of water quality nationwide. The enormity of agricultural pollution must be faced, algal blooms created by fertilizer and organic wastes from dairies, hog and fowl farm runoff must become a major objective for enforcement.

I rejoice in the many successes and am deeply disappointed by the lack of commitment by far too many governors and their water quality agencies. It is time to make the case for clean water a national priority once again!

Following my departure to Washington, Governor Askew appointed Jay Landers to head the Pollution Control Commission. He was a highly competent senior aide to the Secretary of State and a good friend. Shortly thereafter there was a sweeping reorganization of Florida governmental agencies forming the Department of Environmental Regulation.

Due to the successful litigation versus President Nixon's refusal to expend Clean Water Act funding, millions of dollars of federal funds were made available to the states for the construction of sewer lines and advanced sewage treatment facilities. My successors, Jay and Victoria Tschinkel had the pleasure of funding millions of dollars to make much needed improvements. They had the great opportunity to use the efforts of my five years of work, especially in the south Florida and on the west coast, to fund miles of sewage lines, a series of regional treatment plants and ended ocean dumping of raw sewage.

Vicki Tschinkel became a fast friend and went on to become one of Florida's best known environmentalists.

I had the pleasure fifteen years later while serving on the Board of the South Florida Water Management District to vote to require all advanced treated sewage water to be utilized on golf courses and public lands reducing the need to use potable water for irrigation. It was a worthy ending of a five-year struggle!

The Marine Mammal Protection Act

Porpoises were killed by the thousands and great whales were nearly exterminated."

One of my most important roles at the Department of Interior was as its representative at the ongoing Council of Environmental Quality (CEQ) meetings, which were exploring opportunities to lay a new foundation of American environmental law. Congress was committed to environmental reforms on a broad range of subjects – a dedication that now, in this time of partisan rancor, would seem odd.

Although I was late in joining the process, Dr. Lee Talbot invited me to a number of sessions devoted to discussion of a potential Marine Mammal Act. Talbot, an ecologist and geographer with expertise in international environmental affairs, formed the CEQ with Russell Train, who you know by now also a renowned conservationist and one of my most valued colleagues.

We were fortunate to have an astonishing number of federal experts who had spent their careers studying the alarming decrease of all marine mammals, plus an outstanding number of experts from the newly formed non-governmental environmental organizations. They all shared sincere concern over the plight of many of the world's marine mammals, including the vast overharvesting by Japan of great whales. Norway and Iceland had defied informal but very real international agreements to restrain whale harvesting, maintaining their supposed "rights" to exploit small whales such as minkes for food.

The Japanese whalers were active in the Antarctic killing the last of the great whales: the gigantic blue whale (the largest mammal on Earth), humpback, fin and a number of other great whales under the pretext of food necessities. Tons of uneaten whale meat were stored in freezers in Japan. Their whaling fleets were encouraged and subsidized by the government to provide what officials called "vital employment."

In the early 1970s, the mismanagement of marine mammals was brought to the public eye by photos of Canadian seal pups being clubbed on the ice and revelations that thousands of porpoises were being killed for no reason other than convenience by the tuna industry.

Talbot had a number of issues he wanted enshrined in a new law. He believed the key objective of managing wild living resources should be maintaining the ecosystem, and that managing a species for consumption or other purposes should be done consistently with this purpose.

He stressed that marine mammals and other wildlife are of value not just for consumption but also for scientific, educational and aesthetic values while maintaining the ecosystems on which we all rely. He believed there should be independent oversight responsibility and authority over the line agencies to assure their operations were consistent with the law involved, and that management advice should be based on science.

He recommended formation of a scientific committee and said if their recommendations are not followed, agencies must provide a public statement explaining why.

He also believed species should be managed on the "Precautionary Principle," which holds that if an action or policy has a suspected risk of causing harm to the public or environment, the burden of proving it is safe falls on those taking an action. This is exactly the reverse of the resource management policies of the U.S. until that time. Our approach until then was that the burden of proof was on those who questioned the management action. Fishermen, for example, could continue to fish unless challengers could prove that the fishing was harmful.

Debate over the marine act led to two sets of proposed laws, one set (by conservation groups) providing complete protection to marine mammals, and the other (an industry and National Marine Fisheries Service effort) assuring harvest as usual.

The Marine Mammal Act was passed as a science-based compromise between the two bills. Congressman Glenn Anderson introduced the Marine Mammal Act in the House as a reaction to Congressman David Pryor's and Senator Fred Harris' proposed legislation, the Ocean Mammal Protection Act. The latter act would have banned outright the killing of any marine mammal.

Anderson's bill proposed to manage, supervise and restrict the taking of certain marine mammals. A bitter controversy ensued between the dueling pieces of legislation, which was characterized in congressional debates as the battle between protectionists and managers.

Ultimately the Anderson bill, which created a management strategy to protect marine mammals, won and became law. It assumed the name: The Marine Mammal Protection Act of 1972.

The New York Academy of Science examined the act and reported on its progress and failures on its 40th anniversary. Its report is worth careful consideration:

"Passed in 1972, the Marine Mammal Protection Act has two fundamental objectives: to maintain U.S. marine mammal stocks at their optimum sustainable populations and to uphold their ecological role in the ocean. The current status of many marine mammal populations is considerably better than in 1972. Take reduction plans have been largely successful in reducing direct fisheries bycatch, although they have not been prepared for all at-risk stocks, and fisheries continue to place marine mammals as risk. Information on population trends is unknown for most (71%) stocks; more stocks with known trends are improving than declining: 19% increasing, 5% stable, and 5% decreasing. Challenges remain, however, and the act has generally been ineffective in treating indirect impacts, such as noise, disease, and prey depletion. Existing conservation measures have not protected large whales from fisheries interactions or ship strikes in the northwestern Atlantic. Despite these limitations, marine mammals within the U.S. Exclusive Economic Zone appear to be faring better than those outside, with fewer species in at-risk categories and more of least concern.

"The fundamental objectives of the MMPA are (1) to maintain stocks of marine mammals at their optimum sustainable populations (OSP) and (2) to maintain marine mammal stocks as functioning elements of their ecosystems. The act does not define OSP, but the National Marine Fisheries Service (NMFS) has interpreted OSP to be a population level that falls between Maximum Net Productivity Level (MNPL) and carrying capacity (K). In operational terms, therefore, OSP is defined as a population size that falls between 0.5K and K. In addition, there is a clear mandate to protect individual marine mammals from harm, referred to as take."

The report concluded that there were significant successes resulting from the law.

"The MMPA was passed in response to

concern over the conservation status of several species of marine mammals due to unregulated harvest or incidental mortality. Section 2 of the act notes that 'certain species and population stocks of marine mammals are, or may be, in danger of extinction or depletion as a result of man's activities.' The MMPA, buttressed by additional protection from the ESA, has successfully prevented the extirpation of any marine mammal population in the United States in the 40 years since it was enacted. Countless tens of thousands of individual cetaceans, pinniped, and sirenians have been protected from harm since 1972, exactly as intended by those who crafted the legislation. As a consequence, many marine mammal populations, particularly seals and sea lions, have recovered to or near their carrying capacity. The recovery of these stocks has been so successful that fisheries representatives have occasionally advocated for culls. Yet several recent studies have shown that whales, seals, and dolphins are not a threat to human fisheries and even a complete eradication of marine mammals would show little to no benefit and come at an ecological cost. The remarkable recovery of harbor and gray seals in New England and California sea lions, harbor seals, and elephant seals on the Pacific Coast highlights the value of the act and serves as a striking reminder of the magnitude of the persecution of these species before 1972. [43]

The Precautionary Principle has benefited all marine mammals that are covered under the act, and the Endangered Species Act, which followed, applied the principle to all species. While the principle is not always followed – what laws have been? – the results have been of worldwide benefit to wild species.

The Train/Talbot CEQ team deserves remarkable credit for substantively ending an era when porpoises were killed by the thousands in tuna nets and great whales were nearly exterminated. They continued their record of bringing together the "brightest and best" – experts of all ages from government and academia and increasingly expert members of non-government organizations – and providing an atmosphere in which dissident views could be openly discussed and agreements made on proposed language of important efforts to change the status quo.

President Nixon appointed me a member of Chairman Train's official delegation at a vital international whaling conference held within the State Department. The 1971 meeting generated bitter debate over the fact that, in 1961, 66,000 whales had been killed. The kill figures continued to indicate that many of the whale species would be extinct if a significant reduction in whaling was not adopted.

The U.S. delegation failed to end whaling, but we secured a number of concessions and led an international publicity effort to decry the exploitation of these remarkable mammals. It was fascinating to be part of a world conference that was tainted by the Japanese literally bribing countries to allow them to continue whaling by offering money for so-called "fishing concessions."

In 1979, a moratorium on factory ships was enacted but proved to be impossible to enforce.

Finally, in 1982, as the world's whale population neared extinction, the International Whaling Commission declared a moratorium on all whaling – zero limit, the most important decision the generally inept commission ever made. Japanese representatives, whose delegation included owners of a number of whaling ships, continued to vehemently oppose the measure.

To this day, the Japanese government still authorizes killing a number of small whales for scientific purposes, an outright violation of the commission's moratorium. Regrettably, both Iceland and Norway still permit the harvesting of a small number of minke whales, whose populations have rebounded.

There is hope, however, for the majority of the great whales, as recent reports show a substantial increase in humpbacks, right whales and even blue whales. The North Atlantic right whale has the lowest breeding numbers and is in jeopardy of becoming extinct despite significant efforts on its behalf.

It will take another 50 years to know if the commission's final moratorium saved sufficient breeding stock of the great whales for significant recovery. Oceans without whales would be a significant indication of man's lack of stewardship.

Wild Oceans, a non-profit group founded by anglers in 1973 to preserve fishing opportunities for the future, summed up our efforts perfectly in a passage from its spring 2015 newsletter:

"Accounts of predators struggling to find food remind us that it's time to move away, once and for all, from ecologically-harmful policies that manage each species to maximize yields to fisheries, without regard for the impact on other species in the food web or the ecological community as a whole. Ecosystem-based fishery management of forage fish is critical because of their strong interconnections with so many other species."

NOTES – A COMPROMISE: THE MARINE MAMMAL PROTECTION ACT

[43] ANNALS OF THE NEW YORK ACADEMY OF SCIENCES - Issue: The Year in Ecology and Conservation Biology. The Marine Mammal Protection Act at 40: status, recovery, and future of U.S. marine mammals. March 2013.

The Harriman Family and the Railroad Ranch State Park

"I told them, with vehemence, their work was a disgrace, to leave the plan for destruction and to disappear."

Having been deeply involved in the creation of the Railroad Ranch State Park, I invited one of my keen and expert grandsons to accompany me to Henry's Fork of the Snake River, not only to test our fishing skills, but to give me an opportunity to inspect the park.

With that in mind, I made a date to visit with the park's manager. I had not been there since Idaho Gov. Cecil Andrus and I were assigned the responsibilities of developing a master use plan for a state park that would be donated by Mr. Roland Harriman. Roland was the son of the legendary E.R. Harriman who controlled the Union Pacific, Southern Pacific, three additional railroads, the Pacific Mail Steamship Company and Wells Fargo.

The final park master plan had to satisfy Mr. Harriman. The plan had to be completed rapidly, as he was suffering from an aggressive disease. He wanted to be confident that he could protect the environmentally sensitive areas of the Railroad Ranch, yet allow controlled visitation.

Following two days of successful fishing, I visited the park. I was impressed by Keith Hobbs, the park's manager, who seemed to understand his role as steward of one of the most unique areas in Idaho, if not the nation.

We drove around the park, looked at the parking areas, the overnight RV areas, the spotless toilet and showering facilities and the general condition of the road system. In particular, the trails and horseback concession exemplified sound management.

I was privileged to see two pairs of trumpeter swans, one with four cygnets, the other with three. The young birds were actively feeding on the insects in the aquatic grass beds within Silver Lake and were in fine condition.

On return to the office, Hobbs furnished me with a copy of the deed and the area's history, written by Mary E. Reed and Keith Petersen.

The role of former Governor Smylie was fascinating and unknown to me.

Controversy had erupted over Mr. Harriman's demands that a state Department of State Parks be established prior to his donation of the ranch, that the opening day for fishing on June 15th be delayed until the bird nesting season was completed, that only fly fishing be allowed (with mandatory use of flies tied on barbless hooks), and that a rule be imposed requiring catch and release of all trout.

In consecutive legislative sessions, Governor Smylie made every effort to convince the ultra-conservative legislature that the state needed a small but effective State Park Commission to manage unique non-federal areas that were needed for public use near growing communities. Slowly, ever so slowly, debates over the creation of a Utah Board of Parks and the acceptance of the Harriman donation with strict reservations on use became more acceptable. Cecil Andrus, the first democrat to be elected governor in Utah in ages, championed the pair of codicils that were critical to the Harriman donation of the Railroad Ranch.

Andrus' new 'vision' for a growing Utah included his love of fishing. He recognized the incredible importance of the Henry's Fork as an attractant of keen expert fishermen not only from our country but from around the fly fishing world who wished to test their skills on sizable, highly intelligent rainbow and brown trout.

All of that was too much of a hurdle for the ultra-conservative Idaho legislature, and it took multiple legislative sessions for the members to agree to Mr. Harriman's terms, thanks to new Governor Andrus, and despite continuing pressure from Governor Smylie.

Finally, in 1965, the Harriman Railroad Ranch land donation was accepted. Roland Harriman retained control over the ranch until March 31, 1977. He died in 1978, with all of his Railroad Ranch interests legally turned over to the state.

How were Governor Andrus and I, working together, able to produce a land-use map that satisfied Harriman's genuine concerns?

James Dolan, a partner in the great New York law firm of Davis, Polk and Wardwell, handled estate planning for many of our nation's wealthiest citizens and was a counsel to and a confident of Roland Harriman.

Harriman asked Dolan for advice on who should assist him in producing a final plan for the development and preservation of his beloved ranch. Dolan knew Roland's brother, Averill, as both owned winter homes on Jupiter Island. Averill, in turn, was a close friend of my grandfather, Samuel Pryor.

My grandfather had become Percy Rockefeller's partner and had completed a major assignment for the Rockefeller family by developing the Remington Arms Company into one of the major suppliers of weaponry and ammunition for the British army and then the American army during World War I. My grandfather was widely regarded as a model by his Wall Street compatriots – a successful businessman who took the time to be a wonderful husband and father.

Meanwhile, my mother, as a teenager, fell "madly in love with Averill," who spent many weekends at the Pryory, her father's home on Field Point Park in Greenwich, Connecticut. In fact, he spent so many weekends there that he was assigned his own bedroom.

Mother and Averill were devoted to each other and Grandfather Pryor became Averill's wise mentor as he attempted to develop his business skills. Averill remained a lifelong friend of the Reed family, buying a large oceanfront house on Jupiter Island from my father. Dolan met Averill occasionally at dinner parties at the Reed's Florida home, but I was unaware of the Harriman's Railroad Ranch in Idaho.

I am uncertain as to the exact date when I received a telephone call from Dolan, by then a close friend and frequent golf partner, asking if I could assemble a team to produce a very conservative land-use plan for the Railroad Ranch that would be acceptable to Harriman and Governor Andrus.

I was asked to reach Harriman by phone on a certain day and hour, and we enjoyed a lengthy conversation. He discussed Grandfather Pryor's business skills and admired his brilliant management of Remington Arms during World War I. He knew that his brother, Averill, was a close friend of both the Reed and Pryor families. He mentioned that my cousin, Samuel Pryor III, had worked on a number of legal issues for the Harriman family as a member of the Davis, Polk law firm.

He was aware that I had been appointed assistant secretary and, in his words, had a "sound record" in land management.

I was aware that he and his parents were significant philanthropists, whose donations included his mother's gift of the 46,613-acre Harriman State Park, the second largest state park in the New York system. I learned from Dolan that Roland Harriman had made significant contributions to the New York-Cornell Hospital and the American Museum of Natural History, and had served on the board of the American Red Cross, becoming its president in 1950.

Harriman urged me to take leave, fly to Jackson, Wyoming, be driven to the ranch, meet the ranch manager, spend two or three days studying the land, and work with the manager, armed with topography maps and aerial photographs of the ranch and river.

I agreed and received permission from Interior Secretary Rogers Morton to take the assignment. I paid for my own flight to Jackson but did accept being driven to the ranch.

An incredibly knowledgeable cattle-land manager guided me by horseback and vehicle through a great deal of the 15,000 acres. It was a dawn-to-dusk inspection. We were joined by the senior ranch manager. He knew every spot Roland Harriman considered rare, fragile, unusual and worthy of total protection. "This is one of Mr. Harriman's favorite wetlands," he would say. Or ponds, lakes, pastures, favorite lunching sites along the river.

When I dismounted at the end of the day, I was in such pain I wondered if I would ever walk again. That evening, after liberal shots of bourbon, a couple of painkillers and a steak dinner, we poured over the land maps and the massive aerial photographs.

I found it fascinating that the Harriman cabin was such a simple log structure, next to a similar structure owned by one his early partners and within easy range of the cowboy's bunkhouse.

It was easy to see that Roland Harriman wanted a summer of simplicity compared to his more complicated life at his vast Tuxedo Park estate.

Working on an overlay of the aerial photograph of the ranch, we used red marking pens to design a more extensive road system, the location of camp sites and even RV parking areas. There were many "no-no" areas of acute wildlife sensitivity or unique lands that were major bird nesting or feeding areas. The lakes were to be off limits for fishing.

The eight miles along both banks of the Henry's Fork River were the keys to the donation, as this was one of the most productive large rainbow trout habitats in the west. Harriman's insistence on catch and release restrictions were new concepts, especially in Idaho, and were bound to be highly controversial. Single barbless hooks were unheard of and were certain to be considered elitist by the majority of Idaho anglers.

I returned to Washington after two days of intense study and had a supposedly highly qualified team from the then Bureau of Outdoor Recreation (BOR) join me in my meeting room where I briefed them on their new assignment. Buff Bohlen and Douglas Wheeler, my senior deputies and counselors, joined us. My order to the BOR team was that the plan must be "the most conservative, environmentally sensitive plan that they had ever been involved with."

Meanwhile, Dolan informed me that Harriman's

health was deteriorating and he really wanted to be briefed and comfortable with the final plan. It was easy to understand why a wise steward who knew and loved every acre of the Railroad Ranch wanted to make certain that his objectives for long-term management as a state park would be legally defined and that his wishes would be honored forever by the state of Idaho.

Time was of the essence.

The BOR team was ready for a briefing in two weeks. Its plan was the most terrible example of how to turn a pristine area into a high-use public park! I declared that "It looked like Coney Island" and told them, with vehemence, that their work was a disgrace, to leave the plan for destruction and to "disappear."

Bohlen, my wise counsel, noted that it was one of my mightiest "volcanic eruptions," even if somewhat understandably generated by incompetence.

I looked at my two all-knowing deputies and asked: "Where should I turn?" They both agreed that a highly respected senior land-use planner from the National Park Service was capable of forming a team that, in short order and working with my drawings and extensive notes, could produce a plan that would be acceptable to me and, most importantly, to Harriman and Governor Andrus.

I knew the recommended team leader, who frequently and successfully had challenged NPS Director George Hartzog over far too aggressive land-use plans for a number of newly created national parks.

We discussed the mission. He was excited by the opportunity and knew who he wanted to work with on the project. I called Governor Andrus and explained the assignment that was being undertaken. We had developed a friendship and a mutual trust, and he was delighted with the course of action.

Secretary Morton also was supportive, as he knew by reputation the value of the Railroad Ranch.

Within a very short period of time, I was presented with a land-use map that incorporated the entire ranch manager's and wise cowboy's recommendations, as well as some of mine. It was an example of "stewardship and conservation usage."

I notified Dolan that a land-use plan had been prepared and that I considered it an excellent effort that merited Harriman's inspection. The plan took into account the extraordinary wildlife-environmental resources that were included in the 15,000-acre donation with suggestions on how the state could work with the adjacent Caribou-Targhee National Forest to enhance both properties.

Harriman asked me to fly to his vast estate in Tuxedo Park. He provided a plane and we met at his great house. He showed the impact of illness and age. Nevertheless, he became "alive" when I spread out on the dining room table the aerial photograph and the proposed land-use map.

I presented him with a red marking pen and he began to slowly, carefully, review the plan for his beloved ranch. He traced the entry road and the system of existing and potential new roads, trails, campsites and parking areas – and the numerous off limits areas.

He made very few changes, but said, almost in a trance: "No, Nathaniel, the trail should be further away from this marsh not to alarm nesting or feeding sandhill cranes," or "I think the parking area could be expanded in this direction for six additional cars to park."

He knew every inch of his land and took a full hour and a half wandering down memory lane with the red marking pen in his hand, tracing roads, paths, ponds, wetlands and lunching sites along the river.

After the session, he was exhausted, but smiled and declared himself delighted with the plan. He hoped that Governor Andrus would be as pleased and would use his political skills to have the plan and strict deed restrictions accepted by the Idaho legislature.

He mentioned that the governor was going to

have to overcome resistance from many of the state's fishermen, who would demand that the restrictions – even a no-hunting codicil – be removed from the conveyance deed. I assured him that the governor would recognize the importance of the donation and would usher it through the legislature.

Even though he was a very conservative Republican, Harriman admired Governor Andrus, a Democrat, and was delighted that someone "bright" finally was governor. I left him in peace: His dream could become true if Andrus could obtain legislative approval of the proposed donation and assuming that future governors of Idaho would comply with the deeded restrictions and the agreed upon land-use map.

Harriman stated firmly that he was confident that his brother, Averill and his sister, Gladys, would support the donation, the land-use plan and the deed restrictions.

Following Harriman's acceptance of the land-use plan with the legal codicils, I sent the package to Andrus, asking him to review the land-use plan and hopefully agree to the restrictions.

John Hough, one of the governor's most important and environmentally sensitive aides, reviewed the plan with members of the Idaho Park Board and won their approval to present the plan at a public hearing.

The hearing was "exciting," as the plan and the legally binding restrictions were opposed by the spin casters, the bait fishermen and, above all, those who never considered fishing as a sport where one released ones captured trout. Some of Idaho's legislative members bitterly opposed the deeded restrictions.

At that time, there weren't many proponents for the type of restrictions that the Harriman donation contained. We were pleased and comforted to win the support of the Upper Snake River Fly Fishers, which had been formed by Rene Harrop, one of the West's most famous dry fly fishermen and innovative fly tiers, Mike Lawson, who owned a fly fishing shop just yards upstream of the Railroad Ranch, and Will Godfrey a fine angler and a recent appointment by Governor Andrus to the Idaho Fish and Game Commission. The club is still active today and is an affiliate of the Federation of Fly Fishers.

They were joined by the Snake River Cutthroats, an organization that were affiliated with both Trout Unlimited and the Fly Fishers. It was a team effort, but the greatest asset, Mike Lawson repeated, was the constant support of Governor Andrus.

The governor also appointed Keith Stonebreaker to the commission. He was an outspoken supporter of the deeded restrictions and acceptance of the ranch as one of Idaho's premier state parks. With Andrus behind it and with the united support from fly fishing groups, the legislature finally agreed that the trade off of the restrictions was worth the creation of a unique, world class state park.

The incredible challenges of the Henry's Fork fishery have attracted anglers from all over the world, who come to test their skills attempting to match one of the extraordinarily varied mayfly hatches and hook, play and release large rainbow trout.

Before Cecil Andrus completed his term as governor, he was invited by Roland Harriman to inspect the ranch with him so that Andrus could understand Harriman's love affair with the land he had tended for 67 years.

Harriman emphasized that it was his wish, if not commandment, that the Railroad Ranch be the beneficiary of wise management and stewardship. Andrus accepted Harriman's invitation and remembers a "terrifying ride" with Harriman at the wheel as he drove at 40 miles per hour over sand and dirt roads, barely missing tall fir and pines, pointing out the most important areas that needed protection.

Andrus thanked Harriman for his incredible donation and accepted the challenge to protect the park and he has kept his word.

Governor Andrus' career continued as he became U.S. Secretary of Interior in 1977 and served until January 1981. He was the driving force behind President Jimmy Carter's successful withdrawal of 154 million acres of land in Alaska as a part of the Alaska Native Claims Act.

I have always wondered whether the joy and honor of preserving Harriman's Railroad Ranch encouraged Secretary Andrus to be the formidable advocate of the Alaska land withdrawals.

I consider my role working with Harriman and Andrus in the creation of the Railroad Ranch State Park to be one of the highlights of my life. The Railroad Ranch section of the Henry's Fork is rightly fully recognized as one of the greatest tests for highly proficient anglers in the world.

May Roland Harriman's vision forever be honored by the state of Idaho and recognized as a prize worthy of sound management and determined stewardship.

First Battle of the Washington Mall: Those Buildings Must Go

"Teddy Roosevelt would have them out in a day. You might succeed in a year."

When Pierre Charles L'Enfant persuaded President George Washington to let him design the location of our nation's Capitol, it faced a vast marsh extending inland from the Potomac River that was polluted, smelly and may have produced mosquitoes bearing malaria. Although his master plan for our Capitol and the city of Washington had many exceptional features, the president had to relieve L'Enfant of his duties, as he was hesitant to accept recommendations from Congress and a presidential commission to consider changes to his design, even minor ones.

Washington, D.C., still was a city in the making. Vast areas around the Capitol building consisted of undeveloped land. It took years to accumulate the public funds required to clear sites for major federal buildings and to open forests and drain marshes for the growth of both the city and the government.

Following a major public works program, a vast area was cleared, drained, filled and graded. Frederick Law Olmsted, the nation's foremost land-use planner and landscape architect, was commissioned in 1873 to design the enlarged grounds of the Capitol. He created the Mall which, in time, connected the Capitol to the Washington Monument, completed in 1885, and to the Lincoln Memorial in 1922. With construction of these structures, the Mall became one of the world's most impressive urban designs – and one that was and remains deserving of protection.

Working with Calvert Vaux, a renowned architect, Olmstead used the same sense of length and breadth that he employed when he designed New York City's Central Park. From the Capitol almost to the Washington Monument, the Mall now is flanked by an astonishing array of brilliantly designed museums showcasing the history of America. The National Gallery of Art and the Smithsonian Institution, the Air and Space Museum and a series of other buildings and gardens all are major tourist attractions and vital parts of the "American Experience."

The area from the Lincoln Memorial to the river where the Arlington Memorial Bridge crosses the Potomac was left as "green space" for athletic pursuits – soccer, field hockey, softball, even cricket. The space is used daily by hundreds of college students, federal workers and residents who find time to burn off some steam.

That sets the stage for our (first) Washington Mall battle story:

During World War I and long before the Pentagon was completed in 1943, the United States Navy claimed rights to both sides of the reflecting pool, which was built in 1897 below the Washington Monument. The Navy built a series of imposing buildings on the land. Officers and curriers had to cross two footbridges to get messages across the water or join meetings on one side or the other.

When the Pentagon opened in January 1943, the Department of the Navy was ordered to incorporate its headquarters into that massive building. Consequently, the Navy finally consented to raze the vast majority of its aging buildings from the reflecting pool area and marked the occasion with a brass band and a bevy of senior officers and retired admirals who wept at the sight of demolition equipment.

Addressing a large audience, William Brazis, director of the Washington Naval Headquarters Service, paraphrased Ecclesiastes 3:3 and said, "There is a time to build and a time to tear down and it is time to start tearing these buildings down."

But no – not all of the buildings went to the scrap pile. The Navy insisted that, as the nation's "senior service," it should retain a "presence" closer to the White House and the Capitol.

Although the hierarchy of naval officers moved to the Pentagon, they retained a vested interest in staying on the ground where the original Navy headquarters had been. Still, over time, most of the buildings were removed.

By 1971, there remained only two wooden, single-story, hideous buildings – surrounded by piles of wood that contractors had left from previously demolished buildings. It was imperative to remove the last of the "temporary" naval buildings that had been built as we entered World War I. They were in a state of disrepair, ugly and in danger of collapsing

I was astonished when I received a telephone call from the White House and received a presidential order relayed by Nixon aide John Ehrlichman. It was a deceptively simple order:

"The president wants the two ancient naval buildings removed now. The president has become interested in a plan for the construction of a major Mall lake between 17th Street, the Reflecting Pool, the Lincoln Memorial and Constitution Avenue. The proposal cannot move forward until the Mall is clear of those ugly buildings. Get rid of two wooden naval buildings quickly."

The lake proposal had been the brainchild of Nathaniel Owings, a world-acclaimed landscape architect and senior partner of Skidmore, Owings & Merrill.

President Johnson had been keen on the plan, but the Vietnam War's expenses made it impossible for him to request significant funds for such a beautification project.

President Nixon harbored one of his odd suspicions that Owings had received more than his share of projects from Kennedy and Johnson. Nevertheless, he agreed to be briefed on the Owings plan.

I visited Secretary Rogers Morton to determine what steps I should take to follow a "presidential order." The secretary roared with laughter.

"It would seem so simple," he said, though it really wasn't. "Just get the General Services Administration (GSA) to put the buildings' demolition out to bid. Then, call Defense Secretary Melvin Laird and tell him to notify his admirals that the rotting, old buildings are coming down per a presidential order.

"Those damnable buildings sit on the Mall, which is under the ownership and control of the National Capitol Parks, an important component of the National Park Service. I join with the president. Get those buildings off the Mall!

"Nathaniel, neither Mel Laird nor the Navy are totally under the command of the Office of the Presidency. You will have to involve George Hartzog the director of the National Park Service, who has attempted several times to regain ownership of the area on which these two monuments of the past sit without any action by the Navy.

"They insist that the buildings are needed. That's a bunch of nonsense, but no one has forced the issue. Teddy Roosevelt would have them out in a day. You might succeed in a year.

"You know Mel personally. Make a date to see him and inform him of the presidential order and

wait to see what happens. Director George Hartzog is your ally and knows how to nudge the GSA into obtaining a contractor with the proper permits from the District to remove the buildings and the trash the Navy had allowed to accumulate. Let me know what Mel's reaction is to your visit."

I met Hartzog and discussed strategy. I had known Mel Laird for a number of years, as he had been a house guest of Mr. and Mrs. Al Cole, the former "right hand" of Dewitt Wallace, who owned Readers Digest. Al had a lovely home on Jupiter Island and was as devoted a golf nut as Mel Laird.

Despite the Vietnam War, Laird found needed time to relax by flying down for a few days of golf and hours of needed sleep. They played golf every day during Mel's short periods of relaxation. I had dined with him and played a round or two of golf with both of them.

Hartzog was not optimistic. I exclaimed, "George, this is a presidential order!" Hartzog was not completely impressed. He replied, "There have been several presidential orders to clear the site, but two aged buildings and a mountain of trash are still on 'our' Mall."

I called Secretary Laird's secretary and requested a personal appointment. She asked what the subject would be. I replied that I had a presidential order to remove the old naval buildings on the Mall and wanted to consult with Laird for an appropriate time frame for initiation of the demolition project. I heard a muffled laugh and she said, "I will inform the secretary and if his very busy schedule will permit, he will make a date to see you."

A week later my wonderful secretary, Nori Uchida, informed me that I had a date with Laird at his office in the Pentagon the following week. Dutifully, I arrived a few minutes ahead of time and was met by a Navy captain (covered with medals and gold braid) on the steps of the Pentagon. He led me through the labyrinth of floors and offices to the vast office of the Secretary of Defense. Mel's secretary ushered me in.

Mel was sitting behind a huge desk that displayed three red telephones that were obviously "doomsday phones." Behind him was a row of four-drawer steel cabinets with "Top Secret" identification tags on them.

Laird met me graciously, directing me to a pair of comfortable chairs to the left of his desk. We sat and talked about the Coles, my mother and father, and how much his vacations on Jupiter Island had meant to him.

Finally, he asked, "What is it that I can do for you?" I explained my mission. He sat impassively for a full minute before returning to his desk and summoning someone on his intercom.

An admiral in full dress uniform, complete with rows of medals and golden aiguillettes on his shoulder, walked into the office. He was a stunning presence for a young assistant secretary. Following introductions, Laird asked me to give the admiral a synopsis of John Ehrlichman's telephone call and the presidential order.

The admiral stared at me as if I had come from Mars. He responded, "I will set up another meeting, Mr. Secretary, with the appropriate staff present to discuss this order."

Mel gave me his best wishes and I was on my way, recognizing that Mel Laird, for whatever reason, was not going to order the Navy to remove the last vestiges of the "senior service's" former home.

Upon my return to Interior, Secretary Morton asked Director Hartzog and me to join him the following morning. I gave them an accurate description of the lack of enthusiasm by Secretary Laird and what was sure to be a confrontation when the next meeting was scheduled.

Secretary Morton suggested that Hartzog and I pay visits to Capitol Hill to educate key congressional members of the Interior committees about the President's order and the department's full support for removing the buildings from the Mall.

Director Hartzog had a close working relationship with many of the Democratic senators, most importantly with Sen. Alan Bible of Nevada, who considered the National Park Service and system to be under his personal control. He commented after being briefed, "We have tried for years to remove the vestiges of that long period of time when the Navy occupied the Mall. They have long overstayed their welcome. That's why the Pentagon was built, to consolidate the services. I agree with the president, get them off the Mall." We briefed Democratic Sen. Henry Jackson of Washington, one of the most influential members of the Senate and a key force on the Armed Services Committee. His only comment after being briefed was, "About time!"

Chairman Morris Udall of the House Interior Committee and Julia Butler Hansen, chair of the Interior Appropriations Committee, both said, "Get it done!" Director Hartzog's introduction of me to the key members of Congress I would be working with for the next several years was invaluable. One of the chairman's staff members repeated an old admonition, a joke that had been used since the U.S.-Mexican war: "Nothing in Washington is as permanent as a temporary building."

Ten days later, the Secretary, his Naval Commandant and I agreed on a date to meet.

I arrived well ahead of time and was escorted by another impeccably dressed naval captain. I was welcomed by Secretary Laird's secretary, who had a faint smile on her face as I entered the secretary's office.

Laird waved me to the informal part of his immense office and introduced three naval admirals in full dress – medals and aiguillettes. They could not have been more imposing. Rather than have me repeat the White House call and my orders, I was immediately informed by two of the admirals that they had every intention of removing the offending buildings, but it would take another four years for them to fill out the necessary paperwork.

I leaned forward and, as calmly as I could,

stated, "My orders come from your and my commander in chief. I have no other option than to proceed to have the buildings removed."

The third admiral who had watched and listened but not spoken introduced himself as the commandant of all naval facilities in the Washington area. The buildings and this site on the Mall came under his command. He reiterated that the buildings were "important" and could only be removed with the approval of his office.

I asked him how Jack Fish, director of the National Capital Parks Service, or Director Hartzog should proceed to secure an agreement with the Navy and a contract for removal of the buildings and adjacent trash. He replied that he would send me the necessary forms.

Laird thanked the three admirals and walked me to the door. I said ever so quietly, "Mel, this is crazy. You can order the removal of those buildings by lifting your phone." He replied, "It is more difficult than you would think. My role with the joint chiefs and the senior military officers is dependent on good faith in my orders. I use them judiciously."

I returned to Interior and called John Ehrlichman and informed him that the presidential order was "complicated" by the secretary of defense's refusal to order the naval brass to comply. He roared, "That is impossible. Mel Laird thinks he can defy the president at will. Your orders remain the President's: Remove the buildings from the Mall!"

I met again with Secretary Morton and Director Hartzog. The Secretary's orders were short and precise. "George, you have my authority to make a date with a high-ranking member of the GSA and have them prepare a bid document and send it out for bids to be received in 30 days maximum," he said. "I want the buildings removed and the area bulldozed flat and sodded within less than five days following an acceptable bid."

The GSA went along with the request, prepared the documents and received a number of competitive proposals. It was a low-cost effort – a couple of bulldozers, front-end loaders and trucks to carry the debris away.

Just 10 days before demolition day, the Justice Department informed Secretary Morton that an "environmental assessment" might be required, as the commandant of naval real estate in Washington deemed the removal of the buildings to be "a significant environmental action."

The Secretary called Attorney General Edwin Meese, explained the situation and discussed alternatives. Meese called Laird and complained of the admiral's action, but Laird stated that he was "out of the picture" in this dispute between Interior and the Navy. It took 20-plus days to write an environmental assessment that would satisfy a federal judge.

The GSA had to pay a penalty for the delay in the demolition process. But, before long, we watched as U.S. Navy trucks arrived at the buildings and left loaded with ancient chairs, desks and filing cabinets. The mice, rats and cockroaches fled.

Finally, the great day of demolition came. Within eight hours, the contractor had the vast majority of the buildings down and was tearing them up in pieces for the front-end loaders to hoist into trucks that would carry the debris away.

In the late afternoon on demolition day, the Secretary, Director Hartzog, Jack Fish and I met on site and shared some of the Secretary's finest bourbon.

Ehrlichman reported that the president was delighted. He complimented me and the united effort to force the issue to a conclusion that the commander in chief desired.

The first battle of the Mall was won!

Constitution Lake

One day after the naval buildings finally were gone, Secretary Morton invited Nathaniel Owings to lunch in his private dining room in the building. I was invited to attend. Mr. Owings was very entertaining – "a pixie," who kept us laughing about his role in making Skidmore, Owings and Merrill [SOM] one of the nation's foremost architectural firms.

The secretary inquired as to whom SOM would assign the all-important design of the reflection pool now that the Naval buildings were demolished. Owings replied, "I have a brilliant young architect who has great imagination and the ability to understand the importance of the landscape plan to complement the lake."

President and Mrs. Nixon met with Owings and his youthful architect associate, David Childs, to view an astonishing 25-foot-long, panoramic depiction of the proposed lake and the groves of trees that would flank it. The paths were perfectly displayed.

President Nixon, buoyed by Mrs. Nixon's enthusiastic reaction to the display, became unusually animated. He traced the walkways with his fingers. Mrs. Nixon asked Mr. Owings if there were any possibility of a site for a pagoda, as she was fascinated by the ones she had seen on their presidential visit to China. Without hesitation, Owings pointed to a prominent spot on the lake shore and announced, "Mrs. Nixon, this will be the site of a pagoda."

I almost fainted. Owings was a master of speed and ability to adjust within seconds. David Childs' design was acclaimed by all. Secretary Morton, recognizing the growing support of the Nixons, asked Childs a series of leading questions, which he easily answered. The president nodded his head in approval. Mrs. Nixon was obviously thrilled with the proposal.

David Childs had designed a major permanent feature for the improvement of the Mall. It was an astonishing achievement.

I testified before pertinent House and Senate Committees supporting the project. The congressional committees were delighted by this proposed addition to the capital grounds and it was approved and finished during the Ford Administration.

I never drive by Constitution Lake without a smile on my face.

David Childs' career continues as one of the world's most respected architects. After joining the SOM firm in Washington, one of his first assignments was to redevelop Pennsylvania Avenue in 1971. He designed 1201 Pennsylvania Avenue, the Four Seasons Hotel, the U.S. News and World Report headquarters, the new National Geographic Society headquarters, the expansion of the Dulles International Airport's main terminal and the Park Hyatt Hotel.

He was appointed to the Capitol Planning Commission, which he chaired from 1975 to 1981. In 2002, David was appointed to the Commission on Fine Arts and served as chairman from 2003 to 2005.

The Childs moved to New York City in 1984, where he headed the SOM design team there. His New York projects include the World Wide Plaza, 450 Lexington Avenue, the Bertelsmann Tower, Bear Sterns former headquarters, the Time Warner Center, Times Square Tower, 7 World Trade Center and many other major buildings in the city.

Childs also was chosen to design the United States Embassy in Ottawa, Canada.

He has been awarded The Rome Prize and named a Senior Fellow. He has served on the boards of the Municipal Arts Society, the Museum of Modern Art and the American Academy in Rome.

The completion of One World Trade Center in 2014, after years of political bickering and serious infighting by many forces that felt that they should have a role in the design and construction, is an example of his disciplined and brilliant expertise.

David and Annie Childs and their three children are "life friends" of the Nathaniel Reed family, all due to his brilliant plan of Constitution Lake.

Second Battle of the National Mall: Much Ado About Little

"Little victories can be the source of great pleasure."

No sooner had we removed the naval buildings from the National Mall than a second order from President Nixon arrived from John Ehrlichman.

Ehrlichman stated, not asked, "Why the devil does Dillon Ripley think he can have a blacktop parking area behind the 'Smithsonian Castle' on the Mall? Have it removed promptly."

Dillon was a close friend of the Reed family and I thought he would cooperate with a direct order, but I was wrong.

I joined him for lunch at the "Smithsonian Castle," the familiar nickname for the main Smithsonian Institution building. We enjoyed a delicious meal and discussed the Washington Zoo's financial problems and the rumor that turned out to be true – endangered species had been shipped to the zoo, which was under Dillon's authority, without proper clearance from the U.S. Fish and Wildlife Service. He assured me if there were "any further problems at/or with the zoo's management" that they would be corrected within hours.

I finally informed him of the presidential order I had received to have the parking lot behind the Castle removed. It's where my driver had parked my official automobile. There was no question that the blacktop parking lot invaded the Mall, not by much, but if you looked down the Mall, you could see the indentation into the Mall from the parking lot, with cars parked in obvious view. I told him that my orders were to have any and all non-approved incursions onto the Mall removed, including, specifically, the Smithsonian Institution parking lot.

He declared himself "astonished." He insisted that the parking lot was necessary for his most important board members – members of Congress, the Supreme Court, and major donors. Admittedly, when scientist James Smithson donated the Castle, Washington was a very small city and there were no plans to preserve space for a parking lot of any size to service the Castle and its important doyens. When the Mall was completed, there were no plans for parking cars on it. No land was available for parking – none!

I failed to convince him that it was the president who had ordered the parking lot removed. He simply stated: "I have no intention of obeying such an order even if it is delivered in writing. Someone in the White House staff has it in for me. You know very well the president has never seen the institution's much-needed, private parking lot. The parking lot is an important feature of the Castle for important people. It stays."

I returned to the Department of Interior and called Secretary Rogers Morton for a short visit. He said, "Come on up and tell me what is on your mind?" I told him of the telephone call, the luncheon and Dillon Ripley's response.

The secretary called downstairs and asked National Park Service Director George Hartzog to join us on the double. When briefed, Hartzog seemed astonished by Ripley's curt refusal to remove the parking lot from the Mall, which was under the National Capitol Park System. Morton quizzed Hartzog on how the parking lot had been allowed in the first place. Hartzog had a quick reply.

"Dillon asked for permission from a former Secretary of Interior and I complied with the order that a short parking lot be allowed on the Mall, which is under our authority," he said. "It was a mistake. I support an effort to have it removed."

The Secretary asked Hartzog to call Dillon and ask him to comply, as the Mall was under Hartzog's stewardship. Hartzog reported the next day that Dillon has told him, "No way!"

The secretary instructed George to proceed legally with the city and the General Services Agency (GSA) to have a contractor remove the parking lot.

We were just getting used to the requirements of the Environmental Policy Act and I wondered aloud if removal of the parking lot could be construed as a "significant federal action."

I thought that, due to Dillon's intransigence, a well-prepared environmental assessment was in order. Hartzog assured us that it could be prepared rapidly, and the plan for the parking lot's removal would be put out for bid. Hartzog signed a contract and Mayor Washington agreed with a very early morning removal operation.

To our surprise, the Ripley supporters filed suit demanding an environmental assessment, which wasn't quite finished. I told Hartzog that the team preparing the assessment better work a 24-hour day because the contract had penalties for delays in receiving proper permits, including the environmental assessment.

The Justice Department and the Interior Department urged the appropriate court to set a trial date as rapidly as possible, as every day of delay cost taxpayers money. As we anticipated, plaintiffs claimed the National Park Service had not obeyed the environmental impact review process, and a trial date was set promptly.

The Justice Department's and Interior's leading attorney presented the final environmental assessment, which concluded the parking lot had been built illegally and there would be no significant impact on the Castle if it was removed. It took the judge 15 minutes to rule in our favor.

Hartzog received permission from the mayor and ordered the contractor to start demolition at dawn. By 8 a.m., long before Dillon arrived at the Castle, the parking lot had been scooped up by a pair of front-end loaders and trucked away, and the National Capitol Parks crew had sodded the area.

I called John Ehrlichman at the White House and informed him that the Smithsonian Mall parking lot was gone. The area had been sodded and the vista down the Mall was clear of all impediments. Planner and architect Frederick Law Olmstead's vision was restored.

Ehrlichman called back with the following: "Bravo that will keep that SOB in his place."

Secretary Morton, Director Hartzog and I agreed that "little victories" can be the source of great pleasure.

Needless to say, my relationship with Dillon Ripley was significantly damaged. Fortunately, for both of us, it later was repaired, but that is another story for another day.

Saga of the Mississippi Sandhill Crane National Wildlife Refuge

"Damn the governor. Get rid of that turn-off!"

Shortly after the Endangered Species Act became law in 1973, I was faced with a number of delicate issues. Environmental organizations that had pressed for the law were convinced that they had endangered species of wildlife and plants in all 50 states.

They did not show equal enthusiasm for testifying before two congressional appropriations committees on behalf of proper funding and additional manpower for the U.S Fish and Wildlife Service, which was to enforce the new act.

A number of immediate legal actions had been taken against the service for failing to protect rare and endangered species such as the snail darter, which seemingly was the reason for opposition to the construction of the Tellico Dam.

I had opposed construction of the dam on the grounds that it would inundate a major stretch of the Little Tennessee River, one of the most prolific trout-fishing rivers in the east. I visited it and was awe-struck by its beauty and its productivity. The river was flanked by productive farms and grazing areas.

The problem was that the president had given his word to Sen. Howard Baker of Tennessee that the dam would be constructed so that summer homes could be built around the reservoir. The cost-ratio benefits were laughably low.

Presidential aide John Ehrlichman quietly urged me on to oppose the dam's construction. But Senator Baker was implacable and, armed with the president's promise, forced the issue.

The snail darter, a diminutive fish, was said to require a free-flowing Little Tennessee River to survive. The river was deemed to be "critical habitat" for the darter, causing elation among the dam's opponents and fury for Senator Baker and potential developers.

The senator forced state and federal biologists to survey all existing tributaries of the Little 'T' and was relieved when snail darters were discovered. The Little 'T' was not the sole critical habitat of the Tennessee snail darter!

The great battle over the construction of the Tellico Dam was over. Politics beat common sense and a federal "investment" of questionable value.

Shortly thereafter, a pumping scheme in the California desert was shown to be capable of lowering the area's groundwater sufficiently to destroy the springs that supported another small fish, the desert pupfish. Jack Horton, our deputy assistant secretary of lands, denied the pumping plan to protect the endangered pupfish.

The realization that the act required preservation of critical habitat if an endangered species was to be protected became a topic within the Department of Interior, the White House and Congress.

We suffered through a period of intense criticism for what was perceived as a slowdown in officially designating endangered species and their required critical habitat. Our critics claimed political interference, lassitude on my part and within the service's bureaucracy, ignoring the fact that a very small group of experts was working six days a week attempting to publish the first list of highly endangered species.

I was invited to speak about the act before the Garden Club of America. In concluding remarks, I begged them to join, if not galvanize, the conservation organizations and press Congress to adequately fund and increase the manpower needed to handle this new role, a vital one in protecting endangered species.

During the question-and-answer session following my address, a young audience member who was an expert on threatened plant communities argued that I was ignoring the plight of endangered plants in favor of highly visible large animals.

I replied, "With the invaluable assistance of the Smithsonian Institution, we are in the process of assembling a long list of highly endangered plants and their specific locations and would proceed to announce critical habitat as soon as sufficient manpower was achieved. Yes, we had made a point of announcing critical habitat for highly visible mammals so that the public would support the Endangered Species Act."

In future testimony, I made it abundantly clear that on my watch no species, no matter how seemingly insignificant, would be ignored and allowed to slip into the oblivion of extinction.

One afternoon, Wildlife Service Director Lynn Greenwalt asked for an emergency meeting. He explained that the Mississippi Sandhill Crane National Wildlife Refuge had been proposed to protect the remaining 30 to 35 non-migratory cranes. Now, the construction of highway I-10 was rapidly approaching the cranes' critical habitat and a "turn-off" had been authorized by the U.S. Department of Transportation (DOT) at the request of the governor.

The "turn-off" or exit would allow adjacent landowners to significantly invade what was basically wilderness next to the cranes' important critical habitat. The major incursion – including proposed housing developments, a possible shopping center and conversion of the wet prairies into farmland – would mean the end of the highly endangered Mississippi sandhill cranes.

It was vital to stop the politically inspired turn-off from I-10 and protect the area until the service was able to fund a national wildlife refuge.

I immediately signed the paperwork informing the federal DOT that the turn-off would be a violation of the Endangered Species Act and that construction of I-10 as it approached the refuge would have to be halted until the issue was resolved.

You can imagine what a roar went up from DOT Secretary John Volpe. I had attended many governors' conferences when Gov. Claude Kirk of Florida and then-Gov. Volpe of Massachusetts were in office and I had developed a friendship with Gov. Volpe.

He was known to have a "great temper" and when we traveled together, I was amazed that he attended mass twice a day. His Secret Service companion was charged with the responsibility of getting him to early morning and late evening mass daily. I asked him why two masses per day? He replied, "Nathaniel, I get so angry so often each day that I need to clear my soul before I can fall asleep."

I didn't need to hold the telephone anywhere near my ear when Volpe heard that I-10 was on hold until negotiations over the turn-off were resolved. He bellowed, "Nathaniel, you cannot hold up I-10 for ransom! The Mississippi congressional delegation will have your head and mine, too."

I replied, "The hold will be lifted immediately when your federal highway administrator cancels the turn-off that was added to the interstate system at the governor's insistence and will encourage development adjacent to the cranes' critical habitat, dooming the total population of 30-35 cranes – all that exist."

Later in the afternoon, my secretary broke into a meeting, handing me a note stating I had an appointment at 10 a.m. the next day with Sen. John Stennis of Mississippi. The senator had served since 1941 and, due to seniority, was one of the most powerful and respected Democrats on the Hill. He served on all the important committees, had chaired many of them and had a large staff that attended every conceivable Senate committee meeting. He knew everything that was going on. He knew every one of his colleagues by first name and was a force probably unequaled today or even in the future.

I informed our legislative staff that I had been summoned to the Hill to meet with the senator and was told that if I came out of his office alive, I would be lucky. Douglas Wheeler, my legislative deputy secretary, briefed me to be calm and collected and said that, contrary to reports circulating in the Interior building, Senator Stennis was a "rational man, a gentleman of great distinction."

Dutifully, I was sitting in his outer office at 9:50 a.m. the following day.

Promptly at 10 a.m., I was ushered into a seat to the side of the great man's desk and was greeted warmly despite the frowns on the faces of a dour bunch of aides. The senator went right to the subject: "What is going on down in my state that would require a potential holdup of the construction of the vital I-10 highway?"

I explained how the original DOT plan had not included an exit at that spot, that it had been added at the request of the governor and that development of the land adjacent to the Mississippi sandhill cranes' critical habitat and planned national wildlife refuge would without doubt cause their extinction. My final statement hit home. I said, "Senator, these are your birds. They are the remnant of a flock of non-migratory sandhill cranes that once flourished along your coastal wet prairies and wetlands. They were especially good eating and, between poaching and habitat conversion, they are going to go extinct. You should not allow this great Mississippi bird to suffer that fate!"

The senator leaned back in his chair and mused, "Besides canceling that turn-off from I-10, what more needs to be accomplished so that my cranes increase in numbers?"

I replied, "Under the act, there are provisions for mitigation. I know I-10 even without the turn-off will impact on the proposed refuge. Additional lands for mitigation would give the cranes the opportunity to have more food and larger breeding areas. The service has been attempting to secure funds from the Land and Water Conservation Fund since 1972. We need the Mississippi congressional delegation's assistance to protect the last remaining breeding colony of your cranes."

The senator leaned back in his chair and thought quietly about my observations. Suddenly, he called his secretary and asked her to put Secretary of Transportation John Volpe on the line.

He turned on the speaker phone as Volpe offered him best wishes on this beautiful day and ended by asking what he could do for the chairman.

"Well John, Secretary Reed and I have just had a friendly conversation about I-10 and 'my Mississ-ippi cranes' and I want that damn turn-off that threatens them and would halt construction of I-10 canceled by nightfall. Is that understood?"

"Yes, Mr. Chairman," Volpe replied. "I will inform the federal highway officials that the turn-off will be canceled although the governor may not be too happy with the news."

Stennis barked, "Damn the governor. Get rid of that turn-off and, by the way, John, Reed tells me that there ought to be some mitigation for the potential impacts the highway will have on the critical habitat and the cranes."

There was a pause. Then Volpe, in a constrained voice, asked: "Is Secretary Reed with you now?" The senator replied, "Secretary Reed is sitting right beside me and we think additional funds should be made available so my cranes have additional territory to expand their small numbers."

Volpe answered, "Mr. Chairman, it would be a dangerous precedent if we have to add funds for land acquisition as mitigation for routing an interstate highway near or across a potential national wildlife refuge."

"John," Stennis replied, "it's time that DOT took the Endangered Species Act more seriously. I will see to the appropriation when I receive a request from the federal highway commissioner for funds to acquire additional lands for the potential Mississippi Sandhill Crane National Wildlife Refuge, which sustains my cranes – understood?"

"Yes, Mr. Chairman, it will be accomplished," Volpe replied.

I stood and thanked the chairman and stated, "We will do everything in our power to protect and increase the size of the refuge and encourage the existing flock to increase the number of your cranes. Mr. Chairman, I cannot adequately thank you and I speak for myself and the remaining Mississippi sandhill cranes that will be forever known as 'your cranes'!"

With that, we shook hands and I departed. I nearly flew down the corridor to my car. On return to my office, I informed my loyal deputies, the director, refuge staff, the Secretary of Interior and the head of the Office of Legislative Affairs of my warm welcome by the chairman and success in avoiding an additional confrontation over the Endangered Species Act.

The refuge was officially created on November 25, 1975. The Nature Conservancy had acquired another 1,708 acres in September 1974. Under David Morine's leadership as the Conservancy's chief of land acquisition, it acquired six additional tracts totaling 457 acres in 1975. In 1978, the most critical area totaling 6,169 acres was acquired by working out a great deal with the president of the St. Regis Company.

Without Senator Stennis' determined interest in protecting "his cranes" and The Nature Conservancy's gamble to acquire vital areas of the critical habitat before the refuge was formally created, the Mississippi Sandhill Crane National Wildlife Refuge would not exist and the tiny remnant of what was once a common bird would have become extinct.

From humble beginnings, the refuge now exceeds 19,000 acres. But there have been problems with the original interbred cranes.

Captive breeding and new blood have dramatically increased the numbers of cranes. More than 100 Mississippi cranes now prowl the refuge, breed successfully and are at peace.

There always are problems with habitat management and predators. Serious funding and manpower restrictions threaten important management necessities across the nearly 600 refuges and wetland management districts within the National Wildlife Refuge system. Nevertheless, the recovery of the Mississippi sandhill crane represents a major success story of the value of the Endangered Species Act.

The outcome of this particular threat has been duplicated countless times when intervention on behalf of a threatened or endangered species led to a solution, sometimes more expensive or more difficult than anticipated, but worthy of the effort.

Thanks

To refresh my memory and report the results of the expansion of the refuge acreage and the dramatically increased flock of Mississippi cranes, I was ably assisted by members of the U.S. Fish and Wildlife staff, including Martha Nudel, Scott G. Hereford and Danny Moss. They joined to give me the wonderful news of the refuge's continuing expansion and the increase in cranes, thought to be approximately 110, with an increasing number of breeders.

The Today Show and the Illegal Trafficking of Animal Skins

"I flew up the afternoon before the show, examined the maze of skins and felt sick to my stomach."

Shortly after joining the U.S. Department of Interior, I met Dr. Lee Talbot. He was the key science member of Russell Train's brilliant assemblage of talented men and women who formed the newly-created President's Council on Environmental Quality (CEQ). I was in almost daily contact with CEQ members. Russ Train had been a close friend for many years and it was obvious that he was the leader of President Nixon's environmental team.

I studied the proposed Endangered Species Act with my newly appointed deputy secretaries, Buff Bohlen and Douglas Wheeler, so I could become comfortable with every aspect of it. I also worked with Dr. Talbot to produce a draft called "Convention on the International Trade in Endangered Species of Wild Fauna and Flora (CITES)."

I had a lot to learn in a very short period of time. Thankfully, Buff and Doug were masterful instructors. They were joined by Earl Baysinger of the Fish and Wildlife Service, an acknowledged expert on the subject. He spent hours briefing me on the importance of the act and the hope that CITES would curtail the endemic, worldwide exploitation of endangered species. He was the wildlife service's key man in the working group preparing the law, which became a major focus of my first years in Washington.

Russell Train had vast experience regarding the serious poaching that was endemic in East Africa and has spread throughout Africa and Central and South America. Dr. Talbot was his key man. Countless meetings took place before the spring 1973 meeting of the plenipotentiary conference at the State Department. Representing the Department of Interior, I was appointed to the U.S. delegation headed by Train and Talbot.

It was a great scene: hundreds of representatives from 80 countries around the world were present and thoroughly engaged. There were nightly receptions and private working dinners. My wife, Alita, and I enjoyed hosting an early morning breakfast at our Washington home for the representatives from Kenya. I will never forget the sight of my three young children, still dressed in pajamas and bathrobes, sitting on the top steps of our staircase staring at the arriving Kenyan delegation and listening to the laughter and camaraderie that highlighted the breakfast.

My involvement in the lengthy legal and ethical discussions on how to pass the proposed endangered species convention was interrupted on the second day of the official proceedings by a call from Charles Lawrence, chief of the FWS Enforcement Division.

He reported that a crew unloading cargo from a commercial plane that landed at John F. Kennedy International Airport from South America had dropped a crate and spilled out dozens of cat skins. The crate and three similar crates were impounded by FWS enforcement agents, taken to a secure room at an airport federal building and examined. The crates were full of skins from jaguars, ocelots, river otters and caimans, along with thousands of exotic bird feathers.

The announcement of this discovery prompted the producers of the most popular early morning TV program, The Today Show on NBC, to plan a special segment on the discovery for the 7 a.m. time slot the following day. The show was to be hosted by Barbara Walters and Hugh Downs.

I flew up the afternoon before the show, examined the maze of skins and felt sick to my stomach. Working with federal agents and the staff of The Today Show, we filled a room at the airport with piles of the skins from all kinds of animals. We hung skins of magnificent cats and river otters on the walls and chairs.

The television crew arrived in the afternoon to set up and decide how Walters, Downs and I could show off as many skins as possible during a four- to five-minute segment. We planned to mention the CITES wildlife initiative as we discussed the ghastly scene. By nightfall, all seemed ready to go. Hugh Downs called me from the New York studio and went over a possible "script," discussing what entry points Walters could use to show her knowledge of the endangered species act and the potential for CITES to end this type of illegal trade.

I slept in a nearby airport hotel and was at the scene at 5 a.m. I ate breakfast with the television crew and federal agents. Promptly at 6:15 a.m., Ms. Walters arrived in a limousine, accompanied by a makeup artist and hairdresser. Hugh Downs arrived and our chemistry was perfect. He was a quick study, swiftly learning the names of the various animals whose skins were propped up or spread in piles.

The New York master producer called his on-site assistant to turn on the TV cameras at 6:50 a.m. in preparation for joining the program after the initial 7 a.m. news report.

Disaster! Something was wrong with the setup. The feed to the studio didn't connect. At 6:55 a.m., The Today Show producer called to say the section of the show devoted to endangered animals had to be rescheduled. Ms. Walters left in a huff, but Downs was so interested in the booty that he stayed with me and, with the federal agent's assistance, touched the skin of every conceivable animal.

At 7:05 a.m., the television crew announced that the electrical feed was working: "Stay where you are! You are going on the air!"

At 7:10 a.m. the producer called on the hotline and said, "You two will be on in 60 seconds for six minutes."

At a signal, Downs, the master, calmly introduced me, and I explained that at that very moment, representatives from 80 countries around the world were meeting in Washington in an effort to halt the illegal trafficking in endangered species of animals and plants. We then walked slowly around the room pointing out magnificent pelts of jaguars, ocelots and river otters. I remember holding a caiman skin that was destined to be made into belts, handbags or shoes.

The local producer kept waving us to continue well past the six-minute mark. Finally, our sequence was completed. I collapsed into a chair. Downs was very pleased and obtained needed cups of coffee for both of us.

The television crew was preparing to break down its equipment when the New York producer called at 7:25 a.m. saying, "The telephone lines are busting with incoming calls. Repeat the segment at 7:40 a.m." Dutifully, Downs and I rehearsed and added a few anecdotes about the magnificence of these animals that had been killed illegally, often by cruel methods.

We went on air again at 7:40 a.m. The on-site deputy producer waved us on after the six-minute segment was completed. We picked up more skins and held up the glorious coats of the great South

American cats until a signal from the show's master producer allowed us to stop.

I was totally exhausted. Downs delivered another cup of coffee. This was just another fascinating day in the life of that "old pro."

At 7:55 a.m., the studio producer called again. "The telephone lines are still backed up," he said. "The viewers want more on CITES and where the skins were going and what is their value and how are they killed and who are the middlemen that pay the poachers to kill such a wide variety of wonderful creatures?"

At 8:10 a.m., we were back on national television!

I asked a federal agent to join us to discuss how "wildlife purchasers" in some South American countries paid poachers to trap or poison animals to make money. Local "merchants of death" acquired dead animals from trappers and partially cured the skins so they would arrive at overseas tanneries and workshops in good enough shape to be expertly cured. Then, the skins were prepared for cutting into a vast variety of ladies' outer garments, handbags and shoes.

The pelts came from a number of South American countries, chiefly Brazil, and were bound for Italy and Japan, which had the finest facilities for tanning skins of all kinds of animals. They were the best tanners of the thousands of alligator skins that were being killed illegally throughout the south and especially in my home state, Florida.

In a concluding statement, I urged viewers to become aware of the importance of CITES. The producer of The Today Show called to thank me. The segment was among a handful of shows that produced the most responsive telephone calls in the history of the program. The television crew literally hugged me, and Downs said it was one of the best segments with which he ever had been involved.

We all hoped that, collectively, we had made a difference.

Later, I heard that the scene at the New York television center was enlivened by Ms. Walters' reported "explosion." She was convinced that the Kennedy Airport television crew had invented the blackout and cost her a significant television coup.

I returned to Washington and the convention. Dr. Talbot had been informed of the scenes included in The Today Show. Russ Train called the producers and had the clips of the interviews reproduced for members of the countries involved in the discussions.

I suspect that the well-timed "luck" of the dropped crate and the television spots made little difference to the outcome of the act, but the Fish and Wildlife Service can be justifiably proud of its contribution to the passage of CITES. Its enforcement agents have been diligent in the ongoing effort to shut down the illegal trade of endangered species, and that perseverance made the widely seen television show possible.

Dr. Talbot and Russell Train represented our country and the world of endangered fauna and flora with tenacity and skill. My part of the story reflects on the good luck, integrity and vigilance of our airport Fish and Wildlife Service officers.

Bald eagle, photo © James Kozan

Patience and Tenacity: The Endangered Species Act of 1973

"The single most important environmental act passed in the 20th century."

By the end of the 1800s, Americans were confronted with something almost unimaginable – extinction of wildlife species and depletion of natural resources in a country that always had seemed blessed with superabundance.

Bison, which may have numbered more than 30 million and roamed across the continent, were on the brink of disappearing – an American icon of the west becoming as rare as the frontier. The passenger pigeon that darkened the skies with crossings of its enormous flocks was in catastrophic decline; once estimated at 3 billion birds in 1800, the last member of the species, Martha, died in the Cincinnati Zoo in 1914. Fur seal babies, desired by the fashion industry for their white fur, were killed by the thousands, and their parents were killed for fur and oil; despite international agreements, they were hunted to near extinction.

America's great forests were hewn to build and supply burgeoning cities. By 1880, an estimated 75 percent of the country's forests had disappeared, and by 1930 only 13 percent still existed. During the next 60 years, half of these also disappeared. Pines once plentiful in Michigan, Wisconsin and Minnesota were cut to supply the builders of Chicago but were not replanted. In many cases, farmers set fires to former woods to claim lands for agriculture.

As Americans came to realize the extent of their wasteful use of resources, a new idea arose in the late 1800s and early 1900s – the concept of conservation of resources. This belief, that humans should use, protect, and replenish their natural wealth, espoused scientific knowledge and wise management of resources. Forests should be replanted. Bison should be protected. Hunting regulations should be enacted. Perhaps then, future generations would be able to enjoy and use these same assets.

The federal government's legislative concerns for endangered wildlife began with the passage of the Lacey Act in 1900. It was the first federal wildlife act, passed in response to the pending extinction of passenger pigeons. Designed as a tool to help states protect resident species, the Lacey Act prohibited the interstate transportation of wildlife taken in violation of the law.

It was widely supported by members of Audubon Societies that had begun meeting across the country. Initially spurred by excesses of the millinery industry, which used wading bird plumes and colorful bird bodies to adorn women's hats, Audubon Societies lobbied federal and state governments for bird protection laws. They also publicized bird issues and, in some cases, helped establish bird sanctuaries and paid for wardens to guard them.

President Theodore Roosevelt, a progressive Republican, was a reliable champion of conservation.

During his time in office, he not only supported conservation ideals but also created 150.8 million acres of forest reserves. In 1913, the bird-watching president established Pelican Island National Wildlife Refuge – the first in the nation; he would create 52 more before he left office in 1919.

The Migratory Bird Act of 1918, a response to over-hunting and commercial sale of waterfowl, was the next major step taken by Congress to protect wildlife. The convention and subsequent law permitted the pertinent federal wildlife agency to manage waterfowl hunting seasons in collaboration with the states. The act allowed a single federal agency to control the harvest and waterfowl hunting seasons rather than allowing every state to pass differing regulations.

Even the nation's emblem, the bald eagle, was in trouble in the century's early decades. The bald eagle once ranged throughout every state in the Union except Hawaii. When America adopted the bird as its national symbol in 1782, as many as 500,000 eagles flew in the country; by the mid-20th century, there were as few as 500 nesting pairs in the "Lower 48." In response, Congress passed the Bald and Golden Eagle Protection Act of 1940. The law prohibited Americans, except in special circumstances, from killing, possessing, or selling bald or golden eagles or any parts of them. The act was amended with stronger penalties in 1972, but by then the eagles were in trouble for other reasons – the loss of habitat but, especially, the effects of chemicals and pesticides on their reproductive systems.

Although others had been warning about the rampant, indiscriminate use of chemicals in the United States after World War II, author Rachel Carson is the person who woke up the nation to the issue with her stunning 1962 book *Silent Spring.* As discussed in the essay *The Banning of DDT,* Carson warned that too many pesticides were being sprayed across the nation, killing not only intended agricultural pests, but everything that was in the area. She called them "biocides" and warned that the country could wake up one day to a world in which no birds sang – a "silent spring."

Eagles and other raptors were in grave trouble. They ate fish and creatures that contained chemicals, which accumulated in their systems and led to fragile eggshells and reproductive failure. Carson's powerful, fact-based, and well-written bestseller created a huge controversy and ultimately made Americans rethink the hype that chemical companies and the federal government had been providing to justify their actions. Although it took a decade, one of the most powerful chemicals of the era, dichlorodiphenyltrichloroethane – better known as DDT – was banned for use in the U.S. in 1972, largely because of Carson's work.

Carson was also a symbol of the new environmental movement in the United States, one in which the emerging science of ecology played a central role. A series of crises had made it clear that a healthy environment included a variety of species that interacted with each other – and the disruption or removal of one could have a domino effect on the entire system.

Public awareness over the continued rapid development of highly sensitive areas that contained a diminishing number of animal species led to the formation of an expert group of ecologists. They joined with members of the Department of Interior (DOI) to identify species in immediate danger of extinction.

The first Endangered Species Act (ESA) was hastily produced, and it passed Congress with limited debate in 1966. Although its intentions were admirable, it was seriously flawed and needed to be clarified and strengthened. There was a debate within the administration about whether to seek amendments to the act, which passed Congress and were signed into law by President Richard Nixon in 1967.

Valerie Fellows, a member of the U.S. Fish and Wildlife Services Office of Ecological Services, wrote: "The 1966 act lacked protection measures for habitat and foreign species, which promoted the Endangered Species Conservation Act of 1969, which increased prohibitions on illegal animal trade, included the protection of invertebrate species and directed the Secretary of Interior to create a list of species in danger of worldwide extinction. Still not satisfied with the protections the 1969 act provided domestic species, the authors of the ESA made an unmistakably strong statement on national species protection policy. The ESA provided for the protection of ecosystems, the conservation of endangered and threatened species, and the enforcement of all treaties related to wildlife preservation."

In early 1970, Dr. Lee Talbot, one of the first staff members of the newly formed President's Council on Environmental Quality (CEQ), proposed to CEQ Chairman Russell Train that developing a new and strengthened ESA should be one of CEQ's early priorities, along with seeking to negotiate what became the Convention on International Trade in Endangered Species (CITES).

Train was a well-informed wildlife expert who had firsthand knowledge of the plight of many animals that were being over-hunted or illegally hunted or poached for their skins, tusks and horns. He also was universally respected in the Nixon administration and in both houses of Congress. He was attracting an expert staff and welcomed the opportunity to protect wildlife.

Train and Talbot took the ESA proposal to John Ehrlichman and Nixon's domestic staff. They agreed and assigned the role producing a farther-reaching ESA to Russell Train and the CEQ. He took charge and brought together expertise from the pertinent federal agencies and reached out to experts of the leading environmental organizations that long had lobbied for a strong Endangered Species Act. Dr. Lee Talbot was his representative and leader of the working team that was assembled to draft the new act. Environmental organizations lent their experts to share critical input in the lengthy process.

DOI Secretary Walter Hickel, frustrated by the number of "great whales" being slaughtered by the Japanese and international whaling fleets, also lobbied to dramatically strengthen the 1969 act. The whaling industry was another example of the alarming disappearance of creatures once thought to be immune to human activities because of their existence in the vastness of the planet's oceans. Yet, by the 19th century, many whale species were in serious trouble as improved technology – boats and harpoons – slowly gave humans the advantage. Overhunting was hurting the mammals' ability to reproduce, further diminishing their numbers.

Hickel wanted Alaska's native people to be able to continue to hunt a small number of whales as they had for generations, and the realization that whales were being slaughtered into extinction set him into action. He publicly protested Japanese over-hunting of whales and supported international efforts to end or curb it.

The secretary knew that the American public supported stopping the Japanese whaling fleets from pursuing the last of the "great whales"; he also instinctively knew that an "anti-whaling" position was sound, "green" politics. Unfortunately, shortly after he took this stand, Hickel was summarily dismissed by Nixon for leaking a personal letter to the president regarding the highly controversial Vietnam War.

As we have learned, Rep. Rogers C.B. of Maryland subsequently was appointed DOI secretary. Before he could assume the reins of office, there was a senseless coup within the department. Fred Malik, one of Bob Haldeman's deputies, raged through the DOI demanding resignations, including one from Dr. Leslie Glasgow, a much-respected Louisiana State University professor who had been appointed assistant secretary. Malik had a list of Interior employees that an informer among the political appointees had prepared, citing those staff members whose loyalty to the president was in question. *The Washington Post* carried a front-page article on the "Interior Massacre," which ended Malik's vendetta in embarrassment.

Spencer Smith had been on assignment from the U.S. Fish and Wildlife Service's (FWS) Atlanta office and was appointed FWS director. Nixon and Morton requested that I assume the vacancy as DOI Assistant Secretary of for Fish, Wildlife and Parks. During my service as environmental advisor to two Florida governors, I had developed some remarkable contacts and friendships among the federal agencies that were allies of what we were attempting to encourage in Florida.

I was brilliantly supported at DOI by Cleo Layton, a senior official permanently assigned to the office of the assistant secretary. He became not only an ally of every member of our staff but a greatly admired friend whose wisdom, experience and advice were indispensable. Being able to concentrate on national parks and the nation's premier wildlife agency, which included the vast national wildlife refuge system that Roosevelt had created, was like stepping into a well-prepared role.

The DOI team working on a new Endangered Species Act was on a fast track – and I soon joined the effort, contributing to an outline.

The amended act of 1966 and 1967 was deficient as, among other things, it failed to protect the habitat of an endangered species and the category of "threatened" was still in the study period at FWS headquarters.

So, I was well aware of the importance of this new effort. I attended weekly meetings and briefed

The Battle of Endangered Plants

The subject of how to classify and protect endangered plants was a nightmare that FWS biologists simply could not handle. They had no expertise in the subject. Their expertise was in wildlife, not plants. FWS staffing and funding levels made it impossible to attract experts needed to adequately protect myriads of endangered plants.

Thankfully, Dillon Ripley, secretary of the world-renowned Smithsonian Institution, accepted the challenge. The Smithsonian's experts created a very important inventory of endangered plants and explained how the use of Section 7 could preserve vitally important habitat.

By 1975, the FWS faced dozens of legal actions for failure to list everything from rare California butterflies to wolverines on the list of threatened or endangered plants and animals. The cruelest assertion was from expert, passionate botanists who thrashed me for apparently ignoring the fate of many threatened or endangered plants.

My response was, "Please join me when I testify in front of the House subcommittee on appropriations and make your case. I am prevented by presidential order to maintain or even have to reduce manpower quotas for the three services that report to me. I need your assistance if the Endangered Species Act will become more than a vision of what could be."

Congress restrained our efforts by simply restricting the amount of funds and manpower it would allow to create an effective Office for Endangered Species.

It took time and a change in administrations and congressional attitudes to fully comprehend the scope of the mission and the manpower and funds needed to protect threatened and endangered species.

The assignment is never ending, as development in the last wild corners of our country threatens endemic plants that are little known or understood. It requires a combination of patience and tenacity to remind an urban America of the value of rare flora that in many cases existed long before our arrival on the scene.

members of pertinent committees in the House and Senate on the proposed scope of the act. Through that effort, I came to know Rep. John Dingell of Michigan, who became a reliable ally on all subjects that concerned the National Wildlife Refuge System.

In my Florida work, I had become mindful of the incredible number of endangered and threatened mammals, insects, reptiles and plants in the state, especially the wild orchids that made Florida second only to Hawaii for its number of imperiled species. Years of drainage and massive urban development had been converting an ever-widening swath of native Florida into gated golf course communities. Intensive agriculture that overused pesticides eliminated pristine habitats. So when the hearings were held on the proposed ESA, I had support from all of the Florida environmental groups. Some large landowners expressed quiet concern about the ESA requirement about preserving habitat, but the responsible landowners, especially the ranching community, supported efforts to protect the wealth of wildlife that shared the land with their cattle.

Buff Bohlen, who had served Secretary Hickel in a prominent post and was widely respected within the department, accepted my offer to become deputy assistant secretary. Bohlen had worked with Talbot and Earl Baysinger, a brilliant FWS maverick located in the small Office of Endangered Species, to carefully consider the aims, objectives and language of a new ESA, including an outline of proposed measures for the act prepared by Talbot. I was fortunate to be able to enlist Douglas Wheeler, an expert on congressional affairs and legislation, to become my second deputy assistant secretary. He had worked with Bohlen and Talbot and was up to date on the effort to draft a new act. His input was invaluable.

FWS Director Smith was enthusiastic and gave Baysinger his blessing to work with the "Train Working Committee," named after Russell Train, to give the FWS the tools for listing and enforcing the requirements of a final draft of the proposed bill. The "Train Team" worked to produce the draft bill that contained the famous "Section 7" language, which forced compliance of all federal agencies for the protection of habitat needed to preserve an endangered species. The requirement to protect habitat was obvious if there was going to be a genuine effort made to ensure the protection and eventual recovery of an endangered species. This provision was critical – as ecology had taught, you can't protect a plant or animal without guarding its habitat and ecosystem.

A new category of protection titled "threatened" was a carefully considered and well-written addition intended to protect a species before it became endangered. This provision was added and gave the act even more teeth.

We were aided by a superb group of hard-working experts and, above all, we listened carefully to Cleo Layton. We became devoted to Layton, as his knowledge of the workings within the FWS and the National Park Service (NPS) could not be matched. I developed a close working relationship with FWS Director Smith, who had quietly and effectively healed the FWS from the damage of the Malik raid.

Long discussions with my mentors – Dr. Starker Leopold, legendary wildlife ecologist of the University of California, Berkley, and former Assistant Secretary Dr. Stanley Cain – convinced Bohlen, Wheeler and me that the proposed act could be one of the most important wildlife issues of the 20th century. I had met Leopold and Cain through my work in managing America's parks. Cain was an international expert on many land and wildlife issues; Leopold chaired a committee to improve science in the decision-making process in the national parks.

Both were well-respected ecologists and I value my relationships with both of these remarkable scientists; no other DOI assistant secretary ever had such an illustrious combination of expertise. Their superb advice and wise council were integral in my abilities to perform my duties. The endangered species team met frequently at the Council's headquarters at Lafayette Square and exchanged not only ideas but also preliminary language to be carefully drafted in the ESA bill.

During this period, Rep. Dingell of Michigan and his staff also worked on their version of a strengthened ESA, similar in many respects to the emerging administration draft. Dingell, chairman of the fisheries and wildlife conservation sub-committee of the Merchant Marine and Fisheries Committee, was the foremost supporter of wildlife conservation in the House of Representatives. We became close friends and worked on many wildlife-related issues during the next five years.

We took drafts of final administration proposals to the Hill, where we briefed key members of the authorizing committee. Dingell collected 24 sponsors of his proposed bill, which was heard by Democratic Rep. Leonor Sullivan of Missouri, who chaired the parent committee. With Dingell's close friend and ally, Republican Rep. John Saylor, of Pennsylvania, they brought together a bipartisan group with their staffs and forged an agreement to support the draft act. The Republican maverick, Rep. Pete McCloskey, rounded up his allies and gave strong support while serving on the pertinent House committee.

The Senate Commerce Committee, chaired by Sen. Warren Magnuson of Washington, handled the bill. Its main sponsor was Sen. Harrison Williams of New Jersey, and it had eight supporters.

After the Office of Management and Budget (OMB) passed positive judgment on the act, I was designated as its manager. Talbot and Dingell's assistant, Frank Potter, went through the Dingell draft ESA and deleted what they called the "weasel words." These included changing wording such as "the Secretary may ..." to "the Secretary shall...", and they removed all the phrases such as "in so far as practicable" and "in so far as possible." The result was the extraordinarily powerful piece of legislation that Dingell subsequently submitted. I prepared for the hearings with intensive briefings from Bohlen, Wheeler and Baysinger and with briefing books prepared by staff. Other experts called and gave me accurate answers to even the most complicated questions that could be raised by dissident members of either committee.

Hearings were called in both houses of Congress. The committee chairs' opening statements made it abundantly clear that the time for a national effort to protect our endangered species and all forms of life would never come again. Dingell wrote me a note: "Go for it. Its time has come!" We had no greater champion!

The House bill unanimously passed the Senate on a voice vote of 390-12 and the Senate bill passed 92-0. Nixon signed it into law on December 28, 1973.

The national feeling of support to save the increasing number of endangered species was widespread. All of the national environmental organizations were united in their support of the bill. Prominent naturalists spoke out, gave interviews and expressed support for, in many cases, a "vision" they had longed for. State game and fish directors did not object to the federal government taking on the very difficult and often controversial decisions that had to be made in the following years to protect endangered species' habitat from development. Their sentiments were expressed to Spencer Smith by a leading state director: "Better you than me – your decision regarding the protection of endangered species and the habitat needed to protect an endangered species will get the governor off my back."

To counter the initial outcry that Section 7's power was "excessive," the FWS almost immediately announced a list of endangered, highly visible animals and birds to which the vast majority of Americans could relate. The FWS used a series of publications to explain the importance of protecting and enhancing habitat to give endangered species an opportunity to rebound from the void of extinction. The vast majority of Americans understood this challenge.

It was more difficult, however, to convince a private landowner whose land included habitat of an endangered species and was under federal order to maintain a land use compatible with the species. It could seem like the heavy hand of the federal government dictating usage rules over private property rights. Although efforts have been made to provide incentives to private landowners, that issue will continue as long as the act remains the bellwether effort to protect endangered species of flora and fauna.

Section 7 must survive the attacks of individuals and state and federal agencies that find their proposed projects that appears more valuable than some seemingly inconsequential form of life. The ethic of protecting those species, which seeks only to share room on Mother Earth with us, is the essence of the Endangered Species Act. This tenet was the major force of my testimony before Congress.

The team that worked together to produce the act, energize support for its passage and maintain oversight of its application are quietly proud of a major accomplishment.

It was a team effort and came at the right time in the history of America's environmental renaissance.

When President Richard Nixon signed the law on December 28, 1973, he called wildlife "a many-faceted treasure, of value to scientists, scholars, and nature lovers alike, and it forms a vital part of the heritage we all share as Americans." With the ESA's passage, Congress recognized that the nation's rich natural heritage is of "aesthetic, ecological, educational, recreational, and scientific value to our nation and its people." It further expressed concern that many of the nation's native plants and animals were in danger of becoming extinct.

Dr. E.O. Wilson, the universally acclaimed biologist, researcher, theorist, and author, has been quoted as saying, "The Endangered Species Act is the single most important environmental act passed in the 20th century."

The Endangered Species Act, while not perfect legislation, was the first time in the world that a national government enacted a law to protect flora and fauna on the brink. Its subsequent success in saving a number of species, including the bald eagle which now numbers 5,000 nesting pairs, shows that humans can reverse the course of their destructive activities when the government mandates a new dawn in which all creatures have value.

I am very proud to have been part of this groundbreaking law. My greatest hope is that my great-great-grandchildren will be able to see specimens of mammals, reptiles, insects and plants recovered from extinction.

The Convention on International Trade in Endangered Species (CITES)

Simultaneously with the team's efforts to prepare the ESA, we were deeply involved with CEQ and the federal State and Justice Departments preparing our country's position on the forthcoming Convention on the International Trade in Endangered Species of Wild Fauna and Flora (CITES).

Although seemingly obvious, the billion-dollar trade in wild animals and rare plants was a growing concern that reached a crescendo in the 1960s when excessive whaling and the ghastly trade in elephants tusks, rhinoceros horns, and exotic birds – both live and for their feathers – became international issues. The trade is diverse, ranging from live animals and plants to a vast array of wildlife products derived from them, including food products, exotic leather goods, wooden musical instruments, timber, tourist curios and medicine. The combination of trade and the loss of essential habitat are capable of depleting populations and bringing some species close to extinction. Because the trade in wild animals and plants crosses borders between countries, the effort to regulate it requires international cooperation.

In 1961, Talbot was an organizer of the international conference on Conservation in Modern African States held in Arusha, Tanganyika (now Tanzania). He organized a side meeting with wildlife authorities from about 30 African nations to examine poaching of endangered species. It was clear that African game departments could not stop the well-financed demand from developed nations, and there was unanimous agreement with Talbot's suggestion that an international convention was needed to deal with wildlife trade. Talbot worked with Dr. Wolfgang Burhenne to prepare a resolution calling for the convention, and the resolution was adopted in 1963 at the meeting of the World Conservation Union (IUCN) in Nairobi, Kenya. The IUCN subsequently developed a draft convention, building on nearly seven years of repeated consultations with its member states and organizations.

After gaining presidential approval to develop CITES shortly after CEQ was established, CEQ Chair Train set up a team involving most of the same individuals and organizations as the team that developed the ESA. At the start of preparations for the United Nations Conference on the Human Environment, held in Stockholm in 1972, Train and Talbot negotiated a governmental agreement for the U.S. to sponsor the convention at the U.N. conference, as well as host the plenipotentiary conference to negotiate the convention.

In the following months, the CITES team worked within the U.S. government and other nations to achieve agreement on the objectives, wording and responsibilities involved with CITES. To this end, Talbot made negotiating visits to many countries in the developing world and Europe.

Ultimately, participants of the Stockholm Conference endorsed the U.S. proposal for CITES. The State Department agreed to allow its extensive facilities to be used for world wildlife leaders to meet and in many cases the head of respective governments to debate and hopefully agree on a final text of a meaningful convention. Train was named to head the United States delegation. Talbot, Bohlen and I were selected as Train's team members. The text of the convention was finally agreed to at a meeting of 80 countries in Washington, D.C. on March 3, 1973; on July 1, 1975, it entered into force.

The convention is an international agreement that countries adhere to voluntarily. Each party to the convention has to adopt its own domestic legislation to ensure that CITES is implemented at the national level. To achieve this, each state must establish a Scientific Authority to determine the status of species, and a Management Authority to handle the permit process.

Among other measures, the convention has three appendices. Appendix I names seriously endangered species for which no trade is allowed, other than strictly limited conservation purposes. Appendix II includes species that may become endangered by trade. Listed species may be traded, but specific permits are required by the exporting and importing nations to monitor the species and the trade. Changes to the appendices and other CITES business are deliberated at periodic meetings of the parties. Appendix III is for species not on the other appendices, but ones for which the country where they are found wishes to give special protection. Today, 180 countries try to implement CITES, which accords varying degrees of protection to 30,000 species of animals and plants.

Sadly, the optimism I once felt about CITES has turned to despair in recent years, with the ongoing poaching of elephants, rhinoceros and spotted cats that continues on a scale never considered possible.

Poachers flying into remote areas in helicopters armed with automatic rifles have killed hundreds if not thousands of forest elephants for their ivory. The black and white rhinos, valued for their horns, may be extinct in less than 20 years due to poaching. Why? The value of ivory, horns and skins of a range of magnificent wild cats is a lure for many indigenous people who live in poverty and see an opportunity to earn a year's wage or more paid by unscrupulous middleman dealers, particularly Chinese agents in Africa.

A 2015 report in Science Advances estimates that mammals, birds, reptiles, and fish are going extinct 114 times faster than normal. Harvard biologist E.O. Wilson estimates that if current rates continue, half of the Earth's "higher life forms will be extinct by 2100." Many of those will be these beloved African mammals.

Many scientists call this impending doom the "Sixth Extinction," referring to a series of mass losses of biota that have occurred during the Earth's history. The first five, notes journalist Gwynne Dyer, occurred during a half-billion years; four were likely through planetary warming set off by "massive, millennia-long volcanic eruptions."

Now the problem is the human race – the brains that made our species so successful also developed technology that has polluted the planet and threatens to cause another disastrous warming event through climate change. It is compounded by the growing human population and its wants and needs.

"It's fair to say that we are the victims of our own success, but so is the entire biosphere," Dyer wrote. "There were one billion of us in 1800. We are now seven and a half billion, on our way to 10 or 11 billion. We have appropriated the most biologically productive 40 percent of the planet's land surface for our cities, farms and pastures, and there's not much left for other species."

Balancing human needs while still maintaining a diversity of species – which means stopping many from going extinct – will be a daunting, complex task. Dyer concludes by quoting author James Lovelock: "If we continue business as usual, our species may never again see the lush and verdant world we had only one hundred years ago."

All of the effort behind the Endangered Species Act, the work of the most notable scientists in the world, and the promise of the Convention on the International Trade in Endangered Species must be heeded, if, indeed, our generation and the next are ever to be considered wise stewards.

It is past time for the partners in the Convention to enforce animal protection laws and maintain extensive wild habitats. This well may be the most important environmental issue of the 21st century.

And our lives, so intertwined with other species in the web of life, may also depend upon it.

The Whooping Crane Adventure

"My God, we have a problem! We're nearly out of fuel. We cannot get back to the fort."

One of the unexpected highlights of my tenure in Washington was an epic experience flying over the whooping crane breeding grounds in Canada's vast Northwest Territory. I was accompanied by John Tener, director of the Canadian Wildlife Service, and the unique and wonderful Ernie Kuyt, a genuine whooping crane expert.

I was saddened by the news that Ernie passed away on May 21, 2010, as he was a most remarkable figure and a highly respected wildlife biologist. We had met at a conference shortly after I was confirmed as assistant secretary in the spring of 1971. I made an immediate friend. I shared his concerns over the future of the whooping cranes and our mutual desire to do our level best to make every effort to protect the existing flock and increase its numbers. At that time, in 1971, only 57 cranes existed, too small a number to be confident of a major recovery.

Several years later, following a joint Canadian-U.S. conference on the gross industrial and untreated sewage pollution problems of the Great Lakes, Canadian Prime Minister Pierre Trudeau asked me during a State Department reception what I would really like to see in Canada. I replied that I was fascinated by whooping cranes and would "give an eye tooth" to fly over their breeding grounds with John and Ernie as my guides. Without a moment of hesitation, the prime minister replied, "Your wish will be consummated!"

Shortly thereafter, John reached me through the director of the U.S. Fish and Wildlife Service and arranged a firm schedule for the flight.

In the late spring, I flew to Ottawa, dined with John and was the government's guest in a fine hotel. At 2 a.m., the fire alarm went off! The bedside telephone rang with a recorded message: "Do not use the elevator. Walk carefully downstairs to the lobby. Please do not panic." By the way, I was on the 24th floor!

I met a lovely group of hotel guests who were served a small tot of fine Canadian whiskey before the all clear signal was given. Some idiot had set the alarm off and was being removed by Canadian police. I was back asleep within minutes after arriving at my room back on the 24th floor. A good night's exercise!

The next morning, John and I flew to Fort Smith in a Canadian aircraft. We spent the night with the governor general of the territory. A Canadian Beaver aircraft had been chartered for our inspection flight. We were up early, as it was very warm. The Beaver was piloted by a young man who followed Ernie's flight plan carefully.

We lost time at the start of the flight by flying over the flooded Athabasca and Slave Rivers to see the cadavers of a fair number of wood buffalo that had drowned in the major spring flood. That wood buffalo herd is the only pure-blooded species left in the world, a uniquely different animal than the plains buffalo. Flying at low level, we could see wolves feeding on the buffalo carcasses.

We then headed west-northwest to the whooping cranes' breeding areas. Ernie reported that it had been a good nesting season, an early spring, which got the chicks off to a good start. The number of pairs of newborn chicks was high, but because of the unique feature of cranes, the birds are hatched independently, sometimes one or even two days apart.

The delayed hatching of the second egg means that chick No. 2 is smaller than his or her elder. If the food supply is insufficient, the elder crane chick receives 100 percent of its parents' attention, including the vast majority of daily food. The second chick is left to die or is physically assaulted by the eldest chick and is killed.

We enjoyed hours of low-level flying discussing Ernie's discoveries and the gradual increase in successful nesting by an ever-increasing number of cranes. The Aransas-Wood Buffalo whooping crane breeding area was not discovered until 1954 when a low-flying airplane saw the cranes and their young. The adults we saw were on guard for sudden rainstorms that can chill the chicks – and for the occasional predator such as a coyote. The chicks we saw were the size of a large rooster with bright yellow baby feathers.

Their parents paid no attention to the plane and continued to walk sedately, searching for roots, green sprouts and any insect that could be discovered. The parents fed the young what they dug up or caught. Ernie had studied the nesting and feeding territories for a number of years and continually pointed out "old friends" that had colored, identifiable collars and had made long migrations to and from the Northwest Territory to Matagorda Island on the southwest Texas coastline. The perils they face during this long-range Aransas migration are hard to believe. Every successful migration, either way, is a minor miracle.

John and Ernie were sitting in the two rear seats of the cockpit in order to give me maximum viewing. I saw a minimum of 10 pairs of adult cranes with young.

The saddest sight was two pairs of cranes that had lost their eggs or chicks to high water, an improperly made nest or a predator. It was too late to start anew. The time frame from birth to being able to fly great distances is short. There is only one opportunity to nest successfully. Adult whooping cranes are 6 feet tall with a 7- to 8-foot wingspan, and it takes time and adequate food for the young to be strong enough to join their parents in the long migration south. The pairs that had lost the opportunity to produce young birds danced and sang their love and frustration at their failure. It was a heartbreaking scene among the successful additions to the world's only flock of whooping cranes.

We flew on and on, finding a distant successful pair with two young that Ernie had missed the week before. My enthusiasm to see more pairs with young, shared by Ernie, nearly led us to disaster.

Recovering Slowly

The total number of wild whooping cranes in 1971 was 57 birds and, by 1973, 49 birds. Although they had "recovered" from a low of only 21 birds in the 1940s, the flock was significantly endangered. The numbers remained perilously low until 1977-78, when the wild population increased to 76 birds. By 1986-87, their numbers had increased to 110 birds. The figure for 2010-11: 278 birds. As this is written in 2016, despite our gains, only about 400 whooping cranes exist in the wild.

Having flown in Beavers and been checked out in Cessna 170s, I read the fuel gauges as we headed back to Fort Smith. Two gauges indicated that they were empty and the third was perilously close to being empty. Very quietly, I asked the pilot if he had a reserve fuel tank. His response was, "My God, we have a problem! We're nearly out of fuel! We cannot get back to the fort. We have to land either on a marsh or on the river."

That, thankfully, the river was just a few miles ahead of us.

John was very unhappy. The pilot called Fort Smith and declared an emergency. A heated discussion took place about where to land the plane safely. The decision was to land on the flood-swollen river. I was the only one who could open the front right-hand door. After swift instructions on what I had to accomplish on landing, the pilot would taxi to the shoreline, where I would depart the front seat for the pontoon. Within a compartment in the pontoon was a long rope. I was to wrap the rope around my waist, wade ashore and run around the nearest black spruce tree three times, securing the rope and the plane.

The plan worked!

I waded through knee-deep water and raced around a handy spruce tree. The plane swung over to the bank allowing John, Ernie and the pilot an easy exit. It was so warm that I was in no trouble with wet pants, socks and low boots, but the others insisted on building a fire to try to dry my clothing. I wrapped up in a blanket and made myself comfortable while the trio debated whose fault it was that we had overextended the flight.

It was a simple explanation. We were flying at low levels on a very warm day and had added the dead wood buffalo and the long-distance pair of cranes and their young to the agenda. I told the pilot he was not at fault and that it was an experience of a lifetime.

The smoke of the fire kept quantities of a large horsefly, I think they called them "moose flies," from attacking. Those flies could really bite!

Don't ask me why, but I had a copy of John Le Carre's book, *Tinker Tailor Soldier Spy*, in my briefcase. There was a canister of hot coffee and I just settled in, content with an extraordinary adventure.

Although the plane was on the river, it was possible to contact the Fort Smith authorities and give our exact location. Within an hour, a helicopter landed carrying fuel for the plane and retrieving John, Ernie and me. We landed at Fort Smith to be greeted by the news that the prime minister's office had been advised that I was "lost" in the Wood Buffalo Park. Rogers Morton, the secretary of interior, had been notified and the prime minister was described as "furious."

I showered, took a nap and enjoyed dinner, working with Ernie and John on issues that the cranes face on their epic migrations. We discussed the prospects of starting another flock, both non-migratory and migratory, from another suitable breeding area.

After dinner, I was delighted to receive a call from Prime Minister Trudeau, welcoming me to Canada and apologizing for the incident. I told him not to blame the pilot, as it was my vast enthusiasm to see so many nesting sites and pairs with young, combined with very warm weather, that led to a fuel shortage. I remarked that it was a "life experience – unforgettable," and that I deeply appreciated the efforts by his office and the Canadian Wildlife Service to make the unique adventure possible.

Before the prime minister left office, we were together again at another joint Canadian-U.S. meeting at the U.S. State Department. He interrupted the meeting with a wild tale of my exploits in the Wood Buffalo wilderness, bringing howls of laughter from the two delegations and confirming Secretary of State Henry Kissinger's view that I was "dangerously adventurous."

UNTO

The Liberty Bell, Independence Hall and the Japanese Finance Minister

"Off we went into the blizzard."

I was invited to speak at the Philadelphia Academy of Science in January 1972. George Hartzog, director of the National Park Service, urged me to go to Philadelphia to be briefed by what he called one of the services' "superstars," assigned to Independence National Historical Park. His assignment was to rejuvenate historic buildings that had fallen into poor condition due to financial restraints. Members of the congressional appropriation committees and the President wanted the Park to be in splendid condition for the upcoming bicentennial ceremonies in 1976.

Hobart "Hobie" Cawood, the recently appointed director of Independence National Historical Park, had an incredible background, having served in a number of our important military parks. Superintendent Cawood was a born leader, a history buff who had been elected as the man to organize the complicated restoration of not only Independence Hall, where the Declaration of Independence and the United States Constitution were debated and adopted in the late 18th century, but also the complex of associated buildings owned and operated by the National Park Service.

I accepted the speaking invitation, as it was a great opportunity to see Independence Hall again and visit the many buildings that make up the Independence Hall National Historical Park. I decided to take an early morning train from Washington to Philadelphia and arranged for a tour of the park.

The weather forecast was for a strong weather pattern moving eastward. Forecasters had suggested that the oncoming storm contained significant snow. I had packed a tuxedo, dress shirt, black tie and proper shoes. I was dressed in a warm woolen suit with a heavy overcoat, scarf and hat. My faithful driver, Garfield Lawrence, dropped me off at Union Station with a round-trip ticket. I had a seat in the club car for the one-hour-and-forty-minute trip. The return train departing Philadelphia at 10 p.m. fit my dinner and speaking assignment perfectly – or so I thought, as I was supposed to be the grand marshal of a winter parade the following day in Washington.

I had spent sufficient time on my remarks, so I was comfortable that my speech would be brisk and environmentally sound. As planned on arrival in Philadelphia, Superintendent Cawood met me. We immediately bonded.

The first priority was to view the extensive rehabilitation work at Independence Hall. We then visited many areas within the confines of the Historical Park. Cawood had a wealth of historical information regarding the months of heated debates that led to adoption of our nation's Constitution and Bill of Rights. He stressed the importance of not only Liberty Hall, but also the complete complex of our nation's history.

The weather turned increasingly dark and forbidding, proving the weather forecasters correct and heavy snowfall could be expected by 4 p.m. As forecast, a great snowstorm began with intensity.

I needed a place to change into my tuxedo before the 7 p.m. dinner; at 6 p.m. Cawood selected the Tower Room in Independence Hall. It served as the resting place for the Liberty Bell while a new interpretative building was under construction. The previous site for the Bell was in a building that simply could not handle the hundreds of tourists who each day wanted to see the symbol of the Continental Congress's efforts to produce our nation's Constitution and Bill of Rights.

At 6 p.m., I had managed to remove my heavy suit, add a dinner shirt, my tuxedo pants, socks and shoes and was tying my black tie using the reflection from a window pane, when there was a knock on the door. Cawood went to the door and said, firmly, "The park is closed!"

I said: "Hobie, anybody who dares enough to come out in the snowstorm to this building should be made welcome. Open the door and see who's there."

A young Japanese lady and man entered and identified themselves as Georgetown University students: brother and sister. They spoke perfect English. They said their father was outside and had a "life ambition to see the Liberty Bell."

I urged them to lead their father in. I shook hands to a bowing, immaculately dressed gentleman covered in snowflakes. His children translated for him. He stated that it would be a "memorable experience" to see the Liberty Bell, as he had studied the American Revolution and the debates that led to our nation's Constitution and Bill of Rights.

I said, "Forgive my dress; I am changing into a tuxedo, as I am giving an evening speech at the Academy of Sciences. It is probably the first time anyone has ever changed from a suit into a tuxedo in front of the Liberty Bell."

That observation "broke the ice" and produced chuckles. I then said, "May I introduce Hobart Cawood, who is the superintendent of the Independence National Historical Park and a highly respected historian. He will give you a far too short briefing on the Bell and Independence Hall, as he must get me to the society's dinner in time for my speech."

Without a pause, Cawood welcomed them and gave the trio an astonishing, brilliant description of not only the Bell but also of the importance of Independence Hall as the site of our Founding Fathers' debates. He explained that Independence Hall had also served as the site of the second presidential inauguration of George Washington and John Adams.

The two young students interpreted for their father, which took time, but Superintendent Cawood was at his absolute best. The senior gentleman asked for a favor, "Could I touch the Bell?" Hobie replied, "Please do it!"

The father reached with both hands, grasped the Bell and bowed deeply. He then turned and thanked

Hobart "Hobie" Cawood

In 1971, Hobart "Hobie" Cawood was selected to become superintendent of – and supervise restoration of – the Independence Hall National Historical Park for the nation's Bicentennial Celebration in 1976.

Despite budgetary problems, Cawood and his devoted staff were able to present a gleaming Liberty Hall and a restored park. His career spanned 20 years as superintendent of Independence Park: two decades of devoted service to the American people and the thousands of visitors who flock to see the birthplace of our country. He enlisted volunteers when staffing problems that still exist throughout the national park system required loving, caring citizens to interpret and even assist in management of our country's birthplace.

Cawood was a high-profile superintendent, regularly attending meetings ranging from business breakfasts to society dinners. He convinced business and government leaders in Philadelphia that the park was vital to the city's well-being, and his contacts paid off handsomely. During celebrations and times of critical needs at Independence Hall, Cawood's contacts resulted in donations from big business, from the affluent and from average citizens. There were donations to sponsor festivals, costly scaffolding donated by contractors for emergency repair of Independence Hall's roof, and even antiques to furnish the historic rooms.

The visit by Queen Elizabeth and Prince Phillip to Independence Hall during our nation's bicentennial celebrations brought international attention to the park and the restored Independence Hall, one of our nation's most important historical sites.

Cawood's career as a member of the National Park Service spanned 33 years. He served as a historian of five battlefield parks before being promoted to his awesome position at Independence Hall. Following his retirement from the National Park Service, he continued his fascination with American history by becoming the president of Old Salem, N.C., a privately owned, colonial-era village.

The list of Hobie's awards is long. His extraordinary career has been recognized by nearly every leading historical society and organization, which have recognized his professional and courageous performance as superintendent.

The financial and staffing deficits that Cawood faced during his tour of duty are reflective of the tragic loss of faith by members of Congress, who are honor bound to protect and preserve the very best of the wilderness and historical places that the majority of Americans cherish.

The National Park Service needs more leaders identical to Hobart "Hobie" Cawood.

us for the privilege having achieved a "life wish." The trio returned into the driving snowstorm. I said, "Well done, Hobie! You have made a life friend for Independence Hall, the Liberty Bell and the National Park Service!"

We agreed that we had to move quickly, as the streets were surely becoming impassable.

Holding my hanging bag containing my suit and day clothing, I was bundled up in my overcoat, scarf and hat as I jumped into Cawood's sedan. I was driven to the academy through a now-blinding snowstorm. Thankfully he, too, was an honored guest at the dinner.

At the conclusion of my abbreviated remarks to a full house of listeners who had braved the snowstorm, I stated that due to the storm I thought it would be wise for everybody to leave promptly, forgoing dessert and coffee, as the roads were becoming extremely dangerous. My recommendation was received with standing applause. Cawood got me to the Pennsylvania railroad station in time to catch the last train at 10 p.m. from Philadelphia to Washington.

As I thanked him for a splendid day and congratulated him on his fascinating assignment, I urged him to call the National Park Police headquarters in Washington to request a police cruiser be waiting for me at Washington's Union Station.

I entered the club car to find three elderly ladies in full evening dress who had ventured from Washington to Philadelphia to hear my speech. I was flabbergasted! They all congratulated me on my brief remarks and stated they were delighted to be in the club car and anxious to return safely to Washington and their residences.

I stepped into the men's room and changed from my tuxedo, back into my warm suit. The train left on time with just the four of us occupying the very comfortable club car. We were graciously attended to by an expert steward.

Off we went into the blizzard. The ladies dozed while I read a report on the plans and time schedule for the renovation of the Independence Hall complex. There was controversy over the design of the new building to house the Liberty Bell, but it was too late to halt construction of an ill-conceived building that didn't fit its location. At least it would allow far more tourists to see the Bell during the many Bicentennial events.

It was an ambitious schedule filled with challenges – obviously the reason Superintendent Cawood had been selected.

About 45 minutes into our train ride, we came to a sudden stop. Then, the heat went off. Within minutes, it became uncomfortably cold. The steward located blankets and we wrapped the three women up in them. I put on my overcoat. We wondered collectively whether we were going to spend the night in the train's club car.

After 40 minutes of no movement, the steward informed us that a truck had foundered on the tracks but was being removed and we should be on our way in another 30 minutes. He also produced a bottle of Scotch whiskey. I poured three-quarters of an ounce of whiskey into four glasses, added a small amount of water and urged the ladies to partake. They didn't need much persuading! Finally, the heat came on and the train began to move cautiously forward.

We arrived at Union Station at 2 a.m. It was bitterly cold and snow now covered the streets. Thankfully, a Park Service police cruiser was waiting for me. I explained the situation to the officer and moved the three ladies into the backseat of the cruiser. I asked them to give me their addresses in sequence. The first lady was dropped at the Mayflower Hotel, where she had an apartment. We then were driven to two beautiful homes in Georgetown. At each one, a butler was waiting for the home's "lady."

As I slipped into bed at 3 a.m., positively exhausted, my wife rolled over and whispered, "The parade has been called off, so sleep in!"

Soon, I received lovely thank-you notes from my three female charges.

About 30 days later, my wonderful secretary, Nori Uchida, flew into my office and stated, "Dr. Henry Kissinger is on the line." I raised my phone and recognized the gravelly, German-accented voice, which stated, "Well, Reed, you have done the country a great service."

I replied, "Henry I try to do that every day I'm in office."

He bellowed, "This time you excelled yourself. I have a letter from the Japanese minister of finance who was in Washington for an International Monetary Committee meeting. He persuaded his two children who were studying at Georgetown University to take him to Philadelphia to visit Independence Hall.

"When they arrived, the snow had begun and the park appeared to be deserted. They saw lights coming from a small building, knocked on the door and were allowed in. The superintendent of Independence National Historical Park was introduced to them by a tall, thin man who was in the process of donning a tuxedo.

"He welcomed them and arranged for the superintendent to give them a superb briefing. The tall man was apparently in Philadelphia to give a speech. He finished dressing while the briefing continued. He joked that he was the first man to don a tuxedo in front of the Liberty Bell. They thought that was very amusing.

"Nathaniel, you'll never know how appreciative the minister is of your kindness and the excellence of the superintendent's briefing."

What could I possibly say except, "Henry, it was a pleasure!"

The Liberty Bell...

an iconic symbol of American independence.

The Bell was commissioned by Philadelphia city fathers in 1752 from a highly regarded English foundry and placed in a steeple of the Pennsylvania State House (now renamed Independence Hall).

The Bell was used to summon lawmakers to legislative sessions and to alert citizens to public meetings and proclamations. The Bell cracked when first rung, leading to a fascinating history of repair efforts that includes it twice being melted down and recast.

The recast Bell was one of many rung to mark the reading of the Declaration of Independence on July 8th, 1776.

Even the replacement bell cracked – its distinctive fissure occurred sometime in the early 19th century. The Bell's famous crack has long fascinated historians, experts in metal casting and owners of foundries.

A Scripture cast on the original Bell led to its eventual name. A quote from Leviticus 25:10 reads, "Proclaim liberty throughout all the land unto all the inhabitants thereof." Before the Civil War, the Bell became a symbol of freedom for abolitionist societies who wanted to emancipate American slaves. They gave the Bell its name, "the Liberty Bell."

The Bell has crossed the country to be displayed at countless expositions and patriotic gatherings, attracting large crowds wherever it has gone.

The City of Philadelphia initially owned the Bell and loaned it to the National Park Service for display, but after World War II, the city allowed the Service to take custody of the Bell.

It hung in one of the towers at Liberty Hall, but this location restricted the number of visitors who could see it. In 1976, in time for the Bicentennial, it was moved to a new building on the Mall.

As visitors to the National Historical Park dramatically increased, the Liberty Bell Center was built in 2003, allowing for a significant increase in visits per hour. Besides the Bell, the center has copies of the founding articles of our nation.

It has become a major – and vitally important – tourist attraction.

Piping plover

A Bridge That Couldn't Connect Two Angry Rockefellers

"I bet my sister was involved in that!"

When New York Gov. Nelson Rockefeller promised construction unions during the 1960s that he would promote and fund a new bridge over Long Island Sound from a site near Rye, N.Y., to Long Island, it was national news.

The bridge would lead to a new road along the island's north shore, beginning near a public beach in Bayville. Just west of the public beach is the Piping Rock Beach Club, which adjoins the Creek Club beach and golf course. The route would continue about a half mile north of the town of Oyster Bay along West Shore Road. The route then turned inland (northwest) up a quite steep hill through many private properties, then down and across the extensive marsh area. It crossed Mill Neck Creek, more marsh area and then continued northwest to the final point at Bayville Beach, which was one-tenth of a mile east of the Creek Club property. (On the other side of Long Island Sound, the bridge made landfall in Rye and connected with Route 287.)

There were obviously better locations. The governor did not want the mainland site to be in Connecticut, as he did not wish to share the tolls needed to finance the New York State bonds.

The Long Island terminus site was highly controversial and led to a stream of well-earned criticism from the Long Island communities that would be adversely impacted by the new system of roads needed to provide additional routes to the island's extensive road network. It was obvious the proposal would have major adverse impacts on multiple communities.

The members and homeowners that surrounded the Creek Club and the Piping Rock Club were well aware of the governor's plan and they united to defeat it. They formed "The Action Committee Against the Bridge" and, with the assistance of one of New York's best-known law firms, developed their strategy. The key tactic was to donate wetlands owned by the Creek Club and other adjacent private owners to form a small but important addition to the Long Island National Wildlife Refuges, making the construction of a bridge all but impossible.

Once the deeds were in hand, members of the protest group met with then-Secretary of Interior Stewart Udall and explained that the intrusion of a bridge and proposed expansion of connecting roads would harm many homeowners and members of two well-known clubs.

They also argued that the project would diminish the value of the 36-acre wetlands, used by thousands of migrating waterfowl, shorebirds and terrestrial birds. The creation of another refuge to be added to a system of Long Island National Wildlife Refuges was deemed appropriate and valuable.

Secretary Udall immediately ordered the Fish and Wildlife Service's senior refuge staff to verify the importance of this small marsh. He promptly received a scientifically sound field report from refuge professionals, aided by local Audubon chapter members. The wetlands were deemed "significant."

It is well within the constitutional authority for a President or a Secretary of Interior to accept exceptional land or even to create national monuments. The President's and Secretary's rights have been repeatedly challenged before the U.S. Supreme Court, which found that both the President and the Secretary have authority to create national wildlife refuges and national monuments.

Udall formally accepted the 36-acre Amagansett National Wildlife Refuge on December 16, 1968, weeks before Nixon was sworn in as president.

After I was sworn in as Assistant Secretary of Interior in May 1971, I was responsible for millions of acres of national wildlife refuges. I was only dimly aware of the proposed bridge when my secretary announced, "Governor Nelson Rockefeller's sister is on the line."

In a loud, clear voice, she announced that she was holding me personally responsible for any concession that would allow her brother's "monstrous" proposed bridge to be built where it was planned. I begged for time, and an opportunity to be adequately briefed by both my counsel and the pertinent refuge staff as to the proposed bridge's location.

My calendar was full, but I made a date to be briefed two days later and included counsel from the Justice Department. I asked all concerned to bring proof that the creation of a small wildlife refuge days before a change in administrations was legal and binding.

The morning of the scheduled briefing, Mrs. Rockefeller Mauzé was back on the phone to remind me that she was holding me "personally accountable" for my reaction to the forthcoming briefing. She stated that she would not sleep until I called her back following the briefing. There was obviously leakage ongoing between her and members of the refuge staff.

I enjoyed an in-depth briefing by refuge staff and my counsel, complete with photographs of The Creek Club's wonderful golf course built in 1925. The adjacent wetlands were small but were "classic" and worth preserving. We discussed the right of a secretary of interior to create a national wildlife refuge and were reminded that the President and the secretary have extraordinary rights under the Antiquities Act. (President Theodore Roosevelt began by creating The Pelican Island National Wildlife Refuge in Florida's Indian River on March 14, 1903, to protect a large breeding colony of pelicans and great egrets. Secretary of Interior Fred Seaton had created the 12.4-million acre Alaskan National Wildlife Range in the final days of the Eisenhower Administration.)

No sooner had I been briefed, than I informed Secretary Morton that there was a predictable confrontation that would arise if Governor Rockefeller attempted to persuade President Nixon to abandon the refuge.

Two days later, I had the unfortunate duty to appear in the Oval Office to face a pair of irate gentlemen: Governor Rockefeller and President Nixon. I was yelled at simultaneously by them both. Nixon began the attack:

"Those rich bastards gave their wetlands to the National Wildlife Refuge system days before the change in administrations. Surely their act – for heaven's sake, 36 acres of mosquito breeding marsh – is illegal!"

I stood silently until asked to respond. I stated that the wetlands had been surveyed and the deeds legally signed over to the U.S. Fish and Wildlife Refuge System. The 36 acres were to be known as the Amagansett National Wildlife Refuge. I cited the authority for presidential or secretarial action.

Nixon snarled, "Get rid of it! Cancel the conveyance!"

I replied quite calmly that the department's legal staff and a senior member of the Justice Department agreed that the only way the land could be removed from the refuge system would be by an Act of Congress.

There was an alarmingly long silence, followed by Governor Rockefeller stating, "I bet my sister was involved in that donation! It sounds like her."

I was excused.

As I left the Oval Office, the governor asked for time to inform the union leaders it would be impossible to build the bridge at that location. I replied that I was due in Denver for a speech, but a member of my staff would be the contact who would maintain silence until I heard from the White House that we could answer questions regarding the creation of the refuge and its importance.

When I returned to my office, I dutifully called Mrs. Rockefeller Mauzé and reported on the White House meeting. She simply stated, "It never occurred to me or my associates that you could or would be 'rolled.' I am proud of you."

I then asked my staff for the Friday through Monday schedule of who would respond to any requests from the White House or the press corps on the predictable uproar over the bridge decision. My two deputies were either in the field or giving speeches, leaving Dennis Drabelle as the ranking staff member. Denny, our staff's historian and able writer, knew all the details, as he had checked the history of the refuge with our legal counselors.

I warned him that there could be a leak to *The New York Times*, as its key environmental correspondent was aware of Governor Rockefeller's promise to the unions. "Denny, just know nothing and I warn you, he is one of the best investigative reporters on environmental issues in the business," I told him. "Silence is golden."

When I woke at the Brown Palace in Denver the next morning, I had a copy of the *Times* beside my door. There on the front page was the full story of the creation of the refuge, the impossibility of declaring the refuge illegal or surplus and the governor's displeasure.

I called Denny, who was in a mild state of shock. He stated convincingly, "*The New York Times* correspondent knew all the details. He only wanted me to say 'yes' or 'no.' I am sorry to put you in the 'pickle jar,' but he was better briefed than I was."

I laughed and replied, "Denny, the cat was out of the bag. I bet the bridge dies a quiet death."

It did. The president had other problems and never referred to this breach of silence.

The Lead Shot vs. Steel Shot Controversy

"If the ducks had picked up lead shot, they would have died of lead poisoning."

Following my briefings on the subject of lead poisoning of waterfowl, I entered a period where I sought more opinions from leading experts from the main duck hunting states. Each state game commission along the four waterfowl flyways had the expertise and were knowledgeable of outbreaks of significant losses of waterfowl when lead shot accumulated over firm bottoms of lakes, ponds and even marshes and was available as grit for feeding ducks. There was no consensus as to the overall impact of losing a significant number of waterfowl to lead shot poisoning per year. Some directors 'wrote off' the dying birds as annual, 'semi-natural' die off. Other state waterfowl experts were conflicted with the position that more ducks would die from an inefficient shot than from lead poisoning.

I was confident that the federal scientists were accurate but recognized that change of the pellets within a shotgun shell would be considered a 'monumental change' by a majority of keen waterfowlers. Many would have difficulty agreeing with the sound science that lead poisoning was killing millions of ducks, geese and swans.

The sporting press knew about the legal action, my concerns, the concerns of the state game commissioners and were cautiously non-committal. The arms industry began a quiet but efficient campaign challenging the number of dead waterfowl from lead poisoning and the cost per shell of a change over to a nontoxic shot.

I asked Spencer Smith, Director of the U.S. Fish and Wildlife Service to organize a conference to publicly discuss our findings, proposed solutions and open the floor to honest debate.

Director Smith arranged for a series of briefings on the science behind the numerous studies on lead-shot poisoning of waterfowl. The meeting was attended by a small number of FWS experts who specialized in the subject.

There was general agreement that, in certain locations, large numbers of ducks, geese and swans had died from swallowing and ingesting lead shot on a frequent basis. But the extent of lead poisoning down each of the four flyways was the subject of debate.

Publication of the legal action against the FWS for failure to mandate a ban on lead shot precipitated questions from the hunting press and organizations representing duck hunters, who questioned the purported death toll. They contended it was very difficult to accept figures such as 2.5 million birds lost to lead poisoning per year, as the bodies of the ducks were not evident along the shoreline or within the marsh where they had been feeding.

I decided I needed to hear from a broad section of waterfowl scientists. Spencer arranged for a major conference, which was attended by a wide representation of waterfowl experts in the FWS and independent experts. He introduced Frank Bellrose to the meetings.

Frank had spent his life's work on waterfowl as a member of the Illinois Natural Science Survey. He grew up along the Illinois River and became fascinated by the once vast migrations of diving and puddle ducks that halted their southward migrations to feed on aquatic plants in the river.

He had a particular fascination with wood ducks and their high loss of eggs and young to predators. He is credited with developing predator-proof wood duck nesting boxes, which have restored this magnificent duck throughout its range.

In speaking with us, Frank Bellrose was in his niche. He had flown surveys along the Illinois River, once a prolific waterfowl flyway, and was considered an expert on waterfowl deaths attributed to ingested lead shot. His studies on migration patterns led to a series of papers on that subject that are considered vital in understanding waterfowl migrations.

Spencer also invited expertise from the FWS's Northern Prairie Wildlife Research Center. It was an impressive group of very serious scientists – the nation's greatest experts on all facets of waterfowl management.

As the meeting progressed, it became increasingly clear that extensive research data beginning as early as 1894 had proven that waterfowl were dying from lead poisoning. Studies showed waterfowl would ingest lead shot, thinking it was grit needed to digest their food, especially from areas where extensive hunting had taken place and lead shot covered the bottom.

As to the question of why more dying ducks were not visible, the experts contended that a duck dying of lead poisoning swam to a protected area of heavy weed cover or even crawled up on the banks of marshes, lakes and rivers in a futile effort to avoid predators. The main successful predation was from eagles, large hawks, raccoons, foxes, coyotes, wild hogs and even alligators.

At the start of the conference, I made it clear that I could not embark on another controversial battle without significant science supporting a major change in waterfowl shotgun shells. I knew that the three most prominent ammunition makers – Winchester, Remington and Federal – would be leery of a mandated change to nontoxic shot. The FWS was aware that all three major ammunition makers knew about the National Wildlife Federation's lawsuit. They also were aware of the significant scientific evidence supporting the fact that as many as 2.5 million ducks were dying of lead shot each year.

Their likely defense would be that a change from lead to steel shot or another hard, nontoxic shot would cause more wounded ducks than the death toll caused by lead poisoning. It was clear from ballistics experts who joined the conference that all three shotgun shell makers were experimenting with steel shot and other nontoxic materials.

In informal conversations, experts agreed that preliminary results showed nontoxic shot could be developed to duplicate the killing power of a leaded 12-gauge duck load that was in common usage but at a shorter range. The vast majority of field studies of waterfowl hunters indicated that a large percentage could not identify the type of duck they were firing at or how far away the birds were when they were shot.

Years of field studies of accomplished duck hunters proved that they killed the majority of their ducks at 40 yards or less. Furthermore, keen waterfowl hunters had retrievers and lost very few crippled ducks. They reckoned that it would take time to develop a steel-shot shell that could consistently kill a duck or goose beyond 40 yards. I said, "I would never shoot at a duck beyond 40 yards. Is it common for the waterfowlers to shoot beyond that range?" The answer was that many duck hunters only went afield for 10 days or less and shot at any duck that flew by them, regardless of distance.

At the conclusion of the second, all-day educational conference, the scientific data that Frank Bellrose and the FWS's experts presented made it clear that change had to be made. I began the arduous task of holding numerous meetings with ammunition makers and Ducks Unlimited leadership.

We had fascinating meetings, as the ammunition companies already had begun making waterfowl shells loaded with steel shot, but they were not happy. A representative of Winchester made an appointment to show us an arsenal of old double-barreled, 12-gauge shotguns that displayed "bulges" in the barrels. The guns had been fired with several hundred rounds of experimental Winchester waterfowl steel shot loads. It was their "proof positive" that any change to steel loads would make all double-barreled guns obsolete. Furthermore, they claimed their loading machines would have to be significantly modified if a change from lead to steel or another nontoxic shot was mandated.

In 1972 and 1973, our team stayed busy with the industry representatives and their Washington lobby claiming that a change to nontoxic shot – steel shot – would increase the number of lost, wounded ducks.

Frank Bellrose openly challenged this contention. He was utterly fearless and quite demanding. He never left my office without winning my support, even when the world of waterfowl hunters refused to accept the balance between deaths by lead poisonings and wounded ducks lost. During this period, the Justice Department, preparing to oppose the National Wildlife Federation's legal action, became increasingly concerned that if the issue went to court, a federal judge would order a change from lead to a nontoxic shot.

In 1974, I received a telephone call from a representative of the Federal Arms Company requesting a private meeting. I asked that the director of the Fish and Wildlife FWS and my deputy, Buff Bohlen, be included in the meeting. Buff was an ardent waterfowl hunter and knew about the legal action and the results of the conferences. At the meeting, Federal Arms Company representatives indicated that they had achieved a major breakthrough in redesigning waterfowl shells to include a longer plastic sleeve, which minimized the potential of barrel bulging.

They also confirmed that the majority of waterfowl hunters used the cheapest waterfowl shells available. They had devised a system to load steel shot into their waterfowl shells without major modifications to their loading machines. Furthermore, they were aware of a number of startup companies that were in the process of developing substitutes for steel shot using a variety of nontoxic, hard pellets.

Chairman John Olin of Olin Industries, which owned the Winchester Arms Company, also made a date to visit. He was convinced that his competitors' shells would not have the killing ability of Winchester's premier cartridge. He arranged for an experiment using raised captive ducks that were harnessed to a conveyor belt. The ducks traveled slowly in front of an immobilized shotgun that fired automatically when the duck was within range. The yardages for the Winchester steel shot were equal to the lead shot up to 30 yards. There was an insignificant difference from 30-35 yards, but an increasing difference between 35 and 40 yards. Beyond 40 yards, only a few of the steel-shot ducks were killed. Conversely, the vast majority of birds were killed up to 40 yards by use of a Winchester waterfowl shell.

John Olin had powerful influence within the industry and enjoyed close contacts with Ducks Unlimited, an organization that was straddling the issue. Olin had many contacts in Washington and had been a major fundraiser for President Nixon. He maintained that the tests showed that the average waterfowler, who frequently shot at out-of-range ducks, would wound but not kill far more waterfowl with steel shot than with the "normal" leaded Winchester waterfowl load.

I returned from the experiment recognizing that besides the needed support of duck hunters, we had to convince manufacturers that the shift to nontoxic stock was absolutely necessary unless they wanted to defend themselves in federal court. I reported to the Fish and Wildlife Service's working group and Frank Bellrose the results of the experiment.

Within days of my return, I received a telephone call from Winchester's chief ballistician. He claimed the tests were "rigged" and offered to put his allegation in writing. I urged him to do so. He replied that he was leaving for Mexico because he was scared of retribution from Winchester.

I thought that was improbable, but I wanted a written critique of the Winchester experiment. His report said the Winchester shell used in the "experiment" was the most expensive and least used waterfowl shell due to its cost. The steel shot was developed because of Mr. Olin's fascination with ballistics. The informant insisted that the test proved there was very little difference in crippling ducks using steel or lead at up to 40 yards. There was a considerable difference at 50 to 60 yards when the Winchester high-grade shell was used, a range that was judged to be a major crippling factor by inexperienced hunters.

Within a month, the FWS director came to my office saying that Remington Arms officials wished to have a private meeting in my office to discuss their interest in nontoxic waterfowl shells. I invited Frank Bellrose to join the director, Buff Bohlen and me, plus several senior FWS ballisticians to hear the Remington briefing.

The representatives of Remington made it clear they had solved the potential problem with the loading machines that created the Remington waterfowl shells. They noted from their secretive experiments that steel could be fired even in old double-barreled guns without bulging gun barrels due to the innovative plastic sleeves. They were aware that Federal Arms had already prepared to make the changeover. They were also aware of startup companies working to find a nontoxic hard shot able to kill a duck at 35 to 40 yards.

They pointed out from the sales literature that the vast majority of North American waterfowl hunters had rapidly begun to move from old-fashioned double-barreled guns to automatic shotguns that were legally able to carry three shells. They maintained there were ways of making three-inch waterfowl shells with steel shot that had excellent killing potential.

After the meeting, our confidence level rose considerably. Only Winchester had to be persuaded to join in the development of a superior, nontoxic waterfowl shell.

As always, it takes time to change a long-standing belief, including the one that lead shot didn't poison as many waterfowl as sound science showed and that a change to a nontoxic shot would wound far more birds than died of lead poisoning.

I hit the road visiting key sports writers at major newspapers within each of the flyways. I gave talks to many of leaders of private duck-hunting clubs. Regardless of my abilities to explain the needless loss of waterfowl to lead poisoning, I encountered reluctance – even resistance – to a mandated change.

There was some support in the hunting press, but the majority, including the powerful National Rifle Association, remained doubtful.

After reviewing numerous studies on the effectiveness of steel shot, FWS admitted that the number of crippled waterfowl would increase with a shift to steel shot. However, the FWS also concluded that the increase in crippled waterfowl would be offset by the benefits expected from the conversion from lead to steel shot. They stipulated that sound scientific evidence, including years of research and Frank Bellrose's long-term studies, confirmed the high rate of waterfowl loss due to ingested lead shot.

I had kept then-Interior Secretary Tom Kleppe

up to date with the debate and science and the strong rationale to shift the type of allowable shot as rapidly as possible. The secretary wanted to be assured of sound science, even though he was unfamiliar with the issue. After a short briefing by the FWS's experts, he decided to mandate the use of steel shot in what was called "designated problem areas."

We discussed an implementation process beginning with the Atlantic flyway hunting season in 1976, the Mississippi flyway in 1977, and the Central and Pacific flyways in 1978. This schedule would give adequate time for waterfowlers to use up their lead shot cartridges.

It was also clear that a number of small companies were developing their own forms of nontoxic shot that would be competitive on price with the big three ammunition makers.

The FWS published its proposed nontoxic shot regulations for public review and comment in 1974. Many competent observers expressed concern over the issues of crippling versus lead poisoning. The FWS, aided by Bellrose, replied to critics and genuine letters of concern clearly and effectively.

The NRA sought a court injunction against the secretary of interior, claiming the secretary had abused his discretion in mandating the use of steel shot. The NRA claimed there was insufficient scientific evidence to warrant the regulations. The court held that the secretary had properly balanced environmental factors and considered factual mandates included in the Migratory Bird Treaty Act. The court held that "it is not appropriate for a court to substitute its judgment for that of the administrator," therefore the steel shot mandate remained in force.

I authorized an agreement with the Justice Department settling the NWF lawsuit by setting forth an orderly time frame for the changeover from lead to nontoxic shot.

During that period steel shot became available and ballistics improved. No longer was No. 4 lead shot the most used waterfowl load.

Steel had different ballistics from lead and the shot size had to be increased. No. 2 became the standard shot size.

Experts from the Northern Prairie Wildlife Research Center and Frank Bellrose, working with experts in the Washington office and at the Patuxent Research Center, continued their studies. They confirmed that autopsies showed harmless steel shot in the innards of legally killed ducks. The ducks were picking up steel shot to be used as grit. If they had picked up lead shot, they would have died of lead poisoning.

In addition to Spencer Smith, Lynn Greenwalt and Frank Bellrose, there is a significant group of experts that I no longer can name, but who contributed to this very difficult decision.

It is noteworthy that nontoxic shot is mandatory in Great Britain, as experts there have faced the fact that lead poisoning has taken a significant toll on their resident and migratory waterfowl. British anglers known for bottom fishing have had to surrender their lead sinkers, as it has been proven that "the Queen's" swans had suffered from deadly lead poisoning from the angler's sinkers for many years.

During this agonizing period of constant criticism, I am forever grateful for the constant support of my brother, Adrian, and Secretary Rogers Morton, both keen waterfowlers, whose neighbors and friends on the Eastern Shore of Maryland opposed the proposed and eventual change. They took a great deal of heat during this period. All change, especially to competent, concerned hunters, is difficult.

Frank Bellrose deserves great credit for his life's work studying waterfowl and for his determination to end the long era of lead shot poisoning of waterfowl. I also relied on my science advisors and ballisticians and am convinced we made a very important decision. Still, I rejoice that the issue is behind us.

The Point Reyes National Seashore and Cap the Knife

"I know that land – really know it – and I have an abiding love for it."

Point Reyes is the home of the Phillip Burton Wilderness Area, a vast area in northern California, where visitors can explore 33,373 acres of forested ridges, coastal grasslands, sand dunes and rugged shoreline. More than 100 miles of trails wander through the park's designated wilderness. [44]

Wildlife also thrives, and visitors may observe tule elk, harbor seals, waterfowl and shorebirds in the Estero de Limatour and multitudes of marine invertebrates in tidal pools. Incredibly this extraordinary, unique area is within a two-hour drive for more than eight million San Francisco Bay residents. In 1984, in honor of U.S. Rep. Phillip Burton's dedication to the protection and preservation of our nation's natural areas and national parks, the Point Reyes Wilderness Area, first established in 1976, was renamed the "Phillip Burton Wilderness Area." [45]

Congressman Burton, obviously influenced by Edgar Wayburn, the leading figure in the Sierra Club known affectionately as the "Grand Old Man," added language to an appropriations bill directing the assistant interior secretary's office to work with experts from the National Park Service to study the western slopes within sight of the spectacular seashore. Edgar lived near the seashore and was concerned that unwanted development would adversely impact the view eastward from the lagoons and beachfront to the rising headlands.

There were a number of questions that had to be answered by experts from the western region of the National Park Service. I flew out and inspected the truly spectacular seashore. I visited with Dr. Wayburn, experts from the Sierra Club, Norman "Ike" Livermore and his brother, "Put," who chaired the Coastal Advisory Commission, and Congressman Burton's local staff members.

Ike's knowledge of California, especially northern California, was unchallenged. The key questions were: How many acres of a proposed acquisition were already in federal lands? How many acres were in private lands and what was their value? I needed concise information if the Office of Management and Budget and the two appropriations committees agreed to an extension of the seashore protection area eastward.

Besides the Park Service expertise, I called on Edgar to provide me with names he considered to be neutral experts on the landscape, knowing full well he would list only friends and associates who would likely favor a major addition.

Representatives from the National Parks and Conservation Association and the Wilderness Society insisted on being involved. In fact, their knowledge of the landscape was invaluable. Chuck Clusen had left the Sierra Club to head the Wilderness Society and keenly supported a potential major extension of the existing federal ownership. He knew the terrain and the concerns related to potential upslope development.

We held several meetings in my Interior offices and slowly but surely developed a topographical map showing privately owned areas that could be deemed intrusive if development was allowed.

I made a date to report our recommendations to ranking members of the Office of Management and Budget.

I could tell from my reception by a senior OMB staffer that any proposed and extensive enlargement of the seashore would not fit within the National Park Service land acquisition budget.

I laid out the wide topographic map and a black-and-white photograph of the area, highlighted in red ink, depicting our recommended new boundary. I described the need to acquire privately owned land if the seashore was to be protected from unwanted upslope development. The silence from the three OMB staffers was a clear signal that I may have recommended buying more land than they thought necessary.

As they began to express doubts about the bill's language and the experts that had recommended buying the land, the door opened and in walked Casper Weinberger, known as "Cap the Knife." His assigned mission as director of the Office of Management and Budget was to slash billions of dollars from the nation's budget and defend the cuts at congressional hearings – hence his nickname. No proposal from any department or agency went to a congressional committee without review and comment by the Office of Management and Budget.

Cap was a fascinating man – brilliant, incredibly educated, politically savvy and a rising star in the Nixon Administration.

As a native Californian, he was interested in the proposal and made it a point to attend my presentation.

Cap quietly but firmly took a seat next to mine and began with a red marking pen to follow the outlines of the proposed extension. The three staff members sat back, expecting massive reductions in the proposed acreage. Ever so slowly, Cap worked through the proposed additions.

Periodically, he would stop and quietly state, "You should have protected" this rise or this bowl. He continued adding acreage where he felt we had been too conservative. To his employees' shock, he added significant acreage to the proposal and then stood, shook hands all around and said, "Nathaniel, see that the Park Service plan conforms to my lines," and was out the door.

We all sat in a state of shock.

Weeks later, I was at a function with Cap and I had to ask him the key question: "Cap, how do you know that area?" He replied, "I made friends with many northern California men my age while in my teens. We kept up a close friendship to this day. I was invited to join them on wonderful summer pack trips deep into those hills and mountains. We often spent two weeks together discussing the future of our state and the nation. I know that land – really know it – and I have an abiding love for it. It will be a long-term investment in the seashore that, generations from now, visitors will look up and see green slopes and mountain ridges. They won't know how the land was preserved or by who, but we will."

Now, more than 2.5 million people visit the seashore every year. It is an awe-inspiring sight and an important part of the national park system.

Following his tour of duty in the Office of Management and Budget, Cap served as Secretary for Health, Education and Welfare. Later, following President Reagan's election, Cap was confirmed as Secretary of Defense and served six years and 10 months, one of the longest stints in that office in American history.

His personal tragedy was being involved with a group of Reagan advisors who defied a congressional act denying military aid to the Contras fighting in the Nicaraguan Civil War. Money from illicit sales of advanced missile systems to Iran was used to support the Contras. The resulting scandal led to the indictment of 14 members of the president's staff, including Cap, who had retired from the Defense Department.

When George H.W. Bush was sworn in as our nation's president, one of his first acts was to issue Caspar Weinberger a full pardon prior to his trial.

With his devoted wife, Rebecca Jane, Cap joined the Forbes publishing empire and rose to chairman before retiring to his home in Bar Harbor, Maine, where he died on July 12, 2009, at the age of 91.

Our paths crossed frequently and he introduced me several times when I was privileged to speak at the exclusive Pot and Kettle Club in Bar Harbor. We never forgot his role in the extension of the eastern boundary of Point Reyes National Seashore. He once remarked, "In my long years of public service, I look back on that short meeting with you and the topographical map that brought back so many marvelous memories as one of my greatest gifts to my country."

The leaders of the effort to add thousands of acres to the existing park and create the Point Reyes National Seashore are proudest of this language in the accompanying law:

> "...the addition of the following words after the Section 6 (a) of the enabling act concerning management: 'without impairment of its natural values, in a manner that provides for such recreational, educational, historic preservation. Interpretation and scientific opportunities as are consistent with, based upon, and supportive of the maximum protection, restoration and preservation of the natural environment within the area."

That section prevents Point Reyes from ever being developed into a seashore recreation area.

May it always remain the rugged, scenic setting that allows thousands of visitors to explore wilderness and the seashore – rare opportunity to realize the importance of the natural world that once surrounded us.

Notes – The Point Reyes National Seashore and Cap the Knife

[44] Background information on Phillip Burton Wilderness, https://www.nps.gov/pore/planyourvisit/phillip_burton_wilderness.htm.

[45] Ibid.

Lady Bird, the Granite Dome and a Bushel of Texas Peaches

"Lady Bird's only comment: 'Told you so!' "

My wonderful Interior Department senior secretary, Nori Uchida, buzzed me on my intercom with the following message: "Pat Noonan wants you to call Liz Carpenter, Mrs. 'Lady Bird' Johnson's No. 1 assistant."

Even then, Pat was a well-known environmentalist, a president of The Nature Conservancy who later would create The Conservation Fund. I knew Liz, as I often had worked with Lady Bird on her beautification projects in and around our nation's capital city that we were all on a first-name basis.

Dutifully, I asked Nori to call Liz in Texas at the LBJ Library. Liz came on the phone in her normal level of excitement.

She said, "Lady Bird needs your assistance. President Johnson and Lady Bird have admired a huge granite dome that inexplicably rises from flat country southwest of Austin. It is privately owned. The family charges $5 to walk up to the top of the dome, from where you can literally see for miles.

"The owner and his family don't really take care of their property and it is a mess. The Texas Parks and Wildlife Commission wants to acquire the area for a state park, but the owners are playing their cards close to their vests when it comes to the price. The feeling is that if you come with Pat Noonan, you can open the door for negotiations and may be able to transfer some of your Land and Water Conservation funds to the Texas Park and Wildlife Commission to acquire the dome and surrounding land for a new state park."

I looked over my schedule and saw a two-day opportunity to take leave from the department and fly to Austin and inspect the granite dome with Mrs. Johnson. An hour later, Lady Bird called and invited me to have a personalized tour of the LBJ Library before we would be driven to the LBJ Ranch, where we would dine and spend the night. The next morning, we would be driven to the "rock," where I was supposed to call attention to the need to preserve this unique feature of the Texas landscape.

I said, "Lady Bird, don't you think the price of the dome is going to go up with your presence that will be covered by the press? I will attempt to aid Pat in discussions with the owner to fix a price that is within reason, but this is a gamble."

"If the owner," I said, "holds out for far more that his granite dome is worth according to the official appraisal, we will shove off and wait him out." Lady Bird stated that she was confident that my presence and Pat's well-known abilities to "work with his fellow man" would result in a price well within the commission's budget.

I called the Interior Secretary and asked for permission to take leave. Interior was in a state of confusion, as President Nixon had resigned and Secretary Morton had been replaced by Secretary Stanley

Hathaway, former governor of Wyoming. Permission was granted. I called Donald Rumsfeld at the White House, as he had been appointed President Ford's chief of staff. We always had been friendly and he laughed at the thought of a trip all the way to Austin to, in his words, "see a rock." His final words were, "Give that great lady our best wishes. President Ford thinks the world of her."

My wife was not pleased that I was taking unpaid leave, flying to Austin round-trip on personal funds.

But, on the appointed day, I flew to Austin and was met by Liz and taken to the LBJ Library, where a very competent young aide was waiting as a tour guide. I asked her for a favor: "Let me be just one of the next group going through the library. I want to hear and see what the average tourist experiences as a visitor."

Off I went. The library is fascinating, tracing President Johnson's personal and public life. The scenes of him taking the oath of office following President Kennedy's assassination brought tears to my eyes. The long list of his accomplishments as president, especially in the area of civil rights, is an impressive achievement, well worth remembering.

The tragic decisions that led to waging the Vietnam War were painful reminders of our nation's failure to understand Vietnam's strong force of liberation from French domination that doomed our ill-advised intervention. It brought back painful memories of my tour of duty in France during the Algerian conflict, which ended with the loss of thousands of young men and squandering of billions of francs.

The photographs were brutally frank. The war destroyed Johnson's presidency, split the country, added to the national debt and ruined the lives of thousands of young men in addition to the incredible death toll of 58,209. One cannot conclude the visit without being shaken by the incredible series of military and political mistakes for which our country's leadership should be held responsible.

Following my tour, I met Lady Bird and Pat Noonan, who had flown in. A large limousine driven by a Secret Service agent and a companion officer drove us to the LBJ Ranch. They were part of a small group of agents that is assigned to former presidents and their wives for life. We had time to drive around the pastures before arriving at the "ranch." I was assigned a comfortable room upstairs. We had a long cocktail period and then a delicious Texas steak dinner.

The next morning, we assembled for an 8:30 a.m. breakfast and headed for the granite dome rock. We were all in good form on a beautiful, warm, late spring day. I kidded Lady Bird about Texan boasting and she answered about "ignorant easterners."

The drive carried us through the wonderfully rolling countryside. A large sign announced that "Mama Smith's World Famous Texas Peaches" were just ahead. I exclaimed, "Lady Bird that is just another example of Texas boasting. Everyone knows that the best peaches come from the south of France and from New Jersey. Who in heaven's sake ever heard of a Texas peach?"

She called to the driver, "Pull in and let's show 'Mr. Know-It-All' a thing or two about Texas peaches."

The place was a typical roadside stand, but Mama and her four African-American assistants were dressed in long dresses that billowed from their sides, and each had a colored neckerchief covering her hair. It looked like a scene from Gone with the Wind.

After being warmly welcomed by Mama and her staff, Lady Bird addressed the group, "I need your assistance. This tall young man has to be educated in the delights of the world's best peaches. He is an ignorant easterner who has never heard about our Texas peaches!"

The foursome roared with laughter. One assistant selected a peach from a cooler and peeled it with ease. It was handed to me on the end of a firm stick. Pat and Liz followed suit.

I had never eaten such a wonderful peach. It melted in my mouth. Pat and I exclaimed, "Lady

Bird, Mama and ladies – this is the best peach we have ever eaten!"

Lady Bird's only comment: "Told you so!"

I noticed full and half-bushel baskets ready to be filled. I asked Mama if, on return, she would have a half bushel of firm peaches ready for me, as our young family in Washington deserved a taste of the world's best peach. Lady Bird said, "I have an idea. Pack another half bushel and, Nathaniel, you will drop it off at the White House for President and Mrs. Ford."

We continued our odyssey, a car full of engaging conversation and laughter. Lady Bird was one of the most entertaining women I ever met. Her views on conservation, land management and the beautification of Washington, D.C., by raising private funds were enlightening.

We finally reached the parking lot adjacent to an incredible sight – a large, sloping rock formation that rose from the surrounding flat land, a most impressive sight.

We were met by Andy Sansom, a special assistant to Secretary Morton who worked out of my office on a variety of conservation and land-management issues. A native Texan, he was well known by Lady Bird. After a hug and a "Thank you, Andy, for joining Nathaniel and Pat," we started up the sloping rock face.

Lady Bird and Liz stayed in the cool of the limo's air conditioning while Andy, Pat and I climbed the mighty rock. We were wearing light ankle boots and faced no danger of falling, but it was a stiff climb. There were no displays describing the geology or the source of the immense granite boulder. It was a modestly tough climb, but once at the top, it was well worth the exertion. The views were splendid.

On return to the rock's base, we visited with a rather bedraggled owner and listened to his interest in selling what he described as "this great rock, unlike anything in Texas or maybe anywhere else on earth – a real oddity."

I sternly informed him that, as a federal official, I could not be a party to using matching federal funds unless the Texas Parks and Wildlife Commission's appraisal was met.

He seemed uneasy at the thought that there was going to be an appraisal, rather than a negotiated sale that morning.

Pat introduced him to Sansom, labeling him "my key Texas land expert," who would be the negotiator. I emphasized that the owner should take this incredible opportunity to make a deal and sell out. I assured him that Texas had a long list of "priority" land acquisitions and, if he was not a willing seller, the opportunity would be lost. The owner seemed ready to deal.

Before long, Andy Sansom, who later worked on my staff, organized an appraisal and orchestrated the sale of the rock and the surrounding property, creating The Enchanted Rock State Park.

On return to Austin, with just enough time to stop and pick up two half-bushels of the finest peaches, I asked one of the Secret Service officers for writing paper so Lady Bird could send a note to the Fords. She wrote a two-page note, sealed it in an envelope and gave it to me.

The bushel baskets were well covered and carefully packed to withstand clumsy airline handlers. I gave Lady Bird and Liz hugs, laughed about my being named an "effete, ignorant easterner" and, accompanied by one of the officers, was checked into my airline. The two bushel baskets of peaches were marked "Special Handling."

I had time to call Alita to give her my time of arrival at Washington National. Although just beyond the three children's bedtime, the thought that daddy going to the White House was sufficient to have them all piled in our car.

On arrival, I called the White House number and informed the Secret Service evening crew that I had a half-bushel of superb Texas peaches for President and Mrs. Ford as a gift from Lady Bird Johnson. I arrived at the proper gate and the bushel basket was carefully examined and then taken into the White House. The children were impressed when the officers addressed me as "Mr. Secretary, good to see you! We will see that the peaches go to the kitchen immediately."

Luckily, I was in my office at 7:45 a.m. the next morning when Nori informed me that President Ford was on the line. His wonderful voice bellowed, "Nathaniel, where the devil did the peaches come from? I ate three of them at breakfast and told Betty she can only have one. The rest are reserved for me."

I had left Lady Bird's note in my blazer jacket at our Washington house. I told the president the story of visiting the LBJ Library, the rock that Lady Bird loved, the negotiations to acquire it and the story of the "World's Finest Texas Peaches." The president roared with laughter. He added, "I love that Lady Bird; do everything in your power to pull the deal off. I'll call her now to thank her."

"No, no, Mr. President. It is not her wake up time," I said. "There is a two-hour time change."

"But of course," replied the president. "I'll call her later this morning. Do bring her note to me as I just want to see what 'devilment' she wrote."

I sent my driver back to our home on Woodland Drive and my wife retrieved the note and it was delivered to the White House.

At 11 a.m., Nori came in and reported that Mrs. Ford was on the line. She was in one of her irrepressible laughter moods and asked, "Nathaniel, where did those peaches come from?" I retold the story and she added, "I have never eaten a better peach. Did you know that peaches grew in Texas?"

I admitted that I was an "ignorant easterner," per Lady Bird's description, and had never heard of a Texas peach or tasted one that came close to those I brought back. She roared with laughter and added, "There is going to be a family battle on who gets those peaches for future breakfasts!"

In the early afternoon, Nori announced that Lady Bird was on the line. She was at her best, reporting that the president had called her with thanks and hinting that she had written him a note that had "tickled him."

So ends the Texas Peach story.

Andrew Sansom

Andrew Sansom's career is a mixture of extraordinary assignments. In 1974, he served as director of conservation education at the Federal Energy Administration. He became vice president of the Old River Corporation before serving as executive director of the Texas Nature Conservancy. In 1987, he joined the Texas Parks and Wildlife Commission's Department of Coordination and Management. His brilliance and ability to work with all groups of interested parties led to his appointment as executive director in 1990. He served with great distinction until his retirement in 2001, when he established and headed The Rivers Institute Systems at Texas State University, studying and making significant solutions to Texas' continuing water problems.

Andy's career includes authoring a number of books on his beloved state of Texas and a much-loved children's book: *Scout, the Christmas Dog.*

He has been a remarkable friend of mine and a successful leader in dealing with the immensity of water problems that Texas faces.

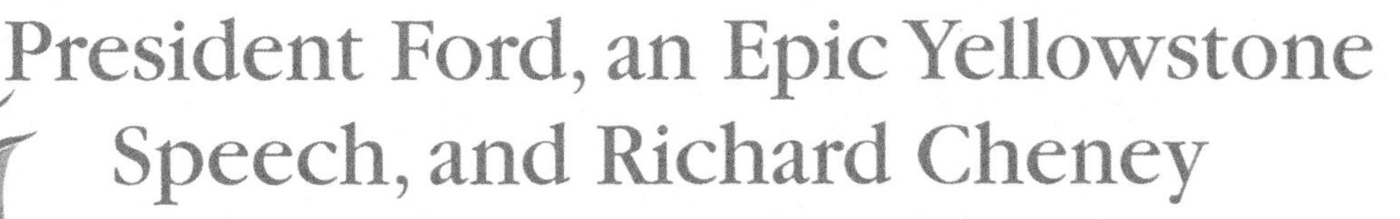

President Ford, an Epic Yellowstone Speech, and Richard Cheney

"Call Dick Cheney. We finished that position paper weeks ago."

During Gerald Ford's term in the office of the Presidency of the United States, I developed a profound sense of loyalty to/and friendship with this wonderful human being. We met shortly after his inauguration in the wake of the Nixon-Watergate debacle.

President Ford asked me to stay on as Assistant Secretary of Interior, as he wanted a smoothly running department that would produce a sound environmental record for his presidency.

Virtually all of Richard Nixon's top aides were dismissed or resigned, so I received my White House orders from Donald Rumsfeld, who had been appointed Ford's Chief of Staff in 1974.

Among the orders I received were requests for briefing papers for the oncoming election of 1976. Senior staff and I prepared a number of environmental issue papers that included the possibility that the president could send a completed package of ambitious Alaskan national parks and refuges to pertinent congressional committees.

There were frequent telephone calls from members of Ford's election staff about the need for "talking points" for campaign speeches. Although the majority of the Republican leadership was rapidly losing interest in environmental issues and the possibility of making additional progress, polls showed that a sizeable proportion of potential Republican voters considered the environment an important issue.

As the Clean Water Act was being funded, the Environmental Protection Agency was beginning to reveal examples of the worst violations of industrial waste disposal, along with major problems regarding raw or grossly under-treated human sewage.

There was a sense that the foundation of environmental protection was built and that good management would be the key issue going forward.

President Ford had appointed many competent managers in various departments, except at the Department of Interior, where Secretary Tom Kleppe had replaced Secretary Stanley Hathaway. Kleppe was a former congressman who had little interest in his widespread secretarial duties and preferred to be on the road, handing out inexpensive pens with his name written on them.

In other words, we all missed former Secretary Rogers Morton!

Stan Hathaway's brief duty as secretary had ended abruptly due to fatigue and family issues. He was beginning to show signs of modifying western views on a series of wildlife, land and water issues that needed to be resolved and modernized. I was beginning to work cooperatively with him before he suddenly resigned. Kleppe was appointed to be a "caretaker," as Ford's senior staff was not convinced that environmental issues were critically important to the president's upcoming campaign.

The three assistant secretaries were enormously grateful to have John Whitaker, formerly John Ehrlichman's aide, become our undersecretary. John Whitaker was a solver of problems between agencies and had good contacts with the White House staff and the Republican members of the Congress.

I received a call from Don Rumsfeld in the fall of 1975, advising me that the president wanted to visit with me the next afternoon. It was to be a "confidential" meeting. At the appointed hour, I was ushered into the Oval Office. The president had his back to me and was looking out the window.

I stood quietly. He turned, waved, stood and shook my hand and offered me a seat beside him.

He said: "Nathaniel, I am embarrassed that I have not paid more attention to the 'green issues' that you champion. I want to make a major speech to the American people about the importance of the National Park System and our nation's environmental issues.

"Do you realize that I worked as an 18-year-old in Yellowstone National Park during the summer when I was a student at the University of Michigan? I worked with the greatest group of young men on rebuilding bridges, repairing trails, cutting up blown-down trees – every imaginable task, often hard physical work. We were housed in bunkhouses and fed large, healthy meals. It was a summer that I can never forget.

"Here is your assignment," he continued. "You will work with two of my aides that have accompanied me from my congressional office, the campaign managers, the officials at OMB and the superintendent of Yellowstone National Park.

"I will want a carefully prepared speech outlining the financial needs for a major effort to catch up on years of inadequate maintenance budgets, and most importantly, a private hamburger luncheon with the members of the crew that I worked with so many years ago. The campaign staff will work with you on the date of the speech. I would like a draft vetted by OMB and my campaign team in 30 days. I will give the speech next fall, depending on my campaign schedule and the schedule of Old Faithful Geyser.

"I have made an appointment for you to meet my staff members tomorrow morning at their new offices in the Executive Office Building," he said. "I would like to keep the whole proposal as confidential as possible, recognizing that the park's management must be given advance notice of my impending visit, speech and the challenge of locating my fellow summer teammates."

Then, he arrived at an important point.

"Now listen carefully," President Ford told me. "I do not want Richard Cheney involved in anything to do with this celebration. Is that clear?"

Dick Cheney was Don Rumsfeld's assistant and a well-known anti-environmentalist.

I was delighted by the order.

Cleo Layton, the "right-hand man" for every assistant secretary, had prepared a wish list of projects from both the National Park Service and the Fish and Wildlife Service. I decided that the president's speech should include the refuges' needs, as they were as pressing as the case for the national parks' needs.

The next morning, I was escorted to the office of two young men in a large office within the OMB complex. They were so different from the Nixon entourage. They were filled with good humor and were looking forward to making sure that the president's "green speech" was a great success.

Their youthful enthusiasm rubbed off on me. I informed them that we had a list of major improvements desperately needed for the National Park System and that I thought the president should include the refuge system's needs as well. They agreed that the nation's national wildlife refuges touched the lives of thousands of concerned citizens and should have the same type of major capital improvements budgeted for the national parks.

We agreed that I would furnish them with a comprehensive list of needed improvements in a variety of parks and refuges, but I also needed a budget. They were puzzled by this request and finally, after discussion, decided that I should furnish them with a list of services that were candidates for major capital improvements and expected costs.

Cleo and I began a series of evening work sessions that lasted for several weeks. We examined the requests for desperately needed capital repairs and improvements, checked on the validity of the requests and the worthiness of each investment. We double-checked the calculated costs of each recommendation. Cleo consulted with pertinent officials in both agencies ever so quietly to verify the need and the value of the improvements.

We turned to my personal secretary, Nori Uchida, whose confidence could never be questioned, to prepare a written "needs document" for study by the White House staff and budget experts at the Office of Management and Budget.

Months later, I was authorized to call Gary Everhardt, the new director of the Park Service, and John Townsley, the new superintendent of Yellowstone National Park. I informed them of the president's decision to make a major effort to gain public support for desperately needed upgrades to the aging infrastructure in our national parks and refuges.

The news was met with rejoicing. I urged them to keep the news as quiet as possible, but as the campaign staff and the Secret Service were now in control of the event, they were to follow instructions as if they came from me. Secretary Kleppe was deliberately kept out of the loop until final preparations were made.

The campaign staff described the scene that they wanted. The president would be flown to West Yellowstone and be brought into a nearby meadow in a helicopter. He would be standing on a high podium with Old Faithful in the background. The Secret Service already was working out the details. The campaign staff had a number of days when the speech could be given, but it had to coincide with an eruption of Old Faithful at the speech's conclusion.

I looked at them in a state of disbelief.

I said, "Old Faithful never erupts exactly on a firm time schedule. It is always consistent within a time frame, but no one can pinpoint an exact time of an eruption."

They answered, "Ask the superintendent for which of these dates Old Faithful can be expected to erupt within a few minutes following the President's 11 o'clock, 15-minute speech."

I doubt that any Yellowstone superintendent had ever been put in such a predicament! A best guess was made and the date for the visit and speech was set at the end of August.

I called Superintendent John Townsley. I briefed him on the need for the podium and chairs for the dignitaries that the presidential advance men would arrange with him weeks before the event. The question of the timing of a critically important Old Faithful eruption was met with a sense of wonderment. He finally answered, "I will have the pertinent expert staff give you a range of days when an eruption should take place at 11:20 to 11:30 a.m."

I could ask for no more.

I insisted that he work with the advance men in selecting a site that could be made absolutely private and safe for the presidential hamburger luncheon. That was easy, as there are a number of sites near the Geyser Basin that a complement of rangers and Secret Service officers could cordon off for privacy.

I reported to my new friends and now associates at the Old Executive Building and presented them with 12 copies of a perfectly typed, formal listing of projects desperately needing capital improvements within parks and refuges.

The paperwork passed through OMB. I made two visits at their request to prioritize some of the millions of dollars of proposed investments.

They were intimately familiar with the vast majority of proposed projects, as either OMB or the appropriations committees were well aware of the years of inadequate capital investment in both national parks and refuges. The speech writers took

President Ford is introduced...

President Ford speaking as Old Faithful erupts the podium.

over and had me join them as they prepared a superb address. The advance men were pleased with the enthusiastic cooperation of Superintendent Townsley and Director Everhart. Using the best advice on when Old Faithful might erupt at 11:15 a.m., the campaign staff selected August 29 as the date for the speech.

Through excellent management by the president's team and our team at Interior, the ceremony was a huge success. President Ford delivered a flawless, well-crafted speech, mentioning many individual projects of acute national interest. He even added a paragraph about the "unfinished business of congressional support for the selection and transference of millions of acres of Alaskan public lands into permanent protection into national parks and refuges."

Old Faithful defied our best calculations by billowing with a mighty eruption in the midst of the presidential speech. The president handled the situation gracefully, turning toward the geyser and saluting it and continuing with his speech. He quietly quipped, "I knew the Park Service was efficient and effective and they proved it a moment ago."

I found this portion of his speech to be particularly worth remembering:

> "For me, this is a moment I have been looking forward to for a long time – to return to Yellowstone, where I spent one of the greatest summers of my life. Being a seasonal park ranger – we used to call them 90-day wonders – I spent one of the greatest summers of my life. It was one of the most challenging experiences, one of the greatest jobs I ever had since graduation from the University of Michigan. Now, it seems more fun than hard work, although we had plenty of both."

He continued by pledging a $1.5 billion investment over the next 10 years. He named the bill the Bicentennial Land Heritage Act, and it was intended to double the acreage of our existing land for national parks, recreation areas and wildlife sanctuaries. He continued:

> "The development of these new lands is intended to make them accessible and enjoyable and bring the benefits of nature to those who live in our cities. I want an acceleration of the development of park lands and sanctuaries now that have been delayed for lack of manpower and money. This national commitment means we may have to tighten our belts elsewhere, but this is the soundest investment in the future of America that I can envision. We must act now to prevent the loss of treasures that can never be replaced for ourselves, our children and for future generations of Americans."

He concluded, "I remember as a ranger for the first time I stood alone from Inspiration Point over Canyon Station, looking over this beautiful land.

I thought to myself how lucky I was that my parents and grandparents had the vision and determination to save it for us."

Later, his picnic luncheon went off perfectly.

The National Park historian had attempted to reach the five men who had worked with President Ford during the summer of 1936 in the Yellowstone backcountry. So, incredibly, Wayne Replogle, George Baggley, Scotty Chapman, Arthur Jacobson and John Thune attended the ceremony and enjoyed lunch.

There are photographs of his summer companions sitting around a table in the woods and "bear hugging" their leader.

The press gave the ceremony maximum exposure. His poll numbers increased dramatically. Rumsfeld was delighted. The campaign manager was full of praise.

What could I say to the departmental directors, their key staff members, the superintendent and above all, Cleo and the two vital White House assistants other than, "Gentlemen, good show! Well done!"

The president called me with a simple message: "Nathaniel, thank you. It was a blast! Old Faithful stuck to its own schedule, but the photographs of me standing in front of the splendid eruption will be among my treasures. Lunching with my fellow rangers was very special. I cannot describe the stories we told on each other, the good fellowship and the recognition that we had spent one of the greatest summers of our lives together. Boundless thanks."

Alas, Richard Cheney had become the president's Chief of Staff in 1975, when Don Rumsfeld became Secretary of Defense. Cheney was an avowed anti-conservationist. He maintained that environmental issues were "Democrats' issues" and support by President Ford of the many projects that were increasingly becoming campaign issues would not require extensive briefings. Yet the campaign staff continued to request briefing statements on environmental topics.

We made every effort to produce a variety of

President Ford has lunch with former Yellowstone National Park rangers.

position papers that made common sense. Often when a senior campaign official would call asking where a certain briefing paper was, I replied, "Call Dick Cheney. We finished that position paper weeks ago."

The once-close working relationship with Donald Rumsfeld had evaporated. Interior Secretary Kleppe had no contact with the White House staff. He spent hours reading and re-reading documents that required his signature. He studied but did not act.

In early October, I received an irate call from Cheney. He demanded to know why a series of important decisions on everything from coal and oil leases to mineral rights and potential Bureau of Reclamation projects had not "moved forward." I acknowledged the fact that the secretary had a stack of documents on his desk and side desk requiring his signature. They had cleared the assistant secretaries and the undersecretary and were ready to go.

Cheney demanded that I confront Secretary Kleppe with the need to assist the campaign by signing off on the documents.

I called the secretary and made a breakfast date for the next morning. Tom Kleppe was a delightful human being, but totally unfit for being Secretary of Interior. I made the key points: The documents had been thoroughly vetted by his senior staff, had passed review at the Office of Management and Budget and required his signature. I mentioned that the president's chief of staff was anxious to use the approved documents as proof that the Interior Department was actively supporting the extraction side of the department. Coal, gas, and timber leases would be appreciated by the Republican business community.

Tom looked hard at me and replied, "Nathaniel, I will know when to sign the documents. I will not sign them until I am ready." I replied, "The presidency might be on the line, as you really must sign the documents to show that the administration is functioning on the Interior's issues."

He stood, thanked me for joining him at breakfast and waved me away. I called Cheney and reported on the breakfast meeting. He started to scream at me. I replied, "Dick, you appointed him. Why don't you call him!" The telephone line went dead.

The paperwork was signed – but not until after the president's electoral loss to Democrat Jimmy Carter.

During the period between President Ford's defeat and President-elect Carter's swearing-in, I made three desperate attempts to get the president to send the lame duck Congress the full package of proposed Alaskan protections of land. Denny Drabelle, a key aide and office historian, prepared a memorandum defining the potential use of the Antiquities Act of 1906, which had been used by Republican and Democratic presidents since Theodore Roosevelt's time. The whole staff came together in one desperate, last-minute attempt to persuade the outgoing president to make his mark on history by expanding the boundaries of existing parks and creating monuments and refuges in Alaska – adding a total of 30 million acres of protected land.

Buff Bohlen, our Alaska specialist, knew every inch that could be covered by a presidential act. The memorandum was vetted by our solicitor and found to be legally sufficient for presidential action. I hand-delivered it to the president's young staff members, who rejoiced at the idea.

"This is the opportunity of a lifetime for our president to leave his mark in the history books!" one of them said. They made sure that the memorandum went to the president.

Cheney, however, persuaded the president that it would be a "mistake, as the creation of expanded or new national parks and refuges was congressional business, not presidential." Our memorandum with all the backup material sat on a side desk until President Ford left the Oval Office.

A few years later, I received a call from President Ford's secretary asking me to join him in a foursome playing golf at the Seminole Golf Club in Juno Beach, Florida – my home course. I gladly accepted and enjoyed a round of golf and a drink with him at the end. I owed him $5, as he was partnered with the club's fine professional. We laughed and chatted, but never mentioned the lost Alaskan opportunity.

Several years later, while at my Florida desk, he called and said, "Betty and I are becoming 'greener' by the week! We are doing all kinds of things to beautify Palm Springs and are involved in interesting Colorado environmental projects."

He added, "Nathaniel, thank you again for organizing my speech in front of Old Faithful. The photographs of my speech and the group of my friends who worked together that great summer of '36 are in my office here."

There was a pause, and then, "I am sincerely pleased that President Carter forced the Alaska withdrawal. It is the last great land preservation effort for our nation. He is to be congratulated. I hate to think that I had the opportunity to send your teams' five years of work to the Congress even after I was defeated. It was a mistake. I think Dick influenced me in making a short-sighted decision. I deeply regret the lost opportunity. Let's stay in touch."

He called three more times, always upbeat, highlighted by laughter, talking about his golf swing, the beauty of the countryside in California and Colorado, and his dreams for "our America."

Every call was deeply appreciated.

President Gerald Ford was one splendid American.

Santa Cruz Island and Hungry Feral Animals

"We helped save this precious piece of our world and we are the better for it."

Noel "Skip" Dunn, an avid conservationist and an ombudsman for the giant AON Insurance Company, received a call from Tom Macy asking when he was going to be in California. As it turned out, Skip was scheduled to be in San Francisco settling problems between insurance companies. As an active member of The Nature Conservancy's board of directors and an eager participant in new "adventures," Skip accepted Tom's invitation to join him on a day's visit of Santa Cruz Island.

Tom, the Conservancy's western field representative, had received "vibrations" that the owner of the majority stock in the Santa Cruz Land Company might be interested in a sale. Tom wanted Skip to see the island, the largest of the Channel Islands lying off the California coast near Santa Barbara and describe its potential to the Conservancy's leadership and board of directors.

In January 1977, I received a telephone call from Pat Noonan, the Conservancy's engaging and incredibly successful president. We had worked together for years on a vast variety of land preservation projects. He announced that my great friends and fellow Conservancy board members, Marian Heiskell and Skip, had accepted Tom's invitation to inspect Santa Cruz Island.

Tom had made all the necessary trip arrangements. He had assured Pat that a maximum effort might result in a sale of the island to the Conservancy. Tom was the perfect example of Noonan's ability to select and retain a remarkable team of the brightest and best in the land conservation campaign.

We met in Santa Barbara and stayed at the beautiful Biltmore Hotel.

Marian and I knew nothing about Santa Cruz Island other than it was located offshore of Santa Barbara. Tom's briefing sheet indicated that the majority of the stock of the Santa Cruz Company was owned by Dr. Carey Stanton, an oil heir, who appeared to be interested in a potential sale of his stock. His nephew, Edwin, showed an equal interest in selling his one-third share of the company's stock.

The briefing sheet described Santa Cruz Island as the largest of the eight offshore Channel Islands, each quite different and yet similar to one another.

The island is 22 miles long and from two to six miles wide. At more than 96 square miles (63,000 acres) in size, Santa Cruz contains two rugged mountain ranges, each rising above 2,000 feet. The coastline has steep cliffs, gigantic sea caves, coves and sandy beaches. [46]

A central valley splits the island along the Santa Cruz Island Fault, with volcanic rock on the north and older sedimentary rock to the south. This volcanic rock was heavily fractured during the uplift phase that formed the island, and more than 100 large sea caves have been carved into the resulting faults. The large central valley/fault system features deep canyons with year-round springs and streams. The 77 miles of craggy coastline cliffs feature the largest and deepest sea caves in the world. Painted Cave is found on the northwest coastline of the island. Named because of its colorful rock type, lichens and algae, Painted Cave is nearly a quarter mile long and 100 feet wide, with an entrance ceiling 160 feet high and a waterfall over the entrance. There are countless tidal pools and expansive beaches. [47]

These varied landforms support more than 160 plant species in 10 plant communities, from marshes and grasslands to chaparral and pine forests. There are 140 land bird species, 11 land mammal species, three amphibian classes and five reptile species. Large colonies of nesting seabirds, breeding seals, sea lions and other diverse marine animals and plants make their home on the island. [48]

It was a prime territory for sea otters before they were wiped out for their fabulously soft pelts. Owing to millions of years of isolation, many distinctive plant and animal species have adapted to the island's unique environment. Those include the island scrub-jay, the diminutive island fox and eight plant species found only on Santa Cruz and nowhere else in the world.

Archaeological investigations indicate that Santa Cruz Island has been occupied for at least 9,000 years. It was known as Limuw (place of the sea) or Michumash in the Chumash language. The people of the Chumash Indian tribe who lived on the island developed a highly complex society dependent on marine harvest, craft specialization and trade with the mainland population. The Santa Cruz Island Chumash produced shell beads that they used for currency, which formed an important part of the overall Chumash economy.

Native villagers had no known contact with Europeans until the 16th and early 17th centuries. Juan Rodríguez Cabrillo, who is credited with the first European exploration of the California coast, observed at least six villages, though he and his crew did not come ashore. Cabrillo named the island San Lucas.

During the long Spanish era before California became a United States possession in the 1848 Treaty of Guadalupe Hidalgo, the island was used for grazing sheep. It changed ownership numerous times.

Dr. Stanton inherited two-thirds of the stock in the Santa Cruz Island Company from his father, Edward, a very successful oil investor. Dr. Stanton's nephew, Edwin, inherited the other one-third.

After an early breakfast at the Biltmore Hotel, Marian, Skip and I flew to the island and were met by our host, Carey Stanton, who insisted that we use our first names. He was a warm, delightful and welcoming host. We drove from the small landing field to his charming, Spanish-styled home. We did not discuss his potential interest in selling his share. We walked around his home and up a path that was dominated by a row of ancient eucalyptus trees that must have been 60 to 70 feet high – an incredible sight.

Carey recounted the long history of the island, from early Native Americans and a lengthy period of Spanish ownership to a legal settlement that allowed title to pass from one owner to another. Edward Stanton, Carey's father, acquired an interest in the island in 1937 from the Caire family, which had owned the island since 1880, and he raised cattle and sheep, both profitable businesses. Caire family members eventually divided the island into seven shares, five of which Edwin Stanton acquired in 1937. The remaining two shares remained with Caire family members, the Gherini family, until the National Park Service acquired the Gherini interest in 1997.

Following a delicious lunch, a strange-looking airplane arrived. It had fixed landing gear, STOL wings, was built in Scotland and was being flown by a very young pilot. Carey wished us a safe flight and informed us that we would be spending the night in a "hunter's bunkhouse." It consisted of two double-

decker wooden beds, an outhouse, wash stand and a hot water shower.

He had his employees deliver a basket containing rib eye steaks, a large bowl of fresh salad, fruit, eggs, bacon, coffee, plates and utensils and two superb bottles of California cabernet. The bunkhouse grill had been prepared and was ready for us to cook our evening meal and breakfast. We departed. The aircraft needed only 35 yards to be safely airborne.

We flew until the late afternoon, landing frequently to admire the rocky coastline, the valleys, the mountain slopes and the vast variety of habitats that had evolved on this isolated island.

The island was unbelievably beautiful.

It was a great experience, with unforgettable sights. We flew over the two mountain ranges. We flew 35 feet above the ocean, climbing back over the ocean cliffs – astonishing! The habitats changed by mile and by elevation. From the tops of the ancient hills to the surf were spellbinding panoramas.

Landing frequently on some of the steep slopes produced momentary terror. Our mutual confidence in our pilot grew with each landing and takeoff. We saw beaches with seals and sea lions sunning themselves. Hundreds of seabirds filled the sky.

We also saw the obvious impact of years of cattle and sheep grazing. The damage of over-grazing was evident, but we agreed that in time the island would heal if the non-native beasts were removed.

We finally landed near the "hunter's cabin." It was plain but with mutual organization we made it work. There was an outdoor "one-hole" toilet and a washstand with a source of freshwater. Skip and Tom insisted they knew far more than me about grilling steaks, so I enjoyed visiting with Marian and drinking copious amounts of the delicious cabernet.

We had a vibrant, amusing and far-reaching conversation sitting around a fire that lasted into the late evening. No subject was taboo. Our sole problem was that we agreed on 99 percent of what ailed

America and the politics of that day. It was a magical time: a foursome of close friends who had collectively worked on numerous, significant Conservancy projects.

We remembered with appreciative laughter many of the successful preservation efforts and the board members who shared our vision of what could be. Late in the evening, we were joined by an indigenous channel island fox the size of a house cat. It was fed the remainder of a steak by hand, dashing off to its lair with its mouth full only to return moments later for a second round.

The three gentlemen took a short walk while Marian washed, brushed her teeth, changed into appropriate night attire and went to bed. We followed and soon we all were asleep.

We followed the same routine when we awoke the next morning. The three men stayed in bed while Marian went outside, completed her morning routine and changed into her day clothes. Then the men arose, shaved and changed into day clothes. Skip and Tom cooked a wonderful breakfast on the handy grill. Fortified by strong coffee, bacon, eggs and toast covered with strawberry jam, we soon heard the sound of the returning airplane.

When the pilot returned from refueling, we continued our inspection flight, noting the extraordinary number of feral sheep, some with dramatically large horns. There were huge feral hogs that dug up yards of earth to find grubs and roots of their favorite plants. The hogs and sheep had reverted to look like their ancestors, complete with massive horns and fangs.

Carey supplemented his income by selling hunting rights to so-called "big game hunters," who flew to the island to kill a trophy feral sheep sporting a large set of horns. The sheep and boars were practically unidentifiable from their ancestors. They could have been among several of the world's sheep populations or even a Russian boar.

The damage to the indigenous plant material was astonishing. The feral sheep's eating habits were identical to those of a domestic sheep. They not only ate a target plant, but they also mowed grass and every indigenous plant down to its roots. The number of hogs indicated that the resident population, which produced two litters a year, was out of control despite heavy hunting pressure.

It was obvious if a purchase could be made, the sheep and hogs had to go.

We returned to the Stanton home for another delicious lunch and got right down to discussing a purchase. Carey was reluctant to lose his ability to enjoy his island with his friends, but was sorely tempted to sell. I asked him if he was aware that he could sell his stock in the company to the Conservancy and retain life use of his home, admittedly at a reduced value, and the right to visit the island at will. He would be able to walk on the preserve as he and his guests pleased. He stared at me and finally replied, "That is a proposition that I would consider."

Marian was at her charming best leading Carey into delightful insights on the subject of the island and his stewardship. She handled her share of the luncheon conversation with grace and ease. She won Carey's heart.

Skip emphasized that this was the opportunity of a lifetime for a man who owned a channel island with one-of-a-kind plant life. To sell to the world's leading land-conservation organization would bring untold honor to him, especially as the island recovered from the feral sheep and hog damage. Its rare, indigenous plants would be available for botanists to study, and their evolution was sure to be fascinating. Visitors who wanted to roam his magnificent island would enjoy properly managed camp sites, discover the vast seashore caves and majesty of the green valleys, and hike to the top of the mountains.

There was a pause in the conversation as Carey thought about Skip's accurate observation that the island was vastly overgrazed. He asked rather plaintively, "Are the animals going to have to go?" Each of us in turn quietly explained the damage the feral animals were doing to the island's unique native plants. Yes, it was a tough decision, but we felt sure that, if the science were sound, he could accept as fact that the animals had to go. As it turned out, hunting the sheep and hogs brought in a surprisingly large income.

After a delicious dessert, we stood to catch the plane that was in the process of landing. Carey stated that he enjoyed our visit and we had left him with some new ideas to ponder. He would be discussing them with his attorneys and, most importantly, with Tom Macy and Henry Little, the Conservancy's western regional director.

We flew back to Santa Barbara, overwhelmed by our aerial and ground visit to a unique island we hoped could be acquired by the Conservancy and perhaps, in time, the National Park Service.

It is all too rare when great friends have an opportunity to meet, inspect, relax, discuss and remember. These are great life moments.

On return from Santa Barbara, I called a great friend and mentor from my years as U.S. Assistant Secretary of Interior. Dr. Starker Leopold was one of the preeminent ecologists of our day and a renowned professor of zoology and forestry at the University of California, Berkley.

Leopold was an expert on sheep grazing problems across our western states, where they had caused serious soil erosion, damaged stream banks and destroyed habitat on Bureau of Land Management and Forest Service public lands.

I described the feral sheep and hog damage we had witnessed. He replied, in lengthy detail, "I know the island well. There is no alternative except a public process to explain the fact that indigenous plant material is being mowed down by non-native species. There is no hope of the indigenous plant recovery without removal of the feral animals. It will take time and money, but it is really the only way to explain the need to remove hundreds of feral animals.

"The Conservancy must be able to show, as you accomplished in Hawaii, that the indigenous plant material will recover when grazing is halted," he said. "The program must be, above all, scientifically sound. The Nature Conservancy staff has the ability to attract that kind of support. It will need well-respected scientists from the California university system and experts on grazing animals from the federal research centers. The Conservancy must make the case that the feral, non-indigenous animals are destroying the island's indigenous plant material which has evolved over centuries. The feral animals must be understood by the public to be predators."

He continued, "By involving sound science and experts in plant ecology, the Conservancy will be able to sway even animal rights advocates that a sane program that eliminates the feral animals is to the benefit of Santa Cruz. I am totally confident that the Conservancy leadership can devise a plan to achieve the desired results.

"The Conservancy should not acquire Santa Cruz without having the ability to remove the feral animals. The recovery of the indigenous plant material will be a fantastic reward, not only for California but for the world."

Months later, it came as a surprise when Pat and Tom called and asked me to return to Santa Cruz, as Carey was impressed by my concept of "retained rights" and wanted me to be present when he consummated a sale. I made the long trip from Florida to Santa Barbara, was met by Tom and flew to the Santa Cruz in time for a walk with Carey, followed by a working lunch. I had very little to do except support what appeared to be Carey's favorite alternative – sale of his stock while retaining lifelong rights to keep the house, along with unlimited visitation rights.

He finally confirmed his intention to sell but wanted to continue working with Tom and the other Conservancy staff members and attorneys. He thanked me for making the trip and reassuring him that "retained rights" was a superb option. He was getting a fair price that would allow him "freedom" from the island. On return to Santa Barbara, I called Pat Noonan with the news. He was ecstatic and was confident that Tom and Henry would complete the deal.

The conservancy's staff, along with California board member Frank Boren, followed up by meeting Carey and his attorneys and reviewing the wording of the retained rights, tax advantages and the resulting "freedom" Carey would have on the mainland rather than being cooped up on the island. It took time, patience and determination to cross the hurdles, but Carey agreed that the proposed sale agreement was in his and the island's best interests.

In the end, Carey Stanton sold his two-thirds interests in the Santa Cruz Island Company for approximately $1.667 million. In the mid-summer of 1977, Conservancy staff members negotiated to buy the one-third interest of Carey Stanton's nephew, Edwin, for $833,000.

The total price for the 55,500 acres was $2.5 million, a bargain and yet another feather in the Conservancy's cap. Both sales were finally consummated in July 1978, with closing in September 1978. Carey Stanton did retain a life estate, but passed away in 1987, thereby consolidating the Conservancy's ownership of the property.

The National Park Service (NPS) eventually acquired the remaining 6,250 acres of the island.

The Conservancy did eliminate the feral hogs and the sheep in the mid-1980s.

The native plant communities have begun to recover. Exotic plants are being removed.

This speck in the great Pacific Ocean will be a reminder of evolutionary processes for generations that will come and study the recovery and natural changes that are part of a warming world.

The Conservancy still controls all of the buildings on the island, including those in the central valley and west end.

In the early 2000s, the Conservancy gave the National Park Service an additional one-sixteenth interest in the island – property immediately adjacent to NPS's existing holding on the island's east end. It was the remainder of the former Gherini property, which NPS purchased in 1997, and included the area surrounding Prisoners' Harbor, where there is a large pier.

NPS now permits visits and limited overnight camping to its portion of the island. Island Packers out of Ventura, California, runs daily trips to the island, with stops at the former Gherini property on the east end, the Scorpion anchorage and Prisoners' Harbor.

The Conservancy controls access to the remaining two-thirds of the island. The University of California maintains a field research station on the Conservancy's property, a facility which has been on the island for many years and predates the Conservancy's ownership.

Speaking for Marian, Skip, Tom, and Henry, we shared a magical moment in our collective lives – unforgettable memories of incredible, beautiful sights.

We helped save this precious piece of our world and we are the better for it.

NOTES – SANTA CRUZ ISLAND AND HUNGRY FERAL ANIMALS

[46] *Wikipedia*, s.v. "Santa Cruz Island", last modified 3 Dec. 2016, https://en.wikipedia.org/wiki/Santa_Cruz_Island.

[47] Ibid.

[48] Additional background information on Santa Cruz Island from the National Park Service, https://www.nps.gov/chis/planyourvisit/santa-cruz-island.htm.

The Garrison Diversion Battle in Never-Never Land

"Greed is a powerful force when left unbridled."

In 1971, after I was newly sworn in, I instructed the Fish and Wildlife Service (FWS) to arrest violators of drainage easements on Waterfowl Production Areas in North Dakota, where the issue is of key importance. This prompted a collective scream that went all the way to Washington.

At a difficult Senate hearing facing both of North Dakota's senators, I responded to their outrage over FWS legal actions by stating simply that the offending property owners had signed legally binding easements on their land agreeing not to drain.

They had been paid. They voluntarily were violating the law. They would be prosecuted before a federal magistrate.

Enforcement continued, though the decision was not popular and caused the FWS considerable pain. It was tough going to enforce the law against some of the state's most important landowners.

Regrettably, successive administrations curtailed both the FWS and EPA's oversight of many of the proposed and initiated drainage projects.

After my service as Assistant Secretary of Interior, I continued my interest in the water problems and politics of North Dakota. I was appointed to the National Audubon Board and met allies who became lifelong friends.

I was infuriated when Interior Secretary Jim Watt persuaded the Reagan administration to support the Garrison Diversion, an agricultural project I had defeated during my tenure with help from the Office of Management and Budget and an impressive group of national and local non-governmental organizations.

It was deemed dead and buried, but – like the Phoenix bird – it rose again.

My earlier presentation to the Office of Management and Budget had resulted in a proposal to cut severely the number of U.S. Army Corps of Engineers and Bureau of Reclamation staff members dealing with multiple drainage proposals throughout North Dakota.

Consequently, I was told I was "unwelcome" in the state, having used every ounce of energy and sound science to defeat an early proposal known as the "Starkweather Watershed Project." It was designed by the Soil Conservation Service and would have had extraordinary adverse impacts on critical waterfowl nesting areas and numerous existing national wildlife refuges.

I discovered by sound staff work that the Bureau of Sport Fisheries and Wildlife (later renamed the U.S. Fish and Wildlife Service) had abdicated its responsibilities to protect critically important wetlands because of threats from the North Dakota congressional delegation and Governor William L. Guy. He had promised to forbid even a willing seller to sell land to a conservation agency.

Our staff, headed by George Gardner, had torn apart the Starkweather Environmental Impact Statement, embarrassing the Soil Conservation Service and delighting the national and state conservation community. The Office of Management and Budget congratulated our staff and made sure the project was "dead on arrival."

I received a tongue lashing from the state's two U.S. senators and its sole representative, but the victory sent a signal to other federal agencies that the Interior Department was going to protect valuable landscapes from additional drainage plans.

Charles Callison, National Audubon's tireless Washington lobbyist, worked with me. National Audubon's board was warned and became deeply concerned that other major drainage projects in North Dakota might be promoted by the Corps or the Bureau of Reclamation (BR).

Incredibly, Secretary Watt had approved BR's Garrison Diversion Plan at the urging of the three-person North Dakota congressional delegation. Watt supported the massive water transfer plan despite opposition from the Office of Management and Budget and, most importantly, from the Interior Department's own Fish and Wildlife Service leadership and the vast majority of the environmental community. It was to be his personal monument.

In the simplest terms, BR proposed to move massive amounts of water from the Garrison Reservoir, which had been built by the Corps for storage on the upper Missouri, to eastern North Dakota to provide irrigation water for a very limited number of private farms. The land was already in productive agriculture and eastern North Dakota is one of the most productive agricultural regions, even without irrigation.

The scheme included massive drainage work, transferring excess polluted water to the Red River that flowed into Canada. It was the most destructive plan ever designed for the future of waterfowl production in the lower 50 states.

At the last meeting of the National Audubon Society during Dr. Elvis Stahr's presidency, the Garrison Diversion was discussed in detail. Donal O'Brien, heir apparent of National Audubon, took a commanding position and insisted that the society move with dispatch to oppose the project "by every conceivable means."

It was my first meeting as an Audubon board member and I remember the enthusiasm that Don evoked among the directors, who felt that Audubon had been "quiet" for far too long. He stated that it was a "moral obligation" to oppose Garrison "by every means possible, regardless of cost."

At the meeting's conclusion, Donal O'Brien was elected chairman of the National Audubon Society. Immediately after taking control, he moved to replace Dr. Stahr as president with Dr. Russ Peterson, the highly regarded former governor of Delaware.

Richard Madsen, a brilliant young man well-versed in Garrison Diversion plans, had been hired as Audubon's eyes and ears in North Dakota. Filled with energy, knowledge and an extraordinary sense of self-righteousness, he began to campaign actively on a series of important issues, especially the constant battle to prevent illegal drainage – all without approval of Audubon's President Peterson. For reasons that no one on the board and especially Donal and myself were aware, Peterson wanted National Audubon to stay out of the water-related proposed projects in North Dakota.

It became clear quickly that Rich had no intention of communicating with the home office or Audubon's regional director. I appreciated his vigor, but he had a way of being in the four primary North Dakota newspapers several times a week excoriating the governor, BR, the Fish and Wildlife Service and even other conservation groups that lacked his vigor.

At a very serious fall board meeting in the Florida Keys, Don and Pete decided after lengthy debate to retire Rich, who was then suffering a near nervous collapse. Don took it upon himself to negotiate Rich's resignation, which ended the issue on a high note. We lost an activist of the highest order. Rich did not fit the Audubon mold, but I have always thought the loss of Richard Madsen was a tragic mistake.

In rapid order, Don, supported by the board, asked me to represent National Audubon as he pressed the Reagan administration to fully examine the wisdom of the project. I agreed to represent National Audubon under the condition that I was to be staffed by the brightest and best experts and a trained lobbyist. Despite the strong national and international opposition to the project, particularly within the environmental community but also from local farmers who were being adversely affected, the state government in North Dakota continued to strongly support the scheme.

We selected David Weiman as the expert to sabotage this environmentally destructive water project. David had a national reputation as one of the greatest lobbyists related to water projects. He was interviewed and, within minutes, Don and I felt David fully understood his role. He was delighted by the opportunity and our ideas were very much the same. He was hired and immediately began to prepare a plan of action to illuminate the idiocy of the Garrison Diversion project.

By now, expensive construction of the project had been halted for exceeding the appropriation and for failing to comply with the need for a NEPA review.

The key question was, "How to raise the issue of Garrison's environmental cost and the ridiculous monetary cost" to the national level. Following the president's overdue firing of Interior Secretary Jim Watt, Garrison's strongest proponent, Don and other key members of the board debated how to make the Reagan administration realize the project was a disaster in the making.

Support began to crumble for Watts' position on the project. William Clark, was a member of the president's most trusted White House staff, was appointed Secretary of Interior. It was vital to convince him that the Interior Department had to face what was becoming a national issue. He had to approve the Garrison Diversion or cancel it.

Donal O'Brien had a "hold card." Leonard Silverstein had been Nelson Rockefeller's Washington attorney and knew everyone, but most importantly, he knew Secretary Clark. Don and Leonard met with the secretary and informed him that National Audubon was prepared to solicit support from all non-governmental organizations and make the Garrison Diversion a national environmental issue. They offered the secretary two alternatives: a Presidential Commission or a Secretarial Commission to study the financial and environmental impacts of the proposed project.

Secretary Clark made a vital decision. Overwhelmed by his new responsibilities, he wisely turned to Ann McLaughlin, a well-respected senior deputy, and asked her to be the conduit between O'Brien and Interior. Audubon's Peterson was cut out of the loop, as it became increasingly clear that he would constantly oppose action to North Dakota's water issues.

Secretary Clark checked in at the White House and, with the director of OMB, received permission to appoint a "Secretarial Review Commission." The Office of Management and Budget pointed out that there were serious flaws in the Bureau of Reclamation's overdue Environmental Impact Statement that surely would produce legal action against the continuation of the proposed project.

Don and Leonard were welcomed back to the Department of Interior to meet with the secretary, who told Don, "I will help Audubon under one condition: Do nothing that would embarrass the president."

Ann McLaughlin would become Interior's representative and co-organizer of the Secretarial Committee. Governor Peterson overtly began a final effort to undermine the involvement of National

Audubon, claiming that the Society would be "overly exposed" if Garrison became a national issue. Peterson and O'Brien traded memorandums, and then at a face-to-face meeting, O'Brien informed Governor Peterson that his tenure as president of National Audubon was in doubt unless he "got on board." He reluctantly complied by simply "taking a pass."

The announcement that the commission would include nine members led to intense debate as to who the commissioners should be. Behind the scenes, Audubon played a key role, working with Ann McLaughlin to appoint "safe votes." They selected John Whitaker, who had been undersecretary of interior and a member of President Nixon's staff. He was a "closet" environmentalist who considered Garrison to be pure lunacy, and he was appointed chairman of the commission.

Pat Noonan, the highly respected president of The Nature Conservancy, was appointed. The secretary asked for nominees that included experts in drainage and Corps projects. Don checked out every one of the proposed members and concluded that we were in good shape. The North Dakota congressional delegation insisted on the appointment of a former director of the Bureau of Reclamation and other potential supporters of the project.

To "balance" the commission, several other appointees that were deemed either opponents or "safe votes" were selected. Among the most intelligent safe votes was Dr. Gary Pearson, a veterinarian living in Jamestown, N.D. He became a lifelong friend of mine. He is one of the most knowledgeable experts on water law and the continuing violations of both state and federal laws, violations that nearly broke his heart because of the lack of serious attention that Audubon, the FWS and other groups had shown on the continuing drainage schemes in North Dakota.

We felt confident we had five negative votes.

Don made an intense effort to attract other non-governmental organizations to join with us in supporting the society's position. Don had been a "life trustee" of Ducks Unlimited and I had been a 35-year supporter of that prestigious organization.

To our mutual shock, the leadership of Ducks Unlimited agreed that the project would damage five National Wildlife Refuges and drain thousands of acres of highly productive wetlands, but as an organization, it refused to be embroiled in political actions south of the Canadian border. We were dumbfounded.

Don wrote personal notes to every current and past member of the Ducks Unlimited Board, life trustee, and major financial supporter, but the hierarchy stayed firm. Group leaders agreed it was a terrible project that would hamper severely their principal goal of preserving productive wetlands in the major waterfowl areas of North America, but they could not face their members if they criticized an administration policy decision south of the Canadian border.

Happily, a great transition took place later and, for years now, Ducks Unlimited has been the most important conservation group working to protect wetlands and grasslands in North Dakota. The pendulum has swung so much, the group is now experiencing the wrath of state government and the North Dakota Congressional delegation, which are trying to prevent Ducks Unlimited from working with the Department of Agriculture at the field level to implement wildlife provisions of the federal farm bill.

Aside from Ducks Unlimited, all other non-governmental organizations such as the National Wildlife Federation, Izaak Walton League and new organizations that specialized in environmental litigation, opposed the Garrison project.

David Weiman was a master of detail. He headed the Audubon team, organized my testimony and identified well-respected opponents to Garrison who were willing to speak under duress at multiple statewide hearings. He produced informative briefings for commission members and used the newspapers, radio and television to champion issues demeaning the proposed project.

I would arrive at least a day before each public hearing and be briefed perfectly by David. He always carefully prepared the "worst question" that could be asked of me with an easily understood answer. This duplicated the many evenings my wife spent reading Interior staff's preparation of potentially difficult questions when preparing for testimony before Congress.

I have rarely been as calm and collected as I was at the first public hearing. The meeting room was jammed with hundreds of Garrison supporters. There were signs supporting Garrison everywhere. There were caps handed out by Bureau of Reclamation (BR) representatives sporting "Yea Garrison!"

Following a BR presentation of the value of the project, I delivered a brilliantly prepared, critical analysis of the project's benefits versus costs both in terms of money and the incredible loss of valuable habitat.

I was personally verbally attacked by the former director of the Bureau of Reclamation, whose explosion prior to and after my testimony at the first hearing doomed him as a meaningful contributor to the debate. He helped our cause as much as my testimony did.

The hearings were packed by proponents, who comprised about three-fourths of the audience. They yelled and carried signs, cheered the proponents and loudly booed as I and other experts challenged their proposals.

As I approached or departed the podium, fists were raised, fingers were pointed and rather nasty comments were made by unruly proponents. I ignored them, which annoyed them even more. I do not remember ever being as calm and collected, despite the personal attacks. They actually strengthened my determination to cancel the Garrison project.

My testimony at each of the public hearings prepared by David and his staff was well-crafted and scientifically, ecologically and fiscally sound, pointing out the terrible impact the project would have on several National Wildlife Refuges and thousands of acres of the best waterfowl breeding grounds in the United States.

Most importantly, I emphasized the monetary cost of the project for such limited benefits. Whitaker and Noonan fearlessly encouraged opponents of the project.

I received death threats so frequently that the governor had me guarded by state police officers even at night in my motel room. Slowly, in hearing after hearing, support for the project began to crumble. The crowds of proponents diminished with each new hearing. More opponents questioned the validity of the project.

The commission brought forth significant findings of the overly expensive, if not illegal, consequences of proceeding with the Garrison Diversion. Clean water violations were a major issue, as Canada would receive polluted water from the proposed project. O'Brien and Weiman worked with the Canadian government and our State Department to challenge the issues of pollution and the migration of unwanted "rough fish" into Canadian waters. Our State Department became nervous and alarmed by Canada's growing list of genuine concerns.

The Environmental Protection Agency (EPA) finally began to seriously question the water pollution problems.

Thanks to Pat Noonan, we picked up an unexpected sixth vote and the project died.

In the National Audubon's long history, the defeat of the Garrison Diversion must be considered a major triumph.

Among the beneficiaries were three Indian tribes, the Mandan, Hidatsa and Arikara, who already had been harmed when the Garrison Reservoir was built.

Although the tribes were granted more than 926,000 acres of land for their reservation, building

Garrison Dam and filling the reservoir buried ancient burial grounds and flooded prime bottom lands where they grew crops to sustain them.

The Commission forced the Bureau of Indian Affairs to pay for pumps to move additional water up onto the reservation's bluffs where grazing land could be irrigated. Weiman invited a Sioux Chief in full Native American regalia to speak at one public hearing. His long white hair, deerskins and quiet revelations of how "their land" had been stolen was a heart breaker. It made national news. It was a stroke of genius.

Drainage remains a vitally important subject in North Dakota, where there are never-ending efforts to drain, legally or illegally. The state closes its eyes to individual farmland drainage ditches that often violate Waterfowl Production Area easements paid for by American taxpayers.

Currently, the state is better named "Never-Never Land," since a single party rules, led by a party boss willing to undertake development at any cost with no regard for the environment.

It apparently bothers the governor little that he allows trains to be sent daily east from the state that contain volatile gases, sometimes resulting in explosions that endanger millions of people across the U.S. and Canada. The technology exists to remove volatile gases from oil cars before shipment, but the governor considers this an unnecessary burden on oil companies operating in the state.

State government in North Dakota encourages petroleum and gas development that brings rapid wealth to a few without regard to the long-term environmental consequences. It also prevents lands to be set aside for conservation. Those who support protecting wetlands and other unique natural treasures of the state are viewed as the enemy.

I was struck by the level of propaganda being tossed about, including outrageous lies that state, oil, and agricultural groups told before the fall 2014 election to defeat the Outdoor Heritage Amendment, which would have taken 5 percent of the oil extraction tax proceeds to fund wildlife conservation in the state.

Millions were spent on television and radio ads claiming that if the amendment passed, there would be no money left for public education, caring for the elderly, repairing roads, etc.

Greed is a powerful force when left unbridled.

North Dakota politicians have been quick to support special interests that profit at the expense of environmental degradation and, like numerous dictators, cover up their deeds through healthy misinformation campaigns as would be expected in Never-Never Land.

Thanks to vigorous new Audubon leadership, the organization has regained its priority status in North Dakota, along with many other non-governmental organizations that are determined to oppose new drainage schemes.

It will be a constant threat, but new voices are being heard in North Dakota that recognize the value of wetlands and the need to become land stewards.

The defeat of the ill-advised Garrison Diversion gives me great pleasure.

Working with Donal O'Brien and the incomparable David Weiman was a highlight of my long vice chairmanship of the National Audubon Society.

Ever Restless: Patrick Noonan

"One of America's greatest conservationists."

The following speech was presented on January 17, 2013, as I presented The Lufkin Award to my friend and frequent partner, Patrick Noonan, during the National Audubon Society's annual dinner in New York City:

Chairman Holt Thrasher, President David Yarnold, members of the National Audubon's Society Board and distinguished friends of the two recipients: Patrick Noonan and Dan Lufkin.

In the late spring of 1971, with my feet barely settled in my office, having been sworn in as Assistant Secretary of Interior in May, the then-president of The Nature Conservancy made an appointment to visit me.

When the day came, the then-president of The Nature Conservancy was joined by a young Patrick Noonan. The president began to tell me of the potential synergy that could exist between his fledging organization and a long list of major land preservation projects that experts within the National Park and the Fish and Wildlife Service had quietly assembled.

Within minutes, the president was called away to take a telephone call. I asked Pat to join me in two comfortable chairs and we began a discussion on his vision of what The Nature Conservancy could become and how it could be the vital link to acquire the incredible variety of lands that were on the National Wildlife Refuge's priority list. He even boldly suggested that new additions to the national park system could be aided by the Conservancy.

His enthusiasm was infectious. Our attitudes matched. I stated, "Let's go. I have access to federal land and water conservation funds that have been reserved for critical land acquisition, but the Fish and Wildlife Service (FWS) has only limited manpower available to consummate a series of vital land acquisitions."

Pat had already assembled a small but superb staff and it went to work. Priorities included uninhabited islands, natural swamps, remnant old-growth forests, wetlands and native grass prairies untouched by plows.

Within weeks, Pat and Walt McAllister, the FWS chief of realty, joined me with a list of potential acquisitions.

I was chairman of the Migratory Bird Commission, which had a list of potential new waterfowl refuges and additions to refuges and was making a massive effort to acquire easements to prevent over-drainage in the key waterfowl production areas in the Dakotas and Montana.

Recognizing this great opportunity and nationwide support, the House and Senate appropriations committees added significant funds to continue this success story. The FWS and The Nature Conservancy became hitched and were in the business of protecting critically needed land.

Patrick Noonan and Nathaniel Reed

The Conservancy was represented by David Morine, who seemed to live in our office and had become the expert director of the Conservancy's land acquisition program.

The Conservancy went through growing pains. There was a change in the presidency. In 1973, Richard Pough, founder of The Nature Conservancy and a highly respected conservationist, requested an appointment to see me. He was joined by a small group of Conservancy board members. The opening question was, "Do you think Pat Noonan is too young to take on the presidency of The Nature Conservancy at age 29?"

I looked them straight in their eyes and said, "Hire him immediately and give him his head. He will continue to attract one of the finest, most knowledgeable, committed staffs of any group devoted to land preservation. He'll raise more money than any of you could dream of and save more land than is possible for any of us to foresee."

Shortly thereafter, the Conservancy board announced his appointment.

America's environmental history will clearly show that Pat's leadership and ability to attract an expert staff made The Nature Conservancy.

From a mostly volunteer organization aided by great staff, he understood the two keys to accomplish land preservation were money and the U.S. tax code.

The Richard King Mellon Foundation fell in love with Pat and his quiver full of exciting projects. Its interest and key land acquisitions generated commitments from many other foundations. Corporations donated land they no longer needed.

As an example, Union Camp gave 50,000-plus acres to create the Great Dismal Swamp National Wildlife Refuge, using its tax deduction to acquire timberlands near their Savannah paper plants. Other major corporations followed suit and, under Pat Noonan's leadership, The Nature Conservancy became the nation's dominant force for land conservation.

Pough also arranged for Pat to meet Katharine Ordway, an heiress of the 3M fortune. The two of them developed a relationship that dominated Pat's next seven working years.

Miss Ordway had become fascinated in preserving native grass prairies and had saved a number of small prairies that had been subject to immediate destruction. Through education, Pat's enthusiasm and calm guidance, she acquired the most amazing collection of the last vast unplowed tallgrass prairies in North America. There are no others like them. They have never been touched by a plow and never will be.

The names of the great prairie acquisitions are magic: Konza, Flint Hills, and the Samuel H. Ordway, Jr. Memorial Prairie that Pat once described as "a jewel in the Ordway prairies system."

Miss Ordway authorized the purchase of the Niobrara grasslands – 54,000 acres of sand hills, mixed grass and tall grass that meet together: another "Ordway Jewel." They kept working together, identifying exquisite lands: the Katharine Ordway Sycan Marsh Preserve and, working with the National Audubon Society, they jointly acquired 6,000 acres of palmetto prairie along Florida's Kissimmee River.

The list goes on and on. The combination of Katherine Ordway and Pat Noonan is one of the great milestones in the history of land preservation and the development of The Nature Conservancy into national prominence.

Following Miss Ordway's death in 1979, Pat desperately needed time off. He had spent years crisscrossing our country, raising funds and examining potential projects. He had attracted a superb staff of experts in land acquisition, all devoted to the aims and goals of The Nature Conservancy. He needed time to spend with his beloved wife, Nancy, and with children who had been growing without him. He just needed a healthy rest and a change in lifestyle.

Within a short period of time, ever restless, Pat took on new responsibilities, creating the American Farmland Trust with the indomitable Peggy Rockefeller and later, the presidency of the Conservation Fund that has already saved well over 7 million acres of land. More recently, working with the National Geographic Society, Pat developed a growing fascination with the Chesapeake Bay. Working with Secretary of Interior Ken Salazar, he created the John Smith Historic Water Trail – America's first national water trail, over 3,000 miles in length across the Chesapeake, now led by the Chesapeake Conservancy.

The Lufkin Award was created to recognize and honor those who have dedicated their entire lives to the environment and on-the-ground conservation. I know of no one who fits that description more than Pat Noonan – a personal friend, a leader, a unique force for land preservation and one of America's greatest conservationists.

I am honored and thrilled to present Patrick Noonan with the first Lufkin Award as a token of respect and admiration for a life well spent and high hopes of continuing successes.

Photo by Michio Hoshino/Minden Pictures, National Geographic Creative

The Noatak River: The Alaska Preservation Campaign Begins

"Each area was absolutely glorious and qualified in every way to be permanently protected."

By 1973, there was widespread knowledge within the conservation community that an Alaskan preservation team had been organized under Deputy Interior Secretary Curtis "Buff" Bohlen. He was my choice due to his knowledge and ability to work collectively to achieve a great environmental victory.

He had assembled experts from two Interior services to examine the very best of Alaska for the permanent protection of new national parks and special refuge areas where millions of waterfowl and wading birds nested.

I held meetings with leaders of every conservation organization, the Smithsonian Institution, the American Museum of Natural History, the Boston Museum of Natural History, the Sierra Club, National Audubon Society, The Wilderness Society and many more experts in Alaska's great landscapes and the areas of maximum importance as refuges.

We found it interesting that many experts suggested that we include the Noatak River in our final recommendations. The major appeal of the Noatak is that it is an unoccupied river valley where people can experience being out in the great outdoors alone. I made a date to join Buff and his team to fully understand the interest in the Noatak.

I learned that the Noatak River's headwaters are on the flank of Mt. Igikpak within the Schwatka Mountains, a part of the spectacular Gates of the Arctic. All peaks are part of the Brooks Range. The river flows westward approximately 425 miles to the Chukchi Sea at Kotzebue Sound.

The national park website notes that the "Noatak is one of America's largest mountain-ringed river basins. The Noatak supports an intact, unaltered ecosystem. The terrain along the river has vast open vistas providing ample opportunities for viewing wildlife and exploring the flora of the arctic tundra."

Many experts considered the wide Noatak valley to be one of the probable routes taken by early man migrating from what is now Siberia to Alaska when our continents touched in a vast land bridge connecting the two continents.

This was an extraordinary opportunity to preserve a complete watershed, one not to be lost.

In early fall 1973, while Interior Secretary Rogers Morton and I enjoyed breakfast, he announced he wanted to take a seven-day trip with me to fly over some of the areas that Bohlen's Alaska team had selected as potential national parks and wildlife refuges. The National Park Service (NPS) would establish a tent camp at the outlet of Walker Lake. I briefed the secretary on the extraordinary interest in protecting the

Noatak and noted that we would fly over it on our way from Kotzebue to Walker Lake.

He had heard that the "natives were restless in Kotzebue" due to the arrest of a number of Eskimos who had participated in illegal polar bear hunts in Soviet territory. The Eskimo skinners and those involved with preserving the pelt and smuggling it down through Canada to the outfitters' Seattle taxidermy shop were under investigation. [For additional details, see *The Most Extraordinary Day of My Life: Russian Polar Bears.*]

Secretary Morton wanted peace among the Eskimos. I wanted to visit the huge series of proposed national wildlife refuges in interior and western Alaska where millions of ducks, geese and water birds successfully nest yearly. The Bohlen team was preparing to recommend adding millions of acres and a new, vast waterfowl refuge to the existing Yukon Delta Refuge.

Staff laid out a plan. Secretary Rogers Morton and I would fly to Anchorage, which would take a full day, stay overnight at the Captain Cook Hotel and fly on a commercial flight to Bethel, where we would meet with Dr. Cal Lensink, one of the great experts of the vast Yukon Flats National Wildlife Refuge.

On arrival at Bethel, we would transfer to the department's turbo-propped Grumman Goose and fly with Cal over the multi-million acres of the existing refuge and the proposed extension. We would land back in Bethel, lunch with leaders of Native American groups and load back onto the Goose for a long flight up the Alaskan coastline to Kotzebue in Alaska's far northwestern corner.

There was no runway at Walker Lake so a "flying boat" was necessary.

The trip involved a great deal of time in the air the first three days, but we could select shorter flights to see proposed national parks once we were at the Walker Lake camp.

After arriving in Anchorage, we were driven to the Captain Cook Hotel, which was owned by former Secretary of Interior Wally Hickel, who had been fired by President Nixon for leaking a personal letter to the president urging him to end the Vietnam War. We enjoyed his company and a good dinner, and went to bed, as we had an early flight to Bethel.

On arrival the next morning, we were met by Cal Lensink, who joined us on the waiting Grumman Goose for a 75-minute flight over the enormity of the Yukon Delta. Thousands of waterfowl flew up to welcome us.

Regrettably, Jim King, the renowned bush pilot and waterfowl expert, was not scheduled to meet us because his summer work schedule was dictated by what the waterfowl – not Washington visitors – were doing. He was the most informed member of the Fish and Wildlife Service on Alaskan waterfowl breeding and resting areas.

We landed and met the leaders of the two Yupik tribes that live within or adjacent to the refuge.

It was very hot. The temperature rose to more than 90 degrees. The natives and the secretary drank a number of cans of beer and we enjoyed a sandwich lunch. They were marvelous people, supportive of plans to extend the refuge. They did hunt waterfowl in the spring nesting period and during the flightless period when ducks and geese are molting. I urged them to set limits on the numbers they killed, especially for the magnificent emperor goose, which showed some signs of declining numbers.

The Fish and Wildlife Service describes the Yukon Delta as the "waters of Yukon and the Kuskokwim Rivers that flow through a vast treeless plain. Almost 70 percent of the refuge is below 100 feet in elevation." It was obviously one of the greatest "duck and goose factories" in the world. The proposed addition would make it the largest of the nation's wildlife refuges, with more than 19 million acres.

Onward in the Grumman Goose we went to Kotzebue along the Alaska coast, deviating eastward to see some spectacular mountain ranges. We were met by a delegation of Eskimos leaders. It was just as

Photo by Nichael Melford, National Geographic Creative

hot in Kotzebue as it was in Bethel. We ate smoked fish and tiny pieces of walrus and seal blubber.

Rogers out-drank everyone by consuming many cans of beer and agreed to end the effort to identify members of the team involved in the illegal Polar Bear poaching ring if there was a solemn promise that no American Eskimo would ever participate in a hunt on Soviet ice. That promise was immediately made by the Eskimo leadership.

Our pilots became increasingly concerned about the time it would take to fly to Walker Lake, so we thanked our hosts and climbed aboard the airplane. Within minutes, the secretary stretched out his 6-foot 8-inch body and fell soundly asleep.

I sat in the jump seat between the two pilots, who had refueled the plane. Off we went to Walker Lake. I was studying the map and as we approached the Noatak, I bellowed, "Rogers, wake up. We are flying over the Noatak!"

He looked up and said, "Nathaniel, if you let me sleep, I promise that I will support the selection of the Noatak and include it in the national park system." I replied, "It's a deal!"

We spent happy days at the camp. We took off from Walker Lake one day and headed for a meeting at the headquarters of the companies developing an oil field known as Pet No. 4.

The flight over the Brooks Range through the Gates of the Arctic was utterly spectacular. We saw the colossal investment in the oil-production facilities and noted the garbage and impacts to the tundra. During our meeting, oil executives promised the secretary that piles of broken equipment and hundreds of discarded barrels would be removed, loaded onto barges and taken south – something I understand was done.

We dodged all questions of their interest in obtaining drilling leases within the Arctic National Wildlife Range.

Following our meeting, we flew east over the

Arctic Wildlife Range, one of the most impressive public lands in our nation. The vastness of the northern slope of the Brooks Range is unforgettable. We rarely talked, overcome by the impact of the great wilderness, which is the home territory of 152,000 porcupine caribou and a smaller herd of 23,000 central arctic caribou.

We were flown over a number of spectacular sights – these were among the greatest territories of high mountains and long valleys I have ever imagined. Rogers and I exclaimed with wild excitement as we passed over certain areas that Buff's team already had selected as potential additions to the national park system. Each was absolutely glorious and qualified in every way to be permanently protected.

One of the highlights was a long flight over the Yukon Flats, far north from the Yukon Delta, one of Jim King's most "special places" for the protection of literally hundreds of thousands of nesting waterfowl. The Flats are created by the confluence of three rivers: the Yukon, the Porcupine, and the Chandalar.

At one time, there was a proposal to build a dam in the area, but it was thwarted by a united front of conservation groups in the lower 48 states and fiscal conservatives, who understood it would have major impacts on waterfowl production and be a gigantic fiscal boondoggle. The Ramparts Dam proposal was defeated in part by the staff of the Bureau of Sports Fishery and Wildlife – the previous name of the Fish and Wildlife Service.

The Yukon Flats includes an astonishing 8,634,512 acres. It was Jim King's highest priority for protection. We gazed over the immensity of the flats in awe. Flanked by the Brooks Range to the north and White Mountains to the south, it was one of the most special places that could be protected in the refuge system. The Bohlen Alaska team made certain that it received priority for permanent protection.

We returned to Walker Lake for another night under the stars, recognizing the joint stewardship responsibilities we and our successors have to protect these great natural resources.

We finally said goodbye to the service staff that had set up the camp and fed us such wonderful food. Roger's supply of ancient bourbon was significantly reduced. We made the long flight back to Anchorage, refueling at Bethel, and spent another night at the Captain Cook Hotel. We were up early and caught the early morning flight back to Washington.

I ended the investigation of the Eskimos suspected of being involved in skinning or preserving the hides of polar bears. They subsequently kept their promise not to hunt on Soviet ice.

After catching up with our crowded desks, we joined Buff Bohlen's Alaska team for further discussion on the proposed land withdrawals. I asked for a special briefing on the Noatak and was delighted that it was included in the priority list of lands to be protected by the National Park Service.

The secretary pointed to our flight pattern and exclaimed with wonderment as to what we had seen firsthand. He shook hands with every member of the Bohlen team and thanked them for their six-day-a-week effort to identify, with precise coordinates, the lands we would recommend be preserved.

Following the 1972 election, there were many changes in all Cabinet departments. The original teams of assistant secretaries were all "retired" except for me.

In 1974, for reasons never fully understood, Secretary of Agriculture Earl Butz was assigned by the president to become "overseer" of the Department of Interior. Butz had held a chair at Purdue University and was an acknowledged expert in agriculture, but he knew absolutely nothing about the roles of the two Interior services. He paid far too little attention to the Forest Service, which was under his responsibility.

Perhaps the rumors of the amount of Alaskan land that the Bohlen team was going to recommend as parks and refuges concerned Senator Ted Stevens of Alaska. He distrusted both Secretary Morton and

Photo by National Geographic Creative

me, as he wished to defeat the proposals for new parks and refuges or, at a minimum, restrict them in size.

Butz knew absolutely nothing of the great challenge and opportunities of preserving major landscapes in Alaska for refuges and parks for American and other people. He asked for a full briefing from the Interior team. He sat next to the secretary and me and watched Buff Bohlen describe the priceless lands that his team was in the process of preparing for future congressional action.

Looking at a blow-up of the Noatak, Butz practically jumped out of his seat. He stated, "Rogers, Nathaniel and you cannot set aside that much river and land."

The secretary seemed frazzled and I immediately stated that we had flown over the upper Noatak, considered it a natural jewel, and received a great many Alaskan experts' advice that the long Noatak River should be preserved – intact.

The secretary gathered himself and, remembering his promise, turned to Butz and said calmly, "Earl, this is one of the highlights of the withdrawal. It may be the corridor through which early man entered North America across the ice bridge connecting Alaska with Siberia. Earl, it is a 'must' withdrawal."

Earl noisily groaned, "You are tying up Alaska."

Rogers answered him, "But, Earl that is what the Congress authorized us to do. We are to select for permanent protection the very best of the great Alaskan ecosystems."

With that Earl said he had seen enough and left us.

He was forced to resign when one of his intemperate, outrageous "jokes" was reported to *The Washington Post*. It came in the midst of President Ford's re-election campaign. Earl apologized but the game was up.

The Noatak is now designated as a National Preserve and a Wild and Scenic River. It welcomes a surprising number of floaters in canoes and kayaks each summer.

Thank you, Mr. Secretary Rogers Morton!

Photo by Bob Smith, National Geographic Creative

Saving Alaska: A Conservation Blockbuster

"Something unprecedented was in the works – one last chance to do things right."

I wonder if anyone with responsibility for managing American land will ever face a challenge as demanding – or rewarding – as the one we undertook in Alaska.

Encompassing 375 million acres, one-fifth the size of the lower 48 states, Alaska graduated from territory to state in 1958. But because of its small and widely dispersed population, remoteness and vastness, Alaska remained a little-known quantity. To give just one example, Aniakchak Caldera, the magnificent namesake of what is now Aniakchak National Monument and Preserve, was not discovered until 1922.

That began to change in 1968, when wildcatters struck oil at Prudhoe Bay, on the north slope of Alaska's Brooks Range. Developing this find, the largest in North American history, promised to be a herculean task. There were extreme local conditions – strong winds and temperatures that could dip to 65 degrees below zero Fahrenheit, a landscape that froze solid in winter and thawed to the consistency of oatmeal in summer, and thick, underlying layers of permafrost. The difficulty of building and maintaining roads in such an unforgiving climate all but ruled out conventional means of moving Prudhoe Bay oil. A consensus developed in favor of an alternative transportation method – an overland pipeline.

Several routes for the pipeline were proposed, including some crossing Canada. The one chosen – south from Prudhoe Bay through the heart of Alaska to Valdez on Prince William Sound, a distance of 800 miles – would penetrate a number of environmentally sensitive regions. But this route had the advantage of being "all-American." At the pipeline's terminus, the oil would be loaded onto tankers and shipped to Washington state.

The newly enacted National Environmental Policy Act required the preparation of an environmental impact statement (EIS) for any major federal action involved in environmentally sensitive lands – a category in which issuing a permit for the pipeline clearly fell.

As the main custodian of federal land, the Interior Department was responsible for preparing that statement and for ruling on the pipeline itself. At the end of a two-year process, the department's EIS delivered a prognosis of moderate but unavoidable adverse environmental impacts. On that basis, a permit to build the pipeline was granted. The consortium of oil companies at Prudhoe Bay was almost ready to start laying pipe when an overlooked constituency weighed in – Alaskan Natives.

Alaska had entered the Union with its land mass almost entirely in federal hands – a legacy of the purchase from Russia in 1867. The Statehood Act authorized Alaska to select about 100 million federal acres as its own but failed to address Alaskan Natives' rights to the land on which they had long subsisted. In 1966, they organized to press claims to more than half of the state's total acreage. That same year, Secretary of the Interior Stewart Udall froze the transfer of federal land to the state pending settlement of the Natives' claims. Thus, the state, the oil companies at Prudhoe Bay, and the Natives themselves now converged on a single goal: speedy resolution of the Native claims.

Meanwhile, one more voice was making itself heard: that of conservationists. The same conditions that had kept Alaska semi-isolated – remoteness, a rugged environment, a small and scattered population – had protected its starkly beautiful scenery and its bountiful wildlife populations from spoliation.

And wild Alaska had its share of eloquent champions.

Wilderness Society founders Robert Marshall, Aldo Leopold and Olaus Murie extolled the pristine grandeur of the Central Brooks Range and gave just the right name to its most striking feature – two spectacular, complementary peaks that they called Gates of the Arctic, now the centerpiece of Gates of the Arctic National Park and Preserve. The National Geographic Society and its widely read magazine were responsible for highlighting areas that became national monuments.

Edgar Wayburn of the Sierra Club made frequent trips to Alaska, becoming an advocate for such out-of-the-way gems as the Chilikadrotna River in what is now Lake Clark National Park and Preserve. A soft-spoken doctor originally from Georgia, Wayburn and his wife, Peggy, documented their excursions in a series of photographic essays.

On one occasion, I took Edgar upstairs to meet my boss, Secretary of the Interior Rogers Morton, the physically imposing former congressman from Maryland who stood 6 feet 8 inches tall, and I invited one of my deputies, Curtis "Buff" Bohlen, to brief us. Soon, all of us were down on the floor of Morton's baronial office, poring over maps and tracing the boundaries of proposed parks, refuges, and wild and scenic rivers. It was a special occasion when Edgar, Rogers, Bohlen and I all "chemically" agreed on priorities for wondrous Alaskan parks.

Federal employees were eager to share what information they had about the parks and wildlife refuges they already managed in Alaska. Outside the parks and refuges, however, millions of acres remained "terra incognita."

We had to get acquainted with those areas quickly because something unprecedented was in the works: the opportunity to make informed decisions on the future of vast quantities of pristine land, as opposed to the haphazard, first-come first-grab way in which the rest of the United States was filled in.

The old regimen was to create national parks and wildlife refuges as afterthoughts, stitched together once roads already had sliced through forests, rivers already had been dammed, and wild species already had been stripped of their natural habitats or hunted to near-extinction. This time, however, it looked as if a more sensible and public-spirited approach might be possible: gathering information about virtually untouched areas and openly debating what should be kept intact and what should be developed. Secretary Morton was excited by the opportunity: Alaska, he said, offered a chance to "do things right the first time."

In 1971, Congress passed and President Richard Nixon signed the Alaska Native Claims Settlement Act (ANCSA). It awarded Alaska's Natives a collective $1 billion and dealt with their claims by creating regional Native corporations, which would manage subsurface rights, and village corporations, which would take title to village lands and traditional hunting and fishing grounds (a grand total of 44 million acres).

The new law also transformed the conservationists' pipe dreams into a distinct possibility. This came about, in large part, thanks to the

Photo (right) by Design Pics Inc, National Geographic Creative

director of the National Park Service, George Hartzog, whose eye had been on Alaska for years. For him, the impetus to legislate on the pipeline and Native claims presented the opportunity of a career: to enhance the national park system with some of Alaska's stupendous scenery and matchless sites for outdoor recreation.

George had an excellent working relationship with U.S. Sen. Alan Bible of Nevada, who was the greatest supporter in Congress of the National Park concept and system. At George's suggestion, Senator Bible had inserted a provision into what was already a long and complicated bill: Section 17(d)(2), which authorized the secretary of interior to withdraw up to 80 million acres of federal land and to advise Congress within two years on the withdrawn parcels' suitability for national parks, wildlife refuges, forests, and wild and scenic rivers. Thus, through what we called the d-2 mandate, what had originated as a quest for a Trans-Alaska Pipeline had not only resolved longstanding Native claims but might also serve as the catalyst for a conservation blockbuster.

There was no guarantee that all the set-aside acres would end up being protected, but the potential was there for the 20th century conservation movement's crowning achievement. That movement had already spawned the Marine Mammal Act, the Wilderness Act, the Clean Air and Water Acts, the Endangered Species Act, the Environmental Protection Agency, the Council on Environmental Quality, and the environmental impact statement (all of which were signed into law by Nixon), not to mention Earth Day.

The d-2 mandate was a chance to bring the philosophy behind these new agencies, programs and procedures to bear on specific cases, applying what we knew about ecology – and what we had learned from past mistakes – to a peerless array of natural resources.

As the Department of Interior would become the lead agency for the determination of what lands were to be reserved for national parks and wildlife refuges, Secretary Morton assigned the task of reviewing the "special and unique areas" for "perpetual preservation" to me and my expert staff as our wing of the Interior Department was strong, unified, competent, seasoned and ready.

The greatest challenge of my federal tenure was advising Congress on the shape of Alaska's future.

Spencer Smith, director of the U.S. Fish and Wildlife Service (FWS), immediately recognized what ANCSA could mean for wildlife. With his support – and at the special request of Secretary Morton – veteran FWS game warden Jim King teamed up with Alaskan refuge expert Cal Lensink to produce a brochure on Alaska's waterfowl in only three weeks.

Called "To Have and to Hold: Alaska's Migratory Birds," the brochure proved to be of immense help in explaining the state's vital role as a habitat for waterfowl and a host of other birds from both the northern and southern hemispheres. Copies were sent to every member of Congress, many of whom asked for additional copies.

The other two bureaus reporting to the assistant secretary for fish and wildlife and parks were equally enthusiastic. They were the National Park Service and the Bureau of Outdoor Recreation, which has since merged with the Park Service. At the time, the BOR was responsible for wild and scenic rivers. The three bureaus were so enthusiastic that, at times, they were working at cross-purposes, each making plans for the same terrain. To coordinate the department's efforts, I asked Buff Bohlen to form the Alaska Planning Group, to which each bureau assigned top-notch personnel. I never made a wiser decision.

Later, we added Interior's Bureau of Land Management to the group, and eventually the Forest Service.

To direct the planning group, we chose a Park Service veteran, Ted Swem, who did a superb job of giving flow and coherence to a staggering amount of work: 28 separate proposals in all with

Photo by Sumio Harada/Miden Pictures, National Geographic Creative

accompanying environmental impact statements. Preparation of the impact statements was assigned to the Park Service's Denver Service Center, which performed admirably. Bill Reffalt of the Fish and Wildlife Service, Randy Jones of the Park Service, Pat Pourchot of the Bureau of Outdoor Recreation and a host of young, determined staff members gave Swem invaluable support. After wrapping up work on the "To Have and to Hold" brochure, King and Lensink stayed on in Washington to advise the group on its wildlife refuge proposals.

The Alaska Planning Group and its staff, as well as my staff, made numerous field trips to fill in gaps in our knowledge. Because time was so short and Alaska so huge, however, the study of little-known areas was fast and furious. Buff Bohlen and his son, Curtis, followed up on Edgar Wayburn's tip about the Chilikadrotna by floating on it together with Pat Pourchot. The river made an eloquent case for itself and was included in the d-2 recommendations.

Those same limitations of immense landscapes and a tight deadline meant that much of our studying had to be done by air. Flying in Alaska can be a dangerous proposition and one trip ended in tragedy. In 1975, as a token of appreciation for their hard work on the d-2 process, seven Interior Department employees were being taken on a tour of what later became Lake Clark National Park and Preserve when their plane crashed into a mountainside, killing everyone on board. Among the deceased was Keith Trexler, a Park Service planner whose knowledge of/and enthusiasm for Alaska was all but irreplaceable.

At my request, my other deputy, Douglas P. Wheeler, made several trips to Alaska, including one to meet with the state's progressive Republican governor, Jay Hammond.

Alaska's two senators and lone representative were adamantly opposed to what they called a conservation "lockup" of their "public lands," but the governor and his lieutenant, Lowell Thomas, Jr. (who was married to my cousin, Tay Pryor Thomas) were quietly supportive.

They asked to be kept informed of our deliberations and offered invaluable advice. Hammond, who became a lifelong friend of mine, asked only one favor in return for very quiet public opposition to/and genuine support behind the scenes for the withdrawals – that the Wood-Tikchik area in southwestern Alaska, renowned for its giant rainbow trout, be left out of the federal withdrawal so he could create a state park. I agreed and today it is Alaska's largest state park.

The morning newspaper, the *Anchorage Daily News*, was owned by Robert Atwood, a highly controversial, reactionary opponent to the concept of withdrawing thousands of acres to be permanently assigned as national parks and wildlife refuges. Kay Fanning, who owned the evening newspaper, the *Anchorage Times*, supported the withdrawals and urged her readers to ignore Atwood's continuing opposition to the proposal. She received needed financial support from committed conservationists in the lower 48 states. The newspaper battle ended with Fanning's victory when the final bill became law. Her dedication was an important step in gaining wider support from Alaskans who cared deeply about their state's future.

At the same time, newly empowered Alaskan Native leaders were frequent visitors to our office in Washington. The Alaska Native Claims Settlement Act had introduced the Natives to unfamiliar corporate structures, but the Natives themselves argued convincingly for the perpetuation of their traditional subsistence lifestyle, and we incorporated their views into our recommendations to Congress.

One of our best decisions had to do with Secretary Morton's reluctance to exceed the 80 million acres mentioned in Section 17(d)(2) as the amount of land to be withdrawn, studied and incorporated into our recommendations. Departmental lawyers advised that this was not a hard-and-fast limit, that if giving Congress our best advice meant sending a bigger package to the Hill, we could do so. Morton was willing to approve three million additional acres, but no more.

This restriction became a problem because, in some cases, it led us to artificially trim a proposed park or refuge. Swem and Bohlen came up with a solution: creating a special category called "areas of ecological concern" – tracts that belonged to ecosystems contained in our proposals but which were left out because we were running up against the 80-million-acre limit.

I approved the idea and sold it to Morton, and those areas were flagged in the material we sent to Congress. If you compare maps of what Congress ultimately enacted as national parks and refuges in 1980 with the 1973 maps showing these areas of "ecological concern," you'll see that the vast majority ended up being included. Congress, at the urging of then-Secretary Andrus and President Jimmy Carter, were given an opportunity that it seized. This early commitment to holistic management of ecosystems and watersheds was a precursor of today's emphasis on "landscape-scale conservation."

We finished our work and sent it to the Hill on time. At this point, conservationists went to work, lobbying Congress to take action. They, too, saw fit to form a special organization in deference to the vastness of Alaska, the number of the proposed new conservation areas, and the multiplicity of interests in play. Drawing on 55 existing groups for its membership, the Alaska Coalition was capably directed by the Sierra Club's Chuck Clusen.

Chuck ran an organized effort. He was respected by the leadership of the conservation community – people who were willing to follow his directions, as they recognized the importance of a unified

Photo by James Forte, National Geographic Creative

effort. Chuck was in daily contact with Buff Bohlen as the joint effort continued. Every member of Congress was assigned a member of a conservation team that was, in turn, in contact with leading conservationists in the congressional member's home districts – all so that maximum effort would be initiated and sustained. The success of the Alaskan campaign was in part due to the incredible national support that Clusen's team developed.

Because federal officials are not supposed to lobby, we couldn't aid this effort openly, but Bohlen met periodically – and unofficially – with coalition members in the basement of a Presbyterian church near the Interior building in downtown Washington. They called themselves "the Presbyterian Group." Meanwhile, popular support for the d-2 proposals was being drummed up by the magnificent images in a traveling show of photographs, known collectively as the Alaska Campaign and bankrolled by a great young environmentalist.

Starting in 1973, the Watergate crisis intervened, and the d-2 package was shunted aside. This was discouraging, but not fatally so. Congress had given itself until 1978 to ratify, amend, or reject the Interior Secretary's d-2 recommendations (a deadline that was later extended).

Gerald Ford succeeded Nixon as president in 1974, and the proposals continued to languish. After Ford lost the 1976 presidential election and with the d-2 proposals still stalled on the Hill, it seemed only reasonable that Ford should make the most of his last few weeks in office. During a campaign speech against the backdrop of Old Faithful at Yellowstone

National Park, Ford had called for Congress to create a new program that would double the acreage devoted to national park and recreation lands. [For more on Ford's Yellowstone speech, see the essay titled, *President Ford, an Epic Yellowstone Speech, and Richard Cheney.*] In our view, the lame-duck period between November and January gave the outgoing president a golden opportunity to double the national park system on his own.

The tool we had in mind was the Antiquities Act of 1906, signed into law on June 8, 1906, which had been used first and often by President Theodore Roosevelt, notably to protect the Grand Canyon decades before it became a national park. The law allows the president, with the stroke of a pen, to designate federal lands as national monuments.

The authority is not unfettered – areas elevated to national monument status are supposed to contain "historic landmarks, historic and prehistoric structures, and other objects of historic or scientific interest." But that language has been given a broad interpretation: scenery and wildlife can qualify as having "scientific interest." In fact, the park system's two largest units in the 1970s – Glacier Bay and Katmai National Monuments, both in Alaska – had been established by presidents applying the Antiquities Act: Calvin Coolidge and Herbert Hoover, respectively.

The act has been used over 100 times, occasionally creating significant controversy. The U.S. Supreme Court has repeatedly upheld presidential proclamations under the Antiquities Act, ruling each time that the act gives the president nearly complete discretion as to the object to be protected and the size of the area reserved.

My staff prepared a post-election memo explaining how Ford could make history by emulating his Republican predecessors. Among our specific recommendations were expanding the boundaries of existing national monuments, such as Craters of the Moon in Idaho; establishing new monuments, such as Wheeler Peak in Nevada (now part of Great Basin National Park); and – the pièce de résistance – creating roughly 30 million acres worth of national monuments or additions in Alaska.

I sent the memo over to the White House in early December of 1976. Generating the necessary paperwork in the seven weeks remaining before Ford left office would have been a formidable task, but we were prepared to work long hours for a great cause.

We waited and waited. I finally called Dick Cheney, at that point President Ford's chief of staff and no friend of conservationists, and asked if the president had seen our memorandum on proposing the use of the Antiquities Act to protect Alaskan lands. Cheney snarled, "Why should he end his presidency by advancing the Alaskan withdrawal prior to the Congress taking its time debating the wisdom of increasing the 'lockup' of Alaska?"

I was dumbfounded but recognized that Cheney was an arch anti-environmentalist and a formidable block on any last-minute presidential action. I reached the Ford former congressional team that had made the Yellowstone ceremony possible and explained the potential of the president's use of the Antiquities Act. They were enthusiastic, but maintained that Cheney had a "lock on the Oval Office door."

They wanted copies of the memorandum prepared by Douglas Wheeler, one of my deputy assistant secretaries, who had a sound legal background and invaluable contacts on both sides of Congress. This carefully prepared memorandum was vital in assuring that the environmental impact statements and Antiquity Act proposals were legal. Senior staff member Dennis Drabelle spent hours preparing a convincing memorandum recommending specific proposals.

But the team was refused admission by Cheney to see or speak to the president. The doors were shut firmly. Ford's great opportunity was lost to an arch conservative who was not a conservationist – a person who didn't have sufficient vision to recognize that the Ford legacy forever would be enhanced if he had used the Antiquities Act to expand existing national monuments, establish new national monuments and create 30 million acres worth of national monuments or additions thereto in Alaska.

Years later, I played golf with President Ford and spoke to him by phone on several occasions. He always brought up our orphaned proposal. He told me repeatedly that he regretted not having pursued our recommendations.

As the new administration prepared to take over, there was speculation that I might be kept on as assistant secretary, but I knew that President Carter would want to appoint his own policy makers – and rightly so. I resigned shortly before Christmas of 1976.

I was happy to return to Washington in January and brief the incoming interior secretary, Governor Cecil Andrus of Idaho, a close friend, on our d-2 proposals and the political situation as I saw it. I was delighted when Andrus kept Buff Bohlen on as his special assistant for Alaska. This was not only a tribute to Buff's expertise, it was also a nod to the Alaska work done by us all, as well as a recognition that, in those halcyon days, conservation was not a partisan cause, but rather a calling for men and women of vision on both sides of the aisle.

Andrus picked up where we left off. I enjoyed a working session with the secretary and Buff. Andrus, now fully briefed and invigorated at the opportunity of a lifetime, exclaimed that "our five years of work" could not be surpassed, but it would have to be modified slightly to become "President Carter's Alaskan Bill."

I understood and immediately replied, "Buff knows all the areas that were not included in our final proposal because of reluctance to increase the acreage to be withdrawn. The additional lands that you can recommend to the president are well identified as 'areas of ecological concern,' ready to be incorporated into your final submission. There are experts who Buff can call on to recognize additional lands for preservation. Don't lose this once-in-a-lifetime opportunity."

In his memoir, *Politics Western Style*, Andrus repeats almost verbatim what Roger Morton had said about Alaska: "One last chance to do things right."

And where Gerald Ford had feared to tread, President Jimmy Carter rushed in. In 1978, after Congress tried and failed to pass an Alaska d-2 bill, the notion of using the Antiquities Act authority occurred to our successors at Interior, just as it had to us. The principal draftsman of our December 1976 memo, Dennis Drabelle of my staff, received a telephone call asking if he had kept a copy of his and Wheeler's memorandum on the Antiquities Act and if he'd be willing to share it. The answer to both questions was a resounding "yes," and in this way we provided guidance for Carter's historic decision.

The president invoked the Antiquities Act to establish 56 million acres' worth of national monuments in Alaska; Carter also directed Andrus to set aside 40 million acres' worth of wildlife refuges under the authority of the 1976 Federal Land Policy and Management Act.

These bold, executive-branch maneuvers put the screws to Congress. Meanwhile, at Andrus's request, I was using my influence with friends and allies on the Hill. Friends made guest rooms available for my two- to three-night stays for weekly visits to lobby my congressional allies.

There was a strong push from Ohio Congressman John Seiberling that was supported by Congressman John Dingell, who took a particular interest in expanding and creating national wildlife refuges. He was ably assisted by Republican Representatives Silvio Conte and Pete McCloskey.

John Chaffee, the highly respected senator from Rhode Island, was a close personal friend and was widely respected by Republican senators. We spent hours together securing important votes from Republican and Democratic senators.

Despite weekly visits and marshaling what we believed would be the necessary majority to pass the legislation, there were periods of doubt. President Carter invited all the members of the conservation groups to the White House Rose Garden to generate even more pressure. There was a strong feeling among us that this was a "life issue" for all of us!

At the conclusion of the reception, the president asked me to step into an anteroom. He complimented me for my years of work and my weekly flights and determination to sign up as many Republican senators and congressman as I could. He then asked why, in my opinion, the legislation was not moving more swiftly. I answered that there was a powerful lobby of oil, mining and forest industries that were actively opposing the withdrawal.

I added, very undiplomatically, that his personal assistant was not a help on the Hill and that Secretary Andrus was fully and capably involved. The president's demeanor changed. He asserted that his assistant had been his most trusted aide during his years as governor of Georgia and remained an important advisor. With that he spun around and left me. I said to myself, "Good going, Nathaniel, you have just cut your ties to the President of the United States!"

Weeks later, our coordinated environmental team effort paid off.

Congress passed the Alaska National Interest Lands Conservation Act (ANILCA), which established 104.3 million acres' worth of new or expanded national parks, refuges, preserves, forests, and recreation areas. (The "preserve" category was a compromise, designed to accommodate Alaska Natives by exempting certain areas within parks or monuments from the generally applicable rules against developing natural resources and hunting game.) By then a lame-duck president himself, Carter signed the bill into law on December 2, 1980.

I was invited to be a guest at the signing ceremony in the White House's great Yellow Room – a great honor. It was filled with chairs that in turn were to be filled with every member of the leading conservation groups who had so fervently prayed and worked for this day. From carefully prepared lists, it appeared that a minimum of 150 members of Congress was to be seated.

Slightly bewildered, I entered the room and immediately was met by an attaché who directed me to the stage: left side, front row, seated between Senator Jackson and Chairman Udall. What an honor!

The audience was loud, cheerfully recognizing an historic event: The last great land withdrawal to create invaluable national parks and wildlife refuges was the product of nine years of effort and a final push by the Carter administration.

The president and Secretary Andrus strode down the center aisle to a standing ovation. On a stage were a lectern and a large desk. The president delivered an outstanding address thanking supportive members of Congress, leaders of environmental organizations for their combined efforts and the working teams that had produced this great legislation that would stand the test of time.

President Carter moved to the desk and invited leaders of the environmental movement and members of Congress who ardently had supported the bill to join him on the stage. There was a mad rush to climb onto the stage and surround the president.

The rest of us stood and clapped and even cheered!

Then, President Carter did something I will never forget. He looked around the mass of supporters and said: "Where is Nathaniel?"

I had not moved from my seating area but was waved onto the stage, far in the rear of members of Congress who wanted to be included in photographs of this epic moment. I held up my hand and he insisted that I come forward and stand in the crowd behind him as he signed the bill into law.

Carter's gracious gesture strikes me as an acknowledgment that our hard work in the early-to-mid 1970s was the backbone of the most dramatic land-conservation measure in American history.

Many dedicated and committed conservations

had worked six days a week for those nine years to complete the preservation of an extraordinary – if not unique – series of national parks and wildlife refuges. There is nothing like this collection of great scenic vistas and vital wildlife areas of such magnitude.

When the president finished signing the bill into law he handed the first pen to Secretary Andrus and then handed pens to members of congress who had supported and shaped a bill that held together during years during heated resistance.

We stood as one and issued a mighty cheer. It was a scene of bipartisan effort that overcame many obstacles and it is President Carter's singular conservation triumph.

The much-talked-about doubling had finally occurred: the Alaska National Interest Lands Conservation Act made both the national park system and the national wildlife refuge system twice as large as they had been before the law's enactment. The act also gave wilderness protection to 56 million acres – more than half of the 104.3-million-acre d-2 total – thereby putting them off-limits to development.

Throughout the d-2 process, two members of Alaska's congressional delegation – Sen. Ted Stevens and Rep. Don Young – continued to gripe and groan that their state was being "locked up," to the lasting detriment of its citizens. (The other senator, Mike Gravel, finally saw the light and switched to supporting the Alaska National Interest Lands Conservation Act.) Time has not been kind to their gloom-and-doom philosophy. Tourism is now Alaska's second-biggest industry, with the top drawing cards being its incomparable wilderness and wildlife – the very natural resources my staff and I did our best to preserve intact.

"Alaska is different from every other destination in the world," Gov. Bill Walker boasts in his welcome message on the state's tourism website.

You bet it is. People don't come to Alaska to see the cathedrals of Anchorage or the art museums of Fairbanks. They come to watch whales and photograph calving glaciers and to fish dozens of rivers for five species of Pacific salmon and rainbow trout and giant halibut and backpack the Valley of Ten Thousand Smokes. They are able to take part in these and a myriad of other outdoor activities because half a century ago a lot of people who loved Alaska put aside their differences to "do things right the first time."

Many people worked six days a week for many years to accomplish the feat. A truly remarkable group of young men directed by Buff Bohlen, Douglas Wheeler, and Dennis Drabelle worked with experts from the National Park Service and the Fish and Wildlife Service to identify the best of Alaska for permanent protection. Their enthusiasm and vision were matched in intensity and expertise by the Andrus staff. They recognized Bohlen's mastery of the opportunities that existed in the Alaska National Interest Lands Conservation Act.

President Carter, fully briefed by Secretary Andrus, took the opportunity to force the issue. Finally, with great support from a coalition of the nation's most prominent environmental groups and influential expert individuals plus the all-important concerned members of both parties, the Act became law.

I rejoice that we had the opportunity to share in the last great land withdrawal in American history: 154 million acres of some of the most extraordinary terrain on Earth.

(Next page) Photo by Michael S. Quinton, National Geographic Creative

Photo by Barrett Hedges, National Geographic Creative

The National Geographic Society: An Extraordinary Group

"The board members complied and I joined one of the greatest institutions in the world."

Like many teenage boys of my era, I learned a great deal about human anatomy from reading copies of the *National Geographic* magazine. The photographs of African tribal women and the dress – or lack of it – by natives in exotic corners of the world were said by the Grosvenor family to have taught anatomy to more young people than ever had access to that sort of thing in high school.

The family and the National Geographic Society are virtually synonymous.

Founded in 1888 by a distinguished group representing many disciplines, the Society's first president was the renowned Garner Greene Hubbard. He was succeeded by Alexander Graham Bell, inventor of the telephone. Gilbert H. Grosvenor was editor of the world-famous magazine from 1889 to 1954. Dr. Melville Bell Grosvenor, Gilbert's son, served the organization for 58 years, starting as an apprentice writer in 1924 and ultimately becoming chairman and chairman emeritus.

The magazine was a staple in the Reed family home, as our father was extremely interested in natural history. Consequently, it was a genuine delight one spring day in 1972 to receive a telephone call from Dr. Grosvenor inviting me to join him for lunch at the National Geographic's magnificent new Washington headquarters.

I was warmly met and we discussed a wide range of his interests and concerns. His primary issue was the plight of Yellowstone National Park's grizzly bears, fully described in the essay, *The Yellowstone Park Grizzly Bear Saga*. I had the dubious distinction of telling him that before the "garbage bears" died of old age, there would be a significant loss of bears that could not be weaned off human garbage.

I told him that the constant accusations from the Craighead brothers that park managers were out to exterminate all grizzly bears from the park represented a grave misrepresentation of the facts. I brought him up to date with former Assistant Secretary Stanley Cain's tough decision to close the numerous garbage dumps within the park as they were an "attractant" that introduced bears to human food, encouraging them to lose their fear of man.

Dr. Grosvenor listened quietly. He was a great admirer of Dr. Starker Leopold, my good friend, and a superior, world-renowned ecologist. I relayed Dr. Leopold's admonition: "Once a grizzly bear tastes human garbage, he is hooked forever. A garbage dump bear will be a dead bear, as it will lose all fear of man and demand to be fed or will seek food in the campgrounds and the trailer areas."

I admitted that we faced a very difficult period when a number of bears, some well beyond normal lifetimes, were reliant on garbage and would have to be put down. He was curious as to what he called

Photo by George F. Mobley, National Geographic Creative

"the war" between the park and the Craighead brothers, who not coincidentally had been featured in a number of *National Geographic* magazine articles. The brothers were fine biologists and extremely photogenic. It was difficult to explain how their study of "garbage bears" was considered by other experts to be seriously flawed.

He brightened when the conversation turned to Alaska and I described the formation of the team to draw and submit boundaries for major national parks and national wildlife refuges in that gorgeous state. He had joined a number of the Society's expeditions and was proud of the number of national monuments that had been created by a series of presidents and secretaries of interior as a result of the Geographic Society's field expeditions, superb photographs, and expert articles. He urged me to "get the best up there preserved, as there is nothing like what exists in Alaska left in the lower 48!"

Separately, I gave him the bad news about the forthcoming major problem of protecting the tall tree corridor within Redwood National Park. As described in *The Battle Over Tall Tree Corridor* essay, the tall Redwood grove had been discovered by a team from the Society and the National Park Service in 1963.

Aerial photographs indicated that there existed on a bend on Redwood Creek what appeared to be a stand of exceptionally tall redwood trees. Shortly after the discovery, he flew out to the site and walked miles over rough country to access the site. He said he was "dumbfounded by the majesty" of the grove of ancient trees, among the tallest in the world.

In the hidden valley, there were specimens of enormous height. The tallest redwood measured 367.8 feet high!

In 1968, the magazine's articles spurred Congress to create the 58,000-acre Redwood National Park. Those federally purchased lands were combined with three adjacent state parks creating a 131,983-acre park including the then-unknown Tall Tree Corridor.

Grosvenor rang for an assistant and asked for a copy of the magazine that described his impressions of the grove. He read: "Throughout the world, it has been my great fortune to see many dramatic panoramas: Fuji by moonlight, Grand Canyon, the Taj Mahal – each is superlative in its own way. Yet for sheer impact, the view of the magnificent grove and Redwood Creek Valley compares with any one of those."

Dr. Grosvenor ended our luncheon with an invitation to meet with him frequently, as he was interested in potential Alaska conservation projects, the continuing controversy regarding the "garbage bears" and the Craighead brothers and whether those bears could be weaned off garbage and "persuaded to become free-ranging wild bears."

Members of his staff with extensive knowledge of Alaska often joined our Alaska working group during the land selection process and were valuable sources of information.

As my needs developed to inform the administration and Congress of superb opportunities to add important acreage to the national park system and wildlife refuges, the magazine editors, at Dr. Grosvenor's direction, responded with superb articles and the usual high standards of incredible photographs.

As my days became fuller and fuller with the vast amount of work on various task forces and the usual, and not so usual, problems with management of the two major land services, our luncheons became rare. But frequent telephone conversations kept his inquisitive mind up to date with every area that fascinated him.

He assembled one of the most powerful and politically influential boards of directors, one that gave the Society a great edge on worldwide conservation issues.

Dr. Grosvenor retired in 1977 and was succeeded by his son, Gilbert.

Many years after my return to Florida, young Gil Grosvenor called me with exciting news. Lady Bird Johnson was retiring from the Society's board. At her final meeting, she asked the board for a "personal favor." Would it avoid the usual selection process for appointing new board members and appoint me? The board members complied and I joined one of the greatest institutions in the world.

I had known Gil during my years at Deerfield Academy. Gil played brilliantly on Deerfield Academy's undefeated 1949 soccer team that surrendered only one goal and were New England champions. Although he was two years older, we became friends and I admired his work ethic on the playing field and his love of Deerfield.

He had become editor of the magazine in 1970, president of the Society in 1980 and served with distinction until retiring and becoming chairman of the Board of Trustees in 1996. President George W. Bush later honored him with the Presidential Medal of Freedom.

So, I joined one of the most distinguished groups of ladies and men devoted to geographic education, exploration, steadily improving the magazine and acquiring a television channel. The newly evolving era when reading material, from newspapers to magazines, suddenly was eclipsed by new forms of communication caused the Society to make a number of very difficult decisions, including a severe reduction in employees and numerous cost-cutting actions.

I served for 20 years on the board and consider those years to have been some of the highlights of my life. Board members and the staff, from the highest positions to the duty officers, all shared a common "esprit de corps." Being a member of the staff of the National Geographic Society was an honor shared by all employees.

I made life friends and pray that the recent reorganization of the Society will not damage its reputation or its ability to complete important research projects, finance exploration and, above all, make a continuing effort to improve the geographic educational standards of our students.

The levels of ignorance of our world's map (even of our country's map and geography), and the location of Canada and Mexico much less Central and South America, Europe, Africa and the Middle East are inexcusable oversights by the American educational system.

I am proud that, under the leadership of Gil and the board, we all spent time and major funds attempting to improve the teaching standards of geographic education.

For me, that one objective was well worth the travel and time spent on the board of one of the world's greatest institutions.

Afterword

"It was an Era of Opportunity."

The five years during which I served as Assistant Secretary of the Department of Interior for Fish, Wildlife and National Parks was one of the most exciting and rewarding periods of my life.

I worked in harmony with the most extraordinary women and men – all devoted to maximizing a moment in time when the American people demanded of their elected officials' solutions to the blight of excessive sewage and industrial waste pollution. There was unanimity regarding the need to acquire rare habitats not only for endangered species but also for recreational and green space.

It was "an era of opportunity." A small group of women and men accepted the challenges and laid the foundation of national environmental law.

The friendships made among our working group can never be duplicated.

The mission was far more important than individual successes.

The era ended with the passage of the Alaska National Interest Conservation Act, a fitting conclusion to 12 years of bipartisan effort on behalf of the American people.

Since retirement from federal service, I have taken a great interest in my home state's continuing environmental challenges.

I have served as an environmental advisor to five Florida governors and on a vast variety of commissions and committees. My 14 years of service on the board of the South Florida Water Management District were extraordinarily rewarding, as the agency was built into one of the finest water management organizations in the country. We developed a fine scientific staff and undertook impressive restoration steps such as the de-channelization of the Kissimmee River.

Despite all of my efforts, combined with the efforts of some of the finest women and men who were appointed to the all-powerful board, we suffered from the extraordinary influence of the all-powerful cane sugar companies that treated the agency as their subsidiary. Our efforts were constantly thwarted by powerful agricultural forces that wanted no obstacles to their demands for irrigation water and drainage, even highly polluted drainage.

Gov. Bob Martinez appointed me to chair the Commission on Florida's Environmental Future, which gave me and a distinguished group of environmental leaders, major landowners and developers the sense that major portions of Florida needed to be preserved forever.

We were well staffed and, after many statewide hearings, the commission issued a brilliant report that led to a succession of bond issues financed by a relatively small tax paid by buyers and sellers of properties. Successive governors included $300 million a year from this source of funding. At least

2.4 million acres of unique lands have been acquired throughout the state. The list of additional unique areas worthy of protection is still long.

Funding was greatly diminished during the recession of the early 2000s and the annual appropriation was dramatically reduced. The environmental community reacted with disbelief, gathered its forces and faced the very difficult process of adding on the 2014 ballot an amendment to the Florida Constitution. Florida's voters passed the amendment by a 75 percent-plus margin, guaranteeing $200 million a year for Everglades land restoration and as much as $500 million for additional land acquisition and management.

The legislature promptly dipped into the approved funds for appropriations for non-related expenditures – and this will be a contentious battle for the foreseeable future.

Also keeping me busy: service on the boards of National Audubon, Nature Conservancy, Natural Resource Defense Council, the Atlantic Salmon Federation, American Rivers, 20 years as a board member of the National Geographic Society, chairman of the National Parks Conservation's National Council, and member of the Maine's Natural Resource Council.

Highlights include formation and leadership of 1000 Friends of Florida, which gained national attention as it attempted to continue the outstanding efforts of Gov. Bob Graham's vision of "controlled development." Overcoming constant problems with adequate funding, a superb board and loyal staff continues the effort to enforce the major achievement: the Comprehensive Planning Act that requires each city and county to prepare and defend its development plan in full view of the public. It ended the overly long period of passing major land use and zoning changes late at night.

Presently led by a brilliant young man, Ryan Smart, and a continuing superb board of concerned citizens, Friends remains one of my passions for sensible development versus "let it rip development" without regard to intrinsic natural lands nor issues regarding our quality of life.

For the past 20 years, I have been thoroughly engaged in the continuing effort to restore a semblance of a functioning Everglades system.

Working with a small group of visionaries who continued George Barley's determined effort to change the gross mismanagement of the Everglades ecosystem, Mary Barley, Paul Tudor Jones, Tom Rumberger, Stuart Strahl, Jon Mills, Doug Pitts and Bill Riley formed the Everglades Foundation, which has become a formidable conservation organization dedicated to restoring a functioning Everglades ecosystem. Fortunately, we were able to attract Kirk Fordham as the first president and he built the organization and attracted a formidable staff. His successor, Eric Eikenberg, has brilliantly directed the organization adding superbly trained staff, attracting additional committed board and council members.

Progress has been slow but steady. The incredible power of the sugarcane lobby and its ability to influence the Florida Legislature through major political contributions will be a continuing challenge. Accepting Big Sugar's contributions and voting to continue its exemption from the cost of cleansing their pollution will become major issues.

The joy of serving with such an outstanding board and staff has enervated me in my final innings.

My business life highlights were becoming vice president of the Hobe Sound Company, responsible for rebuilding our aged golf course and adding new landscaping and facilities. After assuming the presidency, one of the highlights was the rebuilding of the aged Hobe Sound Water Company.

Our family and faithful friends created The Nature Conservancy Blowing Rocks Preserve, one mile of ocean-to-river land, and the nearly five miles of the west side of the Indian River Lagoon as a part of the Hobe Sound National Wildlife Refuge. This compliments my father's gift of 1,100 acres of land at the northern end of the Town of Jupiter Island, where thousands of visitors and mainland residents find peace walking miles of beachfront.

In addition, my years as a trustee of Deerfield Academy and Trinity College were incredibly rewarding.

Best of all, my years as consort to Alita Reed, father of Nathaniel Jr., Lia and Adrian, and grandfather of five bright, articulate, interesting grandchildren have given me incredible pleasure.

I have been granted many opportunities and I mustered the determination to accept the challenges because of my wife Alita's incredible support.

My final sense of thanks is directed at the men and women who I have worked with as partners in saving great landscapes, mandating clean water and air, protecting endangered species, and facing the fact that the earth is warming due to man's impact on our atmosphere.

I refuse to be discouraged.

Another generation will be as determined as my "Band of Brothers and Sisters" have been and will continue our mutual efforts on behalf of Mother Earth.

I am reminded of Brutus' warning to Cassius:

"There is a tide in the affairs of men,
Which, taken at the flood, leads on to fortune;
Omitted, all the voyage of their life,
Is bound in shallows and in miseries.
On such a full sea are we now afloat,
And we must take the current when it serves,
Or lose our ventures."

–Julius Caesar, IV.iii

We lucky few, bound by friendship and the mutual desire to change our nation's course.

We lucky few!

An amusing effort by 'Big Sugar' to compare me with Fidel, as the need to acquire land to cleanse their pollution loads become a priority and ordered by Federal judges.

At home on Jupiter Island with Hobie, Reed reflects on his legacy: "Nixon banning 1080, which was used to kill coyotes all over the West. The banning of DDT. The government helping buy 90 million acres in Alaska as part of a permanent refuge system. In Florida, making the environment such an issue every governor has had a Preservation 2000 chairman. As a legacy, I hope the Republican Party of Florida develops a strong environmental ethic . . . Speaking to teenagers, I see a real awareness across the country and the world of the possibilities and problems they will face. There is the feeling this is one world, one Earth — and we all have to share the responsibility of whether we are going to make it."

NATHANIEL REED

Born July 22, 1933

Florida's conservation conscience

Because his family's wealth would have allowed him to live a life of leisure, but instead he chose to serve: Five years in Washington as assistant secretary of the Interior for two presidents (Nixon and Ford); the state under two governors and as the creator of 1,000 Friends of Florida; the region as a hard-working member of the South Florida Water Management District board.

Because he could have sailed his own boat on peaceful waters but decided he'd rather rock boats in government and the environmental Establishment.

Because he speaks out strongly and often against any assault on the environment, from ugly power poles along U.S. 1 in Hobe Sound to the state's failure to make farmers keep fertilizers out of Lake Okeechobee.

Because his command of the language lights the lives of those who hear him speak or read his letters.

Because his enthusiasm for life's simple pleasures — a "perfect orange" in a picnic lunch — sparks appreciation in others.

Because he cultivates a lifetime hobby that still excites, delights and challenges him: Fishing — for permit in Florida's Keys, for salmon in Russia, Norway and Iceland — and he releases his catches.

Because he recounts his piscatorial adventures in an annual "fishing diary" friends around the globe await with anticipation.

Because he shares his 66-year-old memories of growing up on Jupiter Island with those who didn't have that privilege, painting word pictures of a tropical paradise where the skies were filled with wild birds and the rivers with great sea trout.

Because, while he can be quite elegant and proper, Florida's No. 1 environmentalist lets Hobie, his Brittany spaniel, sleep on the couch in his office.

— SALLY D. SWARTZ

Loxahatchee National Wildlife Refuge; *photo by Clyde Butcher; Clydebutcher.com*

Nathaniel Pryor Reed

Nathaniel Reed received a B.A. from Trinity College in Connecticut and served as an officer in the U.S. Air Force military intelligence throughout Europe, North Africa and the Middle East. Upon returning to Florida, he became Vice President and then President of the Hobe Sound Company, a real estate and holding company, which owned the Jupiter Island Club.

Mr. Reed has served seven governors. He is best known as the Chairman of the Commission on Florida's Environmental Future. He also served as Assistant Secretary of the Interior for Fish and Wildlife and Parks in the Nixon and Ford administrations.

He is a founding member of 1000 Friends of Florida and the Everglades Foundation, which he serves as a current board member.

Mr. Reed is a former board member and Vice Chairman of the National Audubon Society and the Nature Conservancy, board member of the National Parks Conservation Association National Council, American Rivers and serves as emeritus on the boards of the Natural Resources Defense Council, National Geographic Society, Atlantic Salmon Federation and of Hope Rural School, a school for the children of migrant workers.

Acknowledgements

Writing a book of extraordinary memories requires detailed fact checks, rewriting, editing and a keen sense that the project is worthy of a goal rather than just remembrances. My goal for this project: educating another generation that might be energized by my opportunities and, even more importantly, by my willingness to take a chance and accept those opportunities – even if they seemed hopeless at the time.

I cannot conclude this book without boundless thanks to Teresa Lane for her sharp pen in assuring proper use of the English language.

Leslie Poole was a joy to work with as an editor and a collaborator on several chapters that needed to be expertly concluded.

Cindy Foley is much more than my secretary! She has labored for two years while I was often puzzled, out of sorts, searching for correct names, and often wanted to call the project off. Her determination to assist me in producing both history and facts that have never been told are vital to the understanding of a period in our nation's history when the fundamental foundation of our nation's environmental laws were conceived and passed.

Cindy deserves a major award for incredible patience.

Martin Merzer joined my team as the senior editor whose long history with the *Miami Herald*, The Associated Press and several previous book projects made him a "natural" for pulling the book together, making a number of suggestions and decisions that have been accepted by me with gratitude. I have rarely worked with a companion on a project during which a common thread of mutual thoughts and efforts matched each other as well as has been the case with Marty. Besides my joy over his expertise, our friendship knows no bounds.

Alita Reed, my wife and the "keel" of the Reed family, deserves boundless thanks for surviving, often with a smile, my all-too-often explosions when I was interrupted or was not in the mood to write. The book could not have been completed without her support.

CPSIA information can be obtained
at www.ICGtesting.com
Printed in the USA
BVOW05*0758020217
474471BV00009B/2/P